Palaces and Parks
of
Richmond and Kew

VOLUME I

The Palaces of Shene and Richmond

PALACES AND PARKS OF RICHMOND AND KEW

VOLUME I
The Palaces of Shene and Richmond

John Cloake

> FOR MOLLI

1995

Published by
PHILLIMORE & CO. LTD.
Shopwyke Manor Barn, Chichester, West Sussex

© John Cloake, 1995
The reproduction of the illustrations in this book has been assisted by a grant from
The Scouloudi Foundation in association with the Institute of Historical Research

ISBN 0 85033 976 6

Printed and bound in Great Britain by
BUTLER AND TANNER LTD.
Frome and London

Contents

List of Illustrations vii
Acknowledgements x
List of Subscribers xi
Introduction xiii
    I The Manor of Shene, before the Palace 1
   II The Plantagenet Palace 17
  III The Lancastrian Palace 29
  IV The Charterhouse of Shene 35
   V The 'New Park' of Shene 49
  VI The Building of Henry VII's Palace 55
 VII Henry VII's 'New Park of Richmond, County Middlesex' 75
VIII 'The King's Court should have the Excellence' –
        The Tudor Palace 1501-1553 79
  IX The Dissolutions and Refoundation of the Charterhouse 95
   X The Palace under Queen Elizabeth 117
  XI Princesses and Potentates at Kew 151
 XII James I's New Park 169
XIII Richmond as the Seat of the Prince of Wales 179
XIV Charles I's New Park of Richmond 197
 XV Richmond in the Civil War 207

Appendices
   1 The Belet Family in the 12th and Early 13th Centuries 213
   2 The Sites of the Old Manor House and the 14th- and 15th-Century Palaces 219
   3 Priors of Shene Charterhouse 223
   4 The Demesne Lands of the Charterhouse 225
   5 The Water Supply of the Palace and Charterhouse 231
   6 The Richmond Friary 1534-8 236
   7 Plays Performed at Richmond Palace, February 1574/5 to March 1602/3 238
   8 The Acquisition of Land for Charles I's New Park at Richmond 241
   9 Lords, Farmers and Stewards of the Manor up to 1660 255
  10 Palace Officials and Gardeners up to 1660 258
  11 Keepers of the Parks up to 1660 261

Glossary 263
Bibliography 265
Notes 273
Index 283

List of Colour Plates

facing page

I The presentation of a book to Richard II 32
II Anne of Bohemia on her deathbed at Shene Palace 32
II Building the Tower of Babel, showing early 15th-century building techniques 33
IV Model of Richmond Palace in 1562 64
V Richmond Palace from the south east, c.1630 65
VI The young Queen Elizabeth 160
VII Robert Dudley, Earl of Leicester 160
VIII A dance at Queen Elizabeth's Court 161
IX Queen Elizabeth in procession, 1600 161
X Henry, Prince of Wales, at Richmond Palace 192
XI A stag hunt in Richmond Park 193

List of Illustrations

1. Fortified palisade in the Thames bank opposite Brentford Ait 2
2. Gilbert de Clare, 10th Earl of Gloucester 12
3. Sir Otto de Grandison 13
4. King Edward II 16
5. The coronation of King Edward III 18
6. Queen Isabella 19
7. King Edward III, by an unknown artist 20
8. William of Wykeham, effigy 21
9. King Edward III, effigy 23
10. Richard II in coronation robes 24
11. The presentation of a book to Richard II 25
12. Anne of Bohemia on her deathbed at Shene Palace 26
13. Richard II and Anne of Bohemia, effigies 26
14. King Henry V, by an unknown artist 28
15. A brick kiln in Flanders in the mid-15th century 30
16. Building works in the 1430s 30
17. Building the Tower of Babel, showing early 15th-century building techniques 32
18. Herstmonceux Castle 33
19. The Charterhouse of Shene, c.1450 (model in the Museum of Richmond) 35
20. The habit of a Carthusian monk 36
21. Carved stones from the Charterhouse of Shene 38
22. Plan: the Charterhouse of Jesus of Bethlehem of Shene, c.1420 40
23. Plan: Charterhouse land within Shene manor in the 15th century 42
24. The seals of the Charterhouse of Shene 44
25. Dean Colet, by Holbein 46
26. Cardinal Reginald Pole, by an unknown artist 47
27. Stag hunting and hawking 51
28. The burning of Shene Palace 54
29. King Henry VII 56
30. The betrothal of Arthur Prince of Wales and Catherine of Aragon 57
31. The palace from the Green, 1562 58
32. Richmond Palace, c.1562 (model in the Museum of Richmond) 59
33. Plan: Richmond Palace, 1562 60
34. Richmond Palace from the river (A. van Wyngaerde), 1562 .... 62/3
35. The Palace Gate, Gatehouse and Wardrobe, 1805 64
36. Tudor brickwork 64
37. Fountain Court and the privy lodgings (A. van Wyngaerde) 65

vii

38. The kitchen quarters (A. van Wyngaerde) 66
39. Altar-piece from the Chapel of Richmond Palace 67
40. The privy lodgings from the river (A. van Wyngaerde) 68
41. The riverside at Richmond, c.1630, by a Flemish artist 68
42. Richmond Palace from the south east, c.1630 69
43. Windsor Castle, the Horseshoe Cloister 71
44. The Privy Orchard and Privy Garden at Richmond (A. van Wyngaerde) 71
45. Plan: The two parks of Richmond in the 16th century 76
46. Margaret Tudor, Queen of Scots 78
47. King Henry VII, by Michiel Sittow 80
48. Queen Elizabeth (of York), by an unknown artist 80
49. Catherine of Aragon as a young woman 82
50. The tournament held at Westminster, 1511/2 85
51. King Henry VIII, c.1525, by an unknown artist 87
52. Cardinal Wolsey, by an unknown artist 88
53. King Henry VIII with King Henry VII, by Hans Holbein, c.1536-7 90
54. Prince Edward, by Hans Holbein, c.1538 91
55. Anne of Cleves, by J. Houbraken (after Holbein) 91
56. Queen Catherine Parr, by an unknown artist, c.1545 92
57. King Henry VIII and Queen Catherine of Aragon, two portraits, artists unknown   94
58. Edward Seymour, Earl of Hertford and later Duke of Somerset 101
59. John Dudley, Earl of Warwick and later Duke of Northumberland 102
60. Edward Seymour, Duke of Somerset 102
61. Henry Grey, Duke of Suffolk 103
62. Lady Jane Grey 103
63. Lady Jane Grey, attrib. Master John, c.1545 104
64. Queen Mary I, by Antonio Moro 105
65. King Philip II of Spain 106
66. Cardinal Reginald Pole, by Sebastiano del Piombo 107
67. Elizabeth I, as a princess, by an unknown artist 110
68. The tomb of Frances, Duchess of Suffolk 112
69. The remains of the Charterhouse in 1562 (A. van Wyngaerde) 113
70. Thomas Sackville, Lord Buckhurst, later Earl of Dorset 115
71. The young Queen Elizabeth, by an unknown artist 116
72. Robert Dudley, Earl of Leicester, by an unknown artist 118
73. Queen Elizabeth and members of her Court at a hunting picnic 119
74. Richmond Palace in the early 17th century 123
75. Mary, Queen of Scots, 1578 (after Nicholas Hilliard) 125
76. Francis, Duke of Alençon 129
77. Dr. John Dee 131
78. Queen Elizabeth receiving two Dutch Ambassadors in audience 133
79. The 'Armada' portrait of Queen Elizabeth by George Gower, c.1588 135
80. Robert Dudley, Earl of Leicester, 1585 136
81. Robert Devereux, Earl of Essex, by Isaac Oliver, c.1596 137
82. A dance at Queen Elizabeth's Court 139
83. Sir John Harington 141
84. Sir John Harington's water closet 141
85. Queen Elizabeth in procession, 1600 (attributed to Robert Peake the elder) 144

LIST OF ILLUSTRATIONS

86. The funeral of Queen Elizabeth 148/9
87. Plan: Kew, c.1500 150
88. Pedigree: The Grandees of Kew and Shene 153
89. Wedding portrait of Mary Tudor and Charles Brandon, Duke of Suffolk, 1515 .. 155
90. Sir Edward Seymour 156
91. Princess Mary, by Master John 157
92. Robert Dudley, Earl of Leicester, by Nicholas Hilliard 158
93. Thomas Cromwell, 1st Earl of Essex 159
94. Edward Courtenay, Earl of Devon 160
95. Charles Brandon, Duke of Suffolk, by an unknown artist 161
96. Katherine, Baroness Willoughby d'Eresby, by Hans Holbein 161
97. The tomb of Sir John Puckering and his wife 164
98. Monument to Dr. William Awberry 165
99. Memorial brass from the tomb of Sir Arthur Gorges 166
100. Plan: Kew, c.1600 167
101. John, 1st Lord Harington of Exton 168
102. Princess Elizabeth, c.1611, by Marcus Gheeraerts the Younger 168
103. Portrait of a young lady, 1569 (believed to be Helena Snakenbourg) 169
104. Plan: Lands lying to the west of the Kew road, c.1550 170
105. King James I, by Daniel Mytens, 1621 173
106. Helena, Marchioness of Northampton between her two husbands 174
107. Helena, Marchioness of Northampton and Sir Thomas Gorges, effigies 174
108. Plan: King James I's new park at Richmond 1605 175
109. The plan of the lodge in James I's Richmond Park 176
110. Charles, Duke of York, attrib. Robert Peake, 1605 179
111. Henry, Prince of Wales, by Robert Peake, c.1610 180
112. Henry, Prince of Wales with John Harington, by Robert Peake, 1603 182
113. The Thames at Richmond (detail of plate 111) 185
114. Anne of Denmark, c1612 184
115. Inigo Jones's sketch plan of reclamation work outside Richmond Palace 185
116. Richmond Palace, by Wenceslaus Hollar, 1638 186
117. Designs by Solomon de Caus for Richmond Palace gardens 186
118. Giant figures designed by Solomon de Caus for Richmond Palace 187
119. Henry, Prince of Wales, c.1612, by Isaac Oliver 188
120. Charles, Prince of Wales, attrib. A. van Blijenberch 190
121. Brian Duppa, Bishop of Winchester, by R. Reading 194
122. The children of Charles I, 1637, after Sir Anthony van Dyck 195
123. Nicholas Lane's map of Richmond Park 198
124. A stag hunt in Richmond Park 204
125. The Charterhouse, from Moses Glover's map of Isleworth hundred, 1635 210
126. Pedigree: The Belet family 212
127. Plans: The sites of the 14th- and 15th-century palaces 220
128. Plans: The Duke of Somerset's estate, 1547 and 1551 228
129. Plan: Richmond Palace and Shene Charterhouse water supplies 230
130. Tudor water collecting chamber, Mount Ararat Road 233
131. The alleged seal of the Richmond Friary 237
132. Plan: Acquisition of land for the New Park of Richmond 240

Acknowledgements

The portraits from the Royal Collection are reproduced by gracious permission © Her Majesty the Queen (67, 96, 119). The following have given permission for reproduction of illustrations, as shown:

Lionel Pitt, Tewkesbury Abbey, 2
Museum of Berne, 3
The British Library, 4, 11, 12, 15, 16, 17, 27, 106, I, II, III
Bibliothèque Nationale de France, Paris, 5
National Portrait Gallery, London, 7, 14, 47, 48, 51, 52, 53, 55, 56, 57, 63, 71, 72, 75, 81, 83, 91, 92, 93, 95, 105, 111, 113, 114, 120, 122, VI, VII, X
John Crook, 8
Dean and Chapter of Westminster, 9, 10, 13, 68, 97
Museum of Richmond, 19, 20, 32, IV
Society of Antiquaries, London, 24(a)
British Museum, 25, 58, 60, 61, 66, 70, 86, 94
London Library, 28, 39
Magdalen College, Oxford, 30
Ashmolean Museum, Oxford, 31, 34, 37, 38, 40, 44, 69, 116
Fitzwilliam Museum, Cambridge, 41, 42(a), V
Hulton-Deutsch Collection, 46, 62, 90
Kunsthistorischen Museums, Vienna, 49
College of Arms, 50
Board of Trustees, National Gallery of Art, Washington, 54

Private Collection: photograph Courtald Institute of Art, 59
Isabella Stuart Gardner Museum, Boston, 64
National Maritime Museum, 65
Musée Condé, Chantilly, 76
Staatliche Kunstsammlungen, Kassel, 78
Marquess of Tavistock and Trustees of the Bedford Estate, 79
Viscount De L'Isle, 80, 82, VIII
Private Collection, 85, IX
Earl of Yarborough, 89
Victoria Art Gallery, Bath Museums, 101
Palazzo Chiabese, Turin, 102
Tate Gallery, London, 103
Salisbury Cathedral, 107
The Trustees of Sir John Soane's Museum, 109
Bristol Museums and Art Gallery, 110
The Metropolitan Museum of Art, New York, 112
Controller of HM Stationery Office (item in Public Record Office), 115
Richmond Public Library, 121, 130
Museum of London, 123
Trustees of Lamport Hall, 124, XI
Duke of Northumberland, Syon House, 125

Figures 21, 22, 23, 33, 36, 45, 87, 88, 100, 104, 108, 126, 127, 128, 129 and 132 are the author's own copyright, and the engravings at figures 24(b & c), 29, 35, 42(b), 74, 77 and 131 are from his own collection. Figures 1, 73, 84, 98, 99, 117 and 118 are from books, as shown in the captions, no longer in copyright. Every attempt has been made to acknowledge the source of illustrations, and the author regrets any inadvertent omission.

List of Subscribers

Ian Day Adams
Mr. Clive Adamson
Barbara and Dick Allen
Mrs. Rupert Allison
Martin G.L. Andrews
Mr. and Mrs. Hugh Arbuthnott
David and Jill Atkinson
David and Jane Attenborough
Andrew Ayling
Janet Backhouse
Ann Baer
David and Norma Baird-Murray
Maureen Bantock
Mr. and Mrs. David Barnfather
Ken Beard, F.R.I.B.A.
Ron and Marilene Berryman
David Blomfield
Iris Perowne Bolton
Edward Bostock, CBE
Jackie Bower
Charles J. Branchini
Mr. and Mrs. Michael Baxter Brown
Dr. and Mrs. J. D. K. Burton
Rosemary P. Abbott Butts
Patricia M. Byrne
Helena Caletta
Rodney and Liz and Petra Carran
Edward Casaubon
Richard Cashmore
(Mrs.) Gwen Castell and Hugh Roberts
Douglas Chambers
Sir Terence and Lady Clark
Muriel Clayton
Lady Clieve-Roberts
Norman Cloake
Daniel C. Cochran
Vicki and Nigel Colne
David Cons
Andrew James Constantine
Rosalys Coope
Pamela and James Cooper
Cllr. and Mrs. David Cornwell

Mrs. Tom Craig
Dr. J. Critchley and Dr. L.Y. Leach
Dr. Margaret Crowley
William Dacombe
R.N. and E.M. Dales
Ray Desmond
Hazel L. Donovan
J. Earle Dunford, Jr.
George and Betty Dunton
Mr. and Mrs. H.G. East
Peter Edmonds
Graham and Susanna Edwards
Margaret Evans
Anthony and Priscilla Everett
Guity and Abbas Fallah
Judith Filson
Mr. Edward C. Flann
Peter Foote
Paul Forster
Patrick Frazer
Christina and Bamber Gascoigne
Mrs. David Gibson
James Gibson
Mr. and Mrs. Raymond Gill
John and Rosalind Govett
Sir John Gray, KBE, CMG and Lady Gray
James W. Green
David Grenville
David J. Gridley
Ernst J. Grube and Eleanor Sims
Mary E. Gueritz
Johnny van Haeften
Historic Royal Palaces, Hampton Court
Miles Hardie
Mary and David Harper
Jean and Michael Harris
Mr. and Mrs. John Limond Hart
Martin Harty
Donald and Ruth Hawley
Richard and Maria Hebblethwaite
Mr. and Mrs. F. Nigel Hepper
Peter B. Hills

Sheila Hertslet Hodges
A.J. and D.V. Hoolahan
Neal S. Hostettler-Smith
Anne Houben
Diana Howard
Ken and Teresa Howe
Dr. and Mrs. Roy P. Howell
Noel Hughes
Keith Hutton
Donald W. Insall, CBE
M.J. Ireland
John and Judith Jeffreys
Peter M. Johnson
St John and Penelope Brooke Johnson
Derek Jones
Hugh and Peggy Jones
Charles Keggen
C. Knight
Mr. and Mrs. R.S. Knight
Simon Lace
Ian and Mary Lewty
J.O. Lindsay
Prince Rupert Loewenstein
Lady Logan
Robert and Donna McDonald
Patrick and Carroll Macnamara
Massoud and Leila Mahmoud
Julian C. Mancell-Smith
Tom and Irene Manning
Sylvia Marder, MBE, Judge Bernard Marder, QC
Bob and Betty Martin
Laurie Morris
The Hon. Mrs. P.L.E. Morris
J.M. Moses
Marlyn and David Nagli
S. Nikpay
Joy Nosworthy
Canon John Oates
Dr. B.S. Oskoui
Christopher Palmer
John W. Parton
Dr. Stephen Pasmore
Mary and Jim Patton
A.E. Pearson
Clare M. Peckham
Mrs Beryl Pethick
John and Rosalind Pickston
John Royston Plant
Gordon Pocock
Laura Ponsonby
Sir Ghillean and Lady Prance
Roy and Martha Price
Christine Pryer

Norman Radley
Mike and Emma Reeve
Mrs. William Reid
Marjorie and Anthony de Reuck
John Richardson
Theo and Lee Richmond
London Borough of Richmond upon Thames
    Libraries and Arts Services
Royal Parks Richmond
Elizabeth Roberts
I.A. and V. Robertson
Mr. and Mrs. John Samuels
Dennis A. and Roberta Sandberg
Esther and Richard Savinson
John and Sharman Sheaf
Jillian Sinclair-Hill
Mr. Barney Sloane
Ronald Smedley
Mrs. Prudence Spielman
Miss S.L. Starforth
Mrs. Elaine Stokes
David Suratgar
Jack Swanson, Maryann C. Swanson
Richard B. Tait
Mr. Geoffrey Tantum
Nick Tarsh
Ian Compton Taylor
Malcolm and Suzanne Taylor
Dr. Simon Thurley
Professor and Mrs. John Treasure
Edmund de Unger
David and Patricia Urch
Joan and Alan Urwin
Paul and Elizabeth Velluet
Sir Peter and Lady Wakefield
Arthur and Fenella Warden
Jan F. van der Wateren
Euan and Margaret Watson
Christopher and Anna Wayman
Ray and Mary Weber
Dr. Barbara B. Wedgwood
Derek and Pam Wheatley
Ian D. White
Kevin A.S. White
Leah White
Kim Wilkie
Councillor David Williams
Martin and Madeleine Wonfor
Kenneth Woodford
Lord Wright of Richmond, GCMG
Zoë Woolrych York
William and Lynne Young

Introduction

Palaces and Parks sets out to tell the story of the royal estate at Richmond and Kew: the seven palaces, the five parks, the three royal monastic foundations. It is only a part of the history of the area; but it is the central part. At least until the middle of the 19th century, Richmond's history was largely shaped by its royal connections.

Many books have been written on the history of Richmond and Kew, though most are now quite hard to obtain. However, few of their authors have troubled to quote sources – and few have troubled to consult original sources. Though a little new material may have been added, many of those published in the 20th century are mainly rehashes of what had been written before. In the process old mistakes have been repeated – and often exaggerated. Hypotheses have hardened into 'facts', myths into 'history', careless wording into downright error. Incorrect dates have been repeated so often that they have become generally accepted.

This book results from over twenty-five years of (intermittent) research into original sources. Some of the material has never been published before in any form. Much has never before been brought together into one book. There remains a wealth of material that I have not studied – not even looked at. In the Public Record Office, the Surrey Record Office and the Richmond Public Library, to name the three most important repositories of Richmond records, there is enough material to occupy a researcher into Richmond history for three or four full lifetimes.

I believe however that the time has come when I should try to put the results so far of my own research, however incomplete, into a form more durable and coordinated than the odd lectures and articles. I also believe that it will be of great value to future researchers to present a narrative which is fully documented as to sources. I do not doubt that I have made mistakes, but I have tried to draw a clear distinction between facts and hypotheses and to show the evidence on which the hypotheses are based. I have tried to clear up the old misunderstandings and errors.

There are two small exceptions to this policy. To explain the historical context of some of the events which took place in the palaces of Richmond and Kew, I have introduced a number of summary passages of national history which I have not thought it necessary to document. And in dealing with the more recent history, especially of Kew Gardens and of Richmond Park, both of which have been covered in recent well-documented works, it would be tedious to recite all the sources which they have used and quoted. Indeed I have deliberately dealt only in rather summary fashion with these subjects in Chapters 25 and 27 of this book; and have concentrated on the physical, architectural and topographical aspects rather than on the flora and fauna, which have been well covered in these works.[*] I have also omitted sources, such as newspaper reports, for events within recent memory.

---

[*] *Royal Kew* by Ronald King (Constable, London, 1985); *Richmond Park: The History of a Royal Deer Park* by Michael Baxter Brown (Robert Hale, London, 1985).

A book which aims to tell in some detail the story of the palaces of Richmond and Kew is bound to rely to some extent on the same material which has been so expertly researched and ably recorded in the monumental *History of the King's Works*. The first volume of this appeared at about the time when I started my research, but it has been completed only in the last few years. In the meantime I had covered a lot of the same ground. I had worked out and published (in a lecture and in a plan lodged at the Richmond Library) my own reconstruction of the plan of the Tudor Palace some six years before that in the *History of the King's Works* was published in 1982. (I was happy to find that the differences in our conclusions – and there are some – were not too great!)

I owe the compilers of *HKW* a great deal. They had identified and checked out many references in the early account rolls which I had not yet done. On the other hand, they made no use of some of the sources which I explored in detail, such as the manorial documents and the Crown leases. I have never wished to plagiarise what they have written, but in reciting references from sources and often in drawing conclusions from them, some similarity of language is inevitable. To ignore this great work would be folly; however to cite it every time that I have borrowed a source reference would be tedious for the reader. Whenever I have borrowed or cited their conclusions, whether to adopt or to contest them, I have made this clear. For the rest I hope my debt is sufficiently expressed here.

Some parts of this book retell what I have already published in articles and lectures. Plans have been rechecked – and often revised in the light of fresh material or further study. The preparation of the detailed plans for the architectural models of the Tudor Palace and the Charterhouse that are now exhibited in the Museum of Richmond proved a useful stimulus to rethinking about some of the more doubtful points.

For sound commercial reasons this book is being published in two parts at a year's interval – thereby reverting to an old tradition. The subject matter can in fact be divided quite conveniently and logically at 1660, when the great Tudor Palace of Richmond had just been reduced to ruins and before the royal family re-established themselves in the Lodge in the Old Deer Park and later in the palaces at Kew.

Each volume is self-contained, with its own bibliography, notes and index, but the book is conceived as a whole and the story will continue from Volume One to Volume Two with only a pause to draw breath.

The story of the royal estate at Richmond and Kew is of course central to the whole history of the area, but it is only a part of that whole. When I set out to write up the results of my researches I felt convinced that, rather than try to divide a general history into a number of arbitrary periods, it would make more sense – and better reading – to treat a number of themes separately. It remains my aim to follow up the royal history with a book on the economic and social history and another on the rich architectural history of Richmond and Kew.

I must express my especial gratitude to the staffs of the Public Record Office, of the London Library, and of the Local Studies Room of the Richmond Public Library as well as to those of other institutions where I have worked. Above all I must thank my wife who has not only typed (and frequently retyped) my manuscript, but has offered many useful suggestions and unfailing support and encouragement.

I am also extremely grateful for the financial help towards the publication of the book given by the Trustees of the Richmond Parish Lands Charity and by the Scouloudi Foundation in association with the Institute of Historical Research.

Spelling and Quotations

I have so far discovered 25 medieval variants for the name of Shene (the old name of Richmond before 1501), and 30 for Kew. I have adopted the policy of giving the original spelling used, both in quoting directly from a document and also when there is a clear documentary context. Otherwise, I have standardised on 'Shene' as being the commonest early spelling which is both easy to read and provides a useful differentiation from the later use of Sheen and West Sheen to refer to the house and hamlet on the Charterhouse site, and also from East Sheen. The use of 'Kew' where there is no documentary context seemed, however, preferable to the more common early 'Cayho'.

Although most short quotations (and some longer ones) have been reproduced with the original spelling and punctuation, this can soon become wearisome to the modern reader. Many longer quotations have therefore been to some extent modernised. Most of the early documents are in Latin or medieval French, and 'quotations' from them should be understood as translations from the original.

Personal names have usually been given in the form in which they will be most readily recognisable. First names in Latin documents have been translated; and as far as possible the spelling of surnames has been standardised (except in direct quotations). This regard for consistency hardly conveys the flavour of the original documents written by scribes who did not care if they spelled the name of the same individual in several different ways within a single deed!

Dates

Medieval documents were normally dated only by regnal years. These have been translated to calendar years. Later, both systems were often used in parallel.

According to the 'old style' Julian calendar, the year date changed on 25 March. (For example, the day after 31 December 1295 was 1 January 1295, and 24 March 1295 was immediately followed by 25 March 1296.) Although the 'new style' Gregorian calendar, with the year change on 1 January, was first introduced in 1582 and was soon adopted in many countries of Europe, it was not adopted in Britain until September 1752.

Some modern books quote only the original old style dates; others give dates as though the year change had always been on 1 January. To avoid ambiguity, dates between 1 January and 24 March in years up to 1752 should be – and are here – shown with both the original year date and the 'new style' one, in the form: 1 January 1295/6. (The form 1295-6 is used to indicate a spread over the two years.)

The Gregorian calendar also corrected an error in the Julian, which had amounted to 11 days by 1752. Where foreign reports, using the new Gregorian calendar – but dealing with events in England still dated by the Julian – are cited, both dates are given: new style (N.S.) and old style (O.S.).

Chapter I

The Manor of Shene, before the Palace

> With festive treat the court abounds;
> Foams the brisk wine, the hall resounds:
> The pages run, the servants haste,
> And food and verse regale the taste.
> The minstrels sing, the guests commend,
> Whilst all in praise to Christ contend
> The King with pleasure all things sees,
> And all his kind attentions please.

So wrote an unnamed Anglo-Saxon poet, quoted by the chronicler William of Malmesbury, of the scene of the banquet following the coronation in 925 of King Athelstan 'at a royal town which is called Kingston'.[1]

Athelstan was the second of seven Anglo-Saxon kings to be crowned at Kingston between 900 and 979. Kingston was a royal vill; it had one of the early minster churches and had been the scene of an ecclesiastical council in 838 – perhaps because it was on the border between Wessex and Mercia. As the administrative centre of a part of the county of Surrey it must have had a royal manor house from which that administration functioned. Yet there is no tradition of a royal house within the present *town* of Kingston, nor has any trace been found. Within the old *manor* of Kingston, however, there was probably a royal manor house which existed by the early 12th century – that at Shene. It is here that we may perhaps find the site of the chronicler's 'great hall'. It was not unusual for the royal manor house and the minster church, which together formed the secular and religious focus of an Anglo-Saxon administrative area, to be a little distance apart. It would be far more unusual to find two royal houses within the same manor. It is at least a tenable hypothesis that the history of the royal manor house at Shene – later the palace of Richmond – can thus be dated back to the 10th century.

Shene was already a recognised place-name by the middle of that century. The earliest documentary reference so far traced occurs in the will of Theodred, Bishop of London, who died in 951. The estates which Theodred left to his kinsmen were in Suffolk and were presumably his personal property. But as bishop he also held lands in London, Middlesex and Surrey:

> And it is my wish [he wrote] that at London there be left as much as I found in the estate, and that which I have added to it be taken and divided into two, half for the minster and half for my

1

soul, and all the men are to be freed. And the same is to be done at Wunemanedune [Wimbledon] and at Sceon [Shene]. And at Fulham everything is to be left as it now stands, unless one wishes to free any of my men.[2]

The identity and future fate of the bishop's land at Shene is unknown. By the time of the Domesday Survey the canons of St Paul's had only one holding in the county of Surrey – at Barnes, within the manor of Mortlake. If this is to be equated with one of Theodred's holdings it is more likely to be the one at Wimbledon, for Wimbledon and Mortlake were two centres within the same manor and the names may have been virtually interchangeable as a title for the manor as a whole.

That Shene (or Sheen) is a name of Anglo-Saxon origin has long been recognised. The derivation from the Old English *scene*, with the variant West Saxon *sciene*, meaning 'beautiful', which is accepted for the 'sheen' on a material, was for centuries accepted without question. It was adopted, though with reservations, in the Surrey volume produced by the English Place Names Society. But more recently it has been rejected by the *Oxford Dictionary of Place Names* in favour of a more prosaic origin. For the earliest known form of the place-name, Sceon, as used in Theodred's will, appears to be the genitive case of the Old English *sceo*, meaning a shelter or shed. So Shene may have been, to the Anglo-Saxons, a place of shelter rather than a place of beauty.[3]

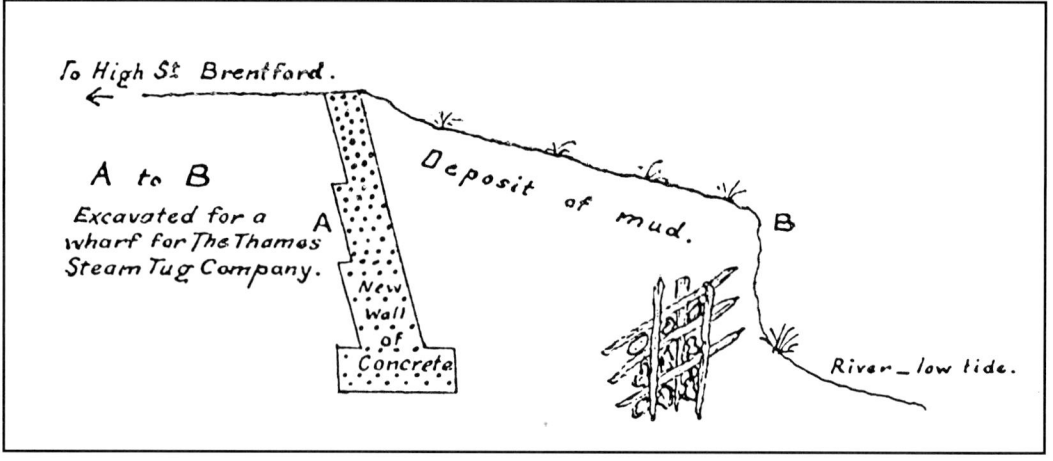

1 Fortified palisade found in the north bank of the Thames opposite Brentford Ait in 1881. (From Montagu Sharp, Middlesex in British, Roman and Saxon Times.*)*

Shene does not itself reappear in surviving documents until the early 12th century. However we must take note in passing of an important topographical feature and a notable event connected with it. The river Thames had of course been bridged at London in Roman times, but the lowest easy fording place was that at Brentford.* The site of the ford was approximately where the Brentford Docks were later built, to the south of the mouth of the river Brent and the Grand Union Canal, across to the Surrey bank at a point about level with the Palm House in Kew Gardens. The Middlesex historian Sir Montagu Sharpe argued strongly – and fairly convincingly – that this was where Caesar crossed the Thames in 54 B.C., and also where the Emperor Claudius and his general Aulus Plautius forced the crossing in A.D. 43, putting the Britons to flight at the sight of a Roman war-elephant.[4]

---

* There was a ford near Westminster, but its approaches on the south bank were through marsh land and difficult to negotiate.

Whether or not those crossings at Brentford can be substantiated, there is clear documentary evidence of the passage of armies and of a battle near the ford some thousand years later. In 1016 the Danes, under King Cnut, besieged London. The young English King Edmund (Ironside) led a relief force from Wessex and, as the Anglo-Saxon Chronicle informs us, 'went to London, all by north of the Thames and so out by Clayhanger [near Tottenham] and relieved the citizens, driving the enemy to their ships'. The Danes crossed to the south bank of the Thames and struck westwards. Edmund and his army rushed back to cut them off. 'It was within two nights after that,' the Chronicle continues, 'that the King went over at Brentford; where he fought with the enemy and put them to flight. But there many of the English were drowned, from their own carelessness; who went before the main army with a design to plunder. After this the King went into Wessex ...'[5]

It is not very clear where the battle took place, but the obvious interpretation is that it was on the Surrey bank of the river – perhaps therefore this should be called the battle of Kew. Not long after, the Danes, having rallied and having again tried in vain to take London, made a raid into Mercia and then retired to the Medway. The Chronicle says; 'Then assembled King Edmund the fourth time all the English nation, and forded over the Thames at Brentford, whence he proceeded into Kent.'[6] He drove the Danes out of Kent across the river into Essex, but was there defeated by them, and he eventually made peace, agreeing to a division of the country. However, before the end of the year Edmund had died, and Cnut had become uncontested King of England.

These references clearly attest to the importance of the ford at Brentford as a crossing point of the Thames, and it is curious that no major road seems to have survived which follows the old route from Kent south of the marshes on the Surrey bank of the Thames to the great ford at Brentford, or to the ferry which later took its place. Perhaps the bridge at London, with the roads radiating from it, had changed an older road pattern and made the ford of less account, save for the passage of large armies. When the Thames was also bridged at Kingston – before the end of the 12th century – the importance of the Brentford crossing would have been further diminished.

That Shene does not feature by name in the Domesday Survey does not disprove its early origins. Many places which certainly existed in 1085 were not mentioned. Brentford and Wimbledon are two nearby examples. Just as the manor of Mortlake had its two centres at Mortlake and Wimbledon, but was listed only under the former name, so the manor of Kingston may have had two centres – the little town by the church and the river crossing, and the royal manor house at Shene – but is listed under the name of the town. Moreover, a royal manor house, while it was in royal hands, was not itself going to yield any revenue, so there was no point in mentioning it specifically in the survey.

There is however confirmation to be found that the manor of Kingston extended at that time up to the borders of Mortlake, for it was recorded that the fishery in Mortlake had been established by force by King Harold before 1066 'on Kingston land and on St Paul's land'.[7] 'Kingston land' in this context can only be Kew meadows. 'St Paul's land' was probably not Barnes, but rather in this instance land belonging to the Bishop of London on the north side of the Thames. The manor of Fulham extended up to the edge of Brentford, so it included Strand-on-the-Green, opposite the Kew Meadows.

There is also evidence in Domesday Book of royal activity around the Kingston area. A villager in the charge of Humphrey the Chamberlain had the task of 'collecting the Queen's wool', a service connected with the holding of a hide of land at Coombe.[8] Walter Fitzother, the governor of Windsor Castle, had a man 'of the jurisdiction of Kingston' who had 'charge of the King's forest mares' and held two hides of land – presumably for their pasture, as 'he had no right in the land'. A fishery of eels was associated with this holding, which points to its being somewhere by the river Thames.[9]

It is possible that these two hides, which included land for one plough held in demesne, together with the 'land for two ploughs held in desmesne' of the main Kingston entry, constituted the nucleus of what was soon to become the separate manor of Shene, based on the royal house there. The hide, originally a measure of land, had become rather a measure of tax assessment by the time of the Domesday Survey and it cannot be equated with confidence to any definite acreage. But both it and the carucate (the amount of land which could be cultivated by a single plough team) probably amounted, in this part of Surrey, to some 80-100 acres. The carucate was four virgates; and the virgate in Shene can – at a later date – be identified as 20 acres. The first indication of the amount of demesne land held by the manor of Shene dates from the end of the 13th century when it was detailed at 400 acres.

If the later Anglo-Saxon kings or the early Norman ones ever actually resided in the manor house at Shene, they left no documentary evidence. The story that King Henry I was at Shene in 1125 or 1126 seems to be entirely without foundation.[10] Indeed, by that date the manor of Kingston may already have been divided and Shene granted into private hands.

The first documentary reference to Shene after the Conquest occurs in the earliest surviving Pipe Roll, that for the 31st year of the reign of Henry I (1130-1). The Pipe Roll (an account of money paid and owed to the royal treasury) records that John Belet owed £67 3s. 4d. for 'having back (*rehabendo*) his land of Sceanes'. He paid £16 and one mark* of the debt during the year and was left owing £50 10s.[11] From this it would appear that he had been paying off the debt for some years already, since it seems certain that the initial 'fine' was fixed at some round sum, most probably £100 – or possibly 120 marks (£80). Thus the actual restoration of the land can be dated to the 1120s. And since it is restoration, not an initial grant, that is here in question, it appears that the original grant to John Belet – for some unspecified reason later resumed by the Crown – could date back to the early years of the century and of Henry I's reign. That it was Henry I who made the grant is stated categorically in a return delivered to the Exchequer in 1212: 'the old King Henry [i.e. Henry I, not Henry II] gave the Manor of Syenes which was part of the royal demesne to the forebears of Michael Belet …'[12]

Shene was not the only property in Surrey held by John Belet. In the same Pipe Roll of 1130-1 he was also assessed in that county for 40 shillings owing for a 'long standing knight's fee', and he was discharged of debts of 40 shillings and 22 shillings arising from unspecified holdings in Surrey.[13] These other properties were probably at Bagshot and Coombe. The 'Book of Fees' records that a part of the manor of Bagshot was given to John Belet by Henry I; and Coombe was certainly in the family by the next generation.

The Belets were an important Norman family. The name occurs in the Battle Abbey roll (which by no means guarantees that they arrived with the Conqueror in 1066, but does indicate an early arrival from Normandy). They were certainly established in Dorset by the time of the Domesday Survey, when William Belet held Frome (Belet), Woodsford, Nutsford, Lyme and other land in that county. John Belet of Shene may have been the son of this William; for in addition to the Surrey holdings he accounts in the Pipe Roll of 1130-1 for three entries in Dorset

---

* The mark was 13s. 4d.

(where a note associates him with holdings in Berkshire) and for one holding in Berkshire – for which he was to account in Surrey.[14] It is likely that the estate at Bagshot extended over the county border into Berkshire.

The relationships of the 12th-century members of the Belet family are not easy to establish, and the descent of the manor of Shene has largely to be deduced from records relating to other places rather than from direct references.[*]

After that single Pipe Roll for 1130-1, no more have survived until the 1150s. Manning's assertion that John Belet was sheriff of Surrey in 1155 cannot be substantiated.[15] We come instead to a new generation – Robert and William. In 1160-1 Robert Belet accounted for a 'new debt' of 40 shillings for forfeiture of his lands.[16] The lands in question were Coombe and Bagshot. The forfeiture appears to have been a voluntary one, and it may have been part of a deal, for in 1164-5 Robert Belet was granted a valuable fishery in Surrey, for which he paid, in instalments over the next 18 years, a fine[**] of 100 marks.[17] The location of the fishery is not recorded, but it was probably the one at Kew which in the 13th and 14th centuries was attached to the manor of Shene and which was later given to the Shene Charterhouse. At almost the same time the 'Brentford fishery' was granted to Merton Priory.

It appears to have been William Belet who inherited the lands in Dorset and the manor of Shene, and to whom Bagshot was restored a couple of years after Robert's forfeiture. William died in 1174-5, leaving a widow Matilda and several sons. Robert inherited the Dorset lands. William or John probably inherited Shene. Half of Bagshot went to Ralph, while the widow Matilda kept the other half (which after her death came back to the heir of Shene).

Shene again changed hands c.1185 when it was inherited by a younger Robert Belet, probably the son of Robert of Coombe. He accounted in 1185-6 for a fine of 30 marks for 'his property' (unspecified).[18] The elder Robert recovered Coombe in 1190 for a fine of 80 marks.[19] In 1194 'Robert Belet of Schene' (thus clearly differentiated from the Robert who held the main Dorset estates) was granted land at Knighton in Dorset.[20]

Robert Belet of Shene died c.1197-8 leaving a young son, Michael, whose wardship was granted to Richard de Heriet.[21] Robert of Coombe died about two years later, and Michael was also his heir – as he was to a part of the Bagshot holding.

Young Michael Belet came of age and gained possession of his lands between 1207 when the wardship debt, taken over by Philip de Oxey, was finally discharged[22] and 1212. In an entry in the 'Red Book of the Exchequer' dating from 1210-12 he is shown as holding 'Shenes' by serjeanty of cupbearer and 'Bagsete' by serjeanty of veltrary (the service of slipping the hounds when the King went hunting).[23]

Serjeanty was a form of direct free feudal tenure, differentiated from the more usual 'knight's service' by the fact that the service due to the King was civil rather than military. 'Grand serjeanty', as in the case of Shene and Bagshot, required a direct personal service to the King on specified occasions; 'petty serjeanty' required the provision of some specified item. The tenure was otherwise very similar to that by knight's service and when money levies were being raised, in the form of 'aids' for civil occasions such as the marriage of the King's daughters or of 'scutages' to finance military operations, the accounts apply a 'knight's fee' equally to serjeanties and to holdings, such as Coombe, by knight's service.

---

[*] These questions are considered in detail in Appendix I. In the narrative that follows, the conclusions of that study, though only tentative, are adopted, since the constant repetition of reservations and qualifications would be tedious.

[**] The word 'fine' in medieval documents seldom has a punitive meaning. It was the sum paid to 'finish' a transaction, such as the purchase of land or of an appointment.

It is probable that the original grant to John Belet of the manor of Shene in the reign of Henry I was as a serjeanty, the service required being to act as cupbearer to the King at his coronation banquet. This was an honorific duty performed only on such state occasions, but the King also had a regular 'cupbearer' who was in effect his wine steward. This latter office came, at least by the mid-12th century, into the hands of another branch of the Belet family whose lands were in Oxfordshire and elsewhere, but not in Surrey. To the confusion of later historians this office was held for two generations by two Michael Belets, the first a judge, the second a lawyer, neither of whom was Michael Belet of Shene.

In 1212 there came a move to convert tenures by serjeanty into money rents. An enquiry was ordered into all existing serjeanties – and in each case a local jury was asked to state the history of the holding. The returns, delivered to the Exchequer on 30 June of that year, are recorded in the 'Book of Fees' (known also as the Testa de Nevill). The jurors for Shene reported that 'Syenes was part of the royal demesne, and the old King Henry [i.e. Henry I] gave the manor of Syenes to the predecessors of Michael Belet who now holds it by serjeanty of cupbearer'.[24] As a result of this exercise the Shene serjeanty was commuted to a regular payment of four shillings per annum rent, though references to the serjeanty of cupbearer continue for many years.

In 1214 Michael Belet 'of Sienes' was called upon to perform military service, being summoned to join the King's abortive military expedition to Poitou, which was abandoned because of the barons' opposition.[25] This summons was presumably based on the knight's service owed for the manor of Coombe, but the fact that Michael is named as 'of Shene' is a strong indication that he was in fact residing there. In the same year he was accused in the King's Bench of having 'unjustly and illegally disseised Roger de Burun and his wife Matilda of common pasture in Scien which belongs to their free tenement in that village.' The court found against Michael who was ordered to return the land and to pay three shillings in damages.[26] He may also have been fined, for the Surrey Pipe Roll of that year records him as paying one mark as a fine 'of the Bench'.[27]

A frequent source of freeholding within a manor was the dowries settled upon daughters of the lord. As the wife of William Belet, Michael's great uncle, had herself been named Matilda, it is very possible that Matilda de Burun was Michael's aunt or cousin.

The Belets and the de Buruns were not the only holders of land in Shene at the beginning of the 13th century of whom a record exists. The King's Bench rolls of 1200 give the names of Hubert de Burgh, Justiciar of England, and of John de Valtort as joint parties in a suit concerning land in Shene, but give no details.[28] A list of Surrey serjeanties drawn up in 1244 but evidently based on earlier information (for it includes, for instance, Michael Belet as holding 'Shenes') mentions that Robert de Bello Campo (or Beauchamp), a supporter of King John and a former ward of Hubert de Burgh, held a virgate of land in 'Shenes', as did also the Order of Templars.[29]

Moreover, the great priory of Merton, founded by Gilbert the Norman, sheriff of Surrey, in 1114-7, had at an early date been granted the church at Kingston with its four chapelries at Ditton, East Molesey, Petersham and Shene, with endowments in land for each. There is unfortunately no surviving record of this grant, which may have been made by Gilbert himself. In 1231, however, a document in the cartulary of Merton Priory describes it as '*a longis retro temporibus*' (from a long time ago).[30]

The earliest surviving document relating to the transfer of a part of the manorial lands of Shene records a grant made by Michael Belet as lord of the manor to one Walkelin de Caneton, conveying to him a virgate of land which had previously been held by widow Wolinne and half a virgate which had belonged to Geoffrey Dipere. This must have been freehold land, but a token annual rent had to be paid: as much hay as could be picked up on one scythe. (This was an interesting but not uncommon form of medieval payment – and using the handle of the scythe as well as the blade quite a lot of hay could be balanced on it.)[31]

Michael Belet of Shene died in 1215, leaving a widow Alice and a young daughter Matilda. Matilda was heir to the estate, for Michael's two sons, Robert and Michael, had both died. If the heir to an estate held 'in chief' (i.e. directly from the King) was under age, the King would appoint a guardian and enjoy the profits of the land during the heir's minority. For a boy the age of majority was 21; a female heir was only considered to be under age if she was not yet 14 – but once made a ward she did not come into enjoyment of her property until she was sixteen. The wardship also included the right to give the heir in marriage. Provided that the proposed match was not 'unequal or disparaging', the heir could forfeit the value of the land if it were refused.

On 17 November 1215 King John 'entrusted' to Hugh de Nevill 'the land which had belonged to Michael Belet, Knight, in Shenes', as well as other property which had belonged to him in Dorset.[32] Hugh de Nevill, who had been Justiciar of the Forests and the King's Treasurer, remained loyal to King John until the latter's death, but then he joined the baronial party and surrendered Marlborough Castle to the invading Louis of France. For this defection he was deprived of his lands and offices, though he quickly made his peace with the King's party and was restored to some of his lands, including Coombe, which then passed for good out of the Belet hands and became known henceforth as Coombe Nevill.

The guardianship of young Matilda Belet 'and her inheritance in Senes, which should be in the wardship of the King and is worth £10 exclusive of two dowries' and which 'is a serjeanty of the King, and of his butlery' was now granted to Wymund de Ralegh, a member of the Devonshire Ralegh family.[33] In 1218 Wymund agreed to pay a fine of 100 marks for the wardship of Matilda, including the right to bestow her in marriage, and of her lands in Surrey, Dorset and Berkshire.[34]

One of the two dowries mentioned in this grant was obviously that of Alice, Michael's widow, who set about cashing in on her claim. On 17 February 1218/9 she reached agreement in the Court of King's Bench with the prior of Merton in respect of six acres of arable land and three acres of meadow in 'Seenes', which she claimed as part of her dowry. She agreed to surrender all rights in this land to the prior in return for a down payment of two marks and an annuity of five shillings for the rest of her life.[35]

That settled, Alice engaged in another suit in 1220, claiming from William de Colevill and his wife Matilda a third share of one carucate and one virgate of land in 'Shenys' (i.e. some hundred acres of arable land, plus an appropriate share of meadow), and from Baldry the Clerk a third share of an income of 67 shillings derived from the holding in Basghset [Bagshot], all as a part of her dowry.[36] It seems probable that this large Colevill holding represented the other of the 'two dowries' mentioned above – and that Matilda de Colevill was none other than Matilda de Burun with a new husband.

In reply Baldry alleged that Michael Belet had granted him the land in Bagshot by charter, which he was able to produce to substantiate his claim. He asked that Wymund de Ralegh, as guardian of the heir Matilda, should be called to testify. Baldry evidently won his case for in 1227 a royal charter was granted to him confirming the gift by Michael Belet of 'all his lands in Baggashit [Bagshot], Windlesham, Estwude and Hoke'.[37]

Of greater interest is the Colevills' reply. They relied in the first instance on a legal quibble. Alice's writ, they pointed out, had referred to lands in 'Cumbe, Bedensford and Shenes'. But they owned no land in Bedensford, so they should not have to answer to the writ as drawn. Alice retorted, through her attorney, that these three villages were 'all in the parish of Senes and in that fee'. That Alice, widow of the principal local landowner and presumably with direct knowledge of the area, should thus refer to the 'parish of Senes' is remarkable. Shene was but a chapelry of the parish of Kingston. One can only infer either that in local eyes the church at Shene was already regarded as a parish church in its own right, or else that 'Kingston' and 'Shene' were virtually synonymous.

A second point of interest is the name Bedensford. What and where was this village? The name has not been found in any other document. The termination '-ford' places it either by the Thames or on a tributary thereof. There were no significant tributaries of the Thames within the actual boundaries of the manor of Shene, but then Coombe was not in fact within that manor either. The likeliest explanation is that the ford referred to was in fact the great ford of the Thames opposite Brentford, and that Bedensford is therefore Kew. The form 'Kayho juxta Braynford' occurs as a name for Kew in the 14th century: on occasion 'Braynford' alone was used when Kew was clearly intended – although Kayho or Cayho was certainly the local name of the hamlet. It seems possible that 'Bedensford' was an error made by a clerk in transcribing a note which should read 'Braynford' or 'Braensford'.*

The outcome of Alice Belet's case against the Colevills is not recorded in the 1220 King's Bench rolls, but it seems that they kept their land. Alice bided her time, and returned to the attack later.

Matilda Belet, the heiress of Shene, died in 1229 still under age and still unwed. She can have been little more than a baby at the time of her father's death 14 years before, for no heiress was likely in those days to remain unmarried once she reached marriageable age. Her uncle John Belet, Michael's brother, succeeded to the estate and paid, in 1229, 10 marks for relief of Matilda's lands.[38]

In the meantime, Michael's widow Alice had married Roger de la Dune. She now stated that her dowry from Michael had amounted to a total of eight and a half virgates of land, with 12 acres of meadow and two shillings' worth of rents in Shene. However, she and her husband agreed to surrender this property to John Belet.[39] This transaction may well have been designed primarily to further her case against the Colevills which she appears to have taken up again at this time, only to be frustrated by the death of John Belet himself, who had been called as a principal witness.[40]

John Belet died in 1230, only one year after coming into the property. Like his brother he had no surviving son. Two sons, John and Thomas, and two daughters, Matilda and Christian, had all died before him,[41] leaving only two other daughters, Emma and Alice, both under age and unmarried, as joint heiresses. John's widow Amabil promptly remarried, and her new husband Henry Fitz Nicholas paid 50 marks for the wardship of the heiresses and their lands.[42] Amabil however took steps to protect her daughters' interests. At her request, the King ordered Henry Fitz Nicholas to assign an appropriate dowry to them out of 'all the lands which had been John Belet's and which are now in his wardship by the King's writ'. That this Surrey branch of the family still held some land in Dorset is evidenced by the fact that instructions were sent on the

---

* The calligraphy of the period would have made it quite easy to misread a carelessly written 'Bra' as 'Bed'.

same day to the sheriffs both of Surrey and of Dorset that, if Henry Fitz Nicholas should not do as instructed in the matter of the dowries, they were to ensure that the King's commands were obeyed.[43]

Meanwhile a 'farm' (i.e. lease) of the Colevill holdings in Shene had been taken by Hubert de Burgh, Earl of Kent, Justiciar of England, and former regent during the years of Henry III's minority. In a coup d'état in the summer of 1232 he was removed from office and charges of dishonesty and treason were brought against him. His lands were seized by the sheriffs of the various counties in which they were located. Hubert tried to seek sanctuary, first at Merton, then at Brentwood, but finally he submitted to the King. The latter ordered the sheriffs to retain only those properties which Hubert had held as tenant-in-chief from the King, but to restore to him his other lands and tenements with all their chattels. The list of lands to be restored included 'land which he held in Shenes by farm from William de Colevill and his wife Matilda'.[44] However, one of the charges brought against the Justiciar was that he had persecuted the foreign priests, mostly Italians, who had recently been flooding into the country. On 7 February 1232/3 the sheriffs were instructed to hand over to Robert Passelewe, the King's clerk, lands of Hubert de Burgh, so that damages could be paid out of their revenue to 'the clerks, Roman, Italian and others, for the injuries done to them by the said Hubert'. Once again the land in Shene is specified among the properties which the sheriff of Surrey was told to surrender.[45] It was of course only the income from these leased lands which was confiscated; the title of ownership was unaffected.

It was perhaps this juggling with what she considered to be her rightful property that inspired Alice to make yet another attempt to claim her dowry lands from the Colevills. A damaged and partly illegible document of the King's Bench dating from the Hilary Term of 1238 refers to the previous calling of John Belet as a witness and his death, to the wardship exercised by Henry Fitz Nicholas over Emma and Alice, who are now to be called, and then to the Court's having summoned Thomas Maubane and his wife Amabil [is this John's widow with yet another husband?] 'in whose custody the aforesaid Emma and Alice are ...'.[46]

It would seem from this that Henry Fitz Nicholas, who was shown in the Book of Fees as holding the King's serjeanty of Shenes, worth £10, in 1235,[47] may have died early in 1238. In that year Emma, the elder of the Belet sisters, married Walter, son of the judge Jordan Oliver. In an entry for 1238 the Book of Fees shows Walter Oliver as holding the manor of Shene from the King 'by serjeanty of cupbearer in the butlery of the King's household'.[48] There is no qualification that this is only one half of the manor, so it is possible that Walter was now himself acting as guardian of Alice. In any case, though the land of the manor was divided between the sisters, it was Emma's portion alone that carried with it the rights of lordship.

Walter Oliver died in 1240/1. In 1241 an inquest was held in Kingston on his lands. A mistake was made, either by the jury or by the recording clerk, for he was described as the son of Jordan Oliver and his wife Emma, holding his *mother's* inheritance of a moiety of the manor of Shene, by joint serjeanty as cupbearer.[49] This mistake, followed by Manning and others who used him as their source, produced a number of impossible relationships. An order to the sheriff of Surrey two years later sets the record straight. The sheriff was told that if, on the death of Walter Oliver, he had taken into royal custody any lands in his bailiwick that had been Walter's but which were part of the inheritance of Emma, former *wife* of the said Walter, which she held in chief from the King, he was forthwith to grant Emma full seisin of such lands.[50]

The official custody of Emma's young sister Alice and her inheritance had meanwhile been granted to Robert de Bello Campo (or Beauchamp), appointed a judge by Henry II in 1234. Robert appears to have been in financial difficulties. On 20 August 1241 the sheriff of Surrey was sent a writ from the King informing him that Robert, guardian of the land and heir of John Belet, had given sureties which had been accepted that he would satisfy Aaron son of Abraham, Jew of London, for whatever debts the said Jew could prove to be owing him by the said Robert in a process to be held before the special justices charged with the care of the Jews. The sheriff was therefore instructed to permit Robert free enjoyment of his land in 'Chenes' which had been taken into the Jew's hands by reason of the debt, and to ensure that any chattels which had been taken therefrom were at once restored to Robert.[51]

In the following year Robert de Bello Campo was in dispute with the prior of Merton over the latter's fishery in the Thames. This was probably the fishery which Harold had set up at Mortlake and which had been granted to the priory by Henry II. It was a source of constant conflict, not only between the priory and the inhabitants of Shene and Kew, but also between the priory and the City of London, for over three hundred years: there were continual complaints of overfishing and of obstruction of the passage of boats. In this particular case Robert de Bello Campo had had his boats and nets seized at the prior's instigation for fishing above the prior's weir. However, Robert had his own fishing rights (derived from the grant to Robert Belet) as part of Alice Belet's share of the manor of Shene. The sheriff was instructed to release the boats and nets to Robert. If the prior objected, the writ went on, he could carry the matter to the King's Justices.[52]

About 1243 Alice Belet married John de Valle Torte, probably a grandson of the John de Valtort who was involved in a land suit in Shene in 1200.[53] Alice's husband can only have been a young man at the time of the marriage, for he lived until 1301. Apart from his wife's inheritance, he held in his own right some thirty acres of land in Shene, in Alice's part of the manor.

Alice's marriage, and her dowry rights, seem to have given rise to a dispute between the sisters. In 1250 Emma sued John and Alice de Valletorte over holdings of land both in Dorset and in 'Westshenes' in Surrey.[54] The case was eventually settled and in 1253 Emma recognised as part of Alice's dowry a carucate of land in Westshenes and other land in Blandford, Knighton, Winfrith Newburgh and Fossil in Dorset. It was agreed that if Alice should die without heirs, this land would revert to Emma; and John and Alice paid to Emma the sum of 30 marks.[55] This case appears to be the first occasion on which the Belet manor was called *West* Shene; and we may infer that this was to distinguish it from the hamlet of East Shene in the manor of Mortlake, which perhaps came into existence at about this time (though it first figures by that name in a Surrey 'fine' nearly a century later – in 1348). The name of Shene, without distinction, however continued to be applied to either locality for a long time to come.

In 1254 John de Valletort paid 20 shillings for half a knight's fee for his serjeanty in the manor of Shene, towards the aid for knighting the King's son.[56] In the following year we learn for the first time that he had been coroner for Middlesex, when he was relieved of this office.[57]

In the civil war which erupted in 1263-5 between the King and the baronial faction led by Simon de Montfort, John de Valletort appears to have supported de Montfort. Perhaps he had little option when Simon's army was encamped in Richard, Earl of Cornwall's park across the river at Isleworth in July 1263. Or perhaps he joined the citizens of London in their attack on Richard's manor house there the following year. When the King triumphed in 1265, the Valletort lands were seized. The great baron, Roger Mortimer, interceded on Alice's behalf. 'John de Vautort, charged with certain transgressions against the King and others during the troubles, had no lands or tenements other than the inheritance of Alice his wife,' Mortimer pointed out. The King was clement. 'The King, wishing to show grace towards the said Alice, grants her all the lands and tenements which are of her own inheritance and which are held by the King on account of the said charges.'[58]

The Manor of Shene, Before the Palace

After that John de Vautort (as the name was now more frequently spelled) settled down and we hear no more of him until his death in 1301, except for two further occasions when he was called on to pay half a knight's fee towards the scutages of Wales in 1278 and 1287.[59]

Emma Oliver, on the other hand, seems not to have lived on her half of the manor, and she made four further marriages. In 1253 she leased 'her whole land in Shene' to Master William de Kilkenny, Archdeacon of Coventry and Keeper of the King's Seal.[60] Later that year or early in 1254 she married a John Belet, presumably a kinsman and possibly from Hungerford, who is stated, rather surprisingly, to be a lay brother. Whether or not he broke the rules of his monastic order by contracting marriage, Emma certainly defied the secular rules by marrying without the King's licence though she was a tenant-in-chief from the King. Her lands in Surrey and Dorset were promptly confiscated and a fine of £20 was levied before they were released.[61]

William de Kilkenny's lease must have been a short one, for on 1 June 1254 John and Emma Belet granted another short lease, to Dom Artaldus de Sancto Romano, of 'the manor of Shene and two virgates of land which had been Roger Prustman's' until Michaelmas 1255 for a rent of £36. The usual royal confirmation was granted in 1255.[62] Then comes a puzzle. Unless John Belet had changed his name to Hake, or unless there was a mistake by scribe or transcriber, Emma seems to have buried two husbands in as many years. In January 1256/7 one Guy de Lezign restored to Emma and her new husband Robert de Meleburn 'the manor of Shene which he had on lease from John Hake, former husband of the said Emma,' for a settlement of £27.[63]

The reason why Emma and her husband wanted to terminate this lease prematurely was presumably in order to grant a new and longer one to a man of great power and influence. A 14-year lease of the manor of Shene 'of the King's serjeanty', with a messuage and a carucate of land, was granted in 1258/9 to John Maunsell (or Mansel), the King's chief counsellor.[64] In 1234 Maunsell had been the very first Chancellor of the Exchequer. Subsequently he was twice Keeper of the Great Seal. He was a busy diplomat who undertook missions to Brabant, Scotland, Castile (where he arranged for the marriage of the Prince of Wales to Princess Eleanor), Scotland again, France, Germany (where he secured the election of the King's brother, Richard of Cornwall, as King of the Romans), Scotland and then again to France. But he became one of the chief targets of baronial opposition and when de Montfort's uprising started in 1263 he was forced into exile in France. His own lands were confiscated and given to Simon de Montfort junior, but Emma's manor of Shene, being only leased, reverted to her.

Immediately before the lease to John Maunsell, Robert de Meleburn and Emma had granted a lease of two virgates of land and one acre of meadow in West Shene to a kinsman, William de Meleburn. The rent was 15 pence a year to be paid at the church of Shene.[65] This reference in early 1258 is the first explicit mention of the church as a building, although its existence is clearly implied at an earlier date in the Merton Priory records and in that 1220 reference already noted to 'the parish of Senes'.

Whether as a result of political pressure or of financial inducement Emma now surrendered her manorial rights to the King for the express purpose that they be regranted by him to Gilbert de Clare, Earl of Gloucester and Hereford, one of de Montfort's principal supporters. The surrender and the new grant to Earl Gilbert were enrolled in October 1264,[66] five months after de Montfort's victory over the King at Lewes, 10 months before his defeat and death at Evesham. Emma, while giving up the manorial title, appears to have kept a large part at least of the real

2 *Gilbert de Clare, 10th Earl of Gloucester and Hertford (from a window in Tewkesbury Abbey).*

estate. In 1270, by then married to a fifth husband, William de Wilburham, she finally sold this property – 'a messuage and one carucate of land in Shenes' – to William La Zuche (who had been sheriff of Surrey from 1261 to 1266 and was a brother of Alan, first Lord Zouche).[67] William and Emma gave their share of the Dorset lands in Knighton, Fossil and Winfrith Newburgh to the nearby Bindon Abbey.[68]

What happened next to Shene Manor, or rather Emma's half of it, is uncertain. Gilbert de Clare had had the discretion, or sound judgment, to change sides before the battle of Evesham in which he commanded a division of the King's army; so neither his head nor his lands were forfeit despite his earlier support of Simon de Montfort. However, within a very short time both the lordship and the real estate seem to have come into the hands of Hugh de Windsor, a direct descendant of that Walter Fitzother, governor of Windsor Castle, who had been responsible for the rearing of the King's forest mares in this area at the time of Domesday. No deed has however been traced showing how Hugh de Windsor acquired the property.

In 1271 another great national figure became lord of Shene. Robert Burnell, a close friend and confidant of Prince Edward, had been acquiring influence, and with it wealth and property, throughout the 1260s. When Prince Edward went off on the crusade in 1270 Burnell was one of three persons (with the Archbishop of York and Roger Mortimer) appointed as the Prince's attorneys in England during his absence from the kingdom. When King Henry III died in November 1272 these three became regents pending Edward's return. In (or just before) 1271 Hugh de Windsor had died and Burnell then bought Shene from his young son and heir, another Hugh.[69] At the same time he bought the manor of Ham from Maurice de Creoun.[70] In 1274 Burnell was made Chancellor of England; in the following year he became Bishop of Bath and Wells. (Twice Edward tried in vain to secure for him the see of Canterbury: once when he was still Prince of Wales, and then again in 1278 after he had become King. On the latter occasion the Pope himself vetoed the appointment, saying that Burnell was not a suitable person. Two years later he again vetoed Burnell's appointment as Bishop of Winchester.)

The Manor of Shene, Before the Palace

Meanwhile, in or about 1275, Emma Belet's former half of the manor of Shene had again changed hands, for Burnell sold both it and Ham to Sir Otto de Grandison, a knight of Swiss origin, who was another close friend and counsellor of the new King Edward I. Along with the half-manor of Shene went an extra 15 acres of meadow which Burnell had purchased from de Valletorte. A condition of the sale to Grandison was that if the latter, who was childless, were to die without heirs the manors should revert to Burnell. The sale of Shene was questioned, and Otto's right to the property held in suspense, though he is mentioned as lord of the manor in 1275.[71] The problem was that the young Hugh de Windsor had become insane, and it was suggested to the King that he had already been of unsound mind when he sold the property to Burnell – which would have rendered that sale, as well as the one to Grandison, invalid and would have meant that wardship of the manor could be claimed by the King. But King Edward 'inspected the late King's confirmation' of the sale to Burnell 'and reflected that no new right in the manor could accrue to him by any reason'. So on 25 January 1278/9 he ordered the sheriff of Surrey to release the manor to Sir Otto,[72] and in the following year he formally confirmed the sale by Robert Burnell and granted that in default of Grandison heirs 'the premises shall revert to the said Robert without claim or hindrance from the Crown.'[73] In December 1279 Otto was granted the right of free warren (i.e. hunting) in his demesne lands of Shene.[74]

Otto de Grandison had been a companion of Prince Edward on the crusade in 1270. In 1275 he was made 'keeper' of Guernsey and Jersey, and two years later was made lord of those islands – a position he then held until his death. In 1285 he was granted the temporary keepership of the archbishopric of York, then vacant, so that he might apply its revenues to the construction of castles in Wales 'as the King had enjoined him'.[75] He had been one of the leaders of Edward's armies in the final campaign to conquer what was left of the formerly independent principality, and he was directly concerned with the building of the castles at Flint, Conway, Harlech and Caernarvon. He was Constable of Caernarvon, the administrative centre, and was appointed to be the first Justiciar of Wales.

3 Sir Otto de Grandison, from an altarcloth given to Lausanne Cathedral (Museum of Berne).

Having spent most of the decade of the 1280s in Wales, he set out on another crusade about 1290, in the course of which he was present at the siege of Acre in 1292. Before he left, being still without heirs, he reinvested Bishop Burnell, conditionally, in the two manors of Shene and Ham. (Manning hopelessly confused the chronology by dating this action with reference to the previous Crusade in 1270.)[76]

While Grandison was still away, Burnell died, on 25 October 1292, in Berwick where he had accompanied King Edward for his arbitration of John Balliol's claim to the Scottish throne. Whatever the defects in his character as a churchman, which had caused the Pope to block his preferment, he had been a shrewd and faithful counsellor to Edward. *The Dictionary of National Biography* says of him:

> Burnell's faithfullness, wisdom and experience must be set against the greediness and the licentiousness and the nepotism that stained his private character. His kindness of heart, his liberality, affability, love of peacemaking and readiness in giving audience to his suitors brought him a good share of his master's popularity.

In the customary manner, inquests were held into Burnell's property. He held no fewer than 82 manors, so it is perhaps unlikely that Shene had seen much of him. The inquest held at Kingston in 1292, on the Tuesday after the feast of St Thomas the Martyr, records that his holding at Shene included a capital messuage with a garden, a dovecote and a park, 200 acres of arable land, 16 acres of meadow, a pasture, a rabbit warren and a free fishery.[77]

Burnell's heir was Philip Burnell, aged 25, son of his brother Hugh. Philip seems to have inherited his uncle's licentiousness without his shrewdness. He had squandered much of his uncle's patrimony before he himself died in 1294, leaving a son Edward, aged only 12, as his heir.[78] Young Edward was soon married off to Alice, daughter of Hugh le Despenser, Earl of Winchester, the next royal counsellor and favourite to dominate the stage at Shene – and one whose part was to be decisive in changing the course of Shene's history.

Edward Burnell's title to Shene was however only temporary, plus an ultimate right of reversion after the death of Otto de Grandison; and by 1296 Otto had returned to England and recovered his manors. He was granted licence to lease them, Shene included, for a period of five years.[79] It seems probable that Shene was now leased to Edward, Prince of Wales, who found the manor in a poor state of repair. On 26 May 1299 it was ordered that 'no person, whether belonging to the King or any other person of whatever state, the King's son only excepted, shall enter, stay or lodge in Otto de Grandison's manor of Shene, or put their baggage or other goods there, against his will or the will of the keeper of the said manor, as it appears that great damage has been done by people lodging in the houses there'.[80]

In that year, 1299, and in the next, the King himself resided for a while at Shene with his court. There are letters patent dated from Shene in 1299 and accounts of the expenses of the royal household there in 1300. In 1305 the King received at Shene the commissioners he had sent to Scotland to establish civil government. In 1309 Edward II held a council there; in 1310 he dated from Shene the grant to the Percys of the barony of Alnwick.

Throughout this period, while Emma Belet's former half of the manor, which included the manor house and the right to hold the manorial court, had been changing hands so frequently, the other half of the manor lands had remained in the hands of John and Alice de Valletort (or

The Manor of Shene, Before the Palace

Vautort). John died in 1301, and was succeeded by his son, another John. The inquest, again held at Kingston, records that he too held 200 acres of arable land,[*] with 12 acres of meadow and a pasture 'in a little island of the Thames called la Wynyard'. His house and garden, with an extra 20 acres of land and one acre of meadow, were however leased from Otto de Grandison.[81]

The younger John de Vautort was not allowed to enjoy his inheritance for very long. In the second year of Edward II's reign (1308/9) he surrendered all his lands 'in West Shene, Cumbe and Baggeshote' to Hugh le Despenser for a payment of 100 marks.[82] After Despenser's fall and execution in 1326 this John's brother and heir, Richard de Vautort, sought in vain the restitution of these lands. His claim alleged that Hugh le Despenser had imprisoned John de Vautort in Newgate on the pretext that he had trespassed in Despenser's park 'at Bokking', and had kept him in close custody until he agreed to surrender his estates. Despenser, the claim continued, had then granted the lands to the King.[83]

Though deprived of their half of the manor, the Vautorts did keep – or regain – a small holding within it. John de Vautort was still described as 'of Shene' when he sold in 1313 the Dorset lands he had inherited from his mother – a house, 91 acres of land, 7 acres of meadow and 60 shillings in rents in Knighton, Fossil and Winfrith Newburgh.[84] In 1314 Richard de Valtort was shown as holding one acre and a quarter in Shene;[85] in 1332 Richard de Vautort was assessed in Shene for 4s. 2d.;[86] and 20 years later another John de Vautort and his wife Joan sold their messuage with four and a quarter acres of arable land and one acre of meadow to John de Gaddesby, clerk.[87]

The process by which the other half of the manor was formally restored to royal ownership began in 1307 when, after the death of his lifelong friend Edward I, Otto de Grandison decided to retire to his ancestral castle of Grandison on the lake of Neuchâtel. He had no desire to remain in, or ever return to, the England of Edward II and Hugh le Despenser, so he obtained a licence from the King for permanent residence abroad. Whether or not he surrendered his title to Shene at this time is not clear, but it was hardly material. There remained Edward Burnell's reversionary right. In February 1312 young Edward was induced to grant this to his father-in-law Hugh le Despenser.[88] Presumably this title too was then transferred to the King. Grandison lived on, still unmarried and without heirs, in his Swiss castle until he died at the age of 90 in 1328. He was buried in Lausanne Cathedral. But from 1312 Edward II could count himself as direct owner of the whole manor of Shene, and in 1316 'the Manor of West Shene and its members' were officially recorded as not only belonging to the King, but 'in his hands'.[89]

---

[*] The assessed value of this only allowed for 100 acres, so there was a mistake either in the amount of land stated or in the calculation.

4 *King Edward II, from a genealogical table in* A chronicle of the Kings of England. *(British Library, Cotton MSS Jul E4 f6 verso)*

Chapter II

The Plantagenet Palace

The grant, on 7 October 1313, to John de Boseham of the custody of the King's manor of Shene, during the King's pleasure,[1] may be taken as signifying the date by which the manor had again become royal property. But almost at once, albeit briefly, it was abandoned by the King.

At the battle of Bannockburn in June 1314 King Edward II had been put to flight by the Scots under Robert Bruce. Hotly pursued by the enemy, he vowed to the Virgin Mary that if he escaped safely he would found a monastery for the Carmelites (known as the 'white friars' from the colour of their habits). Escape he did – and he quickly honoured his pledge.[2] Twenty-four Carmelite friars were housed in the royal manor of Shene, at the King's command, 'to celebrate divine service there'. The buildings of the manor house were repaired for them in 1314-15.[3] On 28 December 1315 the King granted them 120 marks 'for their sustenance until he should make other provision for them'.[4] In the following summer Edward apparently decided that he would let the Carmelites have Shene permanently, and a grant in franc almoin (i.e. without any obligations save the performance of religious duties) was made to them on 12 July 1316 of 'the dwelling place of the King's manor of Shene, with three islands and the enclosures pertaining to the said dwelling place, to hold to them and their successors celebrating divine service there for the souls of the King's progenitors, his soul, and the souls of all Christian people'.[5]

But then the King found them what he considered a better home, granting them a site at Oxford, the King's Hall. Situated by the walls just outside the north gate, at Beaumont, this was a royal house built by Henry I but which Edward II had already despoiled in order to repair Oxford Castle. The grant was dated 1 February 1317/8;[6] by 10 February they had moved from Shene to their new home at Oxford, where the King renewed his maintenance grant to them of 120 marks a year.[7] Their church in the manor of Shene was demolished.[8] So Shene's first monastic foundation had lasted only some two or three years, and the manor house was once again vacant.

On 26 April 1320 the King appointed Humphrey de Waleden to be his seneschal or steward for a long list of royal castles and manors, in 11 counties, including the manors of Shene and Byfleet in Surrey and the manors of 'Istelworth and La Neyte' in Middlesex.[9] Isleworth, a moated house with a hall, chapel and royal apartments, had reverted to the crown on the death of Margaret de Clare, widow of Edmund, Earl of Cornwall, in 1312. (The reference to a manor of La Neyte is of interest in view of later references to royal buildings

5   The Coronation of King Edward III. (Biblothèque Nationale de France, Paris)

on 'La Neyt', i.e. the eyot, at Shene, but this appears to refer to a small royal house near Westminster rather than to any islands between Isleworth and Shene.)[10] On 8 March 1323/4 a similar grant was made jointly to Humphrey de Waleden and Richard de Ikerne;[11] and then on 20 August 1324 another grant named Richard de Wynferthing and Richard de Ikerne as joint stewards.[12] The King is known to have been at Shene in 1324, 1325 and 1326.[13] As a

King's clerk, justice and baron of the exchequer, Humphrey de Waleden (died *c*.1330) was a man of some importance. He was summoned as a member of the Parliament called in January 1326/7 by Queen Isabella and Prince Edward after the overthrow and execution of the Despensers.

The deposition – or forced abdication – of Edward II in favour of his 14-year-old son followed on 25 January 1326/7. On 1 February the new King, Edward III, formally granted the manor of Shene (and those of Isleworth and Byfleet and the farm of Kingston, among many other possessions) to his mother for her lifetime.[14] In effect she had granted them to herself, for during the next few years Queen Isabella and her lover Roger Mortimer governed the country. The young King Edward, who in 1328, at the age of 16, married the 14-year-old Philippa of Hainault, soon began to chafe at his mother's tutelage. In 1330 he asserted himself; Mortimer was arrested and executed, and Queen Isabella was stripped of many of her estates. Among her losses was Isleworth, now granted to Queen Philippa as part of her dowry; but Isabella was allowed to keep some of her manors, sufficient to endow her with £3,000 a year, including Shene (valued at £30 p.a.) and the farm of Kingston (£54 8s. 10d.). A series of grants in 1331 (two), 1334 and 1345 regulated Queen Isabella's endowment and made changes in it; but she retained Shene and Kingston throughout.[15]

6   Queen Isabella, mother of Edward III, from the choir of Bristol Cathedral.

In her retirement, Isabella lived most of the time at her manor of Castle Rising in Norfolk, and how much use she actually made of the house at Shene it is difficult to say. Queen Philippa was there in 1331-2, when she dated some letters patent from Shene,[16] but thereafter we hear little more of the Shene manor house for the next 20 years. From a few surviving accounts it appears that Isabella visited Shene at least in 1349-50 and in 1351-3, when the houses in 'the Douncourt' were prepared for her visits.[17] (From which it can be inferred that there were two courts.) She may have sought refuge at Shene when the Black Death first struck England in 1348-9, but Shene was itself stricken with that dreadful epidemic of plague.

The plague was followed by much social unrest, and in the early 1350s there were at least two occasions when the royal manor house was broken into. A commission of oyer and terminer issued in October 1353[18] gives no details either of the offenders or of the damage, but a second commission issued on 18 June 1354 is more specific. Twelve inhabitants of Twickenham, Brentford and Acton and some others 'entered the manor of Shene, Co. Surrey, which the King's mother, Queen Isabel, holds for life, of his grant', and 'broke her close and houses and hunted in her free warren there, carried away her goods as well as hares, conies, partridges and pheasants from the warren, assaulted her men and servants there and at Kyngeston, followed them to the dwelling place of the manor and besieged them, so that they dared not go forth to serve her, whereby her land remained untilled and other business was left undone for a long time, and hindered other of her ministers so that they could not do their office and make her profit'.[19]

It was no doubt as a result of these depredations that on 24 May 1356 Ralph Thurbarne was instructed 'to take sufficient carpenters, tilers, coverers of houses and other workmen not being in the King's works, for the works of the King's mother Queen Isabel in the manor of Shene, and to put them to work at her wages'.[20] Isabella visited Shene again in the following year, but on 22 August 1358 she died at her castle at Hertford.

Almost immediately after his mother's death, King Edward began to develop the manor house of Shene into a proper royal palace. The house was put into the custody of a salaried keeper: John de Swanton was appointed on 10 October 1358 to hold the office during the King's pleasure, with wages of 6d. a day.[21] Shene was not the only place where the King was embarking on major works, and on 10 July 1359 the King's clerk, William de Wykeham (the future bishop of Winchester), who had already been given charge of works at Henley-on-the-Heath, Easthampstead and Windsor, was appointed 'chief keeper and surveyor' of four royal castles and 12 royal manors, including Shene, 'with full power to ordain and dispose all works at those places'.[22] Some minor work was put in hand immediately: £100 was spent at Shene in the three years from October 1358 to November 1361, some of it on the garden and the planting of vines. £8 4s. 4d. was spent on the construction of a crane – a presage of the major works to follow.[23] The two other large projects at Rotherhithe and Eltham were now nearing completion. In November 1361 Bernard Cook had been appointed clerk of works for these two sites and for Shene, and in the following year he spent £28 at Shene on making a new fishpond, cleaning out an old one and on works on the moat, and a further £59 on buildings there.[24] Then in 1363 he turned his main attention to Shene, and no less than £556 was spent there between November 1362 and November 1363.[25] Unfortunately there are no extant detailed accounts prior to November 1363, so it is only possible to surmise what was entailed in this year of major expenditure. But the detailed 'particulars' which have survived for the works after November 1363 enable us to build up some idea of Edward III's palace.

7   King Edward III, by an unknown artist. (National Portrait Gallery)

8 William of Wykeham (effigy in Winchester Cathedral). (John Crook)

Altogether in the five years from 1363 to 1368 some £1700 were spent on the works at Shene, which included the following features:

(i) The great gate and the bridge (over the moat) before it, and a new chamber beside the gate (which had two fireplaces in it).[26]
(ii) Repairs and modifications to the King's old chamber, evidently on an upper floor, which was given a new plaster wall in front (1363-6) and a new front with two windows and a 'window facing the clock' (1366-7), and beneath which were cut two doorways where a new cloister was made, leading to a new chamber at the end.[27]
(iii) A new chamber for the King in the lower court (apparently on the side facing the Thames),[28] with a doorway below it. This chamber had glass windows and two fireplaces (which were repaired, rather than new-built, so this was probably an adaptation of an existing building).[29] The fact that these two fireplaces were apparently served by four pipes (flues) has led to the suggestion that they may have been pairs of fireplaces built back-to-back to serve two rooms each. A more probable, and simpler, explanation would be that there were in fact four fireplaces of which only two needed repair, but that all four flues were replastered. In either case, it is evident that 'the King's Chamber' should be regarded not as a single room, but as a suite of rooms. A candelabrum for this chamber was wrought in metal in the shape of 'five flowers in the form of roses' and was fixed in (or in front of?) one of the windows.[30]
(iv) The paving of the new cloister and the making of a herb garden in it (1366-7).[31]

(v)   A new 'great house' with nine chambers with latrines, the location of which is not given (1367-8).[32]
(vi) A 'great house' in the cloister, with four fireplaces and four latrines.[32]
(vii) A 'great house' containing three separate buildings for the King's wardrobe, the Queen's wardrobe and the chandlery.[32]
(viii) A new chamber by the garden, with eight fireplaces.[32]
(ix) New larders and kitchen, and a roasting house.[33]
(x)   New stables (105 feet long and 30 feet high), apparently supplemented by more new stables in 1369.[34]
(xi) New walls on the river side of the buildings.[35]
(xii) A wharf by the riverside, on either side of the bridge towards the Thames.[36]

A hall and a chapel were already in existence by November 1363, but whether they had just been built or whether they were the old buildings of the manor house, enlarged and renovated, we cannot tell. For the hall a new fireplace was constructed (1363-6).[37] And in 1374 'eight feet of glass painted with the Last Judgment, purchased from John Brompton of London, the King's glazier', were set 'in the front of the great chapel'.[38]

By 1369 the main works were virtually completed, but further embellishments and some new development continued during the next decade. The King's new chamber was tiled in 1370;[39] some lattice windows 'towards the bridge and the Thames' were inserted in 1371;[40] the moat was cleaned out in 1371[41] and again in 1376;[42] two pools were made on one of the islands in the river in 1371.[43] In 1376 a great barn was purchased in Wimbledon (presumably from the archbishop of Canterbury's manor) and was brought to Shene and rebuilt there to store the King's hay;[44] and in the following year a hall with two chambers was also moved from Wimbledon to Shene and re-erected with new partition walls and a tiled roof.[45] The year 1376 also saw the erection of five new ancillary buildings, all of timber on stone foundations, to provide a chamber for a member of the household, an 'easement next to the outer gate', a coal store, a carpenter's lodge and a chop house.[46] In 1377 a new belfry was built for the palace clock.[47]

The materials used in these works are not very clearly identified, but can often be inferred from the contracts. There is some mention of stonework, of chalk for foundations, of wall tiles and hollow tiles and roof tiles. There is no mention of brick. Whether the main residential buildings were of stone or half-timber is uncertain. The references to the plaster wall of the King's old chamber suggest that that building may well have been of half-timber construction; and certainly many of the subsidiary buildings were of timber and 'daub' on stone foundations (as is evidenced by the contracts for those listed at v to viii above). It is however safe to assume that stone would have been used for the chapel – and probably also for the hall.

The names of some of those involved with the works as craftsmen and as supervisors have survived. The chief mason employed was John Siward; the chief carpenter was William Selot, a local man from Twickenham. William Northorne and William of Yorke were plasterers, Stephen Southwark a tiler, Thomas Shonk a dauber. John Coupere made the lattice windows, Stephen atte Tower the metal candelabrum for the King's chamber. Thomas Bolton of Hampstead was the contractor who cleaned the moat and constructed the pools on the island. When the main work was completed William Selot was given in 1370 the post of 'intendant carpenter', with a life appointment to maintain the manor (and those of Banstead, Isleworth and Babbeworthpond) with a retainer of sixpence a day to be paid from the issues of the manor of Shene. [48]

Among those who acted as purveyors of material was the great architect Henry Yevele, then master mason for Westminster and the Tower of London. In 1366-7 he arranged for paving at

Shene. Whether he played any significant part in the design or supervision of the works is not recorded. It seems unlikely therefore; but he did sign one contract for the repair of two fireplaces in 1367-8, so he appears to have been involved in more than just the supply of paving.[49]

As clerk of works Bernard Cook was succeeded in 1367 by Robert de Sibthorp,[50] who then continued in charge for the rest of Edward III's reign. The supervisory and accounting duties originally entrusted to William of Wykeham were taken over for Shene alone, by Ralph Thurbarn and John Swanton jointly.[51] Both already had a long association with Shene. John Swanton had been keeper of the manor house since 1358 and of the warren since 1361; he was also appointed keeper of the wardrobe in 1377.[52] Ralph Thurbarn had been in charge of the repair works undertaken for Queen Isabella in 1356; from 1361 he had been the farmer (i.e. tenant) of Shene manor.

From 1361 the manor, as distinct from the new palace or manor house itself and its immediate grounds, was let 'in farm' to a series of tenants, usually on 10-year leases. The first such lease, to Ralph Thurbarn, dated 15 November 1361, committed to him for 10 years from Michaelmas just past, 'the keeping of the King's manor of Shene with all the profits and emoluments thereof (except coneys to the value of 10 marks which the King has reserved for the expenses of his household)' at a rental of 52 marks per annum, on condition that he should maintain at his own cost 'all the houses in the upper court, called la Overcourt, set apart for the animals for tilling the land'.[53]

The next farmer appears to have been an Edward Thurbarn, possibly the son of Ralph, whose grant has not been traced.[54] Then, early in the reign of Richard II, there are two grants to Robert de Dyneleye dated 1382 and 1385 (the first does not specify a rent; the second, at 40 marks per annum, describes the leased property as 'the King's manor of Shene called le Touncourt').[55] But only three weeks after the second grant to Dyneleye, in 1385, comes the first of three grants all made in that same year to John Swanton. They all cover the same 10-year period at the same rent of 40 marks per annum, but the terms are progressively refined. John Swanton was receiving for his services as keeper of the house and wardrobe and of the warren allowances of ninepence a day. He was also responsible for the payment of the sixpence daily wage to William Selot the carpenter. These deductions to be allowed from the revenues of the manor were specifically noted in the last of the three grants, as was Swanton's responsibility for 'maintaining the houses and buildings for husbandry in as good a state of repair as they were in at Michaelmas last'.[56]

These grants in farm of the manor, though extending even to the farm buildings in the outer court of the new palace did not of course affect

9 King Edward III (effigy in Westminster Abbey). (Dean & Chapter of Westminster)

the royal right to occupy the palace itself. Indeed Edward III made much use of it in the last years of his reign. It was at Shene that he died on 22 June 1377. During his last illness he evidently continued to conduct affairs of state from his sick-bed, for the clerk of works was called upon to make 'divers forms or benches to be used round the Lord King in the time of his sickness'. The same accounts also record the making of a 'sepulchre' and a hearse to carry the King's body to Westminster for burial.[57]

Edward III's eldest son, the renowned 'Black Prince', had died in the previous year, so the heir to the throne was Edward's 10-year-old grandson, Richard II 'of Bordeaux'. On 22 January 1382/3 Richard married Anne of Bohemia, daughter of the Emperor Charles IV. It was a dynastic alliance, but the young King and Queen promptly turned it into a love match. For the young couple, both still in their mid-teens, the palace of Shene became a favourite residence. Between 1383 and 1389 further works were undertaken:[58] they included repairs to the King's and the Queen's chambers, to the King's closet, the chapel and the gate of the outer court. The King's bathroom was decorated with 2,000 painted tiles, purchased for 15 shillings from Katherine Lightfoot, who was about to become the second wife of Henry Yevele, himself once again active in the procurement of materials for Shene. A new staircase was made for the Queen's chamber, and work was also carried out on chambers for some members of the royal household.

But the greatest scene of activity was the river and the riverside. On 'an island called la Nayght' – probably the largest of the several eyots near the palace – a house was built. It was probably a summer pavilion; but it was of substantial size, though built of the usual timber framing on stone foundations. It contained 'several chambers with fireplaces' and a kitchen. In the King's chamber three trestle tables and three benches were provided.

It was a romantic retreat for the young couple, and it is pleasant to think of them enjoying a brief respite from affairs of state on their island in the Thames. The island's banks were

10   Richard II in coronation robes. (Dean & Chapter of Westminster)

11 The presentation of a book to Richard II. The book, by a Celestine monk of Paris (possibly Philippe de Maizieres, former Chancellor of Cyprus), was originally in the library of Richmond Palace. (British Library, Royal MS 20 B vi, f2)

reinforced with new palings, and new steps were made 'for the King's way to the water'. A new barge and a boat were provided for the crossing from the palace to the island. At a convenient point – probably where 'Crane Wharf' was later – a new jetty for the loading and unloading of goods for the royal household was built.

It was at the beginning of Richard II's reign that the whole system for supervising the various works was reorganised, and a clerk of the King's works with overall responsibility for all works was appointed on a regular basis. Among the early holders of this office, for two years from July 1389 to June 1391, was Geoffrey Chaucer, the poet;[59] but only minor works were done at Shene at this time and there is no record – sadly – of Chaucer making any notable personal contribution.

Suddenly disaster struck – and the idyll of Shene Palace and the young lovers was brought to an abrupt end. On Whit Sunday, 7 June 1394, Queen Anne died at Shene of the plague. The whole nobility of the country were summoned to escort her body from Shene to Westminster.[60] Richard was heart-broken; he cursed the place where she died. Shene, where he and Anne had been so happy together, must perish with her. On 9 April 1395 he ordered John Gedney, Chaucer's successor as clerk of the King's works, to destroy the place entirely, 'as well the houses and buildings in the court within the moat and the court without the moat, as the houses and buildings in La Neyt beside the manor'.[61]

12 Anne of Bohemia on her deathbed at Shene Palace. From a copy of Froissart's Chronicles. *(British Library, Harleian MS 4380, f22)*

13 The effigies of Richard II and Anne of Bohemia from their tomb in Westminster Abbey.

At the anniversary of the Queen's death a statue of her was apparently erected at Shene, for on 3 June 1395 two shillings were paid by the Exchequer for the transport by river from London to Shene of 'the statue made in the likeness of Anne, late Queen of England'.[62] Despite this, the demolition was carried out, and much of the material from Shene was reused at the Tower of London, at the royal manor houses of Windsor and Sutton (in Chiswick) and other places.

For 20 years Shene Palace lay as an abandoned ruin, though the destruction may have been less total than Richard had intended. At least the farm buildings in the 'Overcourt' seem to have been spared, and the manor continued to be leased out to farmers. In 1393 a William Swanton (perhaps a son of John, who in 1390 had handed over the offices of keeper of the manor house, wardrobe and warren to his son Thomas)[63] and a Richard Goion had been jointly granted a 10-year lease on terms similar to those of the last grant to John Swanton.[64] (The Goions were a local family whose name occurs in the Shene manor records as early as 1314 – but with a holding in villenage, so they had clearly risen in the social scale during the century.) Then in 1395, after the demolition, the lease was renewed for its unexpired term to a John Goion, who paid the same rent – but now the clauses concerning the payment of wages for the keeper of the house and wardrobe and for the intendant carpenter are significantly omitted.[65] A separate grant was made to a William Hervey as keeper of the warren.[66] A series of similar grants in farm followed (in 1400, 1404, 1409, 1410 and 1412) of which the only one of interest is that to Thomas Arundel, Archbishop of Canterbury, who held the farm of the manor from 1410 to 1412. But in all these grants the manor was still always referred to as 'the manor of Shene called the Towncourt' and there remained a clause requiring the farmer to maintain the buildings used for husbandry.[67] So it would appear that the agricultural life of the manor carried on even though the manor house was disused.

Even more significant perhaps is the confirmation by Henry IV, when he came to the throne after Richard II's deposition in 1399, of the appointment of William Rockyngham as gardener of the King's garden at Shene.[68] Rockyngham had originally been appointed in 1387, in succession to Robert Gardyner[69] (the first gardener at Shene whose name we know – he was probably 'Robert le Gardyner'). In 1391 Rockyngham's appointment had been confirmed for life.[70] However, this second confirmation by the new King, who need have felt no compulsion to honour his predecessor's grants, seems to indicate that the royal garden at Shene was indeed still being maintained.

14 King Henry V, by an unknown artist. (National Portrait Gallery)

Chapter III

The Lancastrian Palace

Henry IV seems to have taken little or no interest in Shene, but soon after the accession of Henry V (21 March 1412/3) Shene came to life again. Henry had several motives for deciding to restore the ruined palace. There was the obvious one that here was an agreeable site conveniently close to London going to waste; but there was also a more deeply significant consideration. His father had become King by right of conquest; he himself, as the son of a usurper, was surrounded by cousins whose claims to the throne were at least as valid as his own. He needed to achieve legitimacy, and to establish and maintain a sense of continuity with the reigns of Edward III and Richard II. To rebuild Edward III's palace would be a useful gesture.

Moreover, his father had vowed to expiate his sins of involvement in the murders of Richard II and of Archbishop Scroope by the founding of three monasteries. He had died with his vow unfulfilled. Young Henry was concerned for the fate of his father's soul. Henry V, however wild he may have been in his youth, was a pious man with a strong sympathy for ascetic monasticism. For both religious and dynastic reasons it seemed both necessary and appropriate to carry out his father's intentions.

In the two royal manors of Shene and Isleworth, facing each other across the Thames, there was ample room to realise all these projects. In the manor of Isleworth on the Middlesex bank (which then included the whole of Twickenham) Henry would establish two of the new monasteries; in Shene, on the Surrey bank, he would rebuild the palace and found the third religious house, the Charterhouse of Shene. All four jobs could proceed simultaneously, with economies in management and materials, under unified supervision. Thus 'the King's Great Work' was launched.

The work on the monasteries will be described in the following chapter. In considering how to set about the palace project, Henry seems to have rejected the idea of simply restoring the buildings on the old site. Immediately adjacent to it, however, on the south-east side, were the gardens, and what was probably part, if not all, of the original park of Shene. On the site of these gardens, within the circuit of the old moat, the main block of the new palace was to be built; but Henry was impatient to revive Shene and he determined to start by erecting what we might now describe as 'prefabricated buildings' by the riverside, outside the moat, in the park. (See Appendix 2.) He ordered that the buildings of the royal manor house at Byfleet in Surrey, some 12 miles away, should be taken down and rebuilt at Shene.[1] As they were mainly timber or timber-framed lath and plaster buildings this could be done quite easily. Only new stone foundations were required before the timber frames could be re-erected and the plastering renewed.

15 A brick kiln in Flanders in the mid-15th century. (British Library, Add MS 38.122, f78v)

16 Building works in the 1430s: St Edmund directing the building of the town of Hunstanton. (British Library, Harleian MS 2278, f28v)

Preparations for the works began in the winter of 1413-14, when materials and labour were gathered for the job.[2] In charge of the whole 'Great Work' was John Strange, clerk of the King's works,[3] with John Skipton as his deputy[4] and John Hertishorne as comptroller.[5] Stephen Lote was master-mason for the palace.[6] Materials were gathered not only from all over England but also from the English possessions in France. Stone came from Caen in Normandy and young trees for the new gardens from Rouen. Bricks – still a rarity in England – were shipped from Newenden Bridge just outside Calais. (The brickmaker Hugh Brikeman charged £19 for supplying 114,000 bricks; getting them from Calais to Shene cost half as much again.[7]) Equally costly must have been the shipment of stone from Yorkshire and Devon, or of lead and plaster from Lancashire. At least the timber came from woods in Surrey, and the glass was made in London.

The cost of freighting bricks led to the establishment of one of the area's first local industries, for a brick kiln was set up in Petersham;[8] some twenty years later another was set up by William Vesey, brickmaster, in Shene on the royal demesne land north-east of the Charterhouse site.[9]

Another source of building materials was to pull down and cannibalise old houses. In addition to the manor house of Byfleet, the King ordered the demolition of his house at Sutton (in Chiswick) which had itself been built largely with materials taken from the old palace of Shene.[10] So some at least of the materials of Edward III's palace would have reappeared in Henry V's new one. Every item salvaged from the demolished houses was carefully inventoried before being transported to the building site at Shene. Even the plaster could be reused, and 104 cartloads of it were brought from Byfleet to help in making 'the new manor called Byfleet within the manor of Shene'.[11]

While work on re-erecting Byfleet was given priority, work on the main building of the new palace proceeded at the same time. Between 1414 and 1419 over £8,000 had been spent on the two buildings: £5,815 on Byfleet and £2,368 on the 'foundations of the manor of Shene'.[12] Byfleet was a complete royal complex in itself. Although there are only fragmentary details in the accounts, it is known to have included both a King's ward and a Queen's ward, a chapel, a bathhouse and a kitchen. There is no mention of a hall, and it is at least a possibility that the hall from Byfleet was re-erected, not with its fellows on the riverside site, but in the courtyard to the north of the main building, of which it was then considered to be a part (*see* p.34). The buildings were mostly wooden or timber-framed with plaster walls, as is evidenced by a contract for 'ground walls for the support of the new timber building called Byfleet',[13] but stone was certainly used in some buildings. It is uncertain whether the stones 'worked for the main gate of Shene', for windows of the 'great Chapel' and of a tower, and for the stone-vaulted undercroft of the chapel[14] refer to buildings within the Byfleet complex or to the main palace, but two stone towers were certainly built on the east side of Byfleet between 1419 and 1422.[15] The bricks from Calais were used for the walls and chimneys of the 'outer ward'.[16]

Byfleet, moreover, was well ornamented. Over the kitchen was a 'great antelope carved in wood',[17] and a further 80 antelopes and swans were carved by Peter Kervour for the King's parlour and chamber.[18] Lions and fleurs-de-lys adorned the beams and cornices, while 'knots, curiously wrought' formed the decoration of panelling in the chapel.[19]

By the time of Henry V's death in 1422 the reconstruction of Byfleet must have been more or less finished; the main building however was still far from complete.

For the next seven years work was suspended. The total expenditure on Shene from 1422 to 1429 was less than £70.[20] The new King, Henry VI, was only a baby, born a year before his father's death. John, Duke of Bedford, the younger brother of Henry V, was nominally regent, but spent most of his time in France fighting the war in which the tide had turned against the English. His other brother, Humphrey, Duke of Gloucester, acted for him as Protector of the Realm in England – where he quarrelled with the King's Council. In 1429 the Council determined to end

Gloucester's 'protectorate' and arranged for the coronation of the eight-year-old King, followed by a declaration of the end of the protectorate and Gloucester's relegation to 'chief counsellor'.

It was presumably this event which led to a decision to resume work at Shene. The emphasis was now to be on completion of the main block: 'the new building of the manor of Shene'. For the first three years after the issue of the commission in October 1429 to 'take workmen and materials'[21] there are no records of expenditure; then from 1432 to 1435 the clerk of works (now John Ardene) spent £1,560,[22] and from 1436 to 1439 another £1,015.[23] There are details of the work only for these last three years; they indicate that a late stage had by then been reached in the completion of the building. By 1435 wood was being worked for the ceiling of various rooms.[24] In the next three years, the doors were hung for the great hall; an oratory was constructed for the King over the hall porch; the windows of the great chamber, the privy chamber and the oratory were filled in with glass 'wrought with the King's arms and his beasts and other devices';[25] on the south side of the 'great chapel' a new closet was built for the King's use and this was glazed with glass painted with 'figures and flowers curiously wrought'.[26]

There were still some more buildings to be erected. Six skins of parchment were supplied for the master-mason, Robert Westerley, and the master-carpenter, Richard Wheler, to draw 'divers designs for divers buildings thereon'.[27]

17 An illustration of the building of the Tower of Babel, from the Book of Hours of John, Duke of Bedford, shows some of the building techniques and tools used in the early 15th century. (British Library, Add MS 18.850, f17v)

On the north side of the site a new range of chambers was constructed. Some repairs were undertaken to the King's chapel in the Byfleet complex. The sites of the old palace and the new were separated by the digging of a 'great moat', 25 feet wide and eight feet deep. A new palisade was erected 'outside the moat of the manor of Byfleet joined to the said new building of the manor of Shene'.[28]

There seems to have been another lull in the works after 1439, then a further burst of activity from 1444 to 1447 occasioned by the King's marriage in 1445 to Margaret of Anjou. In 1444 the ceiling of the great chapel was adorned with fleur-de-lys crests.[29] At Byfleet a timber screen was being carved for the chapel, and a cloister was built with a lead cistern in the middle, decorated with eight panels showing various royal monograms and other devices.[30] The cistern was supplied from an underground conduit.

However, the main work of this period was the provision of extra accommodation. William Clere, who took over as clerk of works in 1444, was instructed 'to new make the waterbrigge, the

I *The presentation of a book to Richard II. (British Library)*

II *Anne of Bohemia on her deathbed at Shene Palace. (British Library)*

III *Building the Tower of Babel, showing early 15th-century building techniques. (British Library)*

grete quadrangle with a gatehouse all of new to be made for the necessary logging of the worshipful household, with closer of brike toured about [the King's] garden there'.[31]

This reference leads us to a consideration of the layout and design of these Lancastrian buildings, of which there is no first-hand account. Of Byfleet there is little to add to the (obviously incomplete) mentions recited above of particular buildings and accommodation. That its domestic buildings were timber-framed suggests that it was a 'soft' house, undefended except for its outer wall with the two stone towers and its moat with an outer palisade. Its chapel was no doubt of stone and seems to have been located on the side of the site closest to the main palace (if it is, as appears probable, the one building of this period that survived to be drawn by Wyngaerde in 1562 – *see* pp.71 and 73).

If we look at a plan of the palace complex as it existed in Tudor times (*see* p.60), it is noteworthy that the main palace boundary extended much farther from the river than did that of the Byfleet (later friary) area. The north-eastern wall of the latter is approximately on the same line as that of the *middle* court of the Tudor palace. For this anomaly the expansion of the palace in 1444-5 provides a ready explanation. It seems probable that, up until that date, the palace boundary on the side of the Green had been in a straight line with that of Byfleet. The new 'great quadrangle' with a new gateway and lodgings for the household equates to the outer court of the Tudor palace and was probably enclosed from the Green only at this time in the mid-15th century. At the same time the garden was also extended to the same frontage and enclosed by its new wall of brick, with towers.

Another point is remarkable in the Tudor plan. The block of buildings nearest to the river, containing the royal apartments, has a ground plan which looks nothing like a normal Tudor building, but very like an early 15th-century residential castle. The many-windowed bays and towers of the Tudor building echo the typical perimeter towers of, say, Herstmonceux Castle in Sussex – which dates from 1441. The logical inference is that the Tudor rebuilding made use of the Lancastrian foundations, and that its plan followed very closely, if not exactly, that of the Lancastrian palace as it stood when finally completed about 1450.

So we may imagine a moated castle, something like Herstmonceux in appearance, rising by the riverside of Shene in the 1420s and '30s. To its left, as one looks from the Middlesex bank across the river, is the old site of the Plantagenet palace, now planted as an orchard or garden. To its immediate right is another

18 Herstmonceux Castle in Sussex, built in 1441, probably looks something like the palace at Shene built by Henry V and Henry VI. (Taken from Castles in Sussex *by John Guy [Phillimore, 1978])*

stretch of garden, then the less imposing but perhaps more welcoming group of the Byfleet buildings, dominated by the chapel. On the side towards the Green, before 1445, there would have been just a single courtyard with the great chapel and the great hall and a range of lodgings on each side of the gate. The wall of Byfleet stretched off in one direction and the domestic farm buildings of the manor, still surviving from the Plantagenet palace, in the other. Then, after 1445, the palace burst forward into the Green, with a new gateway and courtyard and a new turreted wall around the garden (*see* p.220).

Little work was done on the palace in the troubled years of the latter part of Henry VI's reign or under the Yorkist kings. In 1466 King Edward IV granted the manor and the palace of Shene to his Queen, Elizabeth Woodville,[32] who held it until it was reclaimed from her by Henry VII in 1486. In 1473 we learn of the supply of an iron gibbet for the drawbridge, and of carved crests held in store intended for the parlour of the manor of Shene.[33] In 1479 the moat was cleaned and enlarged. In the following year Shene was visited by William of Worcester, who noted two sets of dimensions. 'The Hall at King's Sheen is 44 paces long and 24 paces wide, and it formerly stood at ___. The Broad Court built around with chambers is 120 paces long and 100 paces wide.'[34] The missing word is presumably Byfleet. If this note is accurate, the hall from Byfleet must have been used as the main hall of the palace, and it may therefore have stood on the same site as the later Tudor hall. There remains of course the possibility that William of Worcester was misinformed, or even a little befuddled, for he participated in 'a banquet at Kingston Sheen on Wednesday after supper. It cost £100 and consisted of 3 courses each of 57 dishes'.

Throughout this period the manor of Shene continued to be leased out to 'farmers' – always excluding the palace or 'mansion house' itself. But now there were two changes in the pattern. The first was that the manors of Ham and Petersham had both come into the hands of the King – Petersham by an exchange of lands with the abbey of Chertsey in 1415 (they received Stanwell in exchange),[35] and Ham in the same year by purchase from Sir Hugh Burnell, the last of his line.[36] All three manors and 'the island of Crowet', belonging to Ham, were thereafter included in the leases. The second change was that from 1425 onwards the farmers were all men who had some direct connection with the palace of Shene. John Ardene, who held the farm from 1425 to 1444,[37] was clerk of the King's works. John Somerset, his successor from 1444 to 1451,[38] was comptroller of the works. He was followed by Thomas Barton (1451-61)[39] who was associated in the lease with a William Hulyn and in his appointments as keeper of the palace and of the wardrobe with John Bury; the latter was also keeper of the park. Then followed Edmund Glase (1461-70),[40] who was keeper of the warren, the park and the gardens; then Thomas Barton again from 1470 to 1484.

Then two grants in quick succession established a new pattern. Henry Davy in 1484 was not only farmer but was separately appointed keeper of the palace, the garden, the warren and the park.[42] He lost the keeperships promptly on Henry VII's accession, but a new farm was not granted until 1486 when Thomas Fysshe and Richard Brampton held it jointly. They were concurrently appointed to the whole range of keeperships.[43] Both men already owned property in Shene.

Chapter IV

The Charterhouse of Shene

At the time when Henry V was deciding to fulfil the charge laid upon his father in 1408 by Pope Gregory XIII – to found three religious houses – the general state of English monasticism was far from healthy. Corrupt and decadent, its abuses were the target of widespread criticism. Henry wanted to set examples of what the monastic life should be. He had an earnest piety, and a great interest in the recluses who combined the life of monk and hermit. This was a type of monasticism which was little known in Western Europe until the Crusaders encountered it in the Middle East and Eastern Europe. There had however been some attempts to found religious orders of an eremitic type in the West.

The most successful of such new strict orders was the Carthusian. Founded by St Bruno in 1084, the first settlement was at a remote spot in the mountains north of Grenoble called Chatrousse. There St Bruno and his six companions built separate little timber chalets – one for each – in which they could lead solitary lives of contemplation and prayer, and a little stone chapel in which they could worship together. This pattern, combining the life of the solitary hermit with the community of worship, was followed by all subsequent Carthusian houses. The mother house

19   The Charterhouse of Shene c.1450 (a model in the Museum of Richmond).

became the 'Grande Chartreuse', and all monasteries of the order bore the name of Chartreuse, or variants by adaptation into other tongues. 'Charterhouse' was the anglicised form. The name of the order itself was derived from the latin form of Chatrousse, 'Cartusia'.

The Carthusian order had been introduced into England in 1178 or 1179. King Henry II, in expiation for the murder of Archbishop Thomas à Becket, had vowed to take the Cross and go on pilgrimage to the Holy Land. Problems in England, including the rebellion of his sons, prevented him from fulfilling his vow so the penance was commuted to the foundation of religious houses. One of these was the Charterhouse at Witham in Somerset, where the King granted his manor to a small group sent by the Grande Chartreuse. In the course of the next two and a half centuries seven more English Charterhouses were established – at Hinton in Somerset, Beauvale in Nottingham, London, Hull, Coventry, Axholme in Lincolnshire and Mount Grace in Yorkshire. The order had remained virtually untouched by scandal and abuse. It was a natural choice for one of Henry V's new foundations.

For his other foundations Henry V chose a reformed branch of the Benedictine order called the Celestines and a new order recently founded in Sweden, the Briggitines. In his choice he was probably influenced by a recluse priest, William of Alnwick, who lived in the precincts of Westminster Abbey and whom the King often visited privately. Another influence was that of his friend and counsellor, Sir Henry Fitzhugh, Baron Ravensworth, newly appointed Constable of England.[1] Ravensworth had been much impressed on a visit to Sweden by the new order for both nuns and monks founded at Vadstena by Princess Bridget, who had already been canonised within twenty years of her death. It was a reformed version of the order of St Augustine. The house had a preponderance of nuns and was ruled by an abbess, but (living of course in a separate enclosure) there were also priests, deacons and lay brothers. There was a strict rule of enclosure, and a strict rule of silence during part of each day. Ravensworth had already planned to found a house of the order in England himself, but King Henry embraced his idea

20 *The habit of a Carthusian monk. This habit was presented to the Museum of Richmond by the Prior and Convent of St Hugh's Charterhouse in Sussex. It was made by a lay brother of the house and although of modern material it follows the exact pattern of the habits worn in the 15th century. (Museum of Richmond)*

and Ravensworth's manor of Hinton in Cambridgeshire was earmarked as one of the endowments for the new foundation, to be called the monastery of St Saviour and St Bridget of Syon. This was to be established on royal land in the manor of Isleworth, directly opposite the site of Shene Palace, on the boundary of the parishes of Isleworth and Twickenham.

For the Celestines, who were to come from France, Henry chose another site in Isleworth manor, by the river just to the north of the village and church of Isleworth. (In the end, the war with France prevented the establishment of the Celestine house, and the Briggitines of Syon took over their site – *see* Chapter VII.)

The site allotted to the Carthusians was on the Surrey bank of the Thames in the river bend a little north of Shene Palace. In the foundation charter of 25 September 1414 it was described as 'land belonging to the King on the north side of his manor at Shene, containing 1,725 feet in length by 1,305 feet and eight inches in breadth, extending from Hakelot by Diversbushe on the south to Arniette's Lot on the north'.[2] Six months later, a revised charter increased the land granted. It was now to measure 3,125 feet by 1,305 feet, extending as before from Hakelot on the south to 'the cross called Crossashe on the north'.[3] The second grant also conferred both the manorial fishery of Shene (which was at Kew) and ownership of and fishery rights at Petersham weir. (The manor of Petersham had just been acquired by the King through an exchange of lands with Chertsey Abbey.)

In these two charters a great endowment in other lands was granted, mostly at the expense of the 'alien priories' which had just been sequestered by Act of Parliament in 1414 as a consequence of the war with France. The alien priories were daughter houses (with their possessions) of monasteries in those parts of France owing allegiance to the King of France.

The actual priories given to the Shene Charterhouse were those of Greenwich and Lewisham, together with the manors of Lewisham, East Greenwich and East Combe in Greenwich (belonging to the abbey of St Peter, Ghent);[4] Ware in Hertfordshire and Noyon and Neufmarché in Normandy (from the abbey of St Évroult in Normandy); Hayling in Hampshire (from the abbey of St Peter at Jumièges); and Carisbrook in the Isle of Wight (from the abbey of Lire in Normandy). Along with these went various lands and the advowsons of numerous parish churches throughout the country.[5] In granting to Shene all the property (except Hinckley Priory) of the abbey of Lire, the King made express provision that if these estates were ever to be restored to the abbey, the Charterhouse was to receive an annual income of 700 marks from various civil sources such as the customs of certain ports.

The foundation stone of the Charterhouse of Jesus of Bethlehem of Shene was laid, probably early in 1415, by Bishop Nicolls of Bangor, acting on behalf of the Bishop of Winchester within whose diocese Shene lay.[6] Under the supervision of John Strange, clerk of the King's works, the master-mason for the Charterhouse was Walter Walton.[7] Walton had worked at Westminster Hall under Henry Yevele, and had held the post of 'chief surveyor of all stone-cutters and masons for the King's works in England' for nearly twenty years. He and his friend and contemporary Stephen Lote, master-mason for Shene Palace, carried on the great tradition of their master Yevele until they died, within a few months of each other, in 1418 with the King's 'great work' at Shene still not completely finished, but no doubt fully designed.[8]

By the autumn of 1415, when King Henry made his first trip to France, the Charterhouse appears to have been consecrated and Henry ordered that its completion should be speeded up.[9] In his will, made at that time, the King bequeathed 1,000 marks for 'the construction of its greater house, which we have sufficiently endowed for the sustenance of forty monks, which said number we wish to be maintained in perpetuity'.[10]

A year later the King gave funds to found a separate reclusory for a monk to live a solitary life of contemplation within the precincts of the Shene Charterhouse. John Kingeslowe was appointed as the first recluse chaplain, and the prior and chapter of the Charterhouse were to keep the building of the reclusory in repair at their own expense and pay the recluse 20 marks a year for the maintenance of himself and two servants. This was to come from the revenues of the manor of Lewisham.[11] Later the monks provided (at an annual rent of 8d) a 'garden newly walled' for the recluse, then one Robert Jacson.[12]

King Henry also saw to it that, from the outset, his new foundation at Shene should be properly equipped with books. In April 1415 the Exchequer paid £100 to the prior and convent of Mount Grace Charterhouse in Yorkshire 'in part payment of a larger sum granted by the King

21 Carved stones from the Charterhouse of Shene, from a number found on the Royal Mid-Surrey golf course in 1929. Top: from a window arcade; bottom left: from a doorhead or gable; bottom right: the springing of an arch.

to them for certain books and other things ordered by them for their Abbey of Shene, now lately ordered to be provided there by the said Lord the King'.[13]

There are not many traceable references to the building work itself. The first occur in March 1417 when Walter Walton and others were authorised to gather workmen of various kinds and to take a boat for the carriage of stone, timber and other materials,[14] and when Arnald Porter, mason, and Henry Briker, tiler, both of Holland, were commissioned to make tiles.[15] It was in 1417 that the General Chapter of the Carthusian Order incorporated the new house and established John Wydrington as prior – a formal step normally delayed until the physical arrangements were considered to be satisfactory.[16] So it may be assumed that the Charterhouse was reasonably complete by that time, although further work continued for some years. There is, for instance, another commission for workmen and a boat in 1422.[17]

The materials used would have been much the same as those for the palace, stone for the most important buildings, the church and chapter-house, brick for most of the others, and almost certainly lath-and-plaster timber-framed out-buildings. We know that some stone was brought from Caen in Normandy,[18] and a stone now in the Museum of Richmond appears to be of Reigate origin. Substantial quantities of ragstone, chalk, tiles, etc., were brought from the demolished royal manor house at Sutton in Chiswick, from which source also came 436 pounds of lead for the roofing of the reclusory.[19]

The site was just to the south of where the King's Observatory now stands in the Old Deer Park, stretching from the river-bank inland for a quarter of a mile. The enclosing wall made a rough rectangle (though its western side by the river was extended and rebuilt more than once as extra land was reclaimed).

The eastern two-fifths of the site were not built on at all. They contained land tilled by the lay brothers for the monastery's food. The western end of the site was where the lay brothers' quarters and the guest-houses and farm buildings were to be found. The great cloister itself was on the northern side of the central section of the site, following the usual Carthusian pattern with the church and the chapter-house on its south side. The main gate was in the south outer wall, from which a walled court stretched up to the inner gate giving access to the lay brothers' court and to a court at the west end of the church from which one could enter the south-west corner of the cloister. Close to this corner would have been the cells of the two monks who needed to have access to the outside world, the prior and the procurator (who was the 'general manager' of the monastery and who, in particular, organised the work and the lives of the lay brothers).

Around the cloister of a Carthusian monastery, on the west, north and east sides (and some perhaps on the south side also, adjacent to the church) stood the cells of the monks – small detached houses with little high-walled gardens. Sometimes, at a corner or in the middle of a side, two houses would be built semi-detached, but the high walls of the gardens ensured isolation from the neighbour. In each house on the ground floor there would be a little lobby with doors both to the cloister and to the private garden, and with a stair to the upper floor. Next to the door into the cloister was an angled hatch so designed that a lay brother could pass in the monk's food without any direct contact being established. Also on the ground floor would be a living room with a fireplace, a small bedroom and an even smaller study and oratory. The upper floor was a workroom. Windows on the ground floor would look out only onto the private garden, those on the upper floor would face only the cloister court, not the outside world beyond the enclosure.

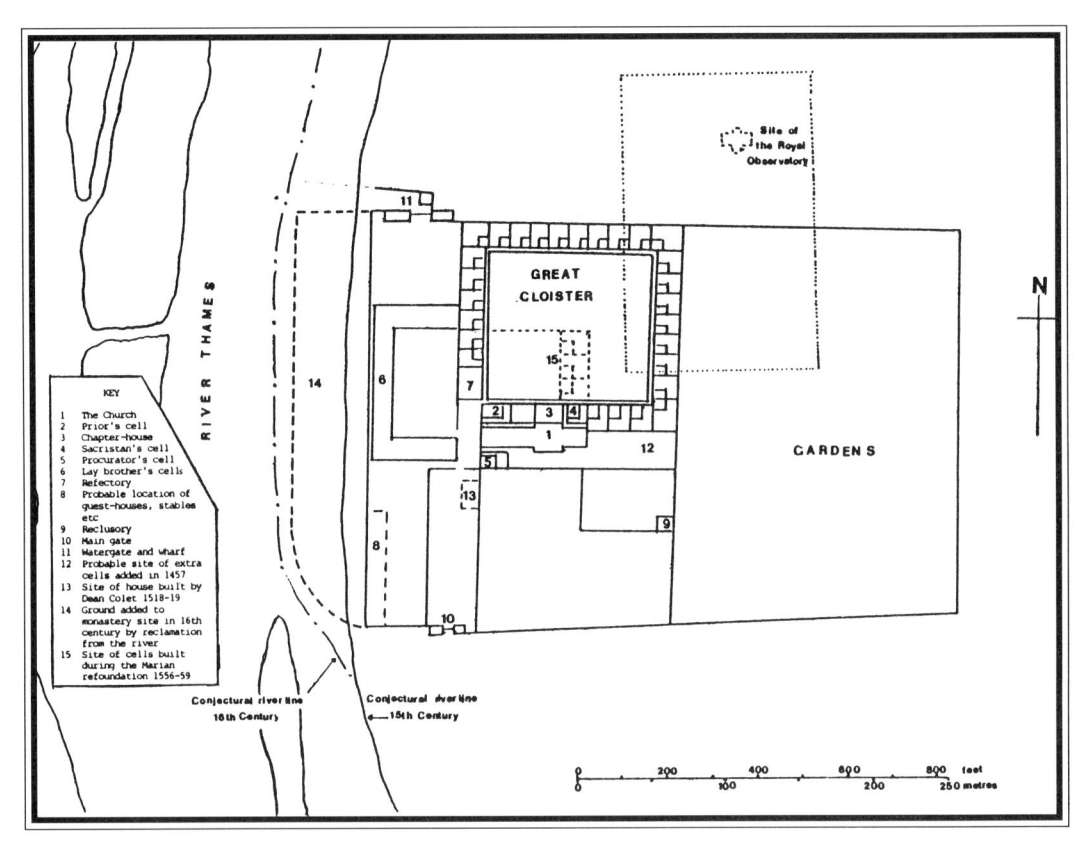

22   The Charterhouse of Jesus of Bethlehem of Shene, c.1420.

Each cell was provided with its own privy at the end of the garden, projecting a little through the outer wall where a flushing drain ran round the circuit. In a house like Mount Grace in Yorkshire where mountain streams could be canalised for this purpose the sanitation must have been quite good for its day; at Shene where such flushing water could only come from the river – and tidal at that – a complicated system of sluice gates must have been used to keep the drains clean. Each privy was linked to its house by a walk with a covered pentice roof, and sometimes this might also be extended round another side or sides of the garden to provide a place for exercise even on rainy days. A larger pentice ran right round the cloister court, linking all the cells by a covered walk to the church, the chapter-house and the refectory.

The refectory was the only communal building, apart from the church and chapter-house. A Carthusian monastery had no work desks in the cloisters, no warming room, sometimes not even an infirmary; its library was probably kept in the chapter-house. Even the refectory was used only on Sundays and feast days, when the monks would be read to while they ate in silence. (After their midday meal on Sundays the monks were allowed a couple of hours conversation.) All other meals were taken in the seclusion of their cells. The refectory was generally a rather smaller hall than in monasteries of other orders, and it stood near the south-west corner of the cloister to be easy of access to the kitchen where the lay brothers worked.

Carthusian lay brothers were divided into two classes: the 'converses' who themselves took lifetime vows almost as rigorous as those of the monks and lived according to a strict rule; and the 'donates' who were somewhat less strictly cloistered and were not pledged to stay indefinitely – some might be scholars or young students for the priesthood. Each lay brother lived in a single cell in the 'lower house' of the monastery. In addition the monastery employed hired labour who came in only for the day.

The livelihood even of a richly endowed house such as Shene depended as much on the farming of its own lands as on rents. As the monks themselves seldom left the enclosure, the services of the lay brothers were essential. They provided not only the supervision of the agricultural labour but also the other services needed to keep the monastery running. The statutes governing the lives of the lay brothers at Shene[20] show that their number included a master of the kitchen and a butler, a separate cook for the kitchen of the lower house, a baker, a cobbler, a smith, a gardener, a carpenter, a master of husbandry and a master of the shepherds. The lay brothers had to attend some of the monks' services and keep the appropriate feasts. They also had their own chapel and chapter-house. They were not allowed to talk to the monks, nor to outsiders save for a minimum courtesy or for the conduct of business; and only when appointed to work on some duty together might they speak 'among themselves or with such as help them, of profitable and necessary things'. (But silence, adds the statute, is 'very ill kept among them'.)

Some further building or alteration was put in hand in 1457 when the General Chapter at La Grande Chartreuse instructed the prior of Mount Grace Charterhouse to send his lay brother William the carpenter to Shene and to let him remain there until the convent could go into new cells.[21] It is possible that extra cells were added at this time beyond the east end of the church, in a separate small court adjacent to the great cloister. Later again the church was enlarged by the addition of a chapel with three altars.[22]

In 1466, perhaps as a result of the building of the new cells, the monastery's water supply from the spring called Hillesden well was acknowledged to have become inadequate and King Edward IV authorised the monks to make a new underground conduit from the spring called 'Welway' or 'Pickwell's well' (probably on the site by the Green now occupied by Old Palace Terrace).[23] These water conduits, both to the Charterhouse and to the palace itself, from springs on the rising ground, are almost certainly the explanation of later tales about secret passages in Richmond.*

The only contemporary information on the size or shape of the buildings comes in a somewhat confused description by William of Worcester who visited Shene in the reign of Edward IV. He recorded that there were about thirty houses for monks within the four-sided cloister, and that 'its length was 200 paces so that it contained 800 paces in all'; the height of the cloister walls was nine feet; and the nave of the church 'apart from the choir' was 60 paces in length.[24] Applying John Harvey's factor of 21 inches as the length of one of these paces[25] gives a cloister enclosure some 350 feet square and a nave 105 feet long. On these dimensions the cloister would have been a little larger than that of the London Charterhouse, and considerably larger than the irregular quadrilateral of the Mount Grace Charterhouse in Yorkshire.[26] Mount Grace, however, was a typical 'single unit' Carthusian house with 12 monks and a prior; London was a double unit, and Shene a triple. The dimensions given for the church at Shene are very much bigger than either London or Mount Grace.

The Charterhouse continued to flourish until Henry VIII's breach with Rome. In turn, Henry VI, Edward IV, Henry VII and Henry VIII confirmed the grants made by their predecessors and granted further lands and privileges.[27]

---

* See Appendix 5.

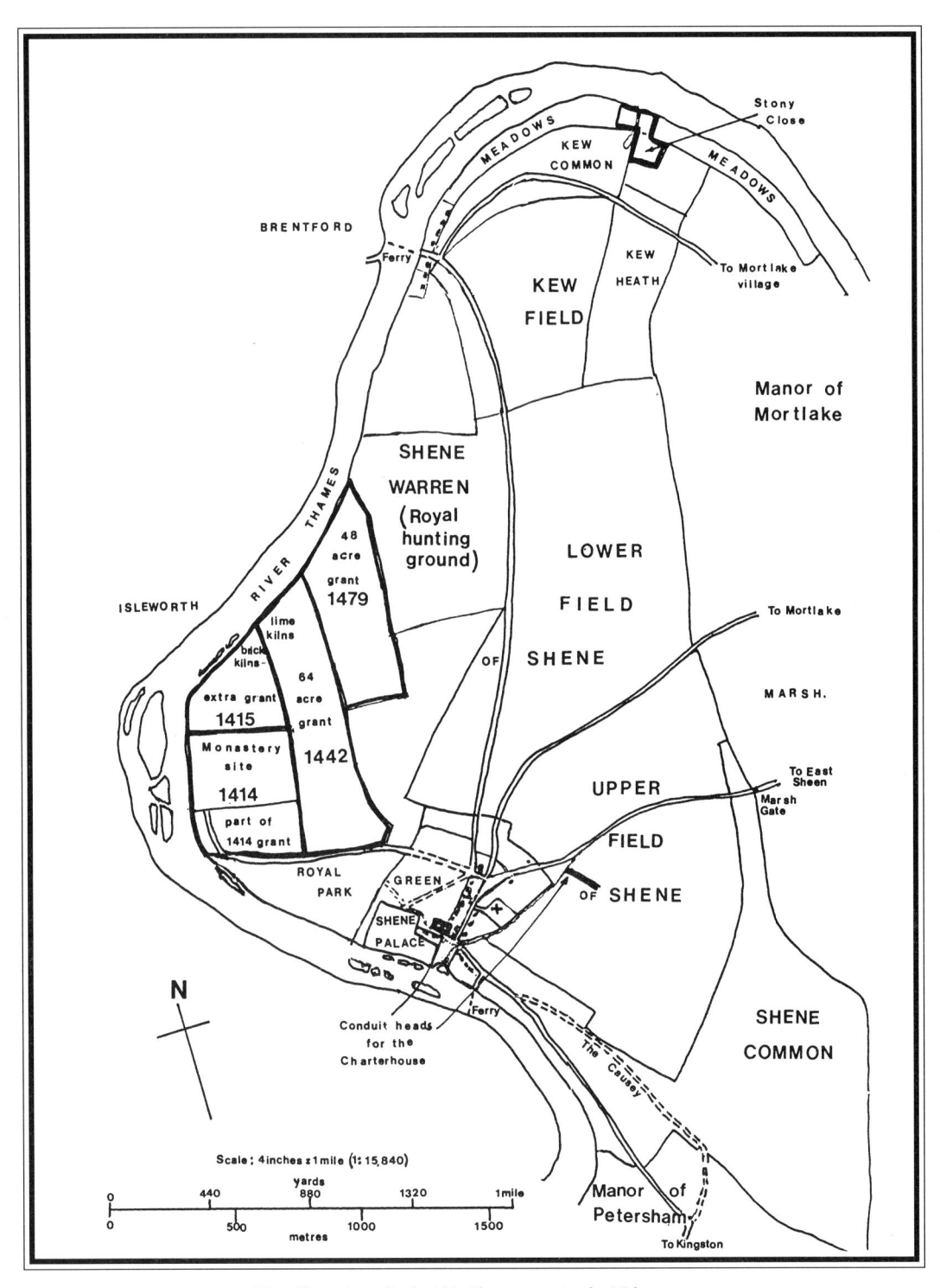

23 *Charterhouse land within Shene manor in the 15th century.*

On 20 March 1442 Henry VI granted to the Charterhouse 64 acres of land in Shene on the eastern side of their previous holdings, 'lying between the road which leads from the said house [the Charterhouse] towards the site of the manor on the south and the water of Thames on the north, and adjoining the land of the Prior and monks on the west'.[28] A further addition to the monastic estate at Shene was made by grant of Queen Elizabeth on 1 April 1479, confirmed by Edward IV on 25 May of that year. (Edward IV had granted the manor of Shene to his wife for her life in 1466.) This was described as '48 acres of land in West Shene parcel of the said manor and lordship lying between the river of Thames on the north and the way leading towards "le Breikhouse" of West Shene on the south and between the land of the said Prior and monks on the west and the warren of Shene on the east, and enclosed with hedges and ditches'.[29]

Among the privileges granted to the Charterhouse was complete exemption from all forms of taxation and service, not only for the monastery but for their tenants.[30] They were also given local powers of jurisdiction with the right to erect gallows and stocks for the punishment of offenders. Perhaps more immediately welcome was the annual grant of four pipes of red Gascony wine.[31] Of course, there was one service required of the monks – 'to pray for the King and his family and for the peace and quiet of the people and the realm'.

While the monks of the Charterhouse passed their time in contemplation and prayer and in work such as the writing and copying of manuscripts, and while the lay brothers worked at their allotted tasks within the monastic enclosure, life was not always untroubled for those who had to deal with the outside world, such as the prior.

There were disputes with other religious houses – some of them prolonged. The Carthusians of Mount Grace, though they seem to have had close links with Shene, were very put out by Henry V's grant to Shene of the alien priory of Ware, which they considered as having already been granted to them. Although Henry had charged Shene to pay Mount Grace £100 a year from the revenues of Ware, it was not for some years, and after an appeal to the Grande Chartreuse, that the dispute was resolved.

Of much greater duration and acerbity were the disputes with the Benedictines of the French monastery of St Évroult and of the Flemish house at Ghent, whose properties had been granted to Shene. There were many appeals to the General Chapter at the Grande Chartreuse, and many injunctions from the General Chapter to the priors of Shene to give up the lands – a matter in which the royal grant hardly gave them any discretion. These disputes dragged on into the 1450s before the continental monasteries finally abandoned their claims.[32]

Later, there was trouble between the Carthusians and the Cistercians over a Cistercian who had become a Carthusian and then, seven years later, decided that he wished to return to the Cistercian order. Henry VII himself intervened in this case, writing in February 1489/90 from Shene Palace a letter to the Pope which was to be carried by the prior of Shene in person, asking the Pope to settle this vexatious question. In his letter the King referred to Shene as a foundation 'we are bound to protect with particular favour and by particular right'.[33]

Two months later, the papal legate to England, Bishop Lionel of Concordia, also wrote to the Pope recommending to him the prior of Shene, 'a person very dear to the King of England who greatly loves that order'. The bishop added that the prior wished to regulate the discipline of his monks in England.[34]

This was John Ingleby who was prior of Shene for nearly twenty years and who, even after being made Bishop of Llandaff in 1496, stayed on at Shene until his death in 1499 supervising the works on the palace. He was the visitor, or senior prior, of the English province of the Carthusian order. The priors of Shene, as the largest English Charterhouse, were frequently

24 The seals of the Charterhouse of Shene, showing the Holy Family in the stable at Bethlehem. Left: *the first seal, from a document of 1416 (a drawing in the collection of the Society of Antiquaries, London);* middle: *the later seal, used in the second half of the 15th century, until the dissolution in 1538;* right: *the seal of the refounded house in the reign of Mary I. (Middle and right – engravings from Brayley's* History of Surrey.*)*

appointed visitors to oversee the other houses in the country, a post which involved considerable travel, including a visit at least once every four years to the Grande Chartreuse to report in person on the state of the English province. Though sometimes feeling somewhat cut off from the Grande Chartreuse and their continental brethren, and complaining of the lack of answers to their letters, the English Carthusians remained strictly obedient to the General Chapter – save over the question of alien priory lands where the King's will and protection had also to be taken into account. John Wydrington, the first prior of Shene, was indeed reprimanded by the General Chapter for trying to introduce variations in the order of service, and that offence was never repeated.[35]

There were also moments when the quiet of Shene was broken by some transgression or by outside factors. What grievous offence had been committed by a Father Anthony in 1426 which caused his immediate banishment to Picardy we do not know – only that the prior was disciplined for getting rid of him without even waiting to ascertain whether another Carthusian house would accept him.[36] (Banishment to another house was a normal punishment for serious offences.) In

June 1498 there must have been some excitement when the pretender Perkin Warbeck, having broken out of custody in Westminster Palace, sought sanctuary at Shene Charterhouse. The prior, Ralph Tracy, interceded with the King for a pardon for him, but he was brought back and shut up in the Tower of London 'under better guard'.[37]

The greatest shock to the peaceful life of Shene Charterhouse came however on 21 March 1502/3 when Prior Tracy and another monk were murdered in the precincts by one of the monks named Godwin.[38] Of this incident nothing else is known, but it may be that Prior Tracy's zeal (he was visitor of the English province) made him enemies even among his own flock.

Another curious interruption in the normal life of the Charterhouse occurred in 1513. The lifeless body of King James IV of Scotland, Henry VIII's brother-in-law, had been picked up on the battlefield of Flodden, embalmed and wrapped in lead, and brought south to England, where it was deposited at Shene while negotiations proceeded as to what should be done with it. The problem was that James had died excommunicated from the Church, and so a papal dispensation would be needed to give him a Christian burial. The excommunication was a direct sanction in accordance with the terms of the Anglo-Scottish treaty of 24 January 1501/2 (*see* p.79), which James had broken by invading England.

Henry wrote to Pope Leo X from Tournai on 12 October. At the end of a long letter about the victory over the Scots, the problems resulting from the death in the battle of the Archbishop of St Andrews and several other Scottish bishops, and the prospect of marrying his widowed sister Queen Margaret to the Prince of Castile, he raised the question of King James's burial. He asked the Pope to grant a licence for him to remove the body from its present 'decent but not sacred' resting place and to bury it with regal dignity in St Paul's Cathedral in London, pointing out that he regarded this as a matter touching on his own honour. The Pope replied promptly on 29 November, granting the desired licence. He said that he had received credible evidence of a last-minute repentance by James IV as he lay dying and could therefore revoke the excommunication. The bishop of London was to announce this before the interment. The pope further proposed that Henry should, in the name of King James, make some appropriate act of penitence, as he thought fit.[39]

Why no action was taken on this remains a mystery. Did King Henry take umbrage at the suggestion that he should make an act of penance in King James's name? This does not seem very probable, for it would presumably have been quite easy for him at this time to arrange, say, for the foundation of some new religious house or charity in Scotland at the expense of the House of Stuart. But it is clear that, for whatever reason, the lead-wrapped body remained unburied. It was still at Shene when the historian Stow visited the place in 1552 after the dissolution. Stow recorded that workmen had later hacked off its head, but that the Queen's glazier 'feeling a sweet savour to come from thence', had finally carried the head off to his house in Wood Street in London and eventually had it buried in the neighbouring church of St Michael.[40]

Some writers have suggested that the body was not that of King James, but the Queen was in no doubt when she wrote from Richmond to Henry (in France) on 14 September 1513 sending him 'a piece of the King of Scots' coat' and passing on the request of the Earl of Surrey – the English commander at Flodden – for the King's instructions 'as to burying the King of Scots' body'.[41] Further credence is given to the story by a report sent by the Venetian *chargé d'affaires* in London to the Signory in October 1532 of another threatened outbreak of war between the Scots and the English. He wrote:

> A herald has come from the King of Scotland defying his Majesty to war. King Henry replied that being his nephew and a King and considering him his son he does not wish for war with him,

but is not afraid nor does he doubt whilst defending himself to be able to injure his enemies. The cause of this stir is said to be that King Henry refused him the body of his father, which is unburied at Richmond.[42]

The ultimate fate of the body is unknown. It seems possible – but this is pure speculation – that Stow's publication of the story may have led Queen Elizabeth or her counsellors to arrange for the covert disposal of the body. It is hardly possible to believe that it could still have been unburied at Shene when James I took over Richmond Palace without someone's bringing it to his notice and without his then arranging for the proper burial of his great-grandfather.

In 1515 King Henry VIII granted the Shene Charterhouse the right to appoint their own coroner for the monastery 'and the River Thames' – a measure that may have been intended to enhance their seclusion from the outside world.[43]

Yet despite their strict rule of enclosure, and their vows of almost complete silence, the separation of the Carthusian monks of Shene from the community was not absolute. Evidence that some family links were allowed to be maintained can be found in the will of William Bracebrigge, citizen and draper of London (who had a house and land in Shene), dated 28 July 1498 and 'done at the Charterhouse of Shene by hand of my son Dom Thomas Bracebrigge'. A legacy was appointed to Thomas 'in the Charterhouse of Shene', so he was clearly a professed monk. William Bracebrigge directed that, if he died in the vicinity, he should be buried in the Charterhouse.[44] Burial at the Charterhouse (or at the house of the Observant Friars in Richmond) was an option chosen by several benefactors of those houses.

In the 1470s, apparently as a fund-raising device, '500 days' pardon' was offered to those who contributed to the repairs of the Charterhouse. In 1472 King Edward IV, his Queen and the Duke of Gloucester, visited the Charterhouse to avail themselves of this offer;[45] and in February 1478/9 William Paston wrote that a young lady whom he knew, and her mother, were to go 'to the pardon of Schene'.[46] The royal patronage was continued by Henry VIII (who visited the Charterhouse in 1510 soon after his accession, and made an offering of two marks,[47] and by Princess Mary – the future Queen Mary I – who made frequent donations, right up to the eve of the dissolution.[48]

The latest addition to the buildings of the Charterhouse had been made by Dr. John Colet,

25   Dean Colet, by Holbein. (British Museum)

the famous Dean of St Paul's, who built a retirement home for himself within the grounds (facing the entrance court, but close to the church) in the early 16th century. Hardly had he finished the house when he fell ill 'of the sweating sickness' and died there in 1519.[49]

In this house two still more notable figures were later to dwell, if but briefly. One already knew Shene well. Reginald Pole, the future Cardinal, cousin of the Tudors and of Plantagenet ancestry, had been left fatherless at the age of five. Two years later, in 1507, he was sent to study at Shene Charterhouse. (Some Charterhouses had established schools by the early 16th century, in which the pupils were probably taught, not by monks or lay brothers, but by specially engaged teachers.) Pole remained at Shene for five years.[50] King Henry VIII interested himself in the boy's education, and granted him an exhibition of £12 in his last year at Shene, before he went on to Oxford in 1512.[51] From Oxford he had gone on to study in Italy, whence he returned in 1527. He wanted to lead a peaceful, academic, contemplative life rather than to join the court. He went back to Shene and was given Colet's house, which remained his home for two years, until he obtained permission to go to the University of Paris in 1529.[52]

Then, in early March 1529/30 the disgraced Cardinal Wolsey moved from the Lodge in the old Richmond Park, where he had briefly stayed on the King's sufferance, to the 'lodging' in the Charterhouse, 'which Doctor Colet … had made for himself', and remained there until he set out for his last journey north on 5 April. Cavendish says that:

26 Cardinal Reginald Pole, by an unknown artist.

> … he had in the same house a secret gallery which went out of his chamber into the Charterhouse church, whither he resorted every day to their service. And at afternoons he would sit in contemplation with one or other of the most ancient fathers of that house in his cell. Among them, by their counsel, [he] was persuaded from the vain glory of this world, and [they] gave him divers shirts of hair, which he often wore afterwards, whereof I am certain. And thus he persevered for the time of his abode there in godly contemplation.[53]

Three months after Wolsey's departure from Shene, Reginald Pole returned from Paris. Latterly he had been engaged – successfully, but with great reluctance – on a mission for the King: to obtain from the theologians of the University of Paris an opinion favourable to the King's cause in the matter of his intended divorce. Pole again attempted to escape to a private life, and resumed his residence in Colet's house at Shene.[54] The King however wanted him to assume an active public role. When Wolsey died in November, Pole – though still a layman* – was offered the vacant archbishopric of York, which he refused. A meeting with the King at which Pole intended to offer some compromise position on the divorce proved a disaster. After attempting to reconcile himself with the King by an explanatory letter, he applied for permission to leave England again. This request was eventually granted, and early in 1532 he left Shene for Avignon.[55] He left some of his goods behind in Colet's house; they were still there when the Charterhouse was dissolved, causing the prior to write to ask Thomas Cromwell what was to be done with 'the stuff of Mr Poole's'.[56]

---

* Reginald Pole was only ordained as a deacon in December 1536, when he was created a cardinal. He was finally ordained as a priest two days before his consecration as Archbishop of Canterbury in March 1556.

Chapter V

The 'New Park' of Shene

The original park of Shene manor house, the existence of which was mentioned in 1293, makes no further appearance in the documents of the 14th or early 15th century. It seems to have been the warren which was used for hunting – an unenclosed area of rough heathland, probably largely covered with underbrush and broom, where rabbits and partridges were bred, or encouraged to breed, both for the lord's entertainment and for his table; and where the lord of the manor and his guests – but only they – could hunt at will.

So we learn that the disturbers of the peace who broke into Queen Isabella's manor in 1354 'hunted in her free warren there, and carried away … hares, conies, partridges and pheasants from the warren'.[1] When the manor came back into the hands of Edward III on his mother's death, there came the first of a series of appointments of 'Keepers of the King's warren of Shene', at the wage of 3d. a day, a series which continues into the reign of Henry VII. The appointment was often held in conjunction with that of keeper of the manor and sometimes along with other appointments.

If the assumption that the land used for the erection of Byfleet-at-Shene was the original park is correct, it is easy to understand why the park did not figure in the documents. It would only have been some four or five acres in extent – more of a garden than a park. There is one indication – and one only – that the original park might have been larger than this. That is the grant, made in April 1499, of land on the slope of the Hill, between the upper and lower roads to Petersham, called 'South Park'. (*See* p.73.) There is no other mention of this name, nor any suggestion of a house in this area to which a park might have been attached. It seems just possible therefore that the original park might have stretched all the way from the manor house between the river and the upper road to Petersham (i.e. Richmond Hill). We do not know the date at which the area between Water Lane and Ferry Hill was first developed, although it was before the time of Henry V. The area between the lower Petersham road and the river south of Ferry Hill was also in private hands by Henry V's reign. But both of these areas might have been granted out, thus isolating 'the south park' on the hillside, only in the late 14th or early 15th century – possibly after Richard II's destruction of the palace. (There are no extant manorial rolls for that period, except for 1404-5.)

Whether or not there is any truth in that conjecture, it is clear that once Henry V had built Byfleet, there was no park left in the vicinity of the palace. A new park was required. By the time that 'the new building of the manor of Shene' had been completed, this new park had been formed – from land to the west of the Green and south of the lane which led from the Green to the site allotted to the Charterhouse. The first mention of it occurs in the grant to John de Bury of the keepership of the manor of Shene on 27 December 1437. He was granted 'a dwelling consisting of a hall, a kitchen, and chambers, with a little garden annexed, adjoining the dwelling of the Clerk of the King's Works on one side and reaching to the King's new park on the other'.[2] Later references enable us to place these two official residences in the middle of the north-west side of the Green, close by the site of the future Fitzwilliam House.

On 29 May 1440 John de Bury was granted additionally the office of keeper of the park called 'le Newe Park' of Shene, Co. Surrey, at wages of 2d. a day, and with the use of seven acres of meadow at the Middlesex end of Chertsey Bridge to provide feed for 'the King's fallow deer within the said park in winter'.[3] So we have confirmation that this was a deer park. John Bury (the 'de' is dropped in later documents) seems to have been neglectful of his duties as keeper; he no doubt protested when complaints were made that he needed an allowance in addition to his 2d. a day, and the 6d. a day he received as keeper of the manor, if he was expected to keep the park and its paling and its deer in tiptop condition. Eventually he was successful.

On 24 July 1447 John Bury, 'keeper of Shene Park which is now in a ruinous state' was granted an additional allowance of 2d. a day (out of the profits of the farm of Kingston) to repair the park 'with pales and hedges and for a house for the King's deer there,' with hay and other food 'in the hard time of winter'.[4] A very full account of John Bury's expenditure on the park from July 1447 until Michaelmas 1450 survives.[5] It shows that 400 stakes were purchased in Chertsey and brought to the park by boat from there, 1,400 stakes came from Eltham and were shipped by river from Deptford, 113 loads of thorn were cut around Kingston and carried by cart, 10 cartloads of elder branches were needed 'for tying and winding' the hedges. With these materials John London, John Kryer, Thomas Body and John Guldeford, presumably local men, 'made 203 rods of hedge around the park in divers places where the master indicated, at a price of 2½d. a rod'. If the standard 16½ foot rod was being used, this gives a total of about 3,350 feet of repairs (at 18 feet per rod, a measure often used, the total would be 3,654 feet). It is clearly not the full circuit of the park, which was said to be 'one mile' in a survey made in the mid-16th century,[6] and was actually about a mile and a furlong.

The park was triangular in shape, and its eastern and northern boundaries by the Green and along the lane to the Charterhouse are clearly defined. Less certain is whether its southern boundary was by the riverside or whether any substantial strip of meadow was left unenclosed between the park and the river. There are just four references to a parcel of land in such a location in the manor records prior to 1603; they are all to the same land and all from the second half of the 16th century. A piece of waste ground of one acre 'between the King's Park of Richmond east and the River Thames west' was granted to John Lovell Senior for a term of 30 years on 27 May 1549; on 1 December of the same year, John Lovell having died, his widow Katherine surrendered the land for the use of herself and her son George Lovell. In 1567 they jointly conveyed the same land to Nicholas Snow, keeper of the wardrobe, and his wife Katherine. After Nicholas Snow's death, Katherine surrendered it in 1583 to Lawrence Snow, who later sold it to Sir Robert Wright.[7] In 1605 Wright sold it to the King for £50, presumably to be enclosed within the new park which King James was then creating (*see* Chapter 12). It was then described as one and a half acres of meadow 'abutting the King's wharf where the Crane stands, and one side abuts the Thames, and the other side abuts the Park to the north'.[8]

This small piece of land was probably in origin just a narrow strip which had been left between the park pale and the river-bank – the winter flooding would have made it imprudent to set the pale right at the water's edge – and which had perhaps grown somewhat by the gradual

27 Stag hunting and hawking: illustrations from Queen Mary's Psalter. (British Library, Royal MS 2B vii, ff150v and 151)

process of embankment and reclamation. It seems therefore reasonable to assume that Henry VI's park extended practically to the river-bank as it was in the 1430s.

※

Brief glimpses of royalty and their guests disporting in the park are afforded by a few documents. In the early days of its existence, Henry VI's Queen, Margaret of Anjou, wrote to 'J. D.' [this must be John de Bury]:

> By the Queen. To my Lord's squier and ours, J. D., Keeper of Shene Park, or his Depute there.
>
> Trusty and well beloved, For as moche as we suppose that in short tyme, we shall come righte nigh unto my Lord's manoir of Shene, we desire and praye you hartly that ye will kepe against our resortinge thedor, for our disport and recreation, two or iii of the grettest bukkes in my Lord's parc there, saving always my Lord's owne commandment there in presence.[9]

In 1480 William of Worcester, during his visit to Shene, made a note about 'a great buck … killed by a band of four men of the German Hansa merchants, with the King's leave, which he gave to them'.[10]

In 1501, Lancaster Herald, writing of the festivities which took place at the newly-renamed Richmond when Catherine of Aragon was married to Henry VII's eldest son, Prince Arthur, described an archery demonstration on Richmond Green, then:

> Afterward, the King's Highnes ledde the estraungers into his parke adjoynyng unto the rehersid manour of Richmonde and there causid wanlaces to be made, and the dere to be brought about, and gave the estraungers free chace wt. bowe and hownde. And there th'Earl of Hispayne strake a dere with his crosse bowe, and great slaughter was of veneson by the said estraungers and brought into the quarrey: the flesshe thereof the King's Grace distributid and gave unto the Espanyards to do therewt. their will and pleasure.[11]

The deer can have had little chance – even against men on foot with crossbows. The park was only about forty-five acres. Hunting in it must have been rather like playing a 'pitch and putt' miniature golf course. One wonders if it was this experience with his Spanish guests that led Henry VII to determine to make a new and larger park on the other side of the river, which he did in the following year. (*See* Chapter 7.)

The park on the Surrey side of the river was however still used and maintained. The appointment of keepers, with their wages of 2d. a day, continued throughout the 16th century. There does not appear however to be any surviving account relating to expenditure on the park or any buildings in it in this period, though it is possible that some such expenditure could have been incurred by Cardinal Wolsey, after he exchanged Hampton Court for Richmond *c.*1525.

Wolsey's brief association with Richmond presents another problem in relation to the park. George Cavendish, Wolsey's 'gentleman usher' and contemporary biographer, states clearly that in the winter of 1529-30, after Wolsey's fall, when the latter applied to the King for permission to leave his house at Esher which 'with continual use … waxed unsavoury', the King

> Was well contented that my Lord should move to Richmond, which place he had a little before repaired to his great cost and charge … My Lord, having licence of the King to remove to Richmond, made haste to prepare himself to go thither. And so he came and lodged within the great park there, which was a very pretty house and neat, lacking no necessary rooms that to so small a house were convenient and necessary. There was also a proper garden garnished with divers pleasant walks and alleys. My Lord continued in this lodge from the time that he came thither, shortly after Candlemas, until it was Lent, with a private number of servants, because of the smallness of the house; and the rest of the family went on board wages … My Lord then in the beginning of Lent moved out of the Lodge into the Charterhouse.[12]

The repeated use of the word 'Lodge' to describe the house where Wolsey stayed is further substantiated by one of his own letters. He wrote on 1 February 1529/30 to Thomas Cromwell, who was negotiating with the King on Wolsey's behalf, a letter which contains the sentence: 'And wher ye wold I shuld thys day remove to Richemond Loge yt ys nat possybyll for me to do so having no provysyon ther …'.[13]

The references by Cavendish clearly cannot be to the palace itself. It seems unlikely, though not wholly impossible, that they refer to a house within the park at Isleworth. This was twice the size of the park at Richmond and might therefore have been described as 'the great park'. But there is a reference in 1550 (*see* p.77) to the Isleworth park as the 'Little Park', which suggests that the Richmond one could have been called the 'Great Park' – perhaps in terms of importance rather than size. Any possibility that the park at Richmond had actually been enlarged seems to be ruled out by the fact that the land adjacent to it was separately leased under the name of 'the Lord's Pieces' throughout this period (*see* p.171-2).

There is no earlier, or later, documentary evidence of a lodge within this park in Richmond,[14] or of any dwelling house closely associated with it other than the residences of the clerk of works and of the keeper of the park which both stood by the park gate leading out of the west side of Richmond Green. The likeliest interpretation is that Wolsey was in fact occupying the keeper's house, which might well have been known as the Lodge. The keepership was at that time held jointly by Massie Villiard and Thomas Brampton, who had a farm of the manor itself for 30 years from 1522. Both were men of substance with their own houses in Richmond, probably larger and more comfortable than the keeper's house. So the latter could well have been vacant and available. That it had a garden is confirmed by a later entry in the manorial court rolls for 1581, when Henry Harvey was presented in court for 'occupying a garden plot … which belonged to the Keeper of the Park'.[15]

In the survey of the manor of Richmond made in 1550, the park is listed among the many items held by David Vincent who had been appointed in 1547 as keeper of the manor (and of those of Petersham and Ham), and keeper of Richmond Park. He was also keeper of the mansion house or palace. 'There is likewise one park adjacent to the said mansion house called Richemount Park containing in circuit by estimation one mile given for the use aforesaid [i.e. the use of the King] into the keeping of the said David, and it is arrented per annum at nothing … And in fees of the said David for the keeping of the park called Richemount Park per annum 60s 10d.'[16]

The greater part of this 'new Park of Shene' (or Richmond) was absorbed into the park created by James I in 1605, but was later detached therefrom to form the grounds of the mansion built on the west side of Richmond Green. The other part, closer to the river, became attached to the mansion on the Charterhouse site. They were eventually recovered by George III.

28   The burning of Shene Palace. A woodcut from the original 1577 edition of Holinshed's Chronicles.

Chapter VI

The Building of Henry VII's Palace

In 1497 King Henry VII and his court came to spend Christmas at the palace of Shene. In the previous years he had ordered some works to be carried out there. We do not know in detail what they were or what they cost, but they were obviously extensive. For some reason – perhaps just his friendship with the King and his proximity to the site – the prior of the Charterhouse, John Ingleby, was in charge of, or at least paymaster for, the operation. In October 1495 he was paid £333 6s. 8d. 'for the finishing of the King's works at Shene',[1] and in the following January he received the final instalment on a bill for £4,803 16s. 3d. 'for beleding' (i.e. the fixing of lead, presumably on roofs).[2] This may well have been a complete re-roofing job; and there also appears to have been some new building or major reconstruction. 'Two large towers' were built, apparently attached to, or adjoining, the chapel.[3]

In the night of 23 December 1497 a fire broke out in the King's lodging. Though discovered at about nine o'clock in the evening it raged for three hours and was not extinguished until around midnight. 'Moch and grete part of the old byldyng of that place was brent' and 'many notable and excellent rych joyallis and other thyngis of superhabundant valu'.[4]

The ambassador of Milan, Raimundo de Raimundis de Soncino, provided his duke with a full report on 30 January 1497/8:

> The King is at his palace eight miles from London with his Queen and all the Court, in good health and merry, thank God.
> They recently celebrated with great triumph and festivities the marriage [*sic* – 'betrothal' would be more correct] between Prince Arthur and Katherine daughter of the Queen of Spain and in this good time they hope she will be brought to England with great splendour.
> Thank God the Kingdom of England was never in such tranquility or so loyal to his Majesty as now, both nobles and people being in great obedience to the King. It is true that the night before Christmas Eve a fire broke out in the place where his Majesty was staying with the Queen and the court, by accident and not by malice, catching a beam, about the ninth hour of the night. It did a great deal of harm and burned the chapel, except two large towers recently erected by his Majesty. The damage is estimated at 60,000 ducats. The King does not attach much importance to the loss by this fire, seeing it was not due to malice. He purposes to rebuild the chapel all in stone and much finer than before.[5]

The ambassador's account makes one wonder just how much of the old palace was in fact destroyed, apart from the chapel. If the King and the court were still residing there in January, it cannot have been a total wreck. Indeed, one reason why the date of the fire has frequently been given as 1499, despite the clear evidence of both the Chronicle and the Milanese despatch, is the

29   King Henry VII

fact that the King was conducting business at Shene in the summer of 1498 (when he received the Spanish ambassador there on 17 July).[6] A likely explanation is that the old Byfleet buildings survived the fire; they were separated from the main palace by a garden and a moat – or two moats. They would have served Henry VII as temporary quarters, as they had done for Henry V, while the main building was unusable.

The privy purse accounts of the Queen, Elizabeth of York, were still carrying echoes of the destruction caused by the fire as late as 1502-3. On 6 June 1502 a payment of 60 shillings was made to Nicholas Grey, clerk of works, 'towards suche losses as he susteigned at the birnyng of his howse at Richemount' and on 7 February 1502/3 Henry Coote, a London goldsmith, was paid £20 'in partie of payment of an hundred marks to him due for certain plate delivered to the Queen's grace at Richemount and there lost and brent at the brennyng of the place there'.[7] In any case, it is clear that the destruction was sufficient to determine the King to step up his existing programme of works into a complete rebuilding project, which was started immediately.

Although there was by this time a resident clerk of works at Shene, the work was of such importance that special arrangements were made for its supervision. John Ingleby, the former prior of Shene, who had been appointed Bishop of Llandaff in July 1496, came back to take charge. When he died in 1499 Sir William Tyler, who had been comptroller of the King's works from 1485 to 1491 and who owned property in the village of Shene, took over from him. In the four years 1498-1501 some £14,500 were spent on the works.[8] In 1501 the work was finished – or nearly so. The Great Chronicle of London records:

> The King, having fynysshid moch of his newe buyldyng at his manoyr of Shene and agayn Furnysshid and Repayrid that before was perysshid wyth Fyre ... [commanded] that From than Forthon it shuld be namyd his manoyr of Rychemount, and not Shene.[9]

That the name Richmond was in celebration of the Yorkshire earldom which Henry had inherited from his father, by which title he had been known before he became King, there can be no doubt. Another chronicler, however, chose to put a different, more cynical, interpretation on it:

> ... For consideracion that in the tyme that the said brennyng greate substance of Richesse was perished and lost; and also that the Reedifying of the said Manoir had cost, and after shuld cost or it was pursued, grete and notable summes of money, where before that season it was ones called and named Shene, from this tyme forward it was commanded by the kyng that it should be called or named Rich mount.[10]

The Building of Henry VII's Palace

Henry VII certainly had a keen awareness of money – but he never seems to have had a sense of humour!

On 14 November 1501 the betrothal between Prince Arthur, elder son of King Henry VII, and Catherine of Aragon, daughter of Ferdinand and Isabella of Spain, was confirmed by their marriage in St Paul's Cathedral in London. Though Arthur was still only 15 years old, and sickly, it was a great dynastic match, to be celebrated suitably; and the King himself had travelled from Richmond down into Hampshire to greet his son's bride. After the festivities of the wedding in London, Henry decided to bring all the court and his Spanish guests to Richmond – his new show-place: 'the bright and shynyng sterre of byldyng; the mirror and paterne of all palaces of delyte, comodite and pleasure, there entendyng to fenyshe, conclude and end the rialties of this moos excellent Prince and Princes' weddyng'.[11] The journey from London was made of course by water. The Lord Mayor and the Livery Companies of the City of London had their barges decorated with 'their standards and stremers, with their conizansis right weel dekkyd'. Peers of the realm, archbishops and bishops, all had their own barges in the procession. In all there were some sixty barges accompanying those of the King and Queen, the Queen Mother, the Prince and Princess and the Duke of York (the future Henry VIII). From Westminster to Mortlake the procession rowed up the river to the accompaniment of music – 'the most goodly and pleasunt mirthe of trumpetts, clarions, shaimewes, tabers, recorders and other dyvers instruments, to whose noyse upon the water hathe not been herd the like'. At Mortlake they were met by horses to finish the last mile of the journey: and they arrived very late in the evening at Richmond where 300 gentlemen and yeomen of the guard were waiting with torches to light them into the palace.

30 The betrothal of Arthur Prince of Wales and Catherine of Aragon, from an early 16th-century Flemish tapestry, now in Magdalen College, Oxford.

Mention has already been made of the hunt in the park on the following day (p.52). Lancaster Herald's description of the palace, which then follows, is worth quoting in full – with the spelling (and a few words) modernised.

> This earthly and second Paradise of our region of England, and, as I credibly suppose, of all the great part and circuit of the world, the … spectacle, and the beauteous exemplar of all proper lodgings, the King's goodly manor of Richmond, is set and built between divers high and pleasant mountains in a valley and goodly plains and fields, where the most wholesome airs and zephyrs obtain their course and access; founded and erected upon the Thames' side and fresh river, eight

31 The palace from the Green in 1562 (detail from Wyngaerde's drawing in the Ashmolean Museum). The length of the plain wall on the right, and the width of the Great Court are much exaggerated.

miles beyond and from the noble city of London. It is quadrate and foursquare; girt and encompassed with a strong and mighty brick wall of great length and curious fashion; which girdle is goodly barred and beset with towers in its each corner and angle, and also in its middle way, of many degrees and stages of height. Its openings be strong gates of double timber and heart of oak, stuck full of nails right thick and crossed with bars of iron.

Within these rehearsed gates there is a fair, large and broad court, raised and banked in the middle for the rain slough having its channels and voidings, to observe and keep it always from soil and foulness. Upon each side of this goodly court there are galleries, with many windows, full lightsome and commodious. Out of the galleries, upon the brick walls, be doors; entering into pleasant chambers, hostels and lodgings, of necessity for such Lords and men of honour that wait, or else make suit, unto the King's grace and highness, as well strangers as of his own liege people and subjects.

Within this outer space and large court there is a lesser curtilage, paved with fine freestone or marble, in whose middle there is a conduit and cistern of stone, four-square, craftily made, with goodly springs and cocks running in its four quarters beneath, that at the will of the drawers of the water open and are closed again. In the upper part there are lions and red dragons, and other goodly beasts; and in the middle certain branches of red roses out of which flowers and roses is evermore running and course of clean and most pure water into the cistern beneath. This profitable conduit serves the chambers with water for their hands, and all other offices as they need to resort.

The pleasant hall is upon the right hand of this curtilage, twelve or sixteen degrees [i.e. yards] in height, paved with goodly tile, whose roof is of timber, not beamed nor braced, but proper knots, craftily carved, joined and shut together with mortices and pinned, hanging pendant from the said roof toward the ground and floor, after the most new invention and craft of the pure practice of geometry; cast out with windows, glazed right lightsome and goodly. In the walls and sides of this hall, between the windows, be the pictures of the noble Kings of this realm, in their harness and robes of gold: as Brutus, Hengest, King William Rufus, King Arthur, King Henry and many other of that name, King Richard, King Edward – and of those names many noble warriors and kings of this royal realm – with their falchions and swords in their hands, visaged and appearing like bold and valiant knights; and so their deeds and acts in the chronicles right evidently be shown and declared. Among this number of famous Kings in the higher part, upon

The Building of Henry VII's Palace

32 Richmond Palace, c.1562 – a model in the Museum of Richmond.

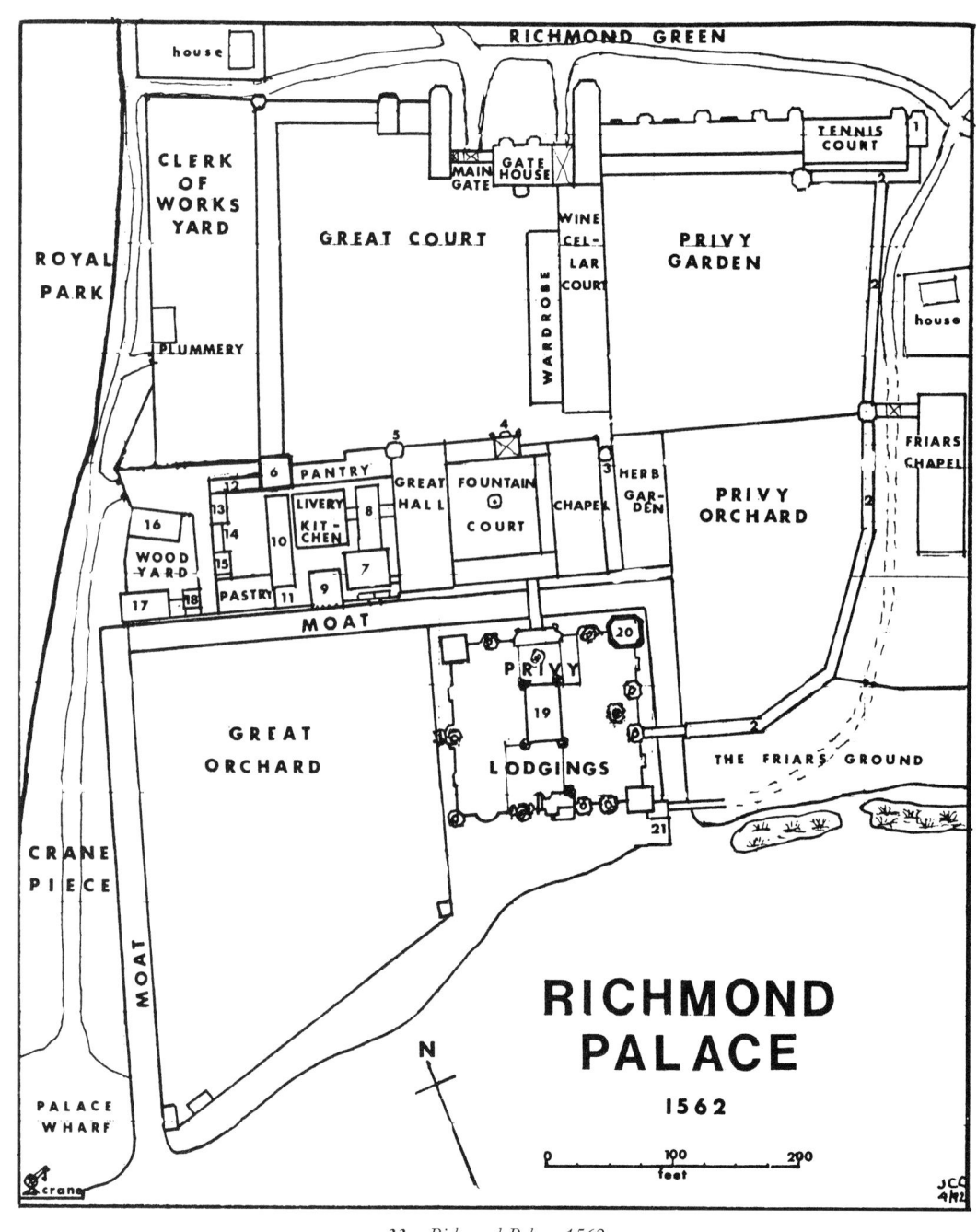

33 Richmond Palace, 1562.

KEY:	1	Banqueting house	8	Cooks' lodgings	15	Ale buttery
	2	Garden galleries	9	House of office	16	Woodyard lodging
	3	Bell tower	10	Fish and flesh larders	17	Coal store
	4	Middle gate	11	Pastry Court	18	Clerk of Woodyard
	5	Clock tower	12	Poultry house	19	Inner court
	6	Kitchen tower	13	Scalding house	20	'The Canted Tower'
	7	Privy kitchen	14	Aumbry	21	Watergate

The Building of Henry VII's Palace

the left hand, is the seemly picture and personage of our most excellent and high Sovereign now reigning upon us his liege people, King Henry VII, as worthy that room and place with those glorious Princes as any King that ever reigned in this land, that with his great manhood and wisdom hath continued nobly and victorious unto this now the eighteenth year of his reign. The walls of this pleasant hall are hung with rich cloth of Arras, their works representing many battles and sieges, as of Jerusalem, Troy, Alba and many others; that this whole apparelment was most glorious and joyful to consider and behold.

On the left side of the curtilage, above every otherlike steps, is the Chapel, well paved, glazed and hung with cloth of Arras, the body and the choir with cloth of gold; and the altars set with many relics, jewels and full rich plate. In the walls of this decent and pleasant Chapel are pictures of Kings of this realm, of those whose life and virtue was so abundant that it hath pleased Almighty God to show by them divers and many miracles and be accounted as Saints: Saint Edward, King Cadwalader, Saint Edmund, and many more, right properly pictured and adorned. In the right side of the Chapel is a goodly and privy closet for the King, richly hung with silk and curtains, carpet and cushions for his noble Grace. The Altar is also hung and plated with rich relics of gold and precious stone. The roof is ceiled, and white-limed and checkered with timber lozengewise, painted with colour of azure, having between every check a red rose of gold or a portcullis. In the other side of the Chapel other like closets for the Queen's Grace and the Princess, my Lady the King's mother, with other persons of estate and gentlewomen.

From the Chapel and closets extended goodly passages and galleries, paved, glazed and painted, beset with badges of gold, as roses, portcullises and such other, unto the King's chambers; the first, second and third, hung all three with rich and costly cloths of Arras, ceiled, white-limed and checkered as the closet was before described, with their goodly bay windows glazed and set out. Divers and many more goodly chambers there be, for the Queen's Grace, the Prince and Princess, my lady the King's mother, the Duke of York, and Lady Margaret, and all the King's noble kindred and progeny; pleasant dancing chambers, and secret closets, most richly hung, decked and adorned. Under and beside the hall are set and ordered the houses of office: the pantry, buttery, cellary, kitchen and scullery, right politicly conveyed and wisely; their coals and fuel in the yard without, nigh unto the said offices.

And in the left side of this goodly lodging, under the King's windows, the Queen's and those of other persons of state, most fair and pleasant gardens, with royal knots, alleyed and herbed; many marvellous beasts, as lions, dragons and such other of divers kinds, properly fashioned and carved in the ground, right well sounded and compassed in with lead; with many vines, seeds and strange fruit, right goodly beset, kept and nourished with much labour and diligence. In the lower end of this garden be pleasant galleries and houses of pleasure to disport in, at chess, tables, dice, cards, billiards; bowling alleys, butts for archers, and goodly tennis plays – as well to use the said plays and disports as to behold them so disporting.

The towers of this excellent place are turreted and pinnacled; the hall, chambers and other offices coved and nobly addressed; and upon each and every one of them, both pinnacles and towers, a vane of the King's arms (painted and gilt, with rich gold and azure) in such exceeding guise and manner that as well as the pleasant sight of them the hearing of them in a windy day was right marvellous to know and understand.[12]

The following day, being Sunday, the King and his guests attended mass 'with pricked song and organs, and goodly ceremonies in the choir and altars'. Then in the afternoon there were all the games in the 'gallery upon the walls' to be sampled, and outside on Richmond Green there was jousting and an acrobatic show, with a Spanish high-wire performer and tumblers.

To the description given by this 16th-century Baedeker, some extra details can be added, both from the drawings made by Antonis van Wyngaerde when he visited Richmond in 1561-2, and

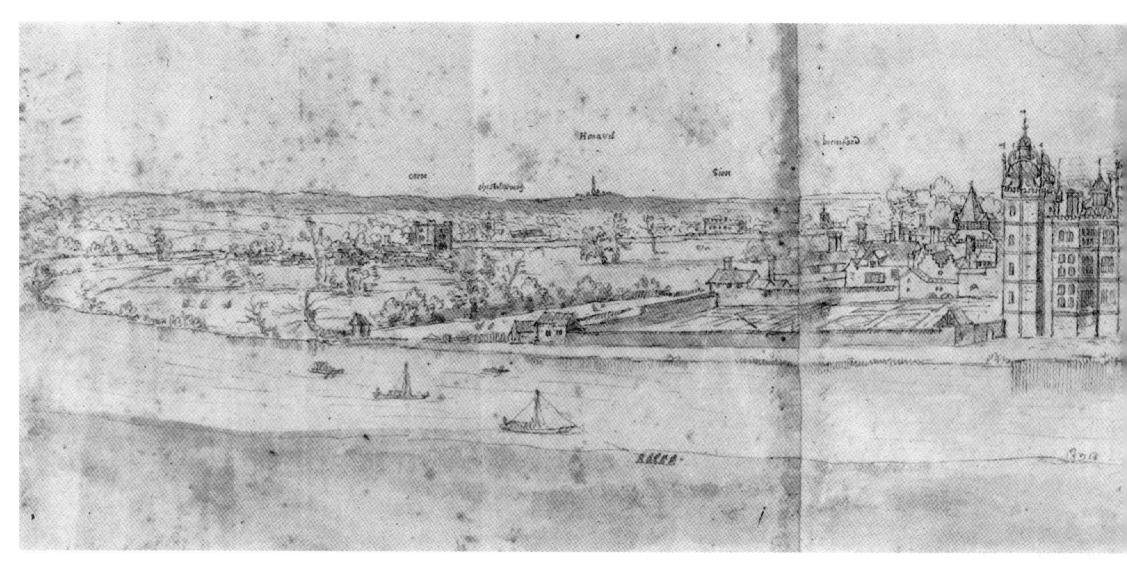

34 *'The beauteous Exemplar of all proper Lodgings'* – Antonis van Wyngaerde's drawing of Richmond Palace from the river, 1562. *(Ashmolean Museum)*

from the Parliamentary Survey of 1649,[13] due allowance being made for the works and alterations which we know to have taken place between 1501 and 1649.

Seen from the Green, the palace was distinctly lopsided. The main gate was well off to the right. A block of tall buildings stood on each side of it, then on the right there was just a blank, battlemented brick wall and quite a low corner tower. On the left was another gate, beside which a range of buildings projected well forward, with a bay at the end. From there, and almost level with the front of this building, a long range of apartments stretched to the left, the wall broken by a series of towers and chimney flues and pierced at first-floor level by sizeable mullioned windows. Then came a section of plain wall (behind which lay the tennis court) and another tower.

The only remains of this complex to be seen today are the main gate itself and a part of the gatehouse to its left (the first tower or bay and the lower part of the next, smaller, bay and some of the wall between them). Just through the gate on the left is a staircase tower which was almost certainly part of the old gatehouse. Another staircase tower at the back of No. 1 Maids of Honour Row is on the site of the tower behind the tennis court, and may contain some part of the old structure.

The gateway into the palace from the Green had, as can still be seen, both a main carriage gate and a small postern. Above the main gate was inset a stone carved with the arms of Henry VII (recently restored). Above the gateway there was originally just a battlemented walkway; the gallery linking the three-storey buildings on either side was probably built at the end of Queen Elizabeth's reign. On entering the courtyard one would see on the left (the east[*] side) a separate range of two-storey building, not then linked to the gatehouse, with a number of wide brick arches at ground-floor level. This was the wardrobe, used for storage of the soft furnishings of the palace as much as for clothing. The wide arches, the brickwork of which can be seen in the front wall, do not form a continuous run such as would suggest an open arcade, but are interrupted by more narrow arches for normal doorways. It seems most likely that the purpose of the wider openings was to allow carts to be backed in to be loaded or unloaded under cover, and that they would have been closed by large wooden double doors.

---

[*] The axis of the palace is in fact from north-east to south-west. For simplicity's sake, this is taken (except where greater accuracy is essential) as north-south.

THE BUILDING OF HENRY VII'S PALACE

Beyond the gatehouse, the north and west sides of the first court had originally only single-storey lodgings and offices, looking inwards to the court, for there were no windows anywhere in the outer walls at ground-floor level.

At the far end of the court, in line with the main gate, was an elaborate three-storey gateway building with a central window bay of two storeys in height projecting as an oriel above the gateway arch. It was surmounted with crenellated battlements, with corner turrets on each of which stood a stone figure of a trumpeter. This was the Middle Gate.

Towards the right side of the buildings at the far, south, end of the front court towered the end of the Great Hall. The hall itself stood on an undercroft to which there was an entrance from the court. The building rose to a total height of some 45 feet, again capped with battlements and with a large domed central lantern to let out the smoke. At one corner, facing the court, was a tall projecting clock tower, which soared above the roof line of the hall. Between the Middle Gate and the hall was a two-storey building containing some apartments and the stairway to the hall. Similar buildings stood to the left of the gate and to the right of the hall (the latter being the pantry).

In the far right-hand corner of the first court was a small tower with an archway which led through to the kitchen quarters and the side ('tradesmen's') entrance to the palace from what is today Old Palace Lane but was then called 'Crane Piece'. Under the archway was the clerk of works' office. On the outside of the range of buildings forming the west side of the main court was the clerk of works' yard where spare building materials and equipment were stored. In this yard was also the plummery, a vital part of the works organisation, for not only the pipes of the palace but the roofs of the main buildings were of lead.

The most impressive building in the kitchen area was the great livery kitchen, which served the royal household, with its tall pyramidal roof with two tiers of gabled louvres, rising well above the surrounding buildings. This was linked to the Great Hall by a passage on each side of which was a range of building containing the cooks' lodgings. To the south of the livery kitchen was the privy kitchen, linked by another passage directly to the screens area of the Great Hall, and through

35 The Palace Gate, Gatehouse and Wardrobe in 1805. (Engraving from Hughson's Description of London.*)*

36 Tudor brickwork in the front of the Wardrobe. The diapered brick pattern can be seen on the left. Two of the large filled-in arches (probably entrances for carts) are visible between the upper and lower windows in the centre of the photograph.

IV *Model of Richmond Palace, c.1562. (Museum of Richmond)*

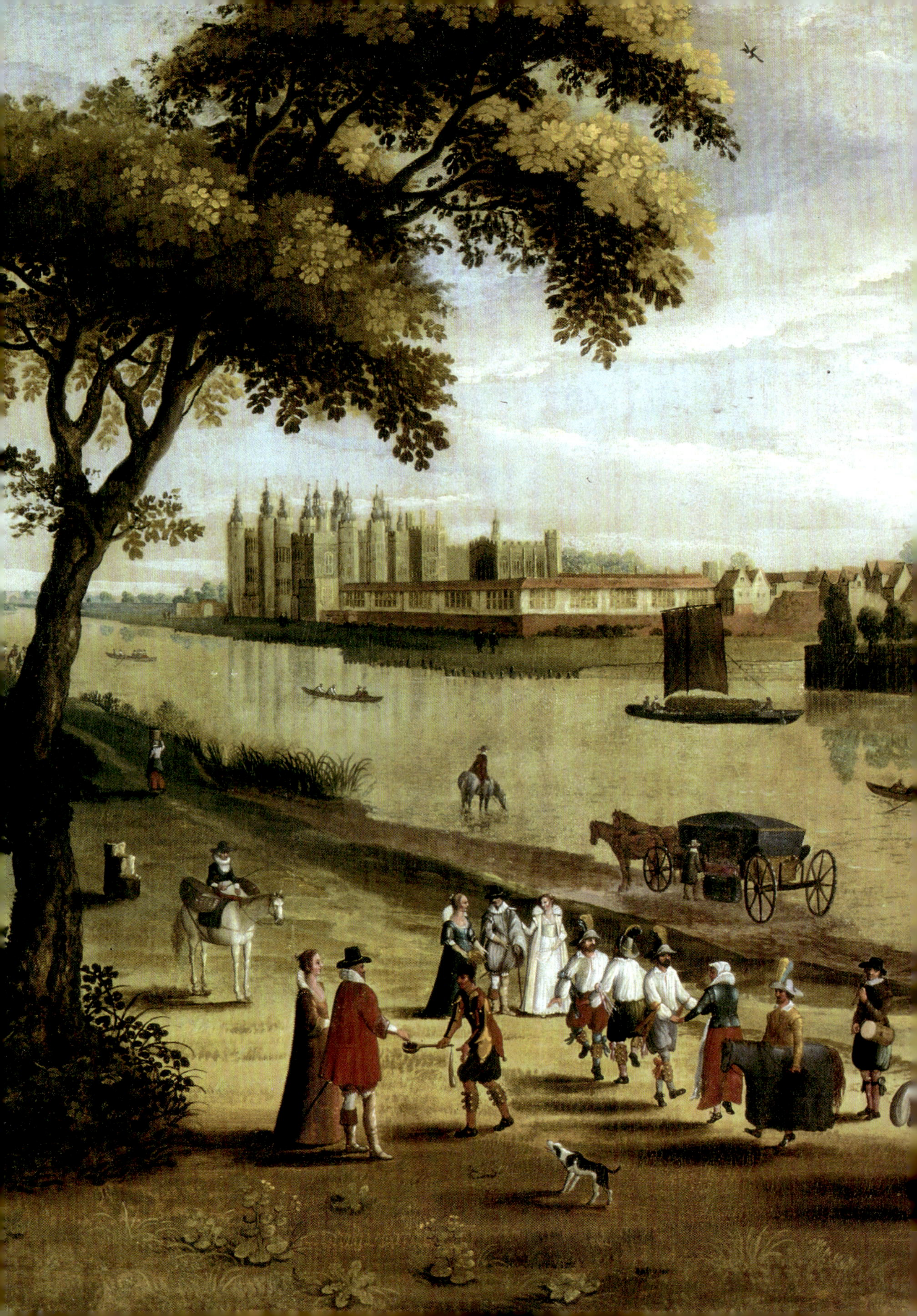

		Canted Tower	Entrance gate tower	Great Hall		The Livery
			of privy lodgings			Kitchen
					Clock tower	
Tower by	The Chapel	Closets, etc.	Passages between			Tower and gate
King's Closet		adjoining Chapel	Chapel and Hall			to Kitchen courts
					Pantry	
The Wardrobe			The Middle Gate	Entrance to		
		Lord Chamberlain's		Staircase	Buttery	Gallery round west
		Lodging		to Hall		side of Great Court

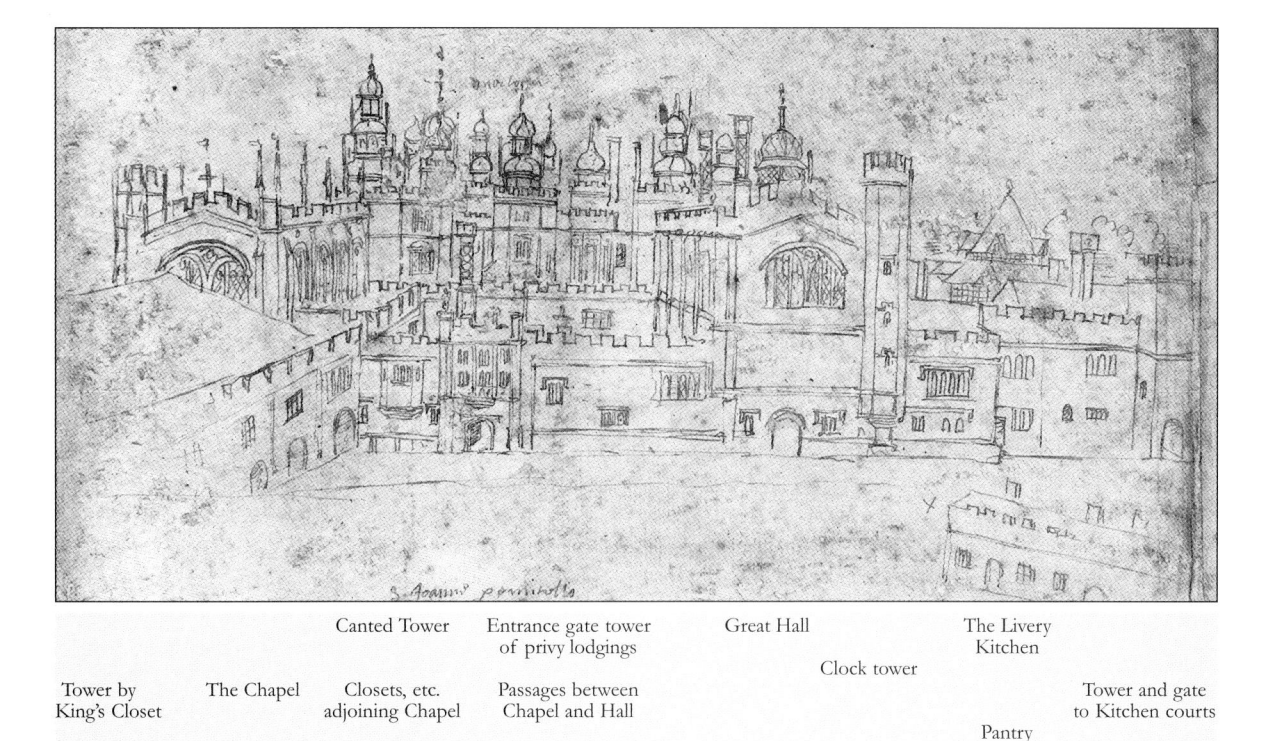

37 Fountain Court and the privy lodgings, sketch by A. van Wyngaerde. (Ashmolean Museum)

them to the gallery and passages which gave access to the privy apartments. Next to, but of course separate from, the privy kitchen was the large 'house of office' (latrines) which stood on arches above a spur of the moat.

The livery kitchen stood in the centre of, and occupied the greater part of, a courtyard which was closed on the west side by the long building of the flesh and fish larders, at the southern end of which was another small courtyard called the Pastry Court. On the farther, west, side of the larders was another large courtyard, the Poultry Court, so named from the poultry house standing on its north side. On the south side of this court was the pastry house, adjoining the Pastry Court. The west side contained the scalding house, the awmbry (storeroom) and the ale buttery. Beyond these was a little lane, separating the kitchen area from the woodyard. On the north side of the woodyard, by the outer gate into Crane Piece, was the large half-timbered Woodyard Lodging; on its south side were the coal store and the office of the clerk of the woodyard.

Returning through the archway into the Great Court one might now turn through the Middle Gate into the middle 'Fountain Court'. This was much smaller than the Great Court – a mere 65 feet square – and it was overshadowed to east and west (left and right respectively as one entered through the gate) by the chapel and the Great Hall. The staircase to the hall was in the north-west corner, that to the chapel in the south-east. At the north-east, within the Middle Gate building, were apartments usually allotted either to the Lord Chamberlain or the Lord Treasurer. Between these and the chapel stairs, and therefore between the court and the chapel itself, was a two-storey

V (facing page)   Richmond Palace from the south west, c.1630. (Detail from a painting in the Fitzwilliam Museum)

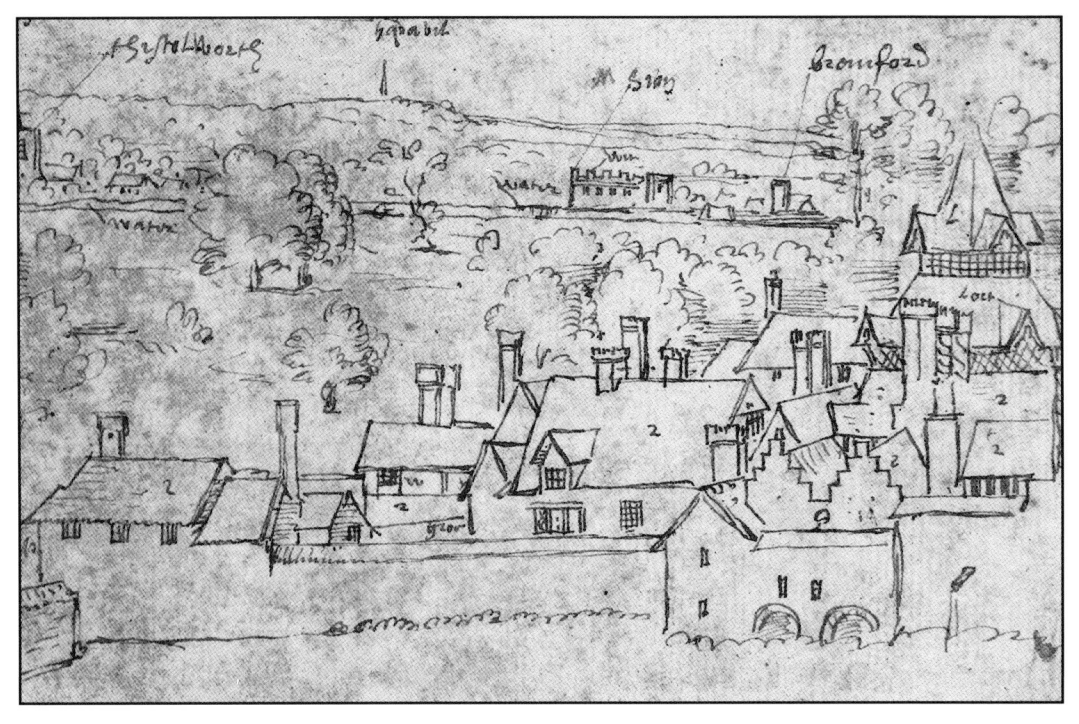

Isleworth Church	Spire of Harrow Church	Syon House	Brentford	
				Livery kitchen
			Poultry house	
	Woodyard lodging Ale buttery	Pastry	Flesh larder	
				Privy kitchen
Coal stores	Clerk of the Woodyard		'House of office'	
			Moat	

38 The kitchen quarters of the Palace, detail of a sketch by A. van Wyngaerde. (Ashmolean Museum)

building on the upper floor of which were the 'closets' or private rooms overlooking the chapel where the Queen and the King's mother and their ladies attended service.

To the Herald's full description of hall and chapel there are but a few points to add. The 'pictures' of Kings – warriors in the hall, saints in the chapel – were probably the statues mentioned in the 1649 Parliamentary Survey. At the end of the hall were screens, with a minstrels' gallery above them. In the centre was a great hearth, on the medieval pattern, the smoke from which would rise among the beams of that splendid roof to escape through the louvred lantern. There were also fireplaces with chimney flues at each end of the building, one of these being no doubt to warm the high table.

Of the decorations of the chapel one painting, now in the Queen's collection, has survived. It was an altar-piece, originally thought by Horace Walpole, in whose collection it was, to represent Henry V and his family, but since determined to be rather Henry VII and his.[14] It was certainly painted in Tudor times and almost certainly dates from the rebuilding of the chapel.

The 'checkered ceiling' of the chapel was evidently no match for its near contemporaries at Westminster Abbey, Windsor Castle and King's College Cambridge. Nevertheless, the chapel was clearly an imposing building in the late perpendicular style, with tall windows on each side and a great broad 'east' window which extended the full width of the building. Its roof line was adorned with the usual crenellations and with a series of pinnacles – or probably royal beasts as at Windsor. By the end of the King's closet on its south-east side stood a tall tower, possibly one of the two that had survived the fire. (The location of the other is a puzzle, for no other tower in close proximity to the chapel appears in any drawing; perhaps it was demolished in the rebuilding.) Below the chapel were a number of rooms for domestic staff, and below these an undercroft – used, in the 17th century at least, as a wine cellar.

The end of the Fountain Court was closed by a gallery or passage building, which may have been rebuilt in the 17th century, and which provided a covered way between the chapel and the hall. It appears to have been of two storeys and was very probably an open arcade at ground level with a closed passage above.

From these passages, and from a passage within the chapel building leading from the royal closets beside the chapel, access could be had to

39 Altar-piece from the Chapel of Richmond Palace showing St George and the dragon, and King Henry VII and his family (thought by Horace Walpole to be Henry V and his family). (Engraving from Walpole's Anecdotes of Painting.*)*

the great block of buildings by the river which contained the royal 'privy apartments'. First, however, the moat had to be crossed – the old moat which had run round Henry V's 'castle'. No existing picture shows how this was achieved. We can assume however that, at least by the time Henry VII had finished his rebuilding, what had once been a drawbridge had been replaced by a covered and enclosed bridge, probably of two levels, leading directly into the entrance tower which was centrally situated on the north side of the 'privy lodgings' block. The moat itself was probably filled in about 1610, as part of the works undertaken for Prince Henry (*see* p.187).

The privy lodgings building was of stone, essentially of three storeys and with 12 rooms (in 1649) on each floor. It was built around a small central courtyard, 40 feet by 24 feet in extent. All around the exterior were a series of towers and bays which, as already noted, produce a ground-plan which resembles that of a 15th-century castle. Some indeed may have appeared more tower-like in 1501 than they did in later drawings, for there was much work on the insertion of bay windows later in the century. Many of the towers were of four storeys and almost every tower and decorative turret was surmounted by its 'pepper pot' dome, though these were of several different designs. There were 14 such 'turrets' left in 1649, but it is likely that some had been taken down since 1501 (*see* p.122). Above the domes came the pinnacles and weather vanes that so pleased Lancaster Herald. Wyngaerde's drawings show what appear to be King's beasts supporting many of these weather vanes, and also some elaborate strap work, which possibly served a practical as well as a decorative purpose, by acting as bracing for the beasts and pinnacles. All this decoration had been cleared away before the 1620s if the depictions of the palace at that time are to be trusted.

The exact arrangement of the rooms within the privy lodgings can only be a matter for informed guesswork. The description of 1649 undoubtedly followed a sequence which makes it

40 The privy lodgings from the river, sketch by A. van Wyngaerde. (Ashmolean Museum)

possible to construct a conjectural plan for that date. But there had obviously been many changes in the use of rooms since 1603, let alone 1501. What is unlikely to have changed is the arrangement whereby the ground-floor rooms would have been given over mainly to the officers of the household. The principal state apartments and the King's chambers would have been on the first floor. That the King's apartments were on the east (actually south-east) side is apparent both from the Herald's description and from a later account for the repair of the bridge over the moat 'out of the King's lodging into the garden'. That the Queen's apartments were on the same side, so

41 The riverside at Richmond, c.1630, by a Flemish artist. (Fitzwilliam Museum)

42   Richmond Palace from the south east, c.1630. Above: detail from the Fitzwilliam painting; right: detail from the engraving of the painting.

most likely on the floor above the King's, also appears from the Herald's account, for both overlooked the gardens.

Another bridge seems to have crossed the moat to the open ground outside 'the Friars' from the small two-storeyed watergate tower at the corner of the river front, as can be seen in both Wyngaerde's and Hollar's drawings.

A notable feature of the privy lodgings was what the Parliamentary Survey of 1649 described as 'one round structure or building of free stone called the Canted Tower, fower stories high covered with lead and battled with stone conteyning one celler and fower hansome roomes one above another and one staire case of stone of one hundred and twentie steps in assent; this tower is a chiefe ornament unto the whole fabrick of Richmond Court'.

The *History of the King's Works* suggests that this was the tower in the middle of the north front.[15] However, this identification is open to objection. The tower in the middle of the north front was indeed canted, as may be seen from Wyngaerde's sketch (*see* p.65), but it was the entrance tower to the privy lodgings. It is surely improbable that, if it were the first feature encountered as the surveyors crossed from the gallery to the lodgings, they should have made no mention of it until they had completed their description of the rest of the lodgings building. And in such a position it is perhaps doubtful whether there would have been space for 'four handsome rooms' and a great staircase.

Another prime candidate for the great canted tower presents itself in a later painting of the palace, that done by a Flemish artist about 1630 which is now in the Fitzwilliam Museum, Cambridge. (It was in Lord Fitzwilliam's collection in his house on Richmond Green and was presented by him to the museum which he founded.) This shows a canted tower, apparently octagonal in plan, at the north-east corner of the privy lodgings block, opposite the chapel. Though only a little higher than the adjacent buildings, and indeed not as high as the many 'turret towers', it is a large and imposing structure with fine big mullioned windows. It is crowned not by a pepper-pot dome but by a number of high pinnacles (or tall chimneys?) at the angles and by what appears to be a small turret – for access to the roof perhaps – at the far side. Wyngaerde's sketch shows a similar feature, but the tower (just to the right of the chapel) appears less imposing and less well fenestrated than in the Fitzwilliam painting, and its roof turret appears to have a small pepper-pot dome. But this Wyngaerde sketch is not very easy to interpret; and there may have been works of alteration and improvement on the tower (though none were specifically recorded) in the seventy or so years between the two depictions. The canted tower can be clearly seen on the right of the Wyngaerde sketch of the privy lodgings from the river (south side), standing up above the water gate. Unfortunately Wyngaerde made no sketch of the palace from the east side, and the Fitzwilliam painting is the only detailed picture of that side. It can leave little doubt, however, that this corner tower is indeed the 'canted tower' of the surveyors' description.*

The canted tower overlooked the palace gardens. The main gardens were divided by a wall (or possibly a walled passage) which ran from the moat to a small tower on the east side of the outer perimeter. This tower was itself linked by a passage, over an archway, to the Friars' chapel. By 1649 the southern part of the gardens had been planted as a privy orchard, and the northern part only was called the 'privy garden', but there is no sign of such a distinction in use in Wyngaerde's drawing, in which both parts appear to have small divided lawns or beds, some planted with the popular 'knots'.

Around the outside of the garden, on each side of the perimeter tower, stretched the garden galleries, of two storeys, open below and closed above, of half-timber construction. They were not unlike the simpler parts of the Horseshoe Cloister at Windsor, which survives today. The southern section of the galleries swept round in a series of obtuse-angled turns to meet the privy lodgings block, to which it was linked in 1517 by a bridge over the moat. North of the tower the galleries continued in a straight line, then turned in at a right angle to terminate in another small tower. This was not on the line of the front walls of the palace, facing the Green, but somewhat behind them. In the space thus left between the galleries and the front wall stood the tennis court. The galleries would have had windows overlooking the court to enable spectators to watch the game. The tennis court cannot have been a building of the size and style of the one which survives at Hampton Court (which was probably built in 1625-6).[16] The Richmond court was probably an open one, for no roof appears in the Wyngaerde drawings.

The long range of pleasure galleries surrounding the gardens was a new feature in English palace architecture, though Edward IV had built a (much smaller) gallery for recreational use at Eltham. Simon Thurley describes them as 'clearly modelled on the Burgundian galleries',[17] and arcaded galleries were indeed a feature of some of the Burgundian palaces of Flanders. There was

---

* I favoured the corner position in my original reconstruction of the palace plan (1975 lecture and in *The Growth of Richmond*, 1981). In preparing the plans for the palace model in the Museum of Richmond I chose, however, to put the canted tower in the centre of the eastern front of the Privy Lodgings building. This I now consider to have been an error. I was misled by using the engraving of the Fitzwilliam picture, which shows the corner tower as square, not canted; and by the evident fact that Wyngaerde shows the highest of the decorative domes as being somewhere on the eastern side, but not at the corner. I am grateful to Simon Thurley of Historic Royal Palaces for drawing my attention to the discrepancy between the engraving and the original Fitzwilliam painting.

43 Windsor Castle: the Horseshoe Cloister.

44 The Privy Orchard and Privy Garden at Richmond, with the Galleries, in 1562; on the right, the Chapel of the Friary. Sketch by A. van Wyngaerde. (Ashmolean Museum)

certainly a strong Burgundian influence at Henry VII's court, and there were already Flemish artists established there,[18] but Henry himself had not visited the Burgundian domains.

He may have been inspired by an example much closer to home. Every monastery in the country had its cloisters – large or small – around a garden. Sometimes such cloistered gardens had been included in palaces: Edward III had one at Shene. At the Shene Charterhouse, which Henry VII took under his special patronage, there was the largest cloister 'gallery' in England, some 1,400 feet of it around the central garth. Henry certainly knew it; he may well have walked in it with the prior. It was only a single-storey construction, probably of timber, but may it not have suggested to the King the concept – novel even in Burgundy – of completely enclosing the open sides of his gardens with such a covered walk? The execution of the concept, with its lower level open to the gardens and a closed viewing gallery above, may indeed have been the contribution of someone who knew the Burgundian exemplars. (Bishop John Ingleby, supervising the works at the palace until his death in 1499, had probably visited the Charterhouse at Bruges when prior of Shene, in the course of his several journeys to report to the Grande Chartreuse.)

On the west side of the privy lodgings, and south of the kitchen quarters from which it was divided by the moat, was the Great Orchard. Its outer walls, facing Crane Piece and the river, were of plain brick, not crenellated. There were small buildings – gardeners' sheds and a barn – in the corners, and a gateway which gave out onto the quite narrow strip of river-bank outside the privy lodgings. It should be borne in mind that the river was much wider then than it is now. The line of the outer wall of the orchard by the riverside can still be seen, in the wall that runs back obliquely in the garden of Trumpeters' Lodge. It serves to give an accurate fix for the corner of the orchard near the palace building. The river frontage of the privy lodgings stood about halfway up the lawn of Trumpeters' House.

✠

The palace buildings that were constructed of stone, or at least faced with stone, were the Great Hall, the Chapel, the Middle Gate and the buildings adjacent to these in Fountain Court, and the privy lodgings. The galleries and some of the domestic and kitchen buildings were of timber-framed construction. The rest were of brick.

Neither the master-mason nor the master-bricklayer for the work of rebuilding the palace are named in the very few accounts that have survived.[19] The local clerk of works, since 1493, was Nicholas Grey. He last appears in that capacity in 1504, after which he seems to have retired to live in Richmond, for in 1514 he was granted 'a tenement in the town of Richmond, near the King's manor, called the Timber Hawe, with a close and two gardens, which said messuage was built by the said Nicholas at his own charge and expense'.[20] Henry Smyth, the clerk of the King's works, took over direct personal responsibility for Richmond from 1505.[21*]

The name we find most frequently mentioned in relation to the works is that of the master-carpenter, Thomas Bynks, who had been Master of the Carpenters' Company in London in 1495-7 and 1500-2.[22] It would be pleasant to be able to credit him unreservedly as the man responsible for that splendid timber roof of the Great Hall so admired by Lancaster Herald, and it may indeed have been his work that the Herald admired. But, alas, some of Bynks's work, including that roof, was not satisfactory. In 1503-5 he had constructed the galleries around the gardens; one section was finished – 'tiled, lathed and pargetted' – in the summer of 1504, and the other a year later.[23] At the end of the gallery behind the tennis court the small tower was

---

* Sir Reginald Bray, the King's closest friend and financial counsellor, may also have played some part. His device of a hemp-bray, found also in St George's Chapel at Windsor, is depicted in one of the few surviving fragments of glass from Richmond Palace (now in the Museum of Richmond).

added.[24] Then in July 1506 a part of the gallery collapsed just an hour after the King and Prince had been walking in it. Bynks was cast into prison, and a rapid investigation was carried out as to the quality of the rest of his work. The job of rebuilding the galleries was given to a new master-carpenter, John Squier, who was also required to repair the roofs of the hall and chapel 'through Bynks' faults'.[25] After that disgrace, it is somewhat surprising to find that Bynks was again Master of the Carpenters' Company in 1510-11 and 1514-15.

Another disaster had been narrowly averted in January 1505/6. On the 5th of that month a fire again broke out in the King's chamber, apparently due to the carelessness of one of his pages. It damaged the beds and hangings and carpets, but was extinguished before it could spread further.[26]

It was not therefore until 1507 that the work of rebuilding the palace can be said to have been satisfactorily completed. This was not however the only work that was being carried out for the King at Richmond during this time. A new religious foundation was established by Henry VII. The Grey Friars of the Franciscan Order had, in the 15th century, been subjected to far-reaching reforms inaugurated in 1421 by their then vicar-general, St Bernardin. In the second half of the century the reform movement reached England – but it was resisted by some houses of the order. Those who accepted the reform were called Observant Friars; those who rejected it were styled Conventuals.

Henry VII was a strong admirer and supporter of the Observant Friars. He suppressed four houses of Conventuals and gave them to the Observants, a grant confirmed by Pope Alexander VI in 1499.[27] In addition he created a new foundation for the Observants adjacent to the palace of Richmond. (A similar foundation at Greenwich Palace, which used to be credited also to Henry VII has now been traced to a gift of Edward IV in 1482.)[28]

No foundation charter exists for the Richmond house. There was no question of endowing such a friary with lands as the Observants were vowed to poverty and could own no property save their own houses. They were of course, like all friars, supposed to be mendicants and to work and preach in the community rather than live the enclosed life of monks. The *History of the King's Works* suggests that the date of foundation was 1501, a deduction drawn from the fact that payments were made in that year to 'the General of the Observants' and to 'Friars Observant of France'.[29] The date fits well with the surviving accounts.

It evidently seemed to King Henry that it would be a convenient plan to make over to the Observant Friars for their new house the old buildings of the 'Byfleet' complex, self-contained and with an existing chapel. If the suggestion above, that these buildings had served as temporary accommodation for the court since the fire, is correct, they would have been in a reasonably good state of repair when vacated in 1501. However some work was needed to adapt them for the friars' use and a contract was made jointly with three master craftsmen to undertake the work: Thomas Bynks, the carpenter; Henry Redman (or Redmayne), a mason of Brentford; and Robert Nevill, who was both a brickmaker and a bricklayer. In April 1499 Nevill had been granted the land, then called 'South Park', but later 'Moorbrook' or 'Smithy Croft', which lay on Cutler's Hill in Richmond, between the upper and lower highways to Petersham. Although no reason for the grant is stated, it may well have been to enable him to set up a new local source of supply, using the clay on the hillside, for the bricks required to rebuild the palace. If so, he appears to have been the first of the long line of brick and tile makers established along the lower Petersham road.[30]

The first payment due on the Bynks-Redman-Nevill contract was made in May 1502.[31] Within the next two years they had received some £1,180.[32] Redman and Nevill (now without Bynks, not yet disgraced but occupied with works at Greenwich) were paid £30 on 17 April 1506 'in full payment upon an indenture for the fynyshing of the freres at Richemonte', with another £3 15s. 5d. 'in addition upon their bill' in the July following.[33] Further relatively small sums were expended on decorative work in the friary, including the painting of the church roof and 'divers tables for the Freres church'.[34] John Oxenbrigge, a cleric who became a canon of Windsor, supervised some of the work of decoration. In 1504 he was paid over £200 'for certain ornaments for the freres at Richemont', for 'adournments' and for 'garnishing' the friary.[35] (Oxenbrigge was another local landowner, acquiring some thirty acres in Richmond in 1506.)[36]

Finally in March 1509 came a payment to Henry Smyth, clerk of the King's works, 'for full fynysshing of the Freres at Richemont'.[37]

Chapter VII

Henry VII's 'New Park of Richmond, County Middlesex'

Of Henry V's three monastic foundations, two – the Briggitines and the Carthusians – thrived. The third project, the introduction of Celestines from France, was abortive as a result of the war between France and England. The buildings remained uncompleted; the site was never formally granted, so there is no document which defines it precisely. In 1425 it was included in a 10-year lease to John Ardene, the clerk of the King's works, of the manors of Shene, Petersham and Ham and 'a close in which a house for religious men of the order of Celestines was lately erected by King Henry V, in the County of Middlesex'.[1]

The Briggitines of Syon were far from happy with their own site, by the river on the borders of the parishes of Isleworth and Twickenham, facing the royal palace. It was too small and too damp. In 1421 King Henry had granted them the whole manor of Isleworth, separated for the purpose from the Duchy of Cornwall estates by a special Act of Parliament.[2] The grant was confirmed by Henry VI in a charter of 1423.[3] However, the abbess and convent of Syon decided that, if the Celestine project was to be abandoned, they would prefer the site which had been intended for them, or somewhere close to it. They secured its transfer to them in October 1426: 'a certain house which the late King built within the said manor with the intention of founding therein other religious persons, an intention never fulfilled'.[4] The first stone of their new church was laid by the Duke of Bedford, regent for the young Henry VI, in that same year.[5]

By 1431 the new buildings were sufficiently advanced for the convent to be able to move, and a petition was sent to the King seeking his formal permission. Their original site, granted by Henry V, was – said the abbess – 'so small and confined in its dimensions that the numerous persons therein were not only incommodiously but dangerously situated, being sixty nuns or sisters, besides twenty-five men of religion (the latter of whom, however, dwelled by themselves in a separate convent … and only officiated as chaplains or clerks …); in consequence thereof the said abbess and convent had chosen a spot within the said Lordship of Isleworth, more meet, healthful and salubrious for them to inhabit, and had begun, and with great cost completed, the erection of a certain edifice more spacious and convenient …' Consent was duly granted,[6] and the move was made on 11 November, St Martin's Day, 1431.[7]

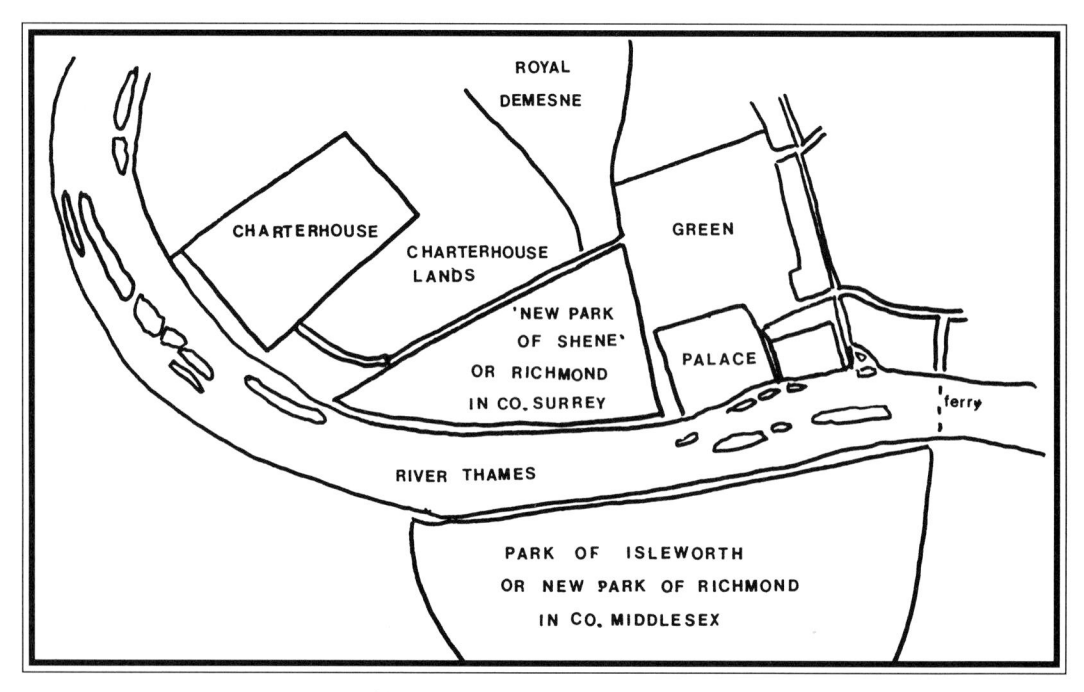

45   The two parks of Richmond in the 16th century.

The abandoned site, opposite the royal palace, was probably cleared of buildings, for the materials would have been reused as far as possible in the new building. If unsuitable for a large convent, it was nevertheless to form the nucleus of another royal project. When Henry VII had completed his rebuilding of the palace of Shene, renamed Richmond, he evidently decided that it needed a larger park than the fifty acres or so enclosed by Henry VI. Perhaps, as suggested above, it was the hunt laid on for the entertainment of his Spanish guests in 1501 that triggered this decision.

In 1503 Henry arranged an exchange with the convent of Syon, who were granted an advowson, chapel and land at Olney in Buckinghamshire and in return surrendered to the King an area of land on the borders of Twickenham and Isleworth which included the old Syon site together with some extra ground around it, to make a rough semicircle. This land was enclosed by the King with a pale 9,642 feet in total circuit.[8] This became the 'New Park of Isleworth, *alias* New Park of Richmond, County Middlesex'.

The name of Richmond was attached to this park because it was dependent on, and an appendage of, the palace. It was the palace and manor, not the village, of Shene that had been formally given this new title – the village just adopted it. However its use in connection with Isleworth Park is a source of confusion, although it is almost always qualified by the addition of 'County Middlesex'. The confusion is increased by the parallel existence of two parks, both having the name of New Park, and both now bearing the name of Richmond. There is, however, another distinguishing feature: the keeper of the park on the Surrey bank continued to receive only 2d. a day as his wages, while the keeper of the larger Middlesex park received 3d. a day.

The first recorded appointment of a keeper for the Isleworth park was that of Sir William Tyler in 1521.[9] In 1529 he was succeeded by Sir Francis Bryan[10] and in 1546 by Robert Bouchier.[11]

A survey of the manor of Richmond made in 1550 shows quite clearly the two different parks and their respective keepers:

> And there is likewise one park adjacent to the said mansion house [Richmond Palace] called Richemount Park containing in circuit by estimation one mile given for the use aforesaid [of the King] into the Keeping of the said David [Vincent] …
>
> And there is likewise one other park belonging to the said mansion house and lying in the parish of Istelworth containing in circuit by estimation [blank] miles given into the keeping of Robert Bocher Esquire for the use aforesaid …[12]

Although the park of Isleworth was certainly larger than the one at Richmond there is an interesting reference to it in 1550/1 as the 'Little Park'. On 22 February the Privy Council sent a letter to 'Robert Boocher' to 'deliver deere in the Lytell Park at Richmond beyonde the water to siche as the Master of Horses shall adress for the same to be sent to Hanworth'.[13]

In 1556 Sir Henry Jernegan, Vice-Chamberlain of Queen Mary's household, was granted for life the offices of 'Master of the hunt of wild beasts in the Park of Isleworth, Co Middlesex, otherwise called the New Park of Richmond' and of keeper of the said park – still with the 3d. a day wage.[14]

It was in 1574 that the park ceased to be a royal hunting ground. In that year Queen Elizabeth granted to Edward Bacon, the third son of Sir Nicholas Bacon, her Keeper of the Great Seal, a 21-year lease of 'our park of Istelworth otherwise called the Newe Parke of Richemonde in our County of Middlesex', containing an estimated eighty-seven acres, as well as the adjoining meadows. One of the conditions of the lease was that Bacon would discharge the Crown of the obligation to pay the keeper's fee, which at 3d. a day amounted to £4 10s. 0d. a year.[15]

The park never returned to royal use. In the 1590s Francis Bacon, Edward's more famous half-brother, was in occupation and referred to it in his letters as 'Twickenham Park', although in a reversionary lease granted to him in 1595 it was still described by the old formula. From this time on it became generally known as Twickenham Park, and its history diverges from that of the palaces and parks of Richmond.[16]

46 *Margaret Tudor, Queen of Scots, daughter of King Henry VII and wife of King James IV of Scotland. (Hulton-Deutsch Collection)*

Chapter VIII

'The King's Court should have the Excellence' – The Tudor Palace 1501-1553

Very shortly after the marriage of Prince Arthur, King Henry VII achieved another dynastic match for one of his children – one that was to prove, though it was hardly to be expected at the time, of far greater significance in British history than the Spanish alliance. At Richmond Palace, on 24 January 1501/2, agreement was reached that the King's eldest daughter Margaret should marry King James IV of Scotland. On the same day a 'treaty of perpetual peace' between England and Scotland was signed at Richmond.

The ratification of these agreements and arrangements for the betrothal ceremony took the best part of a year. In the meantime, less than five months after his wedding, Prince Arthur died at Ludlow, where he had been sent with his bride to make an act of presence as Prince of Wales. Catherine of Aragon, the young widow, was also taken ill at Ludlow, but was brought back to Richmond as soon as she could travel. She was then installed in Durham House in London while her father-in-law pondered over her disposal. He wanted the alliance with Spain; even more he wanted Catherine's dowry.

The Queen, heartbroken at the loss of her elder son, was increasingly unwell. As the date for Margaret's betrothal drew near, Queen Elizabeth was expecting the birth of another child. She went to Richmond on 21 December 1502. On Christmas Day she was sung to by the 'Children of the King's Chapel' and on Boxing Day she drew £5 from her privy purse 'for her disport at cards'.[1] Early in January she went for a week's retreat to the convent of sisters of St John of Jerusalem at Hampton Court. Then she remained at Richmond until the end of the month. Because of her condition it was decided that the ceremony of betrothal should be held at Richmond.

So, on 25 January 1502/3, the betrothal of Princess Margaret to King James IV (represented as proxy by Patrick, Earl of Bothwell) took place at Richmond Palace. Although the Queen's indisposition cast something of a shadow, the occasion was celebrated with much pomp and ceremony. Many lords spiritual and temporal attended, including both the English archbishops; the senior Scottish representative was the Archbishop of Glasgow. The proceedings began with a High Mass in the palace chapel, after which the whole company adjourned to the Queen's Great Chamber, where the actual ceremony of betrothal took place, conducted by the Archbishop of Glasgow.

47 King Henry VII, by Michiel Sittow, 1505. (National Portrait Gallery)

48 Queen Elizabeth (of York), wife of King Henry VII, by an unknown artist. (National Portrait Gallery)

That don, the Trompetters standing on the Leds at the Chamber End, blew upp, and the lowd Noise of Minstrells played, in the best and most joyfullest Manner.

The King went to his owne Chamber to Dynner and had the said Archbishop of Glasco and the Earle of Bothwell att the upper End of his Table … The Queene tooke her Daughter the Q [*sic*] of Scotts by the Hand, and dyned both at one Messe, covered. All the other Ambassadors, with the Archbishops of Canterbury and Yorke, in the Council Chamber.

In the afternoon there was jousting and in the evening 'Sopper' and 'a notable Bankett'. (A 'banquet' in those days was not the meal itself, but a collation of sweetmeats, fruits and wine served either separately or after the main meal, often in a separate 'banqueting house'.) Next day prizes were distributed for the jousting, and 'there was in the Hall a goodly Pageant, curiously wrought with Fenestrallis, having many lights brenning in the same, in Manner of a Lantron, out of which sorted various Sorts of Morisks [morris dancers]. Also a very goodly Disguising of Six Gentlemen and Six Gentlewomen, which danced divers Dances.' Another banquet followed, and after some more jousting on the next day the King presented his gifts to the Scottish visitors.[2]

As soon as the celebrations were over, the Queen moved to the rooms in the Tower of London which had been prepared for her confinement. She was delivered of a daughter, Catherine, on 2 February; but died nine days later. The baby died also.

On 16 June 1503 Princess Margaret set off from Richmond for her journey to Scotland. Exactly one week later Catherine of Aragon was formally betrothed to her late husband's brother

Henry, the new Prince of Wales. Catherine had claimed that her marriage to Arthur had never been consummated; the boy was ill when they were married and had grown steadily weaker. The Princess's duenna confirmed this. All the same, it had seemed wise to King Henry – to make sure of the dowry – to ignore these claims and to obtain a papal dispensation stating that Henry might wed his brother's widow. This had finally been received.

All was now well; except that Henry had demanded another dowry from Spain, and he was not going to allow the marriage to take place until it arrived. Catherine was formally allotted apartments in Richmond Palace which became her principal home, but she saw little of her new husband-to-be, and the years dragged on without any move towards turning the betrothal into a marriage. She was desperately poor, and had to keep writing to her father for funds. Henry VII neglected her, and her Spanish attendants were reduced to living 'in outbuildings at Greenwich, rooms over the stables in Richmond, and a decaying manor house in Fulham'.[3]

There may have been a brief interlude of relief when Catherine's elder sister Joanna, Queen of Castile, with her new husband Philip of Hapsburg, Duke of Burgundy, made an unplanned visit to England in the winter of 1505-6. The ship in which Philip and Joanna were sailing from the Netherlands to their new kingdom of Castile had been driven ashore in Dorset by a storm in the Channel. Henry VII at once seized the opportunity, brought the royal pair to Windsor and there concluded a treaty of alliance with Philip on 9 February. After a brief visit to London the party then moved to Richmond where Philip and Joanna stayed for a short while before setting out to resume their journey to Spain.[4] At Richmond, 'there were many notable feats of arms proved both at the tilt and at the tourney and at the barriers'.[5]

In September 1506 Philip died. Henry VII at once offered to marry the widow Joanna. As she was generally reported to be insane, his motive for this gesture was taken, no doubt correctly, to be a desire to gain control of Castile. (Still, he must have found her not unattractive during her stay in England.) The offer was not taken up by King Ferdinand who was acting as regent for Joanna, his daughter. Henry did not pursue it; but turned his attention to another means of achieving the same end. The plan was now to secure the marriage of his daughter Mary, born in 1496, to Philip's son Charles. Charles was four years younger than Mary, but he was heir to both Aragon and Castile. After involved diplomatic manoeuvring Henry attained his objectives. A large embassy was despatched to England from the Spanish Netherlands, the marriage treaty was agreed, and on 17 December 1508 the betrothal ceremony of Prince Charles of Castile, represented by the Sieur de Bergues, and the Princess Mary was officially celebrated at Richmond.

The ceremony was followed by a banquet in the palace at which Henry paid the rare honour of inviting the Sieur de Bergues and the second most senior Spanish delegate to dine at his own table. The other ambassadors, 'accompanied with dyverse of the grettest Lords spirituell and temporell of the Reame', dined in another chamber 'next adjoynynge'. After the dinner there was jousting, watched by the King, Princess Catherine, and Princess Mary.

> Howe well horsed and harneissed, howe richely appoynted were the said Lords and Knyghts with pavylyons, trappers, bards and other ornaments and appareyll of goldsmyth werke, clothe of gold, silke and other ryche garnysshynge, and with belles of silver, and many diverse devises, it were to longe a processe to wryte. For by the space of thre dayes these Justis continued, and day by day every Lorde and Knyght had dyversitie and chaunge of appareills every day richer than other.

At night there were more banquets, and at one the ambassadors delivered gifts of jewels to Princess Mary from the Emperor and from Prince Charles, while Henry agreed to appoint Prince Charles a Knight of the Garter. 'Att whiche banket there was no cuppe, salte ne layer, but it was of fyne gold, ne yet noo plate of vessayll but it was gilte.' Finally the ambassadors took their leave and departed, laden by the King with gifts of plate, horses, falcons, hawks and hounds.[6]

This dynastic ambition of King Henry had still brought no benefit for the Spanish princess he had firmly in his grip. King Ferdinand had not produced the balance of her dowry; and the unfortunate Catherine was still shamefully neglected by Henry and his son. In September 1508 the court moved from Richmond for fear of the plague; they left Catherine and her suite behind – without even a horse.[7]

The Spanish ambassador was worried about her, not only for her material well-being but because he considered the influence of her confessor, Fray Diego Fernandez, to be unwholesome and unwise. The story which he indignantly related to King Ferdinand, of how this priest made Catherine refuse to visit the ailing King Henry at Richmond while she was staying, with the Princess Mary, at Kew in March 1509 will be told in detail in a later chapter (*see* p.152). On 21 April, in his palace of Richmond, King Henry died. His body lay in state for three days in the hall of the palace and for three days in the chapel, before it was borne away with due ceremony for burial in his chapel at Westminster Abbey.

✠

Henry VIII at once demonstrated that the delay in his marriage with Catherine of Aragon had been entirely of his father's volition and not his own. Seven weeks after Henry VII's death and two weeks before his coronation the young King finally married his fiancée of six years' standing. Christmas of 1509 was spent at Richmond. Early in January a grand tournament was held on Richmond Green. Henry himself took part 'incognito' – and half-killed his unfortunate opponent, Sir William Compton. Queen Catherine was already pregnant, but she suffered a premature labour and the baby, a daughter, was stillborn on 31 January. Soon she was pregnant again.

The court returned to Richmond on 8 November 1510 – to stay until after Christmas. There was jousting, and this time the King made his participation manifest. He issued a challenge that he, with two aides – Charles Brandon and his erstwhile victim William Compton – would take on all comers, 'with spere at the Tylt one daye, and at turney with swordes the other'. On 13 November the King and his two supporters entered the lists.

> Their bases and trappers were of cloth of gold, set with redde roses, ingreyled with gold of brouderye … At these Justes the King brake more staves than any other, and therefore had the pryze: at the Turney in like wise the honor was his.[8]

49   Catherine of Aragon as a young woman. (Kunsthistorisches Museum, Vienna)

The entertainment on the following night was fully recorded in Hall's *Chronicle*, and it gives a vivid picture of the colour and gaiety of Henry's court at Richmond.

> The second night were divers strangers of Maximilian the Emperor's court and Ambassadors of Spain with the King at supper: when they had supped the King willed them to go into the Queen's chamber, who so did. And in the mean time the King with fifteen others, apparelled in Almayn jackets of crimson and purple satin, with long quartered sleeves, with hose of the same suit, their bonnets of white velvet wrapped in flat gold of damask, with visors and white plumes, came in with a mummery, and after a certain time that they had played with the Queen and the strangers, they departed. Then suddenly entered six minstrels, richly apparelled, playing on their instruments, and then followed fourteen Gentlemen, all apparelled in yellow satin, cut like Almaynes, bearing torches. After them came six disguised in white satin and green, embroidered and set with letters and castles of fine gold in bullion; the garments were of strange fashion with also strange cuts, every cut knit with points of fine gold and tassels of the same, their hose cut and tied in like wise, their bonnets of cloth of silver wound with gold. First of these six was the King; [the others were] the Earl of Essex, Charles Brandon, Sir Edward Howard, Sir Thomas Knevet and Sir Henry Guilford. Then part of the Gentlemen bearing torches departed and shortly returned, after whom came in six ladies apparelled in garments of crimson satin embroidered and traversed with cloth of gold, cut in pomegranates and yokes, stringed after the fashion of Spain. Then the said six men danced with these six ladies; and after that they had danced a season, the ladies took off the men's visors, whereby they were known. Whereof the Queen and the strangers much praised the King; and ended the pastime.[9]

On New Year's Day, the first of January, the Queen was delivered of a son. The rejoicing was great – at Richmond and in London. On Sunday 5 January the boy was christened Henry in the chapel of the Richmond Friary, adjoining the palace. 'From the Hall to the Friars was made with barriers and rails a way twenty-four feet wide, strewn with rushes after being new gravelled. All the south side of the way was hangen with cloth of arras, and near the Friars both sides were so hung, as was the body of the Church'.[10] The godparents were the Archbishop of Canterbury, the Earl of Essex, and Katherine Countess of Devon (King Henry's aunt).

On Twelfth Night the Prince's birth was celebrated at Richmond with a pageant:

> … devised like a mountain, glistering by night as though it had been all of gold and set with stones, on the top of which mountain was a tree of gold, the branches and boughs fringed with gold spreading on every side over the mountain, with roses and pomegranates. The which mountain was with vices brought up towards the King, and out of the same came a lady apparelled in cloth of gold, and the children of honour called the Henchmen, which were freshly disguised, and danced a Morris before the King. And that done, re-entered the mountain, and then it was drawn back; and then was the wassail or banquet brought in; and so broke up Christmas.[11]

The heir to the throne was proclaimed Prince of Wales as well as Duke of Cornwall, and had a household appointed to him by his proud father. As a further celebration of the birth a tournament was announced to be held at Candlemas, 2 February, on Richmond Green or wherever the court might then be.[12] In fact it was held at Westminster, for the King and Queen had removed there after the Queen's churching. Henry, bearing the motto 'Loyal Heart', took part – and all his horse trappings and surcoats were embroidered with gold Hs and Ks. There were more pageants and banquets.

Then, to put an abrupt end to all this good humour and rejoicing, came the news that the infant prince, left to nurse at Richmond, had died there, aged seven weeks, on 22 February. He was brought to Westminster for burial. In 1513 Catherine bore Henry another son who lived only a few days, and in November 1514 she again had a premature delivery of a stillborn child.

The King had meanwhile been busy with foreign policy and foreign wars, and was about to effect a remarkable diplomatic revolution. Up until this time the cornerstone of his policy had been the alliance with Spain against France. Egged on by his father-in-law King Ferdinand he had sent a force in 1512 to attack Gascony in concert with the Spaniards. However, he was let down by Ferdinand who, instead of joining the English, took advantage of the French preoccupation with the English attack to conquer Navarre – and the English force, left on their own, mutinied and sailed home. Nevertheless another joint attack on France was planned for 1513, this time with the added assistance of the Emperor Maximilian.

While Henry led his troops in person on an incursion into northern France, Ferdinand negotiated a secret truce which would leave him in possession of Navarre, and Maximilian produced only a token force when he joined Henry in the field. Henry was still campaigning, slowly but successfully, in France when James IV of Scotland launched an attack on his brother-in-law's country in support of Scotland's 'auld alliance' with France. On 9 September James's army was cut to pieces on the battlefield of Flodden by the English forces under the Earl of Surrey. James was killed in the battle and his body, as mentioned above, was brought to Shene Charterhouse. From Richmond Palace, Queen Catherine wrote to her husband on 14 September sending the news, forwarding a piece of King James's coat, and passing on a request from the Earl of Surrey 'to know the King's pleasure as to burying the King of Scots' body'.[13]

Henry's own successes in the war with France were not regarded with much joy by King Ferdinand in Spain, who did however propose renewing the alliance for another attack in 1514. However, the French were now trying to negotiate for peace, and both Ferdinand and Maximilian withdrew from the conflict. When, in mid-1514, Henry proposed that the marriage between Prince Charles of Castile and his sister Mary should now be celebrated, he was met with excuses and delays.

The French King Louis XII was left a widower by the death of his Queen in 1514, and his peace overtures to Henry now included an offer for Mary's hand. Henry, vexed by the behaviour of Ferdinand, and with Wolsey (who had acted as his quartermaster-general during the 1513 campaign) now as his chief counsellor, decided to accept the French offer. On 7 August 1514 peace with France was proclaimed in London; and the reluctant Mary was married to Louis XII,

50 The tournament, planned for Richmond, but actually held at Westminster on 12 February 1511/2, to celebrate the birth of Henry Prince of Wales. (The College of Arms)

34 years her senior, on 9 October. She was Queen of France for just under three months; on 1 January 1514/15 Louis died.

Henry's relationship with Francis I, the young and charismatic new King of France, just three years his junior in age, was to be for a while closer and friendlier – though any prospect of a marriage between Francis and Mary was soon shattered by the unwelcome news that the widowed Queen had married the Duke of Suffolk, sent by Henry as ambassador to congratulate Francis on his accession. French ambassadors came to England; and at Richmond on Easter Monday, 9 April 1515, the treaty of peace between the two countries was formally concluded.[14]

A few days later ambassadors from Venice arrived in London, and Henry announced that he would receive them at Richmond on St George's Day, as a special mark of honour to the Signory, for he would be holding his ceremonies of the Order of the Garter there on that day, St George being the patron saint of the Order.[15] The Venetian despatches give an interesting account of the ceremonies of that day. There are two versions – a despatch from the ambassadors,[16] and a rather more detailed letter written six weeks later by the secretary of the embassy.[17] The two accounts are here interwoven.

The ambassadors were conducted, by water, to Richmond by a prelate and a knight. On entering the palace they were served, according to custom, with bread and wine. Then they were led 'through some other chambers where they saw part of the King's guard consisting of 300 men, all very handsome and in excellent array – never saw finer fellows'. They reached the Presence Chamber where the whole court was assembled. 'The King was standing near a gilt chair – covered with cloth of gold brocade with a cushion of the same material – surrounded by many royal insignia and under a canopy with a gold ground and a raised pile. He was arrayed in the robes of the Garter as were also eight other knights.'

The senior Venetian representative delivered an address in Latin, with 'congratulations on the well-being of the King' and condolences on the death of his brother-in-law King Louis. 'The answer was given by a doctor of the parliament, after which the King went to hear High Mass with the Ambassadors' and all the company. The secretary of the embassy was particularly impressed by 'the King's choristers whose voices are more divine than human'.

> After Mass the King and the nobles with the Ambassadors and their followers returned to the Palace into a hall where a table had been prepared for His Majesty and another for the Knights of the Garter, the Ambassadors and the merchants. After witnessing a display of gold plate of immense value they sat down to table and dined.

It appears that for some years the Garter ceremonies were held at Richmond rather than Windsor. In addition to this well-documented occasion in 1515, there is a reference in 1528 to a meeting of the Order at Richmond on St George's Day.[18] Then in 1534 there was some discussion of the possibility of a distinguished French visitor, Philippe Chabot, Admiral of France, visiting Richmond 'to see the Chapel of the Order'.[19]

In the next few months came several developments which were to have a later effect on the story of Richmond Palace. In August 1515 Wolsey, recently created Archbishop of York and already the King's chief counsellor, received news that he had been made a cardinal; and on 24 December the King appointed him Lord Chancellor. Then on 18 February 1515/6 Queen Catherine gave birth to the Princess Mary, her only child who survived infancy. Henry now had a female heir, but not the son he longed for.

Wolsey had recently acquired a 99-year lease of the manor of Hampton Court from the Order of St John, and he now began to build himself a sumptuous palace, considerably larger than that of the King at nearby Richmond. By May 1516 the work had progressed sufficiently for him to be able to entertain the King and Queen Catherine to dinner there – the first of many such royal visits.

While Wolsey's palace continued to grow in splendour, Henry had a few minor works done at Richmond. In 1517 the timber bridge was built over the moat to give direct access from the King's apartments to the gardens.[20] Two years later Henry Smyth, the clerk of the King's works, received payment for some unspecified work on the Friars' Wharf and the tennis court.[21] It seems that the tennis court could be used by suitable neighbours or courtiers on payment of a small fee (for attendants?): the accounts of Henry Courtenay, Earl of Devon, include an item in February 1518/9 'for costs of the King's tennis court at Richmond when my Lord played there with young Mr Cave 2s 8d'. The earl was soundly beaten – 'to Mr Cave for my Lord's losses at tennis 8s'.[22]

The Venetian embassy secretary, Nicola Sagudino, again gives us a glimpse of Henry's life in Richmond Palace in a letter written in May 1517. He first gives an account of the 'Evil May-day riot', a xenophobic outburst by the London apprentices. Word of it had reached the King. While the Cardinal fortified his London house with troops and cannon, Henry from Richmond issued orders to deploy his troops – 10,000 into the city and 15,000 around it. The riot was quelled and 400 of the conspirators were brought before Henry at Westminster with nooses already round their necks. On Wolsey's intervention they were pardoned. Sagudino then goes on to say that he had spent 10 days at Richmond. He passed the evenings listening to the King sing and play and watching him dance. 'By day the King exhibited his address at running at the ring [jousting practice]. In all these accomplishments he excelled.'[23]

The King was at this period making rather more use than usual of Richmond Palace because there were repeated outbreaks of plague in London. In March 1517/8 he was concerned because three of his pages and another attendant had died of the plague.[24] Again in 1520, 1521 and 1522 we hear that the King went to Richmond because of the plague in London (and at Greenwich).[25]

✠

Meanwhile Henry and Wolsey were again preparing to shift alliances. The infant Princess Mary had been promised in marriage to the French Dauphin in 1518. In June 1520 the alliance with France was apparently further cemented by Henry's meeting with King Francis at the Field of the Cloth of Gold. The four-year-old Princess Mary was left behind at Richmond while her parents went to France. The Lords of the Council wrote to her father on 9 June to say that they had visited her there and she was 'right merry and in prosperous health and state, daily exercising herself in virtuous pastimes and occupations'.[26] Some French visitors a few days later were impressed by 'her skill at playing on the virginals, her tender age considered'.[27]

Henry, however, was playing a double game. King Ferdinand of Spain had died in 1516 and Charles who succeeded him had concluded a treaty with France. The Emperor Maximilian had been trying to rebuild the coalition against France, but when he died in January 1519/20, Charles and Francis were rivals for the election. Henry, instead of backing Francis, had thrown his own hat into the ring. Charles was elected Emperor; and Henry then entered into secret negotiations with him – suggesting that Mary's proposed marriage to the French Dauphin could be changed for an espousal to Charles. On his way to the Cloth of Gold meeting, Henry delayed in Dover to meet the new Emperor who landed there en route for Flanders. They met again in Gravelines in July when Henry was on his way home from France.

In 1521 war broke out between France and the Emperor, and relations between England and France deteriorated. Wolsey was sent to negotiate a new treaty with Charles, including the proposed marriage. In 1522 Charles paid a second, longer, visit to England in May and June, and a treaty of alliance was signed at Windsor. Charles undertook to marry Princess Mary when she reached the age of twelve. The programme for the Emperor's entertainment included a visit to Richmond, described by the Spanish ambassadors as 'the Queen's Palace'.[28] The Emperor and his suite were to stay only one night there, before going on to visit Wolsey at Hampton Court. As Charles was travelling with a retinue of 208 noblemen and gentlemen, 100 household officers and 1,710 servants, the resources of Richmond must have been severely stretched to cope with even one night's stay!

The Spanish ambassadors' reference to 'the Queen's Palace at Richmond' is not substantiated by any evidence of a formal grant, but increasingly that appellation reflected the reality of the situation. There was not yet any very open estrangement between Henry and his wife Catherine, but his attentions had been straying. Elizabeth Blount, one of the Queen's waiting-women, had by him a son Henry Fitzroy (who at the age of six in 1525 was created Duke of Richmond). He had had an affair with Mary Boleyn; his eye had already fallen on her younger sister Anne, and by 1522 the Boleyn family had begun to receive grants and honours from the Crown. Henry continued to use Richmond Palace, but the Queen was now often left there on her own with Princess Mary.

✠

It was in the early 1520s that Cardinal Wolsey's sumptuous establishment at Hampton Court began to become the object of popular attack. Ambassadors and suitors were now flock-

51 King Henry VIII by an unknown artist, c.1525. (National Portrait Gallery)

ing there or to York House, his residence in London, rather than to Richmond or the other royal palaces. John Skelton, the satiric poet, launched pamphlets and verses against the Cardinal. His most famous contains the lines:

> Why come ye not to Court?
> To which court?
> To the King's court
> Or to Hampton court?
> The King's court
> Should have the excellence,
> But Hampton Court
> Hath the preeminence;
> And York's Place
> With my Lord's grace!
> To whose magnificence
> Is all the confluence,
> Suits and supplications,
> Embassades of all nations.[29]

Whether or not there is any truth in the old tale that Wolsey replied to a question from the King as to why he had built Hampton Court with such magnificence, 'To show how noble a palace a subject may offer to his sovereign', it is clear that about 1524 or 1525 he gave Henry the rights of present use and the reversion of title to Hampton Court. The arrangement does not appear to have been formalised by any document, but essentially it involved a sharing of both Hampton Court and Richmond Palace by the King and the Cardinal.

The accepted date for the gift is June 1525. Stow says: 'At this time the said Cardinal gave to the King the lease of the Manor of Hampton Court which he had of the lease of the Lord of St John's, and on which he had done great cost in building. In recognizance whereof the King licensed him to be in his Manor of Richmond at his pleasure; and so he lay there at certain times.'[30] A Spanish diplomatic report of 23 June 1525 records that, 'When the King returned last from Windsor he passed by Hantencourt a house belonging to the Legate which he has presented to him with all the appurtenances, furniture, etc. In future the Cardinal will lodge as any other of the King's subjects.'[31]

Yet the matter is far from clear. As early as August 1524 Wolsey wrote to the King from 'your Grace's Manour of Hamptoncourt'.[32] And yet as late as September 1528 a letter was sent to Wolsey on the King's behalf saying that the King 'wold be glad to bee at your manour of

52   Cardinal Wolsey, by an unknown artist. (National Portrait Gallery)

Hampton Court as upon Saturday next commyng … He wold be verry glad ye shuld remoeve soo as he might bee at your said house on the said Saturday or upon Monday at the farthest, wher he is mynded and desirous to contynue and passe the tyme for 3 or 4 dayes.'[33]

Certainly both Wolsey and the King now used Hampton Court, but Wolsey remained responsible for the expenses of works there until April 1529, when the King assumed full control.[34] Equally certainly both used Richmond, but the Cardinal was now there sometimes in his own right – as when he kept Christmas there in 1526, while the King was at Eltham. Hall's *Chronicle* points out that 'when the common people, and in especial such as had been King Henry VII's servants, saw the Cardinal keep house in the Manor royal of Richmond which by King Henry VII was so highly esteemed, it was a marvel to hear how they grudged and said, "See, a butcher's dog lie in the Manor of Richmond"; these with many opprobrious words were spoken against the Cardinal, whose pride was so high that he nothing regarded; and yet was he hated of most men.'[35]

George Cavendish, Wolsey's gentleman-usher and biographer, states that Wolsey repaired Richmond 'to his great cost and charge',[36] but there are no traceable accounts. It may, however, well have been the question of responsibility for works that was the point at issue when Heneage wrote to Wolsey in August 1528 that 'a little I have moeved the King's Grace for the orderyng of Hampton Court and Richemounte, wherein I find His Grace marvalous towardes and well mynded.'[37]

Wolsey's letters to the King refer consistently to 'your Manour of Richemount'; and the King can be shown to have been there in December 1525 when yet another treaty of peace between England and France was signed at Richmond Palace on 17 December. He was also there in October 1527 and for St George's Day in April 1528.

The peace treaty brought to an end another period of hostilities which had broken out in 1523, and signalled yet another shift in Henry's alliances. The international scene was now about to be further complicated by the long drawn-out negotiations over the King's intended divorce from Catherine of Aragon. The King's breach with his wife was complete by 1529 and Anne Boleyn occupied her place at court. Wolsey had done his best in the King's cause, but Anne was now blaming him for the delay in finding a solution. By July 1529 Wolsey was in disgrace. At the beginning of November a bill of indictment was presented against him and he was told to retire to his house at Esher. Catherine was ordered to remove to Richmond Palace.*

Henry now resumed responsibility for Richmond Palace, and Catherine and her daughter Mary spent some days there in the summer of 1530. In July 1531 the King parted for the last time from Catherine at Windsor, and in August he sent orders that Mary was to leave her mother and take up residence at Richmond. In August 1531 the Venetian ambassador reported, however, that 'The Queen still follows the King [at that time to Greenwich]. The Princess is at Richmond and was lately very ill from what the physicians call hysteria'.[38]

Princess Mary had had another Venetian visitor at Richmond in that same month. Mario Savorgnano wrote an account of his tour in England:

> After seeing the Palace [Richmond] we returned into a hall and having entered a spacious chamber where there were some venerable old men with whom we discoursed, the Princess came forth accompanied by a noble lady advanced in years who is her governess and by six maids of honour … The Princess is not very tall, has a pretty face and is well proportioned with a beautiful complexion, and is fifteen years old. She speaks Spanish, French and Latin, besides her English mother tongue, is well grounded in Greek, and understands Italian but does not venture to speak it. She sings excellently and plays on several instruments, so that she combines every accomplishment. We were then taken to a sumptuous repast, after which we retired to our

---

* The divorce, and the breach with Rome, are dealt with in the following chapter.

53   King Henry VIII with King Henry VII. Cartoon by Hans Holbein, c.1536-7. (National Portrait Gallery)

lodgings, whither, according to the fashion of the country, the Princess sent us a present of wine and ale (which is another beverage of theirs) and white bread. On the next day, the 6th, we returned to London.[39]

Princess Mary's residence at Richmond in the state of a Princess was terminated by the divorce of her mother, pronounced on 27 May 1533. On the following day Henry's marriage to Anne Boleyn, celebrated in secret during the previous winter, was avowed, and confirmed by the Archbishop. On 7 September 1533 Princess Elizabeth was born. Catherine had been ordered to give up using the title of Queen and now Mary, declared illegitimate, was forced to give up the title of Princess. She became a dependent of the household of her infant half-sister.

Henry and Anne were frequently at Richmond in 1534. On one occasion, says the Spanish ambassador, 'came the Lady Anne herself accompanied by the Dukes of Norfolk and Suffolk and others and by a party of ladies on pretence of visiting her own daughter but in reality to see and salute the Princess [i.e. Mary]'.[40] From 1534 to the end of the decade a programme of decoration and improvements to the accommodation at Richmond was carried out. The 'privy bridge' into the gardens and the garden galleries were repaired; wire screens were inserted in front of the windows of the gallery overlooking the tennis court 'for the saving of their breaking with balls'; at the end of the gallery beside the tennis court a new banqueting house was built.[41]

Hampton Court, however, was now Henry's preferred home, and after 1534 his appearances at Richmond were less frequent. Following the trial and execution of Anne Boleyn in May 1536 and his marriage to Jane Seymour, he returned to Richmond in December, where he had a touching reconciliation with his daughter Mary. Catherine of Aragon had died in January 1535/6 and now Mary made her home mainly at Richmond Palace. On 2 March 1537/8 the Spanish ambassador visited her there, 'and stayed a good many hours talking with her and hearing her play on the lute and the spinet in so admirable a manner that I really believe she is the most accomplished musician that could be found.'[42]

Queen Jane died at Richmond Palace on 14 October 1537, two weeks after giving birth at Hampton Court to her son Edward. On 6 January 1539/40 the King married Anne of Cleves. The marriage was not a success. Once again Richmond was to become the abode of Henry's abandoned partner. On 1 July 1540 the French ambassador wrote:

I cannot positively say whether it be in consequence of the King's designs ... or owing to some diminution of the love he once had for his Queen or again because he has placed his affections somewhere else, with some other lady of the court, but the fact is that the King has sent his Queen to Richmond. I know it from the King himself, having promised to follow her thither two days after, he has not moved from Greenwich ... Rumours are current in this city that the Queen has gone to Richmond for fear of the plague raging, as they say, here – but the rumour is entirely false for at present there is no plague here at all.[43]

This time the divorce was rapid and painless. Henry maintained that he had never consummated the marriage. He sent a messenger to Richmond to tell Anne of his intention to have the marriage declared invalid and to settle £3,000 a year on her. She consented. On 9 July Parliament declared the marriage to Anne of Cleves null and void. On 11 July Anne wrote from Richmond formally accepting the declaration of the clergy that the marriage was void.[44] On 3 August Henry married Catherine Howard, niece of the Duke of Norfolk; and on 6 August Henry visited Anne at Richmond Palace – presumably to thank her for her acquiescence.

The lands granted to Anne as alimony included the 'two manors of Richmond and Blechingley, having splendid houses and parks'.[45] The grant of Richmond (including Ham and Petersham and the 'park called Richmond Park') was made on 20 January 1540/1.[46] So Anne now became lady of the manor. How much use she made of Richmond is uncertain, but her presence there twice in 1541 is attested by the Spanish ambassador, Eustace Chapuys, who was evidently enjoying the unfolding drama. His official interest was to oppose any reconciliation between Henry and Anne, for fear of a possible Protestant alliance against Spain. On 4 January 1540/1 Chapuys reported:

Dame Anne of Cleves has been recalled to Richmond, for which reason, added to the fact that she seems happier and more

54 Prince Edward (later Edward VI) by Hans Holbein, c.1538. (Andrew W. Mellon Collection, National Gallery of Art, Washington D.C.)

55 Anne of Cleves, engraving by J. Houbraken after the portrait by Hans Holbein. (National Portrait Gallery)

contented than before and that the present Queen is not yet in the family way, some are of the opinion that some sort of reconciliation may still take place between her and the King. I myself see no chance of this, but should there be any I will seize every opportunity of indirectly threatening it.[47]

By November the accusations of Queen Catherine's adultery had been made and Chapuys wrote to the Emperor that there was 'talk of shutting her up in what was once a nunnery near Richmond' [i.e. Syon]. He added, 'I hear also that Madame Cleves has greatly rejoiced at the event and that in order to be nearer the King she is coming to, if she is not already at, Richmond.'[48]

If Anne really hoped for reinstatement as Queen she was to be disappointed. After the execution of Catherine Howard, Henry made no move towards a further reconciliation with Anne. After two years he married Catherine Parr in July 1543. He lived only for three and a half years after this sixth and last marriage, dying on 28 January 1546/7 and leaving his kingdom to his nine-year-old son Edward. Anne of Cleves outlived him by more than ten years. She spent some time at Richmond during the last years of Henry's reign and was visited there on several occasions by Princess Mary. After young Edward's accession as Edward VI she handed over Richmond Palace to him, and on 3 June 1548 she formally surrendered to him her interest in the manors of Richmond, Petersham and Ham.[49]

56 Queen Catherine Parr, by an unknown artist, c.1545. (National Portrait Gallery)

The practice of leasing out the manor of Shene, now Richmond, together with those of Petersham and Ham, had continued throughout the reigns of Henry VII and Henry VIII. The lease 'in farm' to Thomas Fysshe and Richard Brampton, jointly but in survivorship, was renewed for 20 years in February 1495/6,[50] and then (Thomas Fysshe having died in 1506) to Richard Brampton alone in October 1518.[51] Richard Brampton died in 1520 and his heir Thomas surrendered the old grant in exchange for a new 30-year lease granted jointly to him and Massie Villyard (who rejoiced in the title of 'Serjeant of the King's Pleasure Water') on 29 November 1522.[52] Brampton and Villyard were at the same time officially appointed jointly to the full range of keeperships – the palace, the wardrobe, the garden and the New Park of Shene [in Surrey] – which offices, it is stated in the grant, they had been performing, without wages, for the past two years.[53]

Thomas Brampton died in 1528 and Massie Villyard continued on his own as 'farmer' of the manor. He seems to have been the first inhabitant of Richmond to have had a house on the north-eastern side of Richmond Green. Presumably a grant of land had been made to him,[54] at the corner of the Green north of the end of the lane leading to the Charterhouse, and there two houses were built. After the death of Villyard (which occurred between 1541 and 1546) one of these houses was demolished, but its site with a one-acre close and the other 'fine house with a fine garden' were leased on an annual basis to one Elizabeth Philpot.

On 16 September 1546 Anne of Cleves leased this property, together with the adjacent seven-acre 'Crane's Croft' and 46 acres of demesne land called the 'Lord's Piece' (adjoining on the north side of Crane's Croft) for 80 years to David Vincent.[55] Vincent was a favourite of Henry VIII, who had granted him many offices and lands. He had been keeper of the wardrobe at Richmond since 1531 and lessee of Richmond Ferry since 1536. Anne also granted him a lease of the three manors of Richmond, Petersham and Ham, and all the keepership offices 'as Massye Villyarde lately held the same'.[56] Edward VI confirmed these grants on 27 August 1547.[57]

Vincent surrendered his 80-year lease of the property on the north side of the Green in June 1552 in return for a grant of lands in Long Ditton and elsewhere.[58] However, he appears to have continued as sitting tenant of his house on the Green, paying an annual rent to the new head leaseholder, until his death in August 1565. When the property he had thus surrendered was regranted in December 1555 to Thomas Palmer, the house occupied by Vincent was described as 'a messuage called the Queen's Stable'.[59] This name, not encountered before, then adhered to the house for a century or more, and the stables were probably the origin of what was known in the late 18th century as 'Duke's Yard'. The building of the stable can probably be dated to 1550, when the Privy Council ordered the construction of a new stable for the King at Richmond.[60] It had of course become the 'Queen's Stable' on Mary's accession in 1553.

Vincent surrendered his various keeperships at Richmond on 9 February 1554/5, and they were regranted on 12 March to Gregory Lovell.[61] Ten years later he assigned to Lovell his lease of the three manors of Richmond, Petersham and Ham.[62]

✠

The return of Richmond by Anne of Cleves to Edward VI was the occasion of a major programme of repairs to the palace. No details for the work have survived, but in 1547 and 1548 Lawrence Bradshaw, the surveyor of works, spent over £3,400 on Richmond.[63] Thereafter there was only minor works expenditure until well into the reign of Queen Elizabeth.

The young King made some use of his restored palace. He stayed in Richmond in the summers of 1549, 1550 and 1551. A reminder of the preparations that had to be made for such visits is found in an Exchequer warrant of July 1549 for the payment of £12 'for two years' expenses of wood and coal for breathing [i.e. airing] the King's Majesty's wardrobe at Richmond'.[64]

Occasionally a foreign ambassador would come to Richmond.[65] But the focus of power, in the whole country, as well as in the Richmond area, had now shifted, first to half a mile and then to one mile north of Richmond Palace – to the sites of the former monasteries of Shene and Syon.

57   King Henry VIII and Queen Catherine of Aragon, both by unknown artists. (National Portrait Gallery)

Chapter IX

The Dissolutions and Refoundation of the Charterhouse

King Henry's conviction that he and Catherine of Aragon had been denied a son by the Almighty because he had offended by marrying his brother's widow had become firmly entrenched by 1527, when he first mentioned to a shocked Cardinal Wolsey the idea of an annulment or divorce. His original scheme, that the succession might be settled on his illegitimate son Henry Fitzroy (who might even, by papal dispensation, be married to his legitimate half-sister Mary), was abandoned when the King became infatuated by Anne Boleyn, for Anne would not yield to his advances without a legal marriage. Wolsey's attempts to set up a clandestine tribunal to prepare the way for a divorce were frustrated when Catherine's nephew, the Emperor Charles, sacked Rome and held the Pope prisoner – Charles would never permit the Pope to connive at Catherine's divorce. Henry then announced to Catherine that they had been living in sin and that he intended to divorce her. This was promptly reported to Charles, and the issue soon became a matter of European power politics.

Once Wolsey had succeeded in getting the Pope to send the Anglophile Cardinal Campeggio to London to determine the question, the latter moved so slowly in the matter that Henry tried to force his hand by declaring his problem publicly. Then Catherine hit back with a document sent from Spain which systematically destroyed Henry's legal case which was based on 'flaws' in the original papal dispensation. Following this Henry publicly broke with Catherine, and Anne Boleyn moved into her apartments in London.

In July 1529 Campeggio adjourned his hearings – and soon after messengers arrived from Rome demanding that Henry proceed there so that the Pope himself could try the case. For Henry this was the final straw, and it marked the end of Wolsey. On 19 October 1529 he was ordered to give up the Lord Chancellor's seal. It also marked the beginning of the breach with Rome. Nothing was going to induce Henry to go cap in hand to Rome, and he began to flex his muscles. With a series of measures he attacked the allegiance of the clergy to Rome – the bishops' oaths of loyalty and obedience to the Pope, the fees which new bishops remitted to Rome and the need to consult Rome in the appointment of bishops.

By the summer of 1532 Anne appeared everywhere as Henry's unofficial consort. She was created Marquess of Pembroke in her own right and given precedence over all other marquesses. Late in 1532 she and Henry took matters into their own hands – she became pregnant, and Henry married her in secret. Meanwhile the leading personalities concerned in England had changed, and the tempo changed with them. Thomas More, who had succeeded Wolsey as Chancellor, resigned in May 1532 to be replaced by the tough and vigorous Thomas Cromwell. In August, Archbishop Warham died and Thomas Cranmer's appointment as his successor was confirmed by the Pope. On 10 May 1533, Cranmer opened a special court to hear the King's case. On 23 May he declared that Henry and Catherine had never been married. On the following day he validated the marriage of Henry and Anne. A week later Anne was crowned Queen.

The marriage was unpopular in the country. Most people were in sympathy with Catherine. As Cromwell pushed through Parliament a series of statutes to separate the Church in England from all papal authority and to set it under the direct control of the King, popular opinion began to make itself heard more vociferously. The focal point for the opposition to the divorce and the marriage, was the 'Nun of Kent'. Elizabeth Barton, a servant girl, had some years before enjoyed an apparently miraculous cure from a long-standing disease. She had been shouting and gabbling in delirium, but it was decided first by the local priest and then by a commission of enquiry sent by the Archbishop of Canterbury that she was possessed, not by the Devil, but by the Holy Ghost. She was taken to Canterbury to become a nun. In 1527 she started 'prophesying'. When the issue of the royal divorce became generally known she inveighed against it, and claimed divine inspiration for predictions of a dire fate if the King married Anne Boleyn.

Father Bocking of Christ Church, Canterbury, her confessor and spiritual mentor, Dr. Risby, Warden of the Observant Friars at Canterbury, and Dr. Hugh Rich, Warden of the Richmond Friars, who was a frequent visitor to Canterbury, passed on her prophecies far and wide. Many influential people, including William Warham, the Archbishop of Canterbury, believed them. She had interviews with Wolsey and Thomas More; the King himself gave her an audience. She made several visits to the convent of Syon, and her cause was enthusiastically supported there and by the neighbouring religious of the Shene Charterhouse and the Richmond Friary.

Cromwell could not allow this to continue. Henry, however, had evidently not been struck dead after the marriage with Anne, and belief in the nun's prophetic powers was somewhat shaken. In July 1533, on Cromwell's instructions, Archbishop Cranmer started an investigation of the nun and her close associates. In September he extracted from her a confession of fraud. Bocking, Risby and Rich and some others were arrested. In November they were publicly pilloried as frauds in London and in Canterbury. In March they were condemned for treason by bill of attainder. The nun and her associates were hanged at Tyburn on 20 April 1534.

Some authorities have asserted that Dr. Rich, warden of the Richmond Observants, may have died in prison before the date of execution.[1] There is however a good deal of contemporary evidence that he was indeed executed with the others. Hall's *Chronicle* appears to state clearly that all those who were pilloried in November 1533 (including Rich by name) were executed for treason in April 1534.[2] John Hussee wrote to Lord Lisle on 20 April 1534: 'This day the Nun of Kent, with ii Friars Observants, ii monks, and one secular priest, were drawn from the Tower to Tyburn, and there hanged and headed.'[3] Rich and Risby were the only two Observants condemned with the nun. *The Chronicle of the Grey Friars of London* notes under the year 1534: 'Thys yere was the mayde of Kent with the monkes, freeres and the parsone of Aldermary, draune to Tyborne and there hongyd and heddyd the V day of May, and the monkes burryt at the Blacke freeres, the Observanttes with the holy mayde at the Grey freeres, and the parsone at his church Aldermary.'[4] The Grey Friars' chronicler should surely have known whether one or two Observants were buried in that house's cemetery, although he seems to be in error about the date of execution (possibly 5 May was the date of burial).

Because the Observant Friars at Canterbury and Richmond, the Carthusians at Shene and the Briggitines at Syon had been the nun's strongest supporters, they were singled out (together with the London Charterhouse and the Observants of Greenwich, who were considered potentially equally dangerous) for special attention in the matter of enforcing obedience to the new statutes. The friars were a particular target. Both at Richmond and at Greenwich they had always had the closest relations with the royal palaces; they provided preachers and confessors to the court; they had given support to Catherine after her exclusion from court. As itinerant preachers they were inherently dangerous, the more so as they had attracted to their order some of the brightest conservative theologians in the country. And they were vehement in their public condemnation of the divorce.

Moreover the three orders that were generally perceived to have remained true to a vocation of austerity amid the general laxity and decay of the monastic ideal that had affected most of the country's monasteries were the very three represented in the Richmond area. Of Wolsey's proposed reforms, a Benedictine abbot had complained that if all monasteries had to follow the rule of the Carthusians, the Briggitines or the Observants they would soon be depopulated. Cardinal Pole later picked out the same three orders as praiseworthy.[5]

At the Charterhouse of Shene, Prior John Jonbourne resigned early in 1534 after a priorate lasting over thirty years, and was succeeded by John Michell, formerly the procurator. The monks of Shene had given not only credence but positive encouragement to Elizabeth Barton. Thomas More recorded how Henry Man (who succeeded Michell as procurator) and William Howe, the sexton, visited him to tell him of their admiration of her, and how Henry Man could hardly accept the news of her confession.[6] Henry Man had written gushing letters to Father Bocking; and Henry Ball, the vicar of the Shene Charterhouse, had written to the nun herself praising her virtue and her supernatural gifts, and asking for her prayers.[7]

These letters had been seized when the nun and Father Bocking were arrested, and had been sent to Cromwell. For some reason, no retribution followed. Whether Cromwell used the letters discreetly to put pressure on the leaders of the Shene Charterhouse; or whether they still enjoyed a measure of the King's protection; or whether they simply decided that, having compromised themselves over the nun, they should now, in the interests of the monastery, follow the path of least resistance, is unknown. What is certain is that when the Commissioners visited Shene in the spring of 1534 to require the monks to take an oath to observe the terms of the Act of Succession, whereby Catherine's marriage was pronounced void and Anne Boleyn's issue were pronounced legitimate, they met with no open opposition. The prior and procurator were indeed complaisant.[*]

The Bishop of Coventry, one of the Commissioners, reported to Cromwell on 7 May:

> … Yesterday at afternone we accomplisshed o^r business at Shene and the Prior and the convent with novices and converses and al the servantes of that house have taken the othe … And the said Prior and Procurator of the place with diverse other of the brethren have shewed thaimselfes as honest men and feithful subjectes to the Kinges highnes, nott only in exhibiting their redy obedience to his grace and his lawes in this behalf but also in moving and exhorting the frire observantes of Richmont to do semblably, with which frires by mediacion of thair rulers we have had diverse conferences, and despaired of their reconciliation till this morning, but we hope to bring them to conformity.[8]

---

[*] A letter to Lord Lisle from John Rokewood dated 15 May 1534 stated that the priors of the Charterhouses of London and Shene were both in the Tower (*CLPFD* VII, p.258, no.674). In respect of Shene this seems to have been a complete error.

The ready compliance of Fathers Michell and Man was turned to good use. Man was appointed prior of Witham; then shortly afterwards he and Michell exchanged places and Man returned to be prior of Shene. Both men were also appointed visitors for the English province of Carthusians, so that they might spread the word and influence, or instruct, the other Charterhouses to follow their lead.

The Observant Friars of Richmond were not, however, swayed by their Carthusian neighbours. They held out resolutely against taking the oath. In June 1534 the Bishop of Coventry and his fellow Commissioner, Archdeacon Bedyll, made another attempt to shake them. They arrived at Richmond late in the evening of Saturday 13 June and on the Sunday morning had a session, first with the warden and one of the senior friars, and then with the whole community. The friars would not yield, but agreed to entrust the decision to a committee of four of their senior members who were instructed to meet again with the Commissioners at the friary in Greenwich on the Monday. At Greenwich the Commissioners met with equally stiff resistance both from the friars there and apparently from the Richmond delegates.[9]

It became clear to Cromwell and his helpers that the only course was to break up the whole order of Observant Friars by physically expelling them from their houses and imprisoning them. This they swiftly proceeded to do. On 17 June 'two carts full of Friars' were seen passing through London on their way to the Tower.[10] On 11 August, Ambassador Chapuys reported to Charles V that 'of seven houses of Observants five have already been emptied of Friars, because they have refused to swear to the statutes made against the Pope. Those in the other two expect also to be expelled.'[11] In a further report on 29 August he completed the tale of the Friars' suppression:

> All the Observants of the Kingdom have been driven out of their monasteries for refusing the oath against the Holy See, and have been distributed in several monasteries where they are locked up in chains and worse treated than they could be in prison.[12]

Many of the Observants were to die from their ill treatment in the Tower and in the monastic prisons, though some managed to flee abroad.

Some of the Observant houses were handed over to the Austin Friars (Southampton and Newark) or to the Conventual Franciscans (Greenwich). There is evidence that the Richmond Friary was housing a community of friars in 1537 and 1538, and some indications that these may have been Austin Friars. They would in any case have been dissolved by the end of 1538. The evidence is examined in Appendix 6.

Equally obdurate were the Carthusians of the London Charterhouse where the prior and the whole community initially rejected the oath. Prior John Houghton was taken into custody and was subjected to a month of argument. He was ultimately persuaded that the oath to obey the Act of Succession was not a critical point of faith. He was released, and persuaded his flock to comply. But then they were faced by a further demand to reject the papal authority, and nine refused. In November 1534 this demand was formalised by the passing of the Act of Supremacy and the Act of Treason. By the first the King was declared Supreme Head of the Church of England; the second made it an act of treason to seek to deprive the King or Queen or heir to the throne of any dignity or title (of which, of course, the title of Supreme Head of the Church was now one).

In the spring of 1535 two other Carthusian Priors visited the London Charterhouse, Augustine Webber of Axholme (a former monk of Shene) and Robert Lawrence of Beauvale. Houghton consulted with them and they decided to go together directly to Cromwell to plead that, though willing to declare their loyalty to the King, they could not accept the Act of Supremacy. They were sent straight to the Tower. Together with Dr. Richard Reynolds of Syon, one of the leading theologians in the country, they were tried for the treason of depriving the King of his title of Supreme Head of the Church in England. They were found guilty by a reluctant jury browbeaten by Cromwell; and were hanged, drawn and quartered on 4 May. Their example strengthened rather than weakened the resolve of the other London Carthusians, 15 more of whom chose eventually to suffer martyrdom rather than take the oath.[13]

Exactly what happened at Syon is uncertain. Syon was the tenth wealthiest monastery, and far the wealthiest nunnery, in the country. Many of the sisters were from important aristocratic families. The male community included leading academics and theologians. It needed to be tackled with some delicacy. The Commissioners went on to Syon in May 1534 after getting Shene to accept the oath to the Act of Succession, but there is no record of the outcome. In the autumn Queen Anne visited the convent from Richmond, and received a frosty welcome.[14] Early in 1535 Richard Reynolds, one of the leading members of the male community, was arrested, presumably for refusing to take the oath of obedience to the Act of Supremacy. He suffered martyrdom with the Carthusian priors. After his execution the Commissioners reported that the abbess and nuns and their confessor-general had accepted the royal supremacy, but many of the brethren were recalcitrant and two in particular needed to be 'weeded out'.[15] Eventually, by persuasion, debate and threats the resistance seems to have been worn down. The convent survived until the very end. Syon made no voluntary surrender. From the evidence of Cromwell's memoranda, it was finally suppressed in the autumn of 1539 by the use of a legal quibble under the Act of *Praemunire*.[16] By November 1539 pensions were allotted to the prioress and nuns.

As Supreme Head of the Church of England the King had the ultimate control and disposal of uncounted wealth – the endowments which pious benefactors had for centuries been presenting to cathedrals, churches, chantries, monasteries, religious hospitals. Cromwell set to work to count it. The 'Valor Ecclesiasticus', almost another Domesday Survey, was compiled in 1535. If the suppression of the Observants – poor and unendowed – had been a purely political act and had yielded nothing to the Exchequer but their houses, the suppression of well-endowed monasteries could yield a fortune. The submission of the monks to the anti-papal statutes had broken their spirit; in any case support for the concept of monasticism itself had been weakening as new attitudes and ideas spread through western Europe. In 1536 an Act was passed to suppress the lesser monasteries, those with incomes below £200 per annum. It met with little opposition. King Henry even agreed to exempt two of the smaller Charterhouses, as being deserving cases.

Cromwell now set to work on the priors and abbots of the greater monasteries. Some may have believed, or been led to believe, that the surrender of their lands and possessions could buy the continued existence of their communities. 'Voluntary surrenders' became increasingly common. Shene had already handed over to the King, in 1531/2, the manors of Lewisham and East Greenwich in exchange for less valuable property in Buckinghamshire.[17] Its lands were now valued by Cromwell's assessors at £963 11s. 6d. gross (£777 12s. 0½d. net) annual value – a figure greater than that for the London Charterhouse, and only a little less than that for Merton.

No records have survived of whatever negotiations may have taken place between Cromwell or his staff and the prior of Shene, but Henry Man who took over the priorate in 1535 had already shown himself a compliant tool. He had even, in view of the many journeys he would have to make as visitor of the English Charterhouses, suggested to Cromwell in August 1536 that he, and other Carthusian priors, should preach in favour of the new order 'not only within the houses where they dwell but also in other churches where they come near'.[18]

London was the first Charterhouse to succumb. After the persecution and execution of its leading members the community was left for a while without prior or procurator but under a secular warden appointed by Cromwell. Then William Trafford, the procurator of Beauvale – after a period at Shene when he seems to have been successfully brain-washed by Henry Man – was appointed as prior. On 18 May 1537 he led the community in an act of submission; but even then 10 recusants held out, and were despatched to Newgate prison where they suffered a slow and lingering martyrdom from starvation. This was a final blow; only just over three weeks later, on 10 June 1537, the London Charterhouse formally surrendered itself and all its possessions to the King. Coventry followed in January 1537/8. Shene was probably the next, but this is not certain as for Shene, alone of all the Charterhouses, there is no surviving document of surrender. The date has been surmised, from Prior Man's letters to Cromwell, as being before 5 March 1537/8.

In recognition of his services Henry Man was awarded the enormous pension of £133 6s. 8d. (200 marks) a year. In comparison his fellow visitor John Michell, the prior of Witham, received only a quarter of this amount; Edward Fletewood, the Shene procurator, received £13 6s. 8d. (20 marks); the other monks of Shene got from £5 to £8, perhaps depending on their age and seniority.[19]

Man was soon to receive ecclesiastical preferment also. In 1541 he was made Dean of Chester, in 1546 Bishop of Sodor and Man. In his will, made on the eve of his death on 19 October 1556, he left his books 'to the House of Shene if it shall be hereafter erected again'.[20] One wonders how many of them had come from the monastery's library in the first place.

The remaining Charterhouses all surrendered during 1538 and 1539, together with most of the other major monasteries in the country. The final Act of Suppression of the greater monasteries in 1539 needed to be applied only in a few cases – for the most part it merely validated the *faits accomplis*. Some of the monks found new positions as parish priests, a few chose to go into exile and were received into houses on the Continent. Several of the English Carthusian exiles made a new home in the Val de Grace Charterhouse at Bruges.

At least one former monk of Shene started to campaign against the breach with Rome. On 15 May 1543 the Privy Council committed to the Tower 'one Selby, clarke, who before tyme hadde been monk of the charterhouse in Sheen, upon a lewde writing subscribed with his owne hande ayenst the Primacye of the Kinges highnes, seming neverthelesse to be distracte of his witt'.[21] Blaming nonconformity on mental aberration is not a new technique of the 20th century.

The fortune in goods and lands was now in the hands of the King and his government; it remained to turn it into hard cash. The 'Augmentation Office' was set up to handle this new accretion of wealth through the leasing and sale of property. In the first detailed inventory which the office made of the Sheen Charterhouse lands, the following entries concern property in the immediate area:

> Shene – site and demesne land £5 6s. 0d. per ann.
> Richmond – farm of meadows £3 13s. 4d. per ann.
> Ham, Mortlake, East Shene, Kew and Chiswick – tenements and land £1 12s. 4d. per ann.[22]

The first thing to be sold was the 'surplus plate'; it was bought by one Richard Huchynson.[23] The site and demesne lands were leased, on an annual basis at first, to Edward Seymour, Earl of Hertford, brother of the late Queen Jane and uncle of the heir to the throne Prince Edward. Hertford was already in occupancy by 1540.[24] Then on 7 April 1541 he was given a formal grant 'in farm' by letters patent, at a rent of £5 6s. 0d. per annum, plus an extra 4d. 'for a parcel of land lying at the conduit head'.[25]

Hertford at once started to convert the monastery site into a residence. He evidently obtained permission to demolish many of the buildings and to purchase the materials for re-use. On 26 October 1541 he bought for £168 the 'lead on the buildings of Sheen* Monastery, estimated by the King's plumber at forty-two fodders'.[26]

It is probable that Hertford used as the nucleus for his new mansion the house which had been built by Dean Colet and later occupied by Wolsey and Pole. This would have been more immediately habitable than any of the small cells or the few communal buildings such as the refectory. How much Hertford built anew is not known, for there is no description of the buildings in his period of occupancy. When King Henry died and the nine-year-old Prince Edward came to the throne, his uncle Hertford became 'Lord Protector' (i.e. regent) and was made Duke of Somerset.

58 Edward Seymour, Earl of Hertford, and later Duke of Somerset. (British Museum)

He now arranged a deal. On 16 July 1547 he surrendered his grant 'of the house, site and capital messuage of Shene and lands in Shene and Rychemond' in exchange for a grant of other lands, including 'Osterley and Istelworth, late of Syon'.[27] Syon was not only larger, but probably more easily adaptable as a mansion, than Shene. However, it would need time to carry out the works of conversion so Somerset did not abandon Shene altogether, but planned to remain as tenant on an annual basis until his new house was ready.[28]

In July 1548 the Duchess of Somerset was 'brought to bed of a goodly son' at Shene. The King agreed to be godfather, but when the news was sent to the Lord Admiral, Sir Thomas Seymour, the baby's uncle, on 19 July, it had not yet been decided whether the King should go to Shene for the christening.[29]

In October 1549 the Duke of Somerset was ousted from power by John Dudley, now Earl of Warwick, who – though not taking the title of Lord Protector – assumed all Somerset's powers. After a short period of imprisonment in the Tower, Somerset was released on 6 February 1549/50. The Privy Council ordered that he should 'reside and remain with his family and household at that His Highness' manor of Sheen, or that the said Duke's house commonly called

---

* From about this time, the spelling 'Sheen' begins to appear with increasing frequency – especially in relation to the monastery site – but it did not become the established spelling until late in the 16th century.

59 John Dudley, Earl of Warwick, and later Duke of Northumberland. (Private Collection: photograph Courtauld Institute of Art)

60 Edward Seymour, when Duke of Somerset. (British Museum)

Syon', that he was not to go more than four miles from either house and that he was not to seek access to the King if the latter should come within that four mile limit, for example to Richmond.[30] He was bound in a recognisance of £1,000 to abide by these terms.

On 18 February, however, Somerset was granted a free pardon; and in April he was re-admitted to the Council and his property was restored to him. A reconciliation between Warwick and Somerset was sealed by a marriage at Shene, attended by the King, presumably in the chapel of the Charterhouse – and the same place was used on the following day for the marriage of Warwick's fifth son, Sir Robert Dudley, to Amy Robsart. The young King Edward noted in his journal:

> June 3 The King came to Schein wher was a mariag mad between the Lord Lisle th'erle of Warwic's sone and the ladi Anne daughter to the Duke of Somerset, wich don and a faire diner made and daunsing finished, the King and the ladies went into tow chambers made of bowis wher first he saw six gentlemen of on[e] side and six of another rune the course of the field, twis over … And afterward cam thre mascers of one side and tow of another wich ran foure courses apece … And so after souper he [the King] retorned to Whestminster.
>
> June 4 Sir Robert Dudely third [*sic*] sone to th'erle of Warwic maried Sir John Robsartes daughter, after wich mariage ther were certain gentlemen that did strive who shuld first take away a gose's heade wich was hanged alive on tow crose postes.
>
> June 5 Ther was tilt and tornay on foot with as great staves as the[y] run withal on horseback.[31]

Despite this temporary reconciliation, Somerset's power was broken, and it was not long before Dudley disposed of him finally. On 4 October 1551 Dudley became Duke of

61 Henry Grey, Duke of Suffolk, the father of Lady Jane Grey. (British Museum)

62 Lady Jane Grey. (Hulton-Deutsch Collection)

Northumberland; a few days later reports of a plot to kill him – which Somerset was said to have instigated – were revealed. On 16 October Somerset was arrested and imprisoned in the Tower; on 1 December he was condemned to death for felony; and on 22 January 1551/2 he was beheaded. On 12 April Parliament declared his lands forfeit.

It would seem that Somerset had continued to lease Shene on an annual basis 'at the King's pleasure' until his arrest in October 1549. But Shene was the King's property, not his; and its disposal to another tenant was already determined before Somerset's execution. On 28 December 1551 the Privy Council instructed the Chancellor of the Court of Augmentation 'to make out a book to the Duke of Suffolk for the keeping of the King's Majesty's house at Shene'.[32] On 4 January a detailed account of the property was drawn up, with a new assessment of the rent to be charged – £26 13s. 4d.[33] No actual grant to the Duke of Suffolk has been traced, but he certainly took up occupation with his family at Shene Place, as the mansion was now called, in 1552.

Henry Grey, then Marquess of Dorset, had married in 1534 Frances Brandon, the elder daughter of Charles Brandon, Duke of Suffolk, and Princess Mary, Henry VIII's sister. In 1551 Frances's two brothers both died on the same day, and the dukedom of Suffolk was then bestowed on Grey. He and Frances had three daughters – great-grandchildren of Henry VII. Grey had been a supporter of Dudley in his bid for power, and now he and Dudley – the Duke of Northumberland – were close neighbours, for Northumberland had taken over Somerset's house at Syon. In May 1553 Northumberland's fourth son, Guilford Dudley, and Suffolk's eldest daughter, Lady Jane Grey, were married.

At Syon and Shene, Northumberland worked out with Suffolk his plot to put their children on the throne when Edward VI died. By May he was already very ill and weakening fast. Princess

Mary, though named by Henry VIII's will to succeed if Edward had no children, was a Catholic; moreover she had been declared illegitimate even if that fact had been conveniently overlooked. Elizabeth, the next heir, though Protestant, had also been declared a bastard. Jane was clearly legitimate; she was descended from Henry VII's daughter; she had been named next in succession after Elizabeth; she was Protestant. It must have seemed to Northumberland that, if he could strike fast, the support of the public would be certain. Moreover he had the support of the young King, who favoured Jane over both his sisters, and was determined to safeguard the reformed religion by excluding Mary. Edward drafted a will, with Northumberland's help, proclaiming Jane his rightful successor, and the Privy Council were persuaded, by the King himself, to accept it on 21 June.

Northumberland tried to get control of Mary's person, and ordered her to Greenwich, but she was forewarned and made for her house at Kenninghall in Norfolk. She arrived there on the day that Edward died, 6 July. On 8 July, Jane was proclaimed Queen in London, and two days later she moved, with her husband and father, from Syon to take up residence at the Tower of London. Mary, hearing the news on 9 July, wrote at once to the Council, who rejected her claims; but there was a spontaneous rising in her favour in Norfolk, Suffolk, Buckinghamshire and Oxfordshire, in which counties she was proclaimed Queen. The movement in her favour spread rapidly throughout south-east England. Northumberland hastily organised a force of mercenaries and sent a fleet to Yarmouth to cut off Mary's escape. The fleet mutinied and declared for Mary. Northumberland, leading his troops out of London on 14 July, was struck first by the sullenness of the people, then by the news of the mutiny, then by an exaggerated report of the strength of the forces rallying to Mary at Framlingham in Suffolk where she had set up her headquarters. He lost his resolution, dithered for two days at Cambridge, then set out for Framlingham – and turned back. In London meanwhile a sermon in support of Jane delivered at Paul's Cross by Bishop Nicholas Ridley, had

63 Lady Jane Grey, painting attributed to Master John, c.1545. (National Portrait Gallery)

been shouted down by the crowd. Those members of the Council who had been most unhappy over Jane's accession took heart, and won over to the support of Mary all but their most die-hard radical Protestant colleagues. On 19 July they instructed the Lord Mayor of London to proclaim Mary as Queen. There was an immediate, extraordinary, demonstration of popular support in the capital. That afternoon Suffolk told his daughter that her reign was finished, and went himself to proclaim Mary on Tower Hill. On 20 July Northumberland, also bowing to the inevitable, proclaimed Mary as Queen in the market-place at Cambridge.

Mary was merciful. Most of those who had supported Jane were pardoned – some immediately, some after trial and conviction. Only Northumberland himself and two of his closest aides were actually executed. Jane and Guilford Dudley were convicted of high treason, but Mary would not sign a death warrant. Suffolk and his Duchess, after a brief incarceration in the Tower, were allowed to return to Shene Place.

On the collapse of Queen Jane's reign, Mary set out for London, where she arrived on 3 August. She took up residence in the Tower, but almost at once made known her intention of moving to Richmond after the late King's funeral. King Edward was buried, with Protestant rites, on 8 August. Mary did not attend but held a private memorial mass for her brother.

She moved to Richmond on 16 August. There she received on the following day the congratulations of a special mission of ambassadors from Spain, and those of a similar French mission.[34] On 18 August, from Richmond, she issued her first proclamation on the religious question: a moderate statement calling for toleration for both forms of worship.[35] Within a couple of weeks, mass was being said again openly in many places.[36]

The Emperor Charles V who had for the last 20 years, through his ambassadors in London, been encouraging and, to the best of his ability, protecting Mary, now at once proposed that she should marry his son Philip, King of Spain. The special congratulatory embassy discussed the proposal with the Queen. Mary was much averse to the idea of marriage – she found the thought of sex repugnant – but she was persuaded that the need for her to produce a Catholic heir must be paramount. She eventually agreed to the proposed marriage, but Simon Renard (who was now left in London as resident Spanish ambassador) was given a hard time

64 Queen Mary I, by Antonio Moro. (Isabella Stewart Gardner Museum)

negotiating the details of the marriage treaty. The Spaniards wanted to arrange the marriage as soon as possible in the following year, but nothing would induce Mary to agree to be married during Lent.[37] She returned to Richmond for the Christmas of 1553, and there received the special representatives from Spain who came to complete the negotiations.[38] There was much popular opposition to the Spanish marriage, and the London crowds, who had been so vociferous in Mary's support in July, now demonstrated against the Spanish envoys.

Then in January 1554 Sir Thomas Wyatt raised a rebellion in Kent and marched on London. The inhabitants of Richmond must have been very aware of this event though the Queen had returned to London. Wyatt, finding London Bridge held by citizens loyal to the Queen, marched down to cross the river at Kingston and struck towards London from the west. He entered the city, but was then surrounded and outnumbered, and the rebellion collapsed. The Duke of Suffolk had tried to support it by fomenting another rising in the Midlands, but failed and was arrested.

65 King Philip II of Spain. (National Maritime Museum)

It was after this that Mary finally signed the death warrants for Jane Grey and Guilford Dudley. Suffolk was convicted of high treason, and executed on 23 February 1554. His estates were forfeited, and Mary now restored Shene, not by grant but at least temporarily, to the Dowager Duchess of Somerset. Princess Elizabeth, too, suffered as a result of Wyatt's rebellion. She was arrested on a charge of complicity, and spent two months in the Tower, but despite the urging of the Spanish, and of some of the Council, Mary did not put her on trial. In May 1554 she was brought to Richmond by river (and there were cheers for her from those who saw her pass); and from there she was sent on to Woodstock under house arrest.

By then the plans for Philip's reception in England were completed. While awaiting his arrival Mary moved back to Richmond in June. Philip landed at Southampton on 20 July and Mary went to meet him at Winchester, where the marriage was celebrated on 25 July. On the way back to London they stayed for about a week at Richmond Palace in August.

✠

Wyatt's rebellion was a turning point in Mary's reign. It was after that that she became ruthless in the cause of restoring the Catholic Church in England. She had already been in touch with the Pope, who in November 1554 sent Cardinal Reginald Pole – a distant cousin of Queen Mary –

to England as papal legate. Five days after his arrival, Parliament repealed Henry VIII's Act of Supremacy; and on 30 November Pole, absolving the kingdom from the sin of schism, proclaimed a new holy day in the calendar of the Church – the Feast of the Reconciliation.

There was little reconciliation in the country. The burning of heretics began in February 1554/5 and was to continue until Mary's death nearly four years later.

The reunion with Rome paved the way for a return of monasticism; though Mary and Pole were wise enough to recognise that the vested interests of those who had purchased monastic lands should be safeguarded. There were however still a number of monastic sites in crown ownership. In March 1554/5 Ambassador Renard reported that 'the two monasteries of Franciscans at Greenwich and Richmond are being repaired to receive inmates by Easter.'[39] The Greenwich Friary was indeed restored at a cost of over £1,500, but not the one at Richmond. Whether Renard was – unusually – misinformed, or whether the Queen had actually intended to replace the Observant Friars in Richmond is not known. The works expenditure at Richmond for the year 1554-5 totalled only some £12; there are no surviving accounts for the following years.[40]

66 Cardinal Reginald Pole, engraving from a portrait by Sebastiano del Piombo. (British Museum)

Early in 1555 Father Maurice Chauncey, one of the Carthusians from the London Charterhouse who had taken refuge at Bruges, received instructions from the Grande Chartreuse to return to England and endeavour to refound the order there. He was to take with him another monk, John Foxe, and a lay brother, Hugh Taylor. They arrived in London in May 1555 and were warmly welcomed by Sir Robert Rochester, comptroller of the Queen's household, whose brother John had been one of the martyrs of the London Charterhouse. Rochester found them apartments in the Savoy, and introduced them both to Cardinal Pole and to the Queen. Both Cardinal and Queen encouraged them; the Queen agreed to maintain them at her own expense, and said she would try to restore to them one of the houses of the order.

Shene Charterhouse was the obvious candidate for it was still in royal ownership, but the sitting tenant, the Duchess of Somerset, took a lot of shifting. The Duchess, wrote Chauncey, 'having once set foot in it, neither by prayer nor by a price could thereafter be torn from it'.[41] While the Carthusians waited at the Savoy, Father Foxe died. A replacement was sent – and died also only five weeks after reaching London. Chauncey was in despair, but Rochester encouraged him to persevere, and gradually a number of former Carthusian monks and lay brothers who had stayed in England heard about his mission and came to join him. One was John Michell, the former prior of Shene and Witham, and there were three other former monks of Shene. Finally, by September 1556, the Duchess of Somerset was persuaded to move by the bribe of better accommodation elsewhere. The Venetian ambassador reported:

> The Queen is in good plight, rejoicing to see the monks of St Benedict return to their old abbey at Westminster ... This will be the third monastery and order of regulars, besides one of nuns, which has been hitherto reestablished, to which will soon be added the fourth, of the Carthusians, who have already made their appearance, to return as they will, according to the promise given them, to their ancient abode eight miles hence, although it is now occupied by the Duchess of Somerset, who is however to be recompensed with something else.[42]

On 16 November, the eve of the feast of St Hugh (the one-time prior of Witham Charterhouse who later became Bishop of Lincoln), Cardinal Pole himself, accompanied by Rochester (now Lord High Treasurer) and the Bishop of Ely, escorted Chauncey and his companions 'to the ancient Carthusian place of Shene on the banks of the river near the royal palace of Richmond, to replace in possession, as he did by the royal authority, several fathers of that order'.[43] The Venetian ambassador speaks of Pole's 'infinite pleasure' – and it must indeed have pleased him to see the Charterhouse where he had studied as a boy and where he had later lived for several years restored to its rightful use. After handing Shene over to the Carthusians, the Cardinal went on to Syon to restore the nuns there.

Chauncey was accepted as acting prior of the new community which consisted by this time of nine monks and three lay brothers. The Charterhouse could be occupied almost immediately. On 25 November, wrote Chauncey, 'I led them rejoicing into it'. On 31 December 1556 Pole appointed Chauncey prior; and the Grande Chartreuse confirmed the appointment a few months later, (though chiding the papal legate for venturing to appoint a prior without reference to them). Then on 26 January 1556/7 a formal grant of the house and lands was made by Queen Mary by letters patent to Chauncey and his companions.[44] Five other monks came to join the community during the following months, including the former prior of Mount Grace.

However, there was still a lot of work to do in restoring the buildings to proper monastic use. Chauncey probably made his base in the mansion, which had been Colet's house, for this was later called 'the Prior's Lodging'. Sir Robert Rochester helped with funds for the community's immediate maintenance, and with the repairs. Chauncey records that Rochester 'raised the choir anew from its foundations'; he patched up the rest of the church 'miserably shattered and decayed, the walls only standing and those very ruinous'; he rebuilt the chapter-house. The cloister was partially rebuilt on a reduced scale – there was no point in catering for the 40 monks of the old foundation.

On 25 November 1557 Rochester died. He had just been appointed a Knight of the Garter, but had not been installed. He was buried on 4 December in Shene Charterhouse. Henry Machyn, the London merchant, recorded the event in his diary:

> ... ther was a goodly herse of wax, v prensypalles, with vii dozen penselles, and viii dozen skochyons, and vi dozen torchys and ii whyt [branches]; and a standard, and a penon of armes, and cot armur, elmett, targett, sword, mantylles, and iii baners of emages, and a majeste and valanse, and master Claren [ceux] and master Lankester [h]aroldes, and mony morners in [black]; and the masse and a sermon, and after a grett dener.[45]

Sir Robert bequeathed to the Charterhouse lands in Essex worth £100 a year. These were exchanged by Prior Chauncey in the following year for the manors of Bocking in Essex and Staines in Middlesex and lands in Surrey which included Merton and the site of Merton Priory, the seven acres called Charterhouse Grove near Coombe Park, the manor of Pyrford (which had belonged to Westminster) and the prior's manor at East Horsley (formerly of Christ Church, Canterbury). The transaction was completed only three days before Queen Mary's death.[46]

The Charterhouse had other benefactors. Sir Richard Southwell was given, on 11 November 1558, licence to grant to the Charterhouse two manors and two rectories in Norfolk.[47] Other gifts came from Sir Thomas Englefield, Sir William Roper and Jane Lady Dormer (the sister of another Carthusian martyr). With Rochester, however, the Charterhouse had lost its most practical and devoted friend – on the exact anniversary of the day when the monks had entered rejoicing. Within a year they were to lose also their two most eminent patrons and protectors – the Queen and Cardinal Pole.

✠

Queen Mary had made considerable use of Richmond Palace; in particular she stayed there for quite long periods every summer. The Venetian ambassador found this rather an imposition. So no doubt did some of the other ambassadors, but the Venetian was the only one forthright enough to disclose his feelings quite openly in an official report home. He wrote on 11 June 1555 from Richmond to the Doge and Senate of Venice:

> After going out of London [the Ambassador] determined to remain at Richmond near the court for the purpose of being more frequently with the King [Philip] and the other personages of the palace both Spanish and English, thinking there to hear more about passing events than by remaining at a distance, regardless of personal inconvenience as that of his household owing to the exorbitant cost of everything and the very narrow lodgings as also from being compelled to incur the expense of two houses (one in London and the other in Richmond) which exceeds his means; but for the service and honour of the Signory he will bear it as patiently as he can.[48]

His reports from Richmond that summer were dated from 6 June to 19 August. Two and a half months must have been something like a record for continuous occupancy of any Tudor palace by the Court.

In July 1557 Queen Mary gave a musical entertainment in the gardens of the Palace – and Princess Elizabeth was brought down from Somerset House for the occasion in the royal barge. It 'was hung with garlands of artificial flowers and covered with a canopy of green sarcenet, wrought with branches of eglantine in embroidery and powdered with blossoms of gold'. The barge was attended by six other boats with her retinue 'habited in russet damask and blue embroidered satin, tasseled and spangled with silver, their bonnets cloth of silver with green feathers'. Mary had had a special pavilion erected in the Palace garden, of cloth of gold and purple velvet, in the shape of a castle, and there she received her sister as guest of honour. A sumptuous banquet was served – including a pomegranate tree in confectionery work, bearing the arms of Spain. There was on this occasion no masque or dancing, but an entertainment by a great number of minstrels.[49]

Elizabeth had been restored, if not to her sister's favour, at least to her place at Court, in April 1555. It had been Philip's doing. He had insisted that Mary should treat her sister honourably and affectionately, for she was the heir to the throne and Mary's hoped-for pregnancy had not materialised. Elizabeth had accepted the Catholic restoration, and was attending mass regularly. The only course was to accept that she would probably be the next Queen of England – and to try to win her goodwill and to keep her in the faith.

By the spring of 1558 the matter began to seem actual rather than hypothetical, for Mary was taken seriously ill. She was moreover extremely depressed by the loss of Calais in January, and

67 Elizabeth I, as princess, by an unknown artist. (The Royal Collection © Her Majesty The Queen)

by Philip's absence in Spain. She was worried about the succession and whether Elizabeth would return the country to Protestantism. She was able to visit Richmond in the spring and in the summer of 1558, but on both occasions she suffered from fever and returned to London. On the morning of 17 November she died. Cardinal Pole, who had been sick for many months also, died the same evening.

✠

In her will, made on 30 March 1558, Queen Mary had left bequests of £500 each to the monasteries of Sheen and Syon 'for a further increase of ther lyvyng and to th'entent the said Religious persons may be the more hable to reedifye some part of ther necessary howses that were so subverted and defac'd, and furnish themselves with ornaments and other thyngs mete for Godd's servyce'. She also bequeathed to both houses lands to the clear annual value of £100 which had been part of their possessions before the Dissolution and which remained in the hands of the Crown, requiring the communities of the two houses to pray for the souls of herself, her husband Philip, her mother Catherine 'and all other our Progenitors' (Henry VIII was thus included, but not explicitly!)[50]

In October she was worried that her will would not be honoured, and added a codicil imploring her heir and successor to allow the executors to carry out her wishes – and to honour her intentions even if there were found to be some legal impediment.[51]

Queen Elizabeth did not carry out her sister's intentions. She was soon persuaded to return the country to Protestantism. The first session of Parliament after her accession passed a series of statutes including one which suppressed the monasteries and sequestrated to the Crown all lands and estates that had been given to the restored religious houses. The royal assent was given on 8 May 1559.

When Father Chauncey had first received, in Bruges, his orders to return to England, several of his fellows at the Charterhouse there had, he recorded, cautioned him against undue optimism. 'It may be indeed that it will happen for the moment that things will go prosperously for you; nevertheless no continuous or lasting peace will there be for you now. For quicker than you look for, you will all be hurled suddenly from your dwellings.'[52]

Commissioners were now appointed to enforce the new dissolutions. Chauncey apparently tried to intercede directly at the royal court, but was dissuaded and led away by brother Hugh Taylor. With a more limited aim, and with greater success, the Spanish ambassador, the Count of Feria (who had recently married Jane Dormer), had interceded to secure for the monks safe-conduct back to Flanders. The Bishop of Aquila, who had just replaced him as ambassador, reported from London to King Philip of Spain on 19 June 1559: 'The cloistered monks have all licence to go and have already begun to depart. They are being given alms for the purpose in Your Majesty's name.'[53]

On the third visit of the Commissioners, on 1 July 1559, the monks were expelled from the Charterhouse. The Count of Feria had himself already left England in May, but the Carthusians were probably among the many Catholics who crossed to Bruges in the company of Jane, Countess of Feria, in July. For a while they remained in the Val de Grace Charterhouse there, of which Chauncey was made prior in 1561. In 1568 he was authorised to form the English monks into a separate community, which took the name of 'Sheen Anglorum'. With various changes of home, the community of Sheen Anglorum survived until suppressed, with other monasteries, in 1783 by the Emperor Joseph II.[54]

68 The tomb of Frances, Duchess of Suffolk, in the Chapel of Saints Edmund and Thomas the Martyr in Westminster Abbey. (Dean & Chapter of Westminster)

Queen Elizabeth gave the Shene Charterhouse back to Frances, the Duchess of Suffolk, who had married – two weeks after the execution of the Duke – her young secretary and groom of the chamber, Adrian Stokes. She took up residence immediately. Once more, the monastery was converted into a mansion. The Duchess's tenure of Shene appears to have been, like that of the Duchess of Somerset in Mary's reign, only a temporary grace and favour occupancy. There is no indication of any grant, even in lease. It was soon to end, in any case. On 20 November 1559 the Duchess died at the Charterhouse at the age of fifty-one. She was buried in Westminster Abbey, as befitted a king's granddaughter. After the funeral her two remaining daughters, Catherine and Mary, returned to Shene with their stepfather Adrian Stokes. The Duchess, in a very short will, had made him sole executor and legatee,[55] but he did not inherit Shene.[56]

The next occupant of Shene appears to have been Sir Richard Sackville, Chancellor of the Court of Augmentations. No grant has been traced, but he may have moved in soon after the death of the Duchess of Suffolk. In 1562 he found himself the host and custodian of Margaret, Countess of Lennox and Angus, and her son Henry, Earl of Darnley. They were placed in his charge when Matthew Stewart, the Earl of Lennox, was clapped into the Tower of London by Queen Elizabeth. The Countess was the daughter (by her second husband) of Henry VIII's sister Margaret, and so the Queen's first cousin. Lennox, who had abandoned Scotland for England late in the reign of Henry VIII, had expressed a wish to return. He was excited by a project to marry Henry Darnley to his cousin Mary, the young Queen of Scotland, and then claim the right of succession to the English throne of the Countess Margaret and Henry. The project had alarmed Queen Elizabeth, who was still far from ready to accept the prospect of a Scottish heir.

On 8 June 1562 Sir William Cecil wrote to Sir Thomas Challoner, the English ambassador in Spain:

> At home all things are quiet. The Earl of Lennox remains in the Tower. Lady Lennox and her son are at Sheen, in the household of Sir Richard Sackville. They are charged with two things, one with secret intimation that she has a right to the Crown of England next to the Queen, and the other with secret compassing of marriage betwixt the Scottish queen and her son, which matters they deny, although there are many proofs.[57]

From Shene Lady Margaret kept up a bombardment of letters to Sir William Cecil, trying to secure her husband's release from the Tower. The first was written on 14 May; 11 letters later, on

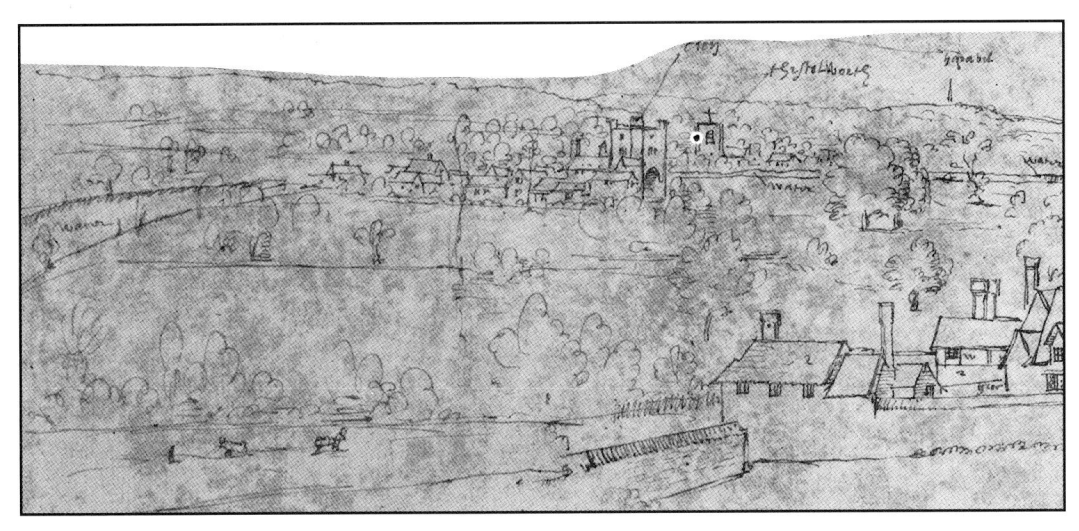

69 *The remains of the Charterhouse in 1562 are in the background, to the left of the large square tower. The tower with a cross is Isleworth Church; in the right foreground are kitchen buildings of Richmond Palace. (Detail from sketch by A. van Wyngaerde.) (Ashmolean Museum)*

24 November, she thanked Cecil for his efforts in securing the Earl's release. She wrote again from Shene in January 1562/3 complaining of the bad treatment they were still receiving, and nine days later to assure Cecil that she wasn't blaming him for this, but realised how grateful she must be for his good offices. The last letter in this series, wanting Cecil to arrange for her and her husband to see the Queen, was written on 3 February 1562/3 from Sackville Place.[58] Whether she had left Shene for good, or only temporarily, is not clear.

After Sir Richard Sackville's death in 1566 his widow continued to occupy Shene. Their son Thomas paid the rent, but had less than full enjoyment of the property. He wrote in 1568 of the domestic arrangements:

> … the occasion of mine abode here hath bene by my mother's suffrance, who under her M[ajesty] hath onlie had the order and keping of the hous, the fourth parte of w[ch] hath not bene possest by me, but onlie such romes as of necessytie I was to crave the use of, and yet I paie the rent of xl markes yerlie to her M., and have bestowed alredy sins my coming above xl li in repairing thos roomes that were delivred unto me. The reste of the hous hath wholie remained in the custodie of my mother, and of my Lord Dacres, who also by her permission had an other portion of the hous assined to him …[59]

Thomas Fiennes, Lord Dacre, was the husband of Thomas Sackville's sister Anne. The rent of 40 marks (£26 13s. 4d.) was the same as that paid by the Duke of Somerset when he had held Shene on an annual basis, so it is likely that, even if there was no formal grant to the Sackvilles, there was an agreement for a similar tenancy at will.

The occasion for these comments by Sackville on the arrangements at Shene was the visit to England in 1568 of Cardinal Chatillon, brother of Admiral Coligny, the Huguenot leader in France, to try to obtain help for the Huguenots. He was at first accommodated by the Bishop of London, then by Sir Thomas Gresham at Osterley. Then it seems that the Queen decided he should be put up at Shene where Thomas Sackville, recently created Lord Buckhurst, was still living with his mother. On 29 September Henry Kingsmill, the official charged with the arrangements, wrote from Shene to the Earl of Leicester and Sir William Cecil that 'the house appointed for the Cardinal Chastillon is too far out of repair for him to occupy'. On the same day Buckhurst wrote to Cecil to express his distress that 'the Queen was displeased with him for not having in better sort entertained the Cardinal at Shene'.[60]

This was followed up by a long letter of explanation addressed on 30 September to the Lords of the Council.[61]

> Returning yesterday to Shene, I receved as from your L., how her highnes stode gretelie displesed w^t me, for that I had not in better sorte entertained the Cardinall who having bene w^t so grete honor receved, not onlie by thos in whos houses he had rested before, but also even by the Quenes Majestie herself, her H. did the rather take it in verie ill parte towards me, especiallie being to her M. as I am. And farther that her H. pleasure was that I shold deliver unto his L. the kaies of all the gates and doores, and the whole hous to be as his comandmente ...
>
> I toke hors w^tin one hower after, I being then xxx mile of Shene, and so rode all the night, and upon my coming thether, being but 2 daies before the Cardinals arivall, I spake w^t her M. officers, w^t whome I had conferens for the better accomodating of the Cardinall ...
>
> And when they required plate of me, I told them as troth, that I had no plate at all. Suche glasse vessell as I had I offred them, which they thought so base; for naperie I cold not satisfie their turne, for they desired damaske worke for a long table, and I had non other but plain linnen for a square table. The table whereon I dine me self I offred them, and for that yt was but a square table they refused it. One onlie tester and bedsted not ocupied I had, and thos I delivered for the Cardinall him self, ... and I assighned them the bedstead on wch my wiefes waiting women did lie, and laid them on the ground. Mine own basen and ewer I lent to the Cardinall and wanted me self ... Long tables formes, brasse for the ketchin etc. we toke order to provide in the towne; hanginges and beds we receved from the yeman of the wardrop at Richemond, and when we saw that naperie and shetes cold no where here be had, I sent word thereof to the officers at the Courte, by wch menes we received from my lord of Leceter 2 pair of fine shetes for the Cardinall, and from my lord Chamberlen, one pair of fine for the bisshop, w^t 2 other courser pair, and order beside for x pair more from London.

On the following day, Sackville continued, the Cardinal, accompanied by the Bishop of London, had arrived at Shene at nine o'clock in the morning. They were welcomed by Sackville, and shown to their lodgings. Sackville, however, had then absented himself on pressing private business – and this was another cause of the Queen's annoyance with him. He explained:

> I thought me self to have fullie performed the mening of your L. letters to me; and because I had tidinges the daie before that a hous of mine in the countri by sodein chaunce of fire was burned ... I toke horse about v a clock in the after none and rode the same night towards thos places where I founde so much of my hous burned as cc markes will not repaire.

The letter Sackville had received with the tidings of the Queen's displeasure had instructed him 'to deliver to the Cardinall the kaies of all the gates and doores, and to leve the whole hous to his pleasure'. This had led him to spell out the arrangements about the use of the house and payment of the rent mentioned above, and then to protest that the Lord St John and Lord Dacres had already delivered the keys and that the Queen's officers had chosen for the Cardinal the most part 'of all such roomes as I enjoyed'. He announced that he was removing 'with as much spede as may be possible' his 'household stuff' and his 'provision of wine, fishe, wood and cole'; and that he would depart for London with his wife and family in a few days.

On 15 October, Kingsmill was able to report that he had 'put the house at Shene in better order for the residence of the Cardinal. There had not been time to do so when Leicester and himself passed that way.'[62] Sackville was rapidly restored to the Queen's favour; but it is uncertain whether he was ever restored to Shene.

Three years later there is a reference to the Shene Charterhouse which may better be described as a 'presence' than an occupation, for it is a pleasing ghost story. Sir Francis Englefield, a Catholic exile from England, was in 1571 visiting Father Maurice Chauncey at the house of 'Sheen Anglorum' in Bruges. He told Chauncey that 'his tenants in England had written unto him that they, dwelling near Sheen, heard for nine nights together the monks that Father Chauncey had buried in Sheen to have sung service with light in the Church; and when they did of purpose set ladders to the Church walls, to see them in the Church, suddenly they ceased. And they heard Father Fletcher's voice, which everyone knew, above them all.'[63]

There seems to be at least a clear implication in this story that the Charterhouse was at that time deserted. It would have been a presumptuous neighbour indeed to bring ladders and set them up against the church walls if the mansion, immediately adjacent to the church, was occupied. While Shene (or Sheen as it was by this time more usually spelled) was retained by the Crown it was used when needed as an annexe to Richmond Palace, and stabling had already been provided there for the court. This was probably converted from a part of the former lay-brothers' cloister.[64] In December 1578 the repair of stables at various places, including Sheen, was authorised.[65]

In November 1583 a new formal lease by grant was finally agreed. The recipients were to be Sir Thomas Gorges and his wife Helena, Marchioness of Northampton (the widow of Catherine Parr's brother). The particulars for the lease include the note that 'many of the rooms and lodgings of the said Priory be used and occupied by divers of the officers of Her Highness's most honourable household during the times of Her Majesty's abode at Richmond'. They also show that at that time the 'church steeple' (i.e. the tower) was still standing, and still had a bell in it.[66] The lease was not actually granted until 23 June 1584; it included a covenant 'that at her Majesty's access to Richmond her officers may have lodging there, saving to the farmer [Gorges] the house called the Prior's House'.[67]

70   Thomas Sackville, Lord Buckhurst, later Earl of Dorset. (British Museum)

71 The young Queen Elizabeth, by an unknown artist. (National Portrait Gallery)

Chapter X

The Palace under Queen Elizabeth

Elizabeth was 25 years old when she became Queen of England. She was faced with two, not wholly unconnected, problems: what to do about the religious future of the country, and what to do about the succession to the throne. Would she marry to bear an heir – and if so, whom would she marry? These questions concerned not only the Queen and her subjects, but also the powers of Europe. King Philip of Spain was the quickest off the mark, with an immediate offer to marry his late wife's sister. But Elizabeth was in no hurry. She told the Spanish ambassador that she appreciated the honour, but had no wish to marry.

She issued an immediate proclamation on religious matters – that no unauthorised alteration in religion should be made. She appointed to her Council many who had served Mary, but leavened them with new men, more Protestant in their outlook, including Sir William Cecil whom she appointed Secretary of State. She moved from Hatfield to London. She gave her sister a good Catholic funeral – then she banned the elevation of the Host in her private chapel, and followed this action with a proclamation ordering that the Litany, the Lord's Prayer, the Ten Commandments and the Lesson for the day should be read in English at all church services.

The bishops – all Catholics – led by the Archbishop of York, pronounced her a heretic and refused to officiate at her coronation, fixed for mid-January. Eventually one, the Bishop of Carlisle, was persuaded to do so. The procession through London on the day before the coronation was an occasion for a great demonstration not only of loyalty to King Henry's daughter but of conviction that she would restore King Henry's religious settlement.

Parliament was summoned and met before the end of January. The elections had been unusually free from governmental influence, and the Commons had a strong Protestant majority. Within a few months the papal supremacy had been abolished, a new Act of Uniformity had been passed, the expelled Protestant clergy were reinstated, the revived monasteries were re-suppressed. Some of these measures barely scraped through the House of Lords, where the bishops' opposition was backed by several temporal peers; but pass they did, and Elizabeth gave her assent to all the new religious legislation on 8 May 1559.

Parliament's first concern, before turning to the religious question, had been to ask the Queen to marry. She told them, in almost the same words she had used to the Spanish ambassador, that she had no intention of ever marrying, and would live and die a virgin.

She was however soon to demonstrate that she was by no means immune to the attractions of the male sex. If her evident delight in the love letters sent to her by King Philip was largely intellectual, her delight in the person and company of Lord Robert Dudley was certainly physical.

72 Robert Dudley, Earl of Leicester (1531-88) by an unknown artist. (National Portrait Gallery)

Lord Robert, son of John Dudley, Duke of Northumberland, had narrowly escaped being executed with his father and his brother Guilford. He had fought in King Philip's army in France, he had returned to England and had already formed a friendship with Elizabeth before Queen Mary's death. On Elizabeth's accession she made him Master of the Horse. He was one year older than the Queen, tall, handsome, strong and an expert jouster. He excelled in the tournaments held by the Queen in the early months of her reign. The Queen, herself a keen rider and huntswoman, spent a lot of time riding and hunting with her Master of the Horse. She made him a Knight of the Garter, she lavished on him grants of patents, money and lands. Within six weeks of her accession she had given him a mansion and lands at Kew.[1]

By the spring of 1559 rumours about the Queen's relationship with Dudley were spreading fast. Sir William Cecil was worried about her intentions. As she rejected proposals of marriage, not only from King Philip but from other suitors such as the Archduke Charles and the King of Sweden, it was said that she meant to marry Lord Robert, if only he were free from his marriage to Amy Robsart (who was left in the country and never came to Court). It was noted that Robert's rooms in Whitehall Palace had been changed to a suite adjacent to the Queen's. It was noted that the Queen was forever singing his praises.

Kew was conveniently close to the palace at Richmond, which Elizabeth now began to use. Sometimes she would ride over to Kew to dine or sup with Lord Robert. On one occasion as she rode back in the evening after supping at Kew she talked to the torchbearers, who were Lord Robert's servants. Their master, she said, was a wonderful man; she would make him greater than any member of his family had ever been. The servants talked and speculated – greater than his father the Duke? – she must mean to make him her husband and King. They gossiped outside the household; they were brought before the Privy Council and confessed their guilt in disseminating 'false rumours'.[2] Nor was that the worst. One Anne Dowe of Brentford was imprisoned for spreading the story that the Queen was already with child by Dudley.[3] Feria, the Spanish ambassador who was on the point of leaving, heard that Lady Dudley was dying of cancer, and the Queen and Robert were just waiting for her death in order to marry.[4]

It was however to be another 18 months before Amy Dudley died; and when she did the circumstances were tragic and mysterious. Alvaro de la Quadra, Bishop of Aquila, the new Spanish ambassador, who had been retailing the gossip about Elizabeth and Dudley with some relish, made the most of it in his first report about the death, written on 11 September 1560:

Cecil tells me that the Queen intends to marry Robert … He ended by saying that Robert was thinking of killing his wife, who was publicly supposed to be ill, although she was quite well and would take very good care they did not poison her … The next day the Queen told me as she returned from hunting that Robert's wife was dead or nearly so, and asked me not to say anything about it …

Since writing the above I hear the Queen has published the death of Robert's [wife] and said, in Italian, 'She broke her neck.' She must have fallen down a staircase.[5]

It was indeed at the foot of a staircase at the Dudleys' house at Cumnor that on Sunday 8 September 1560 Lady Dudley's servants had found her lying dead, with a broken neck, when they returned from an afternoon visit to a local fair. The death, far from making things easy for Robert and Elizabeth, made it virtually impossible for them even to think of marriage. After all the gossip, it at once raised the spectre that Robert had had his wife killed – and that the Queen might have been privy to the deed. As soon as the news reached Windsor on 9 September, the Queen banished Dudley from the Court, with orders to remain at his house at Kew while the matter was investigated. Dudley himself was the keenest to ensure that a full and proper investigation was made, and at once wrote to his kinsman Thomas Blount, who was on the way to visit Cumnor, to urge him to 'use all devices and means you possibly can for learning of the truth, wherein have no respect to any living person'.

73 Queen Elizabeth and members of her Court enjoying a picnic in the course of a hunting party. (From Turbeville's Book of Hunting, *1575.)*

Only Cecil visited the exile at Kew. His worries about the possible match were now dissipated; he could afford to do Robert a kindness – and it was much appreciated.[6] The investigation turned up no evidence of foul play, and the coroner's inquest in due course returned a verdict of accidental death. It was probably correct, though the Queen's enemies were loth to believe it.[7]

A month later the Bishop of Aquila reported that Cecil had told him that the Queen had decided not to marry Lord Robert;[8] although, malicious gossip as he was, he could not forbear from following this up with a rumour that they had been secretly married.[9] However, it would appear that if such a marriage had ever been seriously contemplated by Elizabeth, she abandoned the idea at this juncture. She even postponed, for a time at least, her intention to create Robert Earl of Leicester. However, once cleared by the inquest, Robert returned to Court – and he himself had not yet despaired of eventually winning the Queen's hand.

Within a few months Robert was sufficiently well re-established to be able to joke about his marriage to the Queen. When he gave a water carnival in June 1561, and the Queen invited the Bishop of Aquila onto her barge, Robert suggested that the bishop should marry them at once.

Elizabeth said only that she feared the bishop's English was not good enough to get through the ceremony.[10] This was in jest, but Robert had indeed been trying to enlist the support of the bishop, and through him of King Philip, for his marriage to Elizabeth. He even suggested that if he achieved his goal he would help to restore Catholicism in England and would serve Philip 'at all times and in all things to the full extent of his means and abilities'.[11]

Meanwhile the Queen had engaged in the first military adventure of her reign. Very reluctantly she had been drawn to support the forces of the Protestant Congregation in Scotland in their rebellion against the French Queen Regent – Mary of Guise, King James V's widow and mother of Mary, Queen of Scotland and France. From financial support Elizabeth had moved eventually to armed intervention, when the French had started to reinforce their garrison in Scotland. The intervention had been successful; by the Treaty of Edinburgh, signed just after the death of Mary of Guise, the French had undertaken to withdraw from Scotland, and the religion of that country was to be settled by the Scottish Parliament. On 15 August 1560 Scotland was declared to be a Protestant, Presbyterian state.

Four months later the young French King Francis died and Mary Queen of Scots lost her French kingdom with her husband. However, Mary moved swiftly and staked her claim to the English crown, not immediately but as heir. Back in Scotland she tried to get Elizabeth to name her publicly as her successor, but the English Queen wanted no proclaimed heir presumptive. Mary then tried to arrange a personal meeting with Elizabeth; it was agreed that it should take place in Nottingham, but it was then postponed because of the outbreak of civil religious war in France.

The French Queen Mother, Catherine of Medici, acting as regent for Francis' younger brother Charles IX, had tried a policy of toleration for the French Protestants – Huguenots – led by the King of Navarre, his brother the Prince of Condé, and Gaspard de Coligny the Admiral of France. But the Catholics, led by the Guise family, would not accept toleration, and the Protestants saw the policy as a sign of weakness. Protestant attacks on Catholic churches, Catholic massacres of Protestants, fired religious fanaticism. Early in April 1562 the Huguenots seized Orleans. They were already well established in Normandy and the north. Throckmorton, the English ambassador in Paris, a strong Protestant supporter, urged Elizabeth and Cecil to come to the aid of the Huguenots. Calais, he reminded them, was due to be returned to English rule in 1567, under the provision of the Treaty of Cateau-Cambresis. But by acting now they could secure another French port, Dieppe or Newhaven (Le Havre) which could be then exchanged for Calais without waiting. The Huguenot leaders were reluctant to agree to such terms, but as Guise's forces threatened Rouen and Orleans, they had little choice. In September plenipotentiaries were sent to England to get help on the best terms they could. On 20 September 1562 a secret treaty was signed at Richmond Palace. English troops were to occupy and hold Le Havre until the return of Calais; a further English force would reinforce Condé's garrison at Dieppe; and a loan of 140,000 crowns (repayable when the English were in possession of Calais) was to be made to the Huguenot forces.

To her countrymen Elizabeth proclaimed that she was protecting the Protestant faith; to Philip of Spain, poised to intervene to suppress heresy, she protested that she was only opposed to the house of Guise and concerned with her rights to Calais. An incipient revolt against Spain and Catholic repression in the Low Countries effectively prevented Philip from intervening in France. But even so, the war went badly for the Huguenots and their English allies. Rouen fell to Guise at the end of October, and Dieppe surrendered. Condé and Coligny were defeated at Dreux in December, and Condé was taken prisoner. Guise laid siege to Orleans, but was assassinated in February 1562/3. With Condé prisoner and Guise dead, Catherine de Medici made another attempt, this time successful, to end the fighting. By the Peace of Amboise, signed in March 1562/3, the Huguenots were to be allowed to practice their Protestant religion in the towns they still held, Condé became commander of the French King's army and Coligny was confirmed as Admiral.

The English garrison at Le Havre, commanded by Robert Dudley's brother Ambrose, the Earl of Warwick, was deserted by its allies. Condé even took personal charge of the siege. After a gallant defence throughout the winter and spring of 1562-3, the garrison was smitten with plague in June. In July Warwick had to surrender and the remnants of his army were allowed to take ship to England. They brought the plague with them. A sixth of the population of London died – including the Spanish ambassador. Nor was that the only retribution for the Treaty of Richmond. When the time came for the return of Calais in 1567 Elizabeth was sharply told that she had broken the Treaty of Cateau-Cambresis and its terms were therefore no longer binding. Calais would remain French.

It might indeed have been believed by many that the Queen had also brought a personal divine retribution on herself. Some three weeks after the signature of the Treaty at Richmond, the Queen fell ill at Hampton Court. Soon her affliction was diagnosed as smallpox, and her life was despaired of. She pulled through, and even avoided the disfigurement of pock-marks. But the crisis underlined the insecurity of a kingdom without an heir. The Council had met and decided to ignore the claims of Mary of Scots or Margaret Lennox, and those of the Grey sisters. They settled for Henry Hastings, Earl of Huntingdon, a zealous Protestant who was descended through his mother, Catherine Pole, from Edward IV's brother Clarence. He was married to Robert Dudley's sister – and he was the only serious male candidate.

As the new Parliament, which met in January 1562/3, was forwarding yet further petitions to the Queen to marry and to designate a successor, Elizabeth herself was hatching a most unlikely plan. It was no less than to marry Robert Dudley to the Queen of Scots. This she put forward cautiously, but quite seriously, through Randolph, the English ambassador in Edinburgh. To overcome the initial objection that Dudley, far from royal, was not even a nobleman, she created him Earl of Leicester in October 1564. Randolph did his best to urge the match, and thought he had almost succeeded. But the Queen had not counted on Dudley's own determination not to be exiled to Scotland, even as King of Scots. Perhaps she had been too cynical in assessing Robert's ambition, and he would not be parted from her; perhaps she had not been cynical enough, and he would be King of nowhere but England. While Dudley was holding out against the marriage Elizabeth made the mistake of allowing the Lennoxes' son Henry, Earl of Darnley, to join his father in Scotland. Queen Mary fell in love with him at once; within six months they were married.

Meanwhile at Richmond the chief excitement since the visit of the Huguenots had been the arrival of new ambassadors, and their entertainment. The Queen spent quite a long period there in the spring and summer of 1564. In April peace had been made with France by the Treaty of Troyes, and this was followed by the despatch of a French embassy to London. They were entertained at Richmond on 9 June with three masques 'with divers devisses and a castle for ladies and a harboure for lords and thre harrolds and fower trompetours to bring in the devise with the men at Armes'.[12] On the eighteenth of the same month the new Spanish ambassador, Don Diego Guzman de Silva, arrived in London. On 22 June he had his first audience with the Queen at

Richmond. Arriving by river he 'disembarked near the palace, finding awaiting me on the riverbank Dudley, a relative of Lord Robert'. Lord Darnley met him in the presence chamber, and the Lord Chamberlain conducted him to the Queen, 'She was standing in the chamber listening to a keyed instrument that was being played'.[13]

De Silva was back at Richmond for a second audience a fortnight later and his report to King Philip gives a full account of his reception.

> When I arrived at the house where the Queen was they showed me into a room until Her Majesty knew of my arrival. She was walking in the garden with her ladies and sent the Lord Chamberlain for me to go to her …We then went up into a very large gallery where she took me aside for nearly an hour … We then went to supper which was served with great ceremony as is usual here … After supper … she wished me to see a comedy that was to be acted … The Queen came out to the hall, which was lit with many torches, where the comedy was represented. I should not have understood much of it if the Queen had not interpreted … The comedy ended, and then there was a masque of certain gentlemen who entered dressed in black and white …
>
> This ended the feast, and the Queen entered a gallery where there was a very long table with every sort and kind of preserved and candied fruit that can be imagined, according to the English custom. It must have been two in the morning, and the Queen had to return to Westminster by water, although it was very windy. She sent me back to my lodgings accompanied by the same gentleman as had brought me, as I had come by land.[14]

The unnamed comedy to which poor de Silva was subjected is the first known record of a play to be presented at Richmond, and it is ten years before we hear of another, but the Queen was fond of theatrical productions, and was now spending several months a year at Richmond, so it is probable that there were other plays performed in the palace in the 1560s and '70s.

The most important embassy to visit in the following year was a special mission from the Emperor, to resume negotiations for a marriage between Elizabeth and the Archduke Charles. This was Cecil's goal – in which he was strongly supported by the Duke of Norfolk, and as strongly opposed by Leicester. The Queen by turns encouraged and discouraged the Emperor's representative, who was accompanied by de Silva on several of his visits to Richmond that summer – and the next.[15] For the Queen, though apparently quite pleased by the reports she received of Charles, and impressed by his portrait, and though she once actually told de Silva that she was about to accept the Archduke's proposal, managed to drag on the negotiations for seven years without giving a firm answer.

In the 1560s Richmond Palace underwent a change in appearance. The visit by Anthonis van Wyngaerde to Richmond in 1561-2 was just in time for him to record in his drawings the wealth of decoration above the roof-line – the strapwork adorning many of the domes, the King's beasts and pinnacles, and the weather vanes. And also to record the crumbling chapel of the friary, formerly of Byfleet, now deserted with boarded-up windows and holes in the roof.

The works in 1565-7 included the 'taking down the ymbosses upon the types and th'olde turrets wch were redy to falle over the Queene's Maiestie's lodginges'.[16] It was probably at this time that the roof-line of the palace took on the appearance recorded in the 17th-century depictions: all (or most) of the pepper-pot domes still remained, but unadorned save for the weather vanes which still surmounted some of them. The effect was still picturesque, but it had lost a lot of the breathtaking fantasy of the original.

74 Richmond Palace in the early 17th century (a print engraved 'from an antient drawing in the possession of the Earl of Cardigan').

There is no record of the final demolition of the friars' chapel which must have taken place soon after Wyngaerde's visit – if not during it (for he omitted it altogether in his view of the palace from the Green, though this may have been merely an oversight). It may well be that the building was finally demolished by a tenant rather than by the royal works organisation.

Almost at once after the dissolution of the friary in 1534, the friary site had been leased out. A small part, containing half an acre and lying towards the river, was assigned to George Lovell, the palace gardener, who lived in a house next to the palace at the Green end of Friars' Lane.

It seems possible that the land in the corner where the chapel stood may have been retained for a while in royal hands and that the chapel was used as a school for choristers of the Chapel Royal. One of the 14 articles in a presentment (i.e. indictment) brought in the Manor Court in 1581 against Henry Harvey, a former under-keeper of the palace, was that he had built a barn and shed for himself 'on the Queen's ground, formerly part of the garden belonging to the school for the choristers of the Chapel'.[17] As Harvey had a house on the adjacent land just outside the garden galleries, and as several of his other transgressions apparently relate to the friary site, there is some likelihood that this item referred to the ground around the old chapel.

This piece of ground, which adjoined George Lovell's house and garden, may later have been granted to him or his heirs in exchange for his original half-acre by the river. The latter, mentioned in a grant in July 1572, is not mentioned in a similar grant the following December (see below). Although there is no clear 16th-century evidence, a whole series of grants from the mid-17th century onwards show this parcel of land where the chapel had once stood as leased to the occupants of the house now called 'Old Friars', which was partly built on the former Lovell holding.

In a similar way, the larger part of the friary site was leased to occupants of the three houses that were later put together to become 'Old Palace Place'. Here the evidence goes well back into the 16th century. There were two leases of the site granted in 1572. The first, to Percival Gunston on 5 July,[18] recites the names of three previous tenants of the ground: Sir Anthony Winkfield, John Hall and Thomas Dover. Thomas Dover, from 1538 until his death in 1559, and then until 1571 his widow Alice, were the owners of two of the three houses on the 'Old Palace Place' site. Percival Gunston, a Yorkshireman, seems to have been in the business of finding 'concealed royal properties' and then claiming a lease on them, so it may be that these three predecessors in occupation of the land had no proper leases or titles. Certainly no grants to them have been traced. Gunston's ownership was very brief; he probably assigned his rights for a quick profit as soon as they were granted. Only five months later a new lease was granted to Jeffrey French, who had just taken over Thomas Dover's property[19] (in which he had held a reversionary interest since 1559).[20]

The new lease[21] provided a quite new description of the friary site, which was now said to contain 'a farmhouse and stables' and about three acres of land 'within and without the walls'. (Gunston's lease had said 'two acres'.) It makes no mention of Lovell's portion of land near the riverside, presumably part of the extra ground now added to the lease. Surprisingly, it makes no mention at all of Gunston's grant; but it repeats that Thomas Dover was the previous occupant. French's lease was for 21 years, but by 1581 Henry Harvey was apparently in occupation.

Harvey had been granted, on 15 April 1569, the 'land between the Thames and the Friars' Wall abutting the manor house of the Queen on the north and the house of Massie Stanton on the south'.[22] He built a house on this land, up against the outside of the gallery round the garden. It is a fruitful source of later confusion that this ground, *outside* the friary site, was known as 'The Friars' Ground' and that Harvey's house came to be called 'The Friars'. The confusion grew still worse when a new house was built on the actual friary site in the 17th century (see Chapter 16), and when in the 19th century another house, between the friary walls and the Green, acquired the name of 'Old Friars'.

✠

In Scotland Mary's marriage to Henry Darnley had proved a disaster – not only as a marriage but also as the trigger of a series of disasters which followed in rapid succession. Although she bore Darnley's child – Prince James was born in June 1566 – she fell out of love with her dissolute young husband as quickly as she had fallen into it. In 1567 the murder, in her presence, of her secretary Riccio by Darnley and other lords, was followed by the murder of Darnley himself – and then by Mary's marriage, by Protestant rites, to the Earl of Bothwell, generally supposed to be Darnley's murderer. A month later the Lords of the Covenant defeated the Queen's army at Carbery Hill; Bothwell escaped, but Mary was taken prisoner, and forced to abdicate in favour of the infant James. When she escaped from Loch Leven Castle in 1568, her supporters were again defeated. Having failed to make a getaway to France, she crossed into England and threw herself on Elizabeth's mercy.

Elizabeth and the Council were in a dilemma: they could not send her back nor did they dare risk sending her on to France or Spain. Their solution was to grant her asylum in England, but

75   Mary, Queen of Scots, 1578. Painting after Nicholas Hilliard. (National Portrait Gallery)

under close surveillance – Mary was herself accused of complicity in Darnley's death. Elizabeth proposed mediation, which was accepted; and a Commission under the Duke of Norfolk was set up in York to hear both sides of the story, and to report back to the English Queen. Maitland, the former Scottish ambassador in London, suggested to Norfolk that a way out of the problem would be that Mary should divorce Bothwell and marry Norfolk himself. She could then be allowed to resume the Scottish throne. Norfolk allowed himself to embrace the idea. His apparent partiality towards the Queen of Scots caused Elizabeth to transfer the Commission to Westminster, and to question him about the rumours she had heard of his matrimonial plans. He flatly denied there was any truth in them.

Leicester and Norfolk now combined to try to unseat Cecil – a move that was effectively scotched by the Queen – and were privy to a conspiracy of the Earls of Northumberland and Westmoreland to raise the banner of Catholic revolt in the North of England, rescue Mary, marry her to Norfolk and restore her to the Scottish throne.

The scene shifted briefly to Richmond in August 1569, when the Court moved there from Greenwich. Norfolk, passing by Leicester's house at Kew, found Leicester fishing in the Thames. Leicester told him that his intention to marry the Queen of Scots was common talk among the Queen's ladies. Elizabeth believed he meant to do this behind her back. He advised Norfolk strongly to tell the Queen at once what was in his mind. At Richmond, Cecil bearded him to give him the same advice. In the gardens of Richmond Palace, the Queen asked him what news he had. He pretended to misunderstand; she persisted: 'You come from London and can tell no news of a marriage?' He had not the nerve to tell her and seized an opportunity, when her attention was diverted, to creep away.[23]

The plotters had probably meant to tell Elizabeth of the plan once the agreement of Mary and of the Scottish regent were assured, but Leicester now broke down and revealed the whole story to the Queen. Mary was moved to isolation in a fortress; Norfolk, summoned to Windsor, sent a message to the northern earls telling them to abort their uprising – but he was too late to stop them. They took over, restored the Catholic rite at Durham Cathedral, then at Ripon, and marched to rescue Mary, but she had already been whisked away. They marched on towards London, but no one joined them and having got as far as Staffordshire, they turned back. By the end of November they had been chased over the Scottish border.

Too late to be of any help in fomenting rebellion in England, Pope Pius V issued a papal bull excommunicating Elizabeth. Its only result was the introduction of new more repressive legislation against the Catholics, who had hitherto enjoyed a quite tolerant regime. Norfolk confessed and after 10 months in prison was released, only to get involved in another plot, this time counting on Spanish intervention – the 'Ridolfi Conspiracy' – which was exposed by the discovery of documents in Norfolk's house. He was put on trial for treason and executed in June 1572. Cecil and Parliament were clamouring for Mary's head as well. Elizabeth stoutly refused. When Parliament tried to bring in a bill of attainder, she stopped it. When it passed a bill excluding Mary from the succession, she vetoed it and dissolved the Parliament. But in April 1572 she was again gravely ill; and the question of her marriage and the succession would not go away.

The negotiations for a marriage with Archduke Charles had finally foundered on the issue of the extent to which he should be allowed the free practice of his Catholic religion. Elizabeth did not wait long before resuming her game of matrimonial negotiation. In 1570 she cast a fly to the French ambassador, who rose to it. He came back with Catherine de Medici's suggestion that Henry of Anjou, the younger brother of Charles IX, might be a suitable bridegroom. When those negotiations broke down on the same issue, for Anjou insisted that not only he but his entire household must be free to follow the Catholic rite, Catherine changed horses and put forward the still younger brother, Francis Duke of Alençon, as a 'more flexible' candidate. In April 1572 the Treaty of Blois established a defensive alliance between England and France, and France accepted the *status quo* in Scotland. The negotiations proceeded well; Francis was short, pock-marked and less than half the Queen's age, but he wrote splendid love letters. Then came the Massacre of St Bartholomew in France, and renewed savage repression of the Huguenots. Alençon was imprisoned for Huguenot sympathies and the matrimonial negotiations were temporarily abandoned.

During the 1570s and '80s further repair works and renovation were carried out at Richmond Palace. The galleries round the gardens, already reported to have been in a dangerous state years before,[24] were thoroughly repaired in 1573-4, with:

> newe makinge of twoe new houses in the Banketting howse in the gardeyne. Also in frayminge raringe and settinge upp new howses in the garden for the stayenge uprighte of the Gallarie Roffe to bringe it to a perfecte levell, new bourdinge and joystinge of the gallerie and furringe the seelinge Joystes of yt … layinge of gutters of leade in the new howses and watertables upon the gallerie wyndowes.[25]

(The term 'howses' in this context probably referred to the bays of building of which the gallery was constructed.) In 1584-5 a new brick staircase was made at the end of the gallery.[26] The garden 'that lieth by the coffer chamber' was improved in 1580-1 by being levelled and set with 'Baises, Eglantine and Jasmine and Rosemarie'.[27]

In 1574-5 the walls and windows of the palace were made 'as fayre as when they were first mad'. A lot of new glass was put into the Queen's lodging, and the old white glass was reused elsewhere in the palace, while the painted and coloured glass taken out was given to Cecil, who had now been made Lord Burghley.[28] Some of it may have gone to Theobalds, which was finished about this time, or to Burghley House where the west front was built in 1575-7. In 1583-4 new bay windows were added, and nine 'new' windows were painted.[29] Also adorned with big new bay windows were the lodging of the recently appointed Vice Chamberlain, Sir Christopher Hatton, in 1579-80,[30] and the Lord Treasurer's study in 1590-1.[31] Hatton also got a new staircase.[32]

Nor were the domestic and other more functional buildings neglected. A new livery kitchen and a new 'clock house' were built in 1574-5, as was a new 'bridge' or landing stage.[33] The erection of a brick chimney for the livery kitchen in 1585-6[34] suggests that this building was of timber or half-timber, as was probably the new privy bakehouse put up in 1588-9.[35] The stables at Shene Place, then being used as an annexe to the palace, were repaired in 1578.[36]

In 1590-1 the rood loft in the chapel was enlarged to take a new organ,[37] and John Chappington, a renowned organ-builder, was paid 'for the charges and labour about the setting up of the organs at Richmond'.[38] The use of the plural 'organs' suggest that there may have been one installed somewhere in the royal apartments as well as the one in the chapel. Another facility for entertainment was the construction in 1588-9 of a stage, 14 feet square, 'for the plaiers to plaie on' and of hallpaces (stands) 'for the lords and ladies to sitt on and iii other halepaces for the people to stand on'.[39]

From at least 1574 until the end of Elizabeth's reign plays were a regular feature of life at Richmond Palace when the Court was there at Christmas or at 'Shrovetide'. Two surviving series of accounts, one from the Office of Revels, and the other from the Chamber accounts, provide the dates and places of performances and the names of the companies of actors involved, sometimes the titles of the plays, and occasionally some details of the stage properties or scenery provided.[40] A full list of the performances known to have taken place at Richmond is at Appendix 7.

Thus we know that for the play given before the Queen by the children of the Queen's Chapel, under the direction of their master William Hunnis, on Shrove Sunday 1574/5, Her Majesty paid £13 6s. 8d. 'Holly, ivye, four poles and moss' were provided for 'the Rock in Mr Hunneyes play', and 'hornes iii, collars iii, leashes iii, dogghookes iii, with bawdrickes for the hornes'. Unspecified 'tymber work' had to be carried down to the riverside. A reward was paid 'to the french woman for her paynes and her Daughters paynes that went to Richemond and there attended upon Mr Hunnyes his Children and dressed their heades, etc, when they played before her Majestiye'.[41]

Some elaborate scenery was required for the two plays given at Shrove-tide 1582/3, but it would seem that the Earl of Leicester's men and the Merchant Taylors' schoolboys had sufficiently similar plays for the same scenery to be used for both! On Shrove Sunday the Master of the Revels provided 'one Citty, one Battlement of canvas, iii ells of sarcenet and viii paire of gloves … and sundry other garmentes of the store of the office'. The Merchant Taylors had a larger company, for they needed 'one Citty, one Battlement of canvas, vii ells of sarcenet and ii dozen paire of gloves. The whole furniture for the reste was of the store of this office, whereof sundrey garmentes for fytting of the Children were altered and translated.'[42] An unusual item of expenditure was recorded on 4 January 1578/9 – 'the hier [hire] of a horse ii daies to the courte to furnishe my Lord of Leicester's players the frost being so grate no bote could goe'.[43]

There were nine recorded occasions on which the company of which William Shakespeare was a member played before Queen Elizabeth at Richmond: once at Christmas 1590, three times at Christmas 1595, once at Shrovetide and twice at Christmas 1599, again at Shrovetide 1599/1600, and finally at Candlemas (2 February) 1602/3, just seven weeks before the Queen's death. Unfortunately, none of the plays they presented is named, so we do not know which, if any, of Shakespeare's plays were performed in the palace. Nor do we know whether the performances at Richmond by the Lord Admiral's company, for which Christopher Marlowe had been a playwright, featured any of the latter's plays.

The townsfolk of Richmond must have grown well used to the comings and goings of the Court, the visits of statesmen and of foreign ambassadors, and of all manner of suitors for Her Majesty's favour. Some of the courtiers bought houses in the town, many others rented accommodation if they could not be housed in the palace or at Shene. The town already had several large inns – and many alehouses – to cater for the visitors. Even so, 1581 must have been a memorable year. The King of France's brother came to Richmond in person to seek the Queen's hand in marriage and the town's two main inns were requisitioned for his accommodation.

The project of a French marriage had seemed quite dead after the events of 1572. Two years later King Charles IX died and Henry of Anjou (who had meanwhile been elected King of Poland) returned to succeed his brother as Henry III. The Anjou title passed to Francis of Alençon, who – released from prison – was engaged in wooing a daughter of Philip of Spain. However, Elizabeth's support for the Dutch revolt against Spanish rule and the depredations of Sir Francis Drake among the Spanish treasure ships in the West Indies had severely strained relations with Spain, whose King was still in principle committed to rescuing Mary Queen of Scots and to restoring Catholicism in both Scotland and England. England needed to maintain, and if possible strengthen, the defensive alliance with France. When Alençon, or Anjou as he should now be called, was elected 'Defender of Belgic Liberty' to lead the revolt against Spain in the southern Netherlands, Elizabeth determined that he had better be brought under her control. Negotiations were reopened for a marriage with Anjou. The prince himself was pleased and flattered; he sent a personal emissary, Jean de Simier, to Elizabeth's Court to woo her by proxy (which Simier did very successfully); he wrote more of his love letters which so delighted the Queen.

Leicester was strongly opposed to the match. His influence with Elizabeth was however shattered when Simier uncovered the secret of Leicester's marriage to Lettice Knollys, widow of the Earl of Essex. Leicester was, for a time, banished from Court. Elizabeth was however determined to see her suitor before coming to any decision. In August 1579 Anjou came privately to Greenwich and stayed there for 12 days with the Queen, who was very much attracted by her 'little Frog'. She was twice his age and far taller than he, and they made an unlikely couple, but she was quite captivated by his conversation, his manners and his love-making. She seems to have genuinely fallen at least a little in love with him. Despite her age, her doctors were confident that she could bear a child safely. The one snag was that the idea of her marriage to this ill-favoured French prince aroused much overt hostility among her people. The Queen decided to put the matter to the Council. They discussed it several times, on the last occasion for 11 hours at a stretch, but Burghley was not able to muster a majority in favour of the marriage. The Council would only say they could not advise in favour of it, but would assent if it were Her Majesty's wish. This was the death-blow to the project, but it was resolved that the French should be kept in play. The Queen told them that the marriage must be delayed until she could win more general support for it.

76 Francis, Duke of Alençon (later Duke of Anjou). (Musée Condé, Chantilly, France)

When Spain conquered Portugal in 1580, it was felt that a strike against England might be imminent. Relations had been brought to an even lower ebb by Francis Drake's successful pillaging of Spanish treasure ships during his two-year 'voyage of exploration' in the course of which he circumnavigated the world. The Queen herself and some members of the Council, including Leicester, Walsingham and Hatton, had invested in Drake's expedition. With his return to England on 26 September 1580 it was rumoured that the return on this investment might be as high as fifty-fold. The Spanish ambassador, Mendoza, was protesting vehemently, repeatedly demanding return of the stolen treasure and punishment of the thief, but the Queen would not receive him. Some of the Council who were not investors urged that the treasure should be restored, but the Queen blithely instructed Drake to bring it to her. She was at Richmond by late October and from there she sent secret instructions to one Edward Tremayne to assist Drake in bringing up the bullion, but 'to leave so much in Drake's hands as shall amount to £10,000'.[44] The spoils were duly loaded on a train of packhorses and by 5 November they were on their way. Perhaps to avoid undue publicity, the treasure was apparently held at Syon House, while Drake reported to the Queen at Richmond – where he is said to have spent six hours closeted with her detailing his adventures and acquisitions. He was allotted a further £10,000 for his associates and crew; the rest was moved to the Jewel House at the Tower of London pending a final decision on its disposal. Lord Burghley himself endorsed the receipt on 24 December for '22,899 lbs 5 oz of silver bullion, 512 lbs 6 oz of coarse silver and 101 lbs 10 oz of gold bullion'.[45] Mendoza continued to demand an audience of the Queen; he was told she was 'too busy'.

As the Spanish threat loomed ever larger, Elizabeth and her Council wanted to counter it by achieving a full alliance with France. They did not want the French marriage, but could only move towards the alliance by renewing the matrimonial negotiations. From April to June 1581 French ambassadors were in England discussing the marriage treaty, but made little headway. In October Anjou decided to come himself, openly this time and in great style. He left his troops in winter quarters and set out for England, arriving at Richmond where the Court then was on 2 November.

The palace had been made ready for his reception. For the protection of the Prince and his suite, a 'high paile' was erected. The *Red Lion Inn*, the *Bell* and two other houses were taken over for other members of the suite.[46]

Again Elizabeth fell under the spell of her ardent wooer. Within days Anjou was assured of his success. In a letter written from Richmond to his brother the King of France on 8 November he said, 'one may without doubt hope for the success which has been long awaited'. He went on to ask for the immediate despatch of 50,000 crowns, 'to provide for payment for the presents which I shall have to give, which I shall find more conveniently in London than having them chosen in Paris. Moreover one would not know how many will be required as that may be determined at any moment by the number of people who will be present at my marriage.'[47]

Anjou's confidence appeared fully justified when on 22 November at Whitehall Elizabeth exchanged rings with him, kissed him in public, and told the French ambassador that 'the Duke of Anjou shall be my husband'. She cannot have been only toying with the unfortunate Prince, but she was quickly persuaded to change her mind. Whether or not it is true that Leicester and Hatton, as has been suggested, got the Queen's ladies to make a scene and bewail the imminent death of their beloved sovereign who would surely die in childbirth, it is certain that she changed her mind, told Anjou that she had been overwrought, and that she had decided to sacrifice her personal happiness for her people's welfare, and could not marry him, at least at present. The way out with the French Court, who had announced and celebrated the news of the coming nuptials, was found by making impossible demands over the proposed treaty of alliance. Henry III had to turn them down – and the marriage was off. Anjou stayed on in England for another three months, being feasted and banqueted, but was eventually sent on his way in February 1581/2 with a present of £10,000 and a promise of another £50,000 to follow. Elizabeth went with him as far as Canterbury and wept as they said their farewells. She wrote to him fondly and frequently, but never saw him again. He died of a fever in 1584 in France while on leave from a campaign against the Spaniards.

The 'secret' arrival and departure of 'Monsieur' in 1579 and his departure from Richmond to Whitehall with the Queen on 16 November 1581 were both recorded in the diary of Dr. John Dee of Mortlake, the Queen's faithful friend, astrologer and alchemist.

John Dee had been taken into the Queen's service almost immediately after her accession, as a protégé of William, Earl of Pembroke, and Robert Dudley. Though he spent some time abroad, he had in 1564 instructed the Queen at Greenwich in some of his 'mysteries'. By 1569 he was established in his house by the riverside in Mortlake. From there he was occasionally summoned to Court – at Windsor, Richmond or elsewhere; and the Queen, when travelling to or from Richmond, or when staying at the palace, would pay visits to him.

On 16 March 1575 the Queen arrived, unexpectedly, wanting to see his famous library; but her timing was bad. Dr. Dee had just buried his first wife, but four hours before. 'Her Majestie refused to come in; but willed to fetch my glass so famous, and to show unto her some of the properties of it, which I did; her Majestie being taken down from her horse by the Earle of Leicester, Master of the Horse, at the church wall of Mortlake, did see some of the properties of that glass, to her Majestie's great contentment and delight.'[48]

In November 1577 Dee was summoned to Windsor, where the Court were worried about the sudden appearance of a comet. While he was there, 'I declared to the Quene her title to Greenland, Estetiland and Friseland'.[49] This was his latest hobby-horse, apparently based on the conquest of 'Gelindia, lately called Friseland' by King Arthur.[50] He had a two-hour conference with the Queen at Richmond Palace on 8 October 1578 – and a week later was consulted by Dr. Bayly about the Queen's illness.[51]

77   Dr. John Dee.

On 17 September 1580, 'the Quene's Majestie cam from Rychemond in her coach, the higher way of Mortlak felde, and when she cam right against the church, she turned down toward my howse: and when she was against my garden in the felde she stood there a good while, and then cam into the street at the great gate of the felde, where she espyed me at my doore making obeysains to her Mesjestie'. The Queen called him to her coach and bade him come to the Court – and to let her know when he was coming.[52] Elizabeth had evidently not forgotten the business of her supposed titles, for when Dee went to Richmond Palace on 3 October he 'delivered my two rolls of the Quene's Majesties title unto herself in the garden of Richemond, who appointed after dynner to heare furder of the matter'. Lord Burghley, who was present at the at the subsequent discussion in the Queen's Privy Chamber, expressed some doubts, but had two further sessions with Dee himself to go into it further. On 10 October Dee's mother died – and the Queen called on him herself to express her condolences:

> The Quene's Majestie, to my great comfort ... cam with her trayn from the court and at my dore graciously calling me to her, on horsebak, exhorted me briefly to take my mother's death patiently, and withall told me that the Lord Threasorer had gretly commended my doings for her title, which he had to examyn, which title in two rolls he had browght home two hours before; she remembered also how at my wive's death it was her fortune likewise to call upon me.[53]

The Queen called again at Dr. Dee's on 11 February 1582/3, when going from Richmond to dine with Secretary Walsingham at Barn Elms. Dee walked for a way beside the Queen's horse and she 'asked me obscurely of Monsieur's state';[54] the Queen had not forgotten her 'little Frog'. Dee made this entry in his diary, as he sometimes did with more sensitive matters, in Greek characters. In the following year she passed by his door again on the way from Greenwich to Sion, and sent him 40 angels to assist in his expenses in entertaining the Polish Prince Laski,[55] who was interested in Dee's alchemic experiments.

Dee went abroad shortly after that, for some five years, pursuing his search for the philosopher's stone. The Queen summoned him home in 1589 and received him 'very favourably' at Richmond Palace on 19 December.[56] He settled back into his house at Mortlake, though this had been broken into by a mob soon after his departure for the Continent, and some of his furniture and books had been destroyed. He had always been feared and resented as a 'magician' by the locals. In 1590 the Queen summoned him to the palace when she was at Richmond in November, and promised him 100 angels (£50) 'to kepe Christmas with'. On 4 December she called on him again at his house, 'and I met her at Estshene gate, where she graciously, putting down her mask, did say with mery chere, "I thank thee, Dee; there was never promise made, but it was broken or kept"'. She kept him on tenterhooks another 48 hours, but then sent the £50. On 14 December she called again, 'at my dore as she rod by to take ayre, and I met her at Estshene gate'. She sent word two days later to say that he should practise his philosophy and alchemy freely and no one should be allowed to control or molest him – and promising another £50 (which however never materialised).[57]

Dr. William Awberry of Kew (see Chapter 11), who was a kinsman of Dee's, was pressing the Queen on his behalf to grant him an appointment as warden of the St Cross Hospital near Winchester. Dee saw her in 1594 at Greenwich, and later, on 3 June, took his wife and seven children to call on her when she made a brief visit to Syon. This seems to have been Dee's last meeting with Elizabeth, though his wife delivered a petition to her that December. After an abortive suggestion of the Deanship of St Paul's, he was granted in April 1595 the wardenship of Manchester College. He did not return to Mortlake until 1604, after the Queen's death.

✠

It was during Anjou's visit that the Queen finally granted an audience to the Spanish ambassador. On 11 October 1581 Richmond Palace echoed to some most undiplomatic language. To Mendoza's demands for the restitution of Drake's plunder and the cessation of piratical attacks on Spanish vessels, the Queen denied all knowledge of the alleged offences and counter-attacked by treating him to a lecture on the law of nations and demanding an apology from King Philip for his interference in Ireland. Tempers got somewhat heated. Mendoza started to bluster; in the words of his own report to King Philip: 'I said I had been here for more than three years and a half and had been constantly telling her of these things, but as it appeared that during all this time she had heard nothing about them and would find no remedy for them now it would be necessary to see whether cannons would not make her hear better. She told me I need not think to threaten and frighten her, for if I did she would put me in a place where I could not say a word.'[58]

That the danger of war with Spain remained an imminent rather than an actual threat was largely due to the Spanish preoccupation with the revolt in the Netherlands. The threat however constrained Elizabeth to deal cautiously with the Dutch appeals for assistance.

A month after Anjou's death, William of Orange, the leader of the Dutch revolt, was assassinated. The Duke of Parma laid siege to Antwerp and captured Ghent. The States-General sent envoys to Paris to ask Henry III to become their King; but he refused. They turned to Elizabeth. On 7 March 1584/5 the Queen told them that, while she was not prepared to accept the sovereignty of the Netherlands, she would protect them and their freedom, and – if given three ports as a

78 Queen Elizabeth receiving two Dutch Ambassadors in audience. (Staatliche Kunstsammlungen, Kassel)

pledge (for she had not forgotten her betrayal by the French Protestants) – would send an army to defend them against the Spaniards. The Dutch did not care for these terms; negotiations proceeded slowly, and it was not until Antwerp had fallen that a treaty was signed at Nonesuch in August 1585. Leicester was appointed to command the English expeditionary force. After his arrival the States-General invited him to become Governor in the Queen's name. After initial hesitation, he accepted and was installed as Governor of the Netherlands and Captain-General of the States' armies. Elizabeth was furious, but eventually told the States-General that he could remain until she made other arrangements.

The assassination of William of Orange, following a plot to murder Henry of Navarre, the Protestant leader in France and heir to the childless Henry III, underlined the danger of another Catholic plot to murder Elizabeth and put Mary of Scots on the throne not only of Scotland, but of England also. Nor were such plots mere figments of the imagination. The Throckmorton conspiracy, in which both Guise and Mendoza, the Spanish ambassador in London, were implicated, had been discovered in January 1583/4. In the autumn of 1584 English Protestants formed the 'Bond of Association' and swore that if any attempt were made to kill Queen Elizabeth, they would kill not only those involved in the plot but also whomever the plotters intended to place on the throne and anyone else who might claim the throne through such a person. In 1585 Parliament gave the Association and its oath statutory authority.

Such was the climate in which Secretary Walsingham succeeded in infiltrating several agents into another group of Catholic plotters. Communications between the plotters and Mary were intercepted and deciphered for a long time without anything really incriminating coming to light. Then came a letter from Anthony Babington, giving details of a plot to liberate Mary, assassinate

Elizabeth and assist the landing of a Spanish army in England. Mary replied proposing that the assassination team of six gentlemen should be 'set to work' before her own liberation. Babington was lured into naming his fellow conspirators. Walsingham now laid the evidence before Elizabeth, who agreed to the arrest and trial of the conspirators and to the appointment of Commissioners to investigate Mary's part in the plot. In September 1586 all the conspirators were executed – but Elizabeth would still not agree to send Mary to the Tower or to put her on trial. Not only were Henry III and James VI protesting, but she had the deep feeling that an anointed Queen, even when she had abdicated, should not be put on public trial, let alone executed.

The Commissioners went to Fotheringay Castle, where Mary was being held, on 14 and 15 October, heard the evidence and found her guilty. However, Elizabeth had instructed them to reserve sentence. On 25 October, after a counter-productive intervention by the French ambassador, she authorised the Commissioners to pronounce their sentence; they declared that Mary was guilty of attempting to assassinate the Queen. Under the law passed in 1585 this offence carried the death penalty, but it could not be enforced unless the Queen issued a proclamation naming her.

Parliament, summoned in this crisis, finally met – after two postponements ordered by Elizabeth – on 29 October. They at once joined the Council in demanding that Mary be put to death. The Queen did her best to distance herself from the outcry by staying at Richmond instead of moving to Whitehall as was customary when Parliament was sitting. So a deputation of 20 peers and 40 members of the House of Commons was despatched to Richmond to put their views to the Queen. She received them on 12 November, and in a long speech thanked them for their loyalty, confessed her distate for the whole subject, and promised an answer. After 12 days a second deputation went to Richmond to receive the answer; they were treated to another long and emotional speech which ended, 'excuse my doubtfulness and take in good part my answer answerless'.

For another six days Elizabeth refused to sign the proclamation. She finally did so on 1 December and it was published on 4 December. No one however was anxious to kill Queen Mary without a direct authority from the Queen, and still Elizabeth delayed to sign a warrant of execution. Then yet another plot was revealed, this time implicating the French ambassador in London and the brother of the English ambassador in Paris. This, added to the constant pressure from her Council, may have been the last straw. On 1 February, at Greenwich, Elizabeth signed the warrant. On 8 February Mary was beheaded.

At the last moment, after signing the warrant, Elizabeth had instructed that Mary should be murdered quietly rather than executed officially. When she learned of the execution her fury was as great, or greater, than that expressed at the French Court and in Scotland and Spain. In France and Scotland the indignation gradually burnt itself out. Slowly relations with Henry III and James VI were restored.

Not so with Spain. Although Elizabeth's relations with the Dutch became increasingly strained and she pursued negotiations with the Duke of Parma for a settlement in the Netherlands (where the only English successes had been those of Sir Philip Sidney, who had died of a wound at Zutphen), her intervention in the Netherlands had been yet another *casus belli* for Philip. When he had news of Drake's depredations in the West Indies and the sacking of Cartagena in 1586, he decided to invade England. Mary's execution placed him, he felt, under an obligation to punish Elizabeth – moreover Mary had bequeathed her claim to the English throne to Philip if her son James was still a heretic. Philip began to prepare his great Armada – the fleet that was to seize control of the Channel and to convoy Parma's forces across to England. Elizabeth was persuaded

79 The 'Armada' portrait of Queen Elizabeth by George Gower, c.1588. (Marquess of Tavistock and Trustees of the Bedford Estate)

that Parma was merely spinning out negotiations until the Armada was ready, and authorised a 'pre-emptive strike' by Francis Drake with a fleet of 27 ships. Drake sailed into Cadiz harbour and bombarded and burned the Spanish ships there, inflicted more damage on further ships along the coast, and then intercepted and plundered the Spanish fleet returning from the East Indies.

Drake's action delayed the sailing of the Armada in 1587, but Philip still hoped to strike early in 1588. In January however Parma reported that a third of his army were ill, and Dutch ships were patrolling the coasts. The Armada would have to deal with them as well as the English before he could set out in his transports. He continued the negotiations with Elizabeth's Commissioners, but neither side was really keen to achieve a settlement.

The Armada sailed on 30 May. On 19 July it was sighted off the Lizard. Elizabeth had moved to Richmond a fortnight earlier, and it was there that the defence of England against the threatened invasion was planned. A Council of War was established, with Leicester, who had returned from Holland, as Captain-General of the Land Forces, his stepson the Earl of Essex, recently appointed Master of the Horse, as commander of the cavalry, and with Lord Howard of Effingham as Lord Admiral, with Drake as his second-in-command.

The Council were well aware of Parma's preparations, but expected him to land in Essex and march on London (whereas the Spaniards' actual first target was Margate). They therefore decided

80 Robert Dudley, Earl of Leicester, in 1585, three years before his death. (Penshurst Place, Kent)

to assemble the bulk of the army, which was being hastily mustered, at Tilbury, while building a bridge of boats across to Gravesend in case the landings were after all in Kent. Other forces were to remain in readiness in the south-eastern counties. On 23 July instructions were sent to the Deputy Lieutenants of Surrey (the Lord Lieutenant of the county being the High Admiral, who was otherwise engaged):

> ... the forces of that county ... be directed to come to such place or places as hath been heretofore thought meet, or as you shall thincke fittest to be in readiness upon the fyeringe of the Beacons, to resort to impeache such attempte as the enemie maie make to set on lande his forces in any place ...
>
> And because the greatest doubte is that the enemy will attempt to land in some place of Essex, to wch place her Matie hath sent our verie good Lo. the Erle of Leycester ... to have the charge of such an armye as is appointed to encounter with them there in that county, her pleasure is that you shall forthwith send into Essex, to the town of Burntwood, the number of 8 lances ande 99 light horse ... to be there the 27th of this monethe ...
>
> Furthermore ... you shall send from thence the number of 1000 footmen, to be ledd by the captens and officers, to be at Stratford on the Bowe near London, on the border of Essex, by the 29th of this moneth.[59]

After sending a further 500 footmen to London, the Surrey forces were supposed to be disposed, by 8 August, as follows: 836 soldiers at each of three bases in Godstone, Reigate and Dorking, with 120 horse and 2500 footmen at Croydon.[60]

On 29 July, as the English fleet battered the Spaniards off Gravelines, the Queen and the Court moved back to London, for Elizabeth wanted to be closer to the people and the army. It was from Westminster that she set out on 8 August for Tilbury where next day she gave her famous speech:

> ... I know I have the body of a weak and feeble woman, but I have the heart and stomach of a King, and of a King of England too ...

Although the Armada had been beaten again at Calais by Drake's fire ships, and had run northwards into the North Sea, thus effectively destroying any chance of Parma's invasion fleet sailing, it had still seemed possible that they might regroup and return south. But the Queen had not yet left Tilbury when she received the news that they had been seen in full flight northwards off Newcastle. She knew then that the danger was past. Later the gales completed what Howard and Drake had begun.

When the Court came back to Richmond for Christmas there was one conspicuous place unfilled. Leicester had died, of a renewed attack of malaria contracted some years before, on 4 September. His relationship with Elizabeth had had its ups and downs – from the excitement of young courtship to fury and temporary alienation; the Queen had had other favourites – Thomas Heneage, Christopher Hatton, recently young Walter Raleigh – and other more trusted counsellors, such as Burghley; but Leicester had always been the one to whom she returned, on whom she ultimately relied, the husband *manqué*. When brought the news of his death she shut herself away in a private chamber for two days and would let no one in, until Burghley broke open the door.

Leicester's place was now to be filled by his stepson: the young, handsome, impetuous Robert Devereux, Earl of Essex. Leicester had pushed him forward to counter Raleigh's increasing influence. In 1587 he had been given Leicester's old post of Master of the Horse; after the Armada he had been made a Knight of the Garter, and was invited by the Queen to take over Leicester's apartments at St James's, adjacent to the Queen's.

The war against Spain continued and in 1589 Drake and Norris led an expedition to Portugal. Essex went with them, without the Queen's permission, and she wrote to insist on his return to Court. The expedition achieved little towards its main purpose of restoring the Portuguese claimant, but it inflicted some further damage on the Spanish fleet.

The central focus of Elizabeth's attention in foreign affairs now shifted to France. In December 1588 the Duke of Guise and one of his brothers had been murdered by order of Henry III who was trying to defeat the rebellious fanatic Catholic 'Holy League' which the Guises had formed to stamp out Protestantism in France. In April 1589 Henry compacted with his heir presumptive, the Huguenot Henry of Navarre, to join in crushing the rebels, who held Paris, Normandy and the Channel ports. They inflicted several defeats on the rebels and advanced to Paris. Henry III had asked Elizabeth for a loan. As she feared that the Spaniards were about to intervene in France in support of the League – and as she was concerned that the Spaniards might then be installed all along the southern coast of the Channel, she agreed to help. Then Henry III in his turn was assassinated on 1 August 1589. Henry of Navarre was proclaimed King as Henry IV, but many of the Catholics in the royal army, though willing to serve under a Catholic King with Navarre as his ally, were unwilling to serve directly under a Huguenot. The army began to melt away and

81 Robert Devereux, Earl of Essex. Miniature by Isaac Oliver, c.1596. (National Portrait Gallery)

Navarre had to fall back. He left Paris and marched to Dieppe, which he occupied – for he believed that Elizabeth was his only hope, and for her aid to be effective he needed to hold at least one Channel port.

He sent an ambassador to ask Elizabeth's help, but it was not until September 1590 that she agreed to send an army of 4,000 men under Lord Willoughby d'Eresby. Essex might have had the command, but he was in temporary disgrace for having secretly married Sir Philip Sidney's widow. Henry's fortunes in the war improved, but then Philip of Spain ordered Parma to attack from the Netherlands. Though Henry won the battle of Ivry in March 1590/1 he was unable to prevent Parma from relieving Paris. He continued to appeal for help, financial and military, from Elizabeth. She sent some money and then, in July 1591, another army of 6,000 men, the command of which, with much reluctance, she finally gave to the importunate Essex. Essex achieved little in France, to the Queen's annoyance; and in May of the following year she recalled her army and its general.

In December 1592 Parma died, and in July 1593 Henry IV agreed to adopt the Catholic religion. Paris surrendered to him the following March. Elizabeth played no further significant part in the war in France; in 1596 she was offered the chance of reoccupying Calais which had been attacked by the Spaniards. Essex was again to command the force. But Elizabeth delayed too long – and Calais capitulated to the Spanish before she had sanctioned the dispatch of Essex's force from Dover. Essex was then unleashed in an attack on Cadiz which had been planned for some time. A large and well-equipped fleet with over 6,000 troops achieved complete surprise – captured and sacked Cadiz and would have captured the Spanish fleet had it not been deliberately burned to prevent its capture. In April 1598 Henry IV issued the Edict of Nantes granting limited religious freedom to Protestants; and in May he signed a peace treaty with Philip II. The English remained at war with Spain, but Philip died in September 1598.

✠

In the 1580s Elizabeth had largely given up the annual 'progresses' during which she had toured the counties within comparatively easy reach of London (she never went more than 150 miles from the capital) staying with the noblemen and rich gentry in their houses. Instead, she moved throughout the year from palace to palace: Whitehall, St James's, Somerset House, Greenwich, Richmond, Oatlands, Nonesuch, Hampton Court, making occasional brief forays from these bases. She therefore came at least twice in most years to spend some weeks at Richmond, very often in the late autumn, frequently for Christmas, sometimes in the spring or summer.

Richmond had the reputation of being the warmest of the palaces, perhaps because its royal apartments were more compact and therefore easier to heat. It became her 'warm winter box, to shelter her old age'.[61] Dr. Dee advised her against the chill of Whitehall and urged her to come to Richmond for the winter. Certainly it seemed to suit her: John Stanhope, writing from Richmond in December 1589, said, 'The Queen is so well, six or seven galliards in a morning, besides singing and music, is her ordinary exercise.'[62]

Although the progresses were resumed in 1591 and 1592, in 1593 the Court stayed close to home, moving to Richmond in the autumn for fear of the plague in London. In 1594 only a brief journey was made to Loughborough, and in 1595 a proposed progress got no further than Richmond because of an outbreak of measles and smallpox at Chertsey and Weybridge which were on the intended itinerary.[63] The last progress was made in 1597.

82 A dance at Queen Elizabeth's Court, detail from a painting by an unknown artist. (Penshurst Place, Kent)

The Queen, though generally in good health, was becoming conscious of her age. It was during Lent 1596/7, while the Court was at Richmond, that Dr. Rudd, Bishop of St David's, was invited to preach in the chapel of the palace. The Queen was sixty-three. He announced his text, from Psalm 90: 'So teach us to number our days, that we may apply our hearts unto wisdom.' He then started to discourse on the sacred and mystical numbers. When he got to '7 x 9 = 63 the Great Climacterical Year', he noticed that the Queen was very angry and quickly moved on to less contentious numbers such as 88, the triumph over the Armada. At the end of the sermon the Queen, who had been sitting in her private pew, opened the window onto the chapel and instead of thanking the preacher as was customary, shouted that the bishop should have kept his arithmetic to himself, adding, 'I see the greatest clerks are not the wisest men'.[64] But when some of her ladies-in-waiting criticised the sermon, Elizabeth rebuked them and added that she was not as old at 63 as the bishop supposed, and that her appetite, her singing voice and her eyesight were as good as ever.[65]

In the last few years of the Queen's life there was another burst of improvement works at Richmond Palace. In 1595-6 a new bridge (landing stage) was built with 'a paire of flyeing Staires with a retorne, railes, hallpace and turned Ballusters'.[66] In the next year the roofs of the Flesh Larder and some other buildings were repaired and a new set of rooms for the porters was constructed by the main gate.[67] Then a lot of painting was undertaken, and the gardens must have been brightened by the repainting of posts and rails and seats and arbours. Leonard Fryer, appointed Sergeant Painter in 1598, was a specialist in illusionist painting and imitative finishes. He painted window frames to look like Caen stone, a frame with turned pillars in the library to resemble 'the tissewe of that room' and foot-paces 'stonnework like unto the pavements'. His most impressive work at Richmond must however have been the 'greate diall in the utter court', 12 feet wide by 14 feet deep, 'with greate Romaine letters in fyne gold with an ordenance of Jasper and stone woorke in oyle colours'.[68] The purpose of this is not very clear; was it a painted clock dial, or merely an ornamentation in the centre of the paving?

Another striking piece of decorative work was the renovation of the fountain in Fountain Court, with 'pylasters and carved pillars' fitted and soldered in 1597[69] and with the figure of a dragon fixed on top in 1600-1.[70]

Over £1,000 was spent in both years 1598-9 and 1599-1600. In the latter year the Lord Treasurer's lodging was enlarged.[71] Lord Burghley had died in 1598; the new Lord Treasurer was Thomas Sackville, Lord Buckhurst (once of Shene Place).

Although the works accounts make no mention of it, there can be no doubt that at least one of the newly-invented flushing water-closets was installed at Richmond. The inventor was John Harington, godson of the Queen. Harington (a cousin of the John Haringtons of the Exton family who figure in later chapters) was a man of letters, a poet and an irrepressible wit. At his home at Kelston in Somerset he devised and installed the prototype. Perhaps Her Majesty was introduced to it when she visited him at Kelston in 1592.

Harington (under the pseudonym 'Misacmos' – filth-hater) introduced his invention to the public in 1596 in a book called *The Metamorphosis of Ajax* (jakes was the common term at that time for what was properly called a stool-closet or euphemistically a privy). He wrote that his 'invention may be beneficial, not only to my private friends, but to townes and Cities, yea even to her Majesties service for some of her houses … If I should fortune to effect so good a reformation, in the pallace of Richmond, or Greenwich … I doubt not but some pleasant witted Courtier of either sex would grace me so much at least: as to say, that I were worthy for my rare invention, to be made one of the Privie … chamber.'[72]

That the possibility of installing water-closets in the royal palaces was in the front of his mind is further demonstrated when later in the book he stated that he would appraise its value 'in my house to bee worth 100 pounds, in yours 300 poundes, in Wollerton 500 pounds; in Tibals, Burley and Holmbie 1000 pounds, in Greenwich, Richmond and Hampton Court 10,000'.[73]

The Queen was not entirely amused – the book had contained what was construed as 'a shaft aimed at Leicester'. By the end of 1598, however, Harington's uncle, Robert Markham, wrote to him that 'you have been spoke of, and with no ill will, both by the nobles and the Queene herself. Your book is almoste forgiven, and I may say forgotten … tho' her Highnesse signified displeasure in outwarde sorte, yet did she like the marrowe of your booke … The Queen is minded to take you to her favour, but she sweareth that she believes you will make epigrams and write *misacmos* again on her and all the courte.'[74]

Among Harington's epigrams is the one 'To the Queene when she was pacified and had sent *Misacmos* thanks for the invention', and another that serves as evidence that a water-closet had

The Palace under Queen Elizabeth

83 (above) Sir John Harington, the Queen's godson. (National Portrait Gallery)

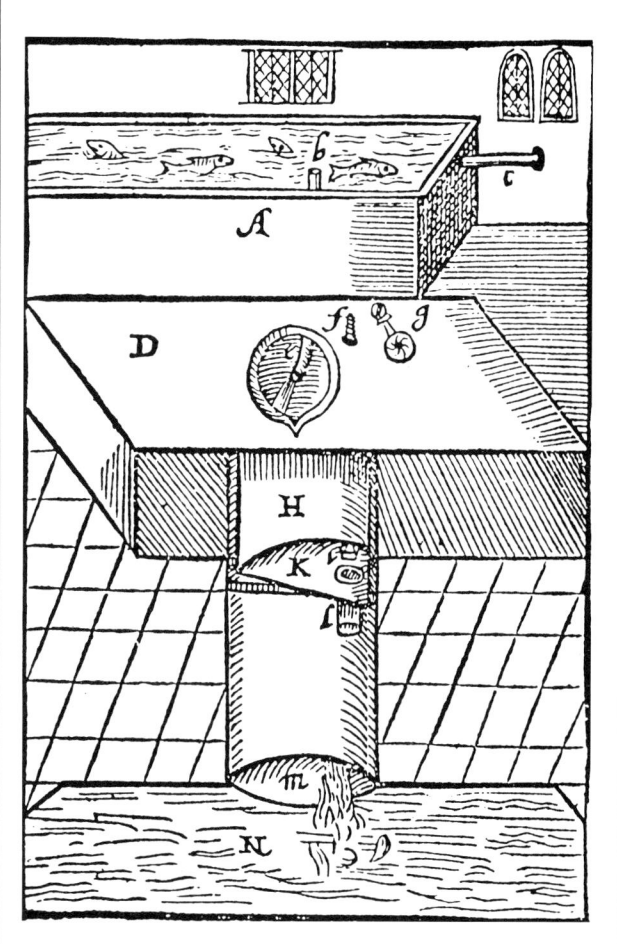

A the Cesterne
B the little washer
C the wast pipe
D the seate boord
E the pipe that comes from the Cesterne
F the Screw
G the Scallop shell to cover it when it is shut downe
H the stoole pot
I the stopple
K the current
L the sluce
M N the vault into which it falles: always remember that at noone and at night, emptie it and leave it halfe a foote deepe in fayre water. And this being well done, and orderly kept, your worst privie may be as sweet as your best chamber

84 (right) Sir John Harington's water closet. (From The Metamorphosis of Ajax.*)*

indeed been installed at Richmond Palace, with a copy of *The Metamorphosis of Ajax* hanging from the wall beside it.

> To the Ladies of the Queenes Privy Chamber, at the making of their perfumed privy at Richmond, The Booke hanged in chaines saith thus:
>
> Faire Dames, if any tooke in scorne, and spite
> Me, that *Misacmos* Muse in mirth did write,
> To satisfie the sinne, loe, here in chaines,
> For aye to hang, my Master me ordaines.
> Yet deeme the deed to him no derogation,
> But deigne to this device new commendation,
> Sith here you see, feele, smell that his conveyance
> Hath freed this noysome place from all annoyance.
> Now judge you, that the work mock, envie, taunt,
> Whose service in this place may make most vaunt:
> If us, or you, to praise it, were most meet,
> You, that made sowre, or us, that make it sweet?[75]

※

The Queen's favour towards her merry godson extended to commending him to the Earl of Essex, who took Harington with him on his expedition to Ireland in March 1599. Harington served as a captain of horse under the Earl of Southampton and was one of those knighted in the field by Essex. The expedition, the primary purpose of which had been to quell the rebellion in Ulster of Hugh O'Neill, Earl of Tyrone, who had been in arms against the Crown since 1593, was a disaster for Essex. It had begun badly.

In August 1598 Tyrone had shattered the English force sent against him, at the fort on the Blackwater which commanded Ulster's communications with the south. This success was followed by the outbreak of further rebellion in other provinces. The Council determined to appoint a new general in Ireland, and Essex demanded that the appointment should be given to Sir George Carew. The Queen would not agree. Essex turned his back on her, and she boxed his ear. He clapped his hand to his sword, but was restrained by the Lord Admiral. He rushed out of the room and sulked at home for weeks, refusing to apologise for his insolence. However, by October he was back at Court and forgiven. In a few months, whether he wanted it or not, he was himself given the Irish appointment, with the title of Lieutenant and Governor-General of Ireland.

Once he arrived in Ireland, he kept putting off a campaign against Tyrone, preferring to deal first with the lesser rebels. The Queen ordered him to invade Ulster immediately, but he still delayed. Elizabeth, who had initially told him that he could return to England whenever he wished, now forbade him to do so. When he finally marched north towards Ulster he made a truce with Tyrone instead of fighting him – and then, in defiance of the Queen's order, returned to England to explain it all to her, riding pell-mell across the country and bursting unannounced into her bedroom at Nonesuch on 28 September. The Queen insisted he explain himself to the Council, not to her. The Council placed him under house arrest. On 2 October he was dismissed from all his offices. Lord Mountjoy, appointed in his place, had by the end of 1602 defeated both Tyrone and a Spanish force sent to help him.

Essex was sent, not to the Tower, but to confinement in York House, next door to his own house in the Strand. It was not until May 1600 that he was allowed to return to Essex House, and not until August that the restrictions on his movements were lifted. Meanwhile the Queen retired to Richmond where she stayed for six weeks over Christmas. She was back there again in March and September, and for a month in October-November 1600; the local inhabitants must have been unusually excited when she received there on 14 October 'a great ambassador come from Muscovie'.[76] When he took his departure the following May, John Chamberlain wrote that 'the Moscovie Ambassador took his leave like a dancing beare, and is gon homeward.'[77]

In February 1600/1 Essex, still brooding in Essex House over his disgrace, planned a *coup d'état*. The Queen, who was at Richmond, was to be detained there by some of his followers while he seized control of London. He called all those he could trust to gather at Essex House. But news of his plan reached the Court and on 7 February he was summoned to the Privy Council. He refused to go and when a party came to arrest him the following morning, he shut them up in the house and – though he had lost all element of surprise and all chance of seizing the Queen – he set out with some 200 armed followers to rouse the populace of London. Not a single person came to join him. He returned home; and when the Lord Admiral threatened to blow up Essex House (after the ladies had been allowed out) he surrendered. He was quickly put on trial and condemned to death for treason. On 25 February he was executed. When the news was brought to Elizabeth, she was playing the virginals. She said nothing – and began to play again.

Elizabeth was deeply afflicted by Essex's rebellion and deeply grieved by his death, but there is no shred of evidence to support the old story that she delayed signing the death warrant in the hope that Essex would send to her a ring which she had once given him with the promise that it would save him if he should ever send it back to her.

In March 1601/2 the Comte de Beaumont, the newly arrived French ambassador, visited the Queen at Richmond, and noted that she walked daily on Richmond Green with greater spirit and activity than could be expected of her years.[78] When the Duke of Nevers paid a visit to her at Richmond from 16 to 23 April, she entertained him with a banquet and dancing. John Chamberlain wrote to his friend Dudley Carleton at the embassy in Paris on 26 April: 'The French gallants are gone, having somewhat redeemed the rascal report that Biron and his train left behind. The Duke of Nevers is especially commended, except that the Queen's musicians and other inferior Officers complain that he was dry-handed. The Queen graced him much and danced with him.'[79]

In October 1602 the Court was back again at Richmond, 'where the Queen findes herself so well that she will not easilie remove'.[80] She had to return to Whitehall in November, but she intended to spend Christmas 1602 at Richmond. However, the entertainments planned for her by Secretary of State Robert Cecil and by the Lord Admiral kept her in Whitehall, 'though most of the cariages were well onward on theire waye to Richmond'.[81] Elizabeth was feeling her age and her melancholy. She kept up a front for the Court, at the dancing and the feasts and the revels, she went riding and hunting as usual, but she did not deceive those closest to her such as her godson John Harington. 'Our deare Queene … dothe now bear shew of human infirmitie', he wrote to his wife, 'too faste for that evil which we shall get by her dethe; and too slow for that good which shee shall get by her releasement from pains and miserye'.[82]

When the Queen asked Harington what he had been writing, he read her some verses. 'She smiled once,' and said, 'When thou doste feele creeping tyme at thye gate, these fooleries will please thee less; I am past my relishe for suche matters; thou seeste my bodilie meate dothe not suite me well; I have eaten but one ill tastede cake since yesternighte.'[83]

On 21 January the Queen finally left Whitehall for Richmond, 'in very fowle and wet weather'.[84] She had had a cold, but seemed to throw it off. The Lord Chamberlain's Company performed for her at Candlemas (2 February), when Shakespeare may have made his last

85 Queen Elizabeth in procession, 1600. Detail from a painting attributed to Robert Peake the Elder. (Private Collection)

appearance before her. At Shrovetide it was the Lord Admiral's Company which put on the usual two plays.[85]

At the end of January a new Venetian diplomat arrived in London. He was not an ambassador but a secretary or *chargé d'affaires*. His principal task was to seek redress for the damages inflicted on Venetian shipping by British pirates. However, he was the first official representative of the Venetian republic in London for very many years. Elizabeth was still quite well and perverse enough to enjoy teasing him in her well-established manner. He reported in a despatch dated 13 February [3 February O.S.][*]:

> I arrived in London on the 7th and found that the Queen had gone eight days ago to Richmond, a palace suited to the season ... My audience was fixed for yesterday, the first day of Lent ... When I was on the point of getting into my carriage to reach Richmond at two o'clock in the afternoon according to instructions received from the Lord Chamberlain, a gentleman in waiting on the Queen arrived post haste to say that urgent business which had unexpectedly arisen

---

[*] The Venetians were already using the new style Gregorian calendar, introduced in 1582. The dates in England, which still – owing to the opposition of the bishops – used the old style (O.S.) Julian calendar, would have been ten days earlier than those mentioned in the despatch.

compelled her Majesty to postpone my audience till next Sunday. I am told by the Italians who were with me at the moment that it is almost the invariable custom to act so here for no other reason than haughtiness, and that Her Majesty has sometimes treated the French Ambassador in this fashion, and quite recently the Duke of Bracciano and the Duke of Nevers when they were over here …

The Queen who is in the seventy first year is in excellent health as I hear on all sides and in perfect possession of all her senses; as she neither eats nor sleeps except at the call of nature everyone hopes and believes that her life is much further from its close than is expected elsewhere.[86]

Scaramelli, the Venetian Secretary, was granted his audience on 16 February [6 February O.S.]. It was the last formal occasion of the reign, and the Queen was in good form. Scaramelli was escorted to Richmond from his lodgings in London by 'one of the Queen's fifty pensioners', and was met on arrival by 'several gentlemen'. Then the Lord Chamberlain took him into the Presence Chamber and from there into the room – probably the Privy Chamber – where the Queen was.

The scene, and particularly the appearance of the Queen, were described by Scaramelli in his report:

The Queen was clad in taffety of silver and white, trimmed with gold; her dress was somewhat open in front and showed her throat encircled with pearls and rubies down to her breast. Her skirts were much fuller and began lower down than is the fashion in France. Her hair was of a light colour never made by nature, and she wore great pearls like pears round the forehead; she had a coif arched round her head and an Imperial crown, and displayed a vast quantity of gems and pearls upon her person; even under her stomacher she was covered with golden jewelled girdles and single gems, carbuncles, balas-rubies, diamonds; round her wrists in place of bracelets she wore double rows of pearls of more than medium size. Her Majesty was seated on a chair placed on a small square platform with two steps, and round about on the floor and uncovered were the Archbishop of Canterbury, Metropolitan of England, the Lord Chancellor, the Lord Treasurer, the Lord High Admiral, the Secretary of State and all the Privy Council; the remainder of the Chamber was all full of ladies and gentlemen and the musicians who had been playing dance music up to that moment.

At my entry the Queen rose, and I advanced with reverences made in due order, and reaching her was in act to kneel down upon the first step and to kiss her robe, but her Majesty would not allow it, and with both hands almost raised me up and extended her right hand, which I kissed with effusion, and at the same moment she said, "Welcome to England, Mr. Secretary. It was high time that the Republic sent to visit a Queen who has always honoured it on every possible occasion."

Then Scaramelli made his set speech and presented his credentials. There followed a discussion of his business, in which the Queen scored another point or two, remarking that she 'could not help feeling that the Republic of Venice, during the forty four years of my reign, has never made herself heard by me except to ask for something'. However, she promised to appoint Commissioners promptly to pursue the details of the matter with Scaramelli. She had conducted the whole audience in Italian without an interpreter. At the close, as she gave him her hand to kiss, she smiled at Scaramelli and said, 'I do not know if I have spoken Italian well; still I think so, for I learnt it as a child, and I believe I have not forgotten it'.[87]

At the beginning of March the Queen again seemed to have a bad cold, but she refused to take to her bed. Then, while her resistance was lowered, she suffered a quite unexpected blow. Her favourite lady-in-waiting and kinswoman, Catherine Countess of Nottingham, the wife of the Lord Admiral, died quite suddenly, and Elizabeth was grievously affected.

The story, mentioned above, about Lord Essex and the ring makes out that Essex had indeed sent the ring to the Queen by Lady Nottingham, and that on her deathbed she confessed to

Elizabeth that, at her husband's behest, she had withheld it – and that that was the cause of the Queen's breakdown. Scaramelli however had another explanation to offer in a despatch of 20 March [10 March O.S.]:

> The Queen for many days has not left her chamber. And although they say that the reason for this is her sorrow for the death of the Countess, nevertheless the truer cause is ... the business of Lady Arabella.[88]

Arabella Stewart was the granddaughter of Lady Lennox, and was next in succession to the English throne after James VI of Scotland and his children. She had just been arrested as the result of a report that a marriage was being planned between her and William Seymour, grandson of Catherine Grey.

A week later Scaramelli reported that:

> I was right when in my last despatch I said that Her Majesty's mind was overwhelmed by a grief greater than she could bear. It reached such a pitch she passed three days and three nights without sleep and with scarcely any food. Her attention was fixed not only on the affair of Lady Arabella who now is, or feigns herself to be, half mad, but also on the pardon which she has given at last to the Earl of Tyrone ... She fell to considering that the Earl of Essex, who used to be her dear intimate, might have been quite innocent after all ... He concluded an agreement with Tyrone that was both more advantageous for the kingdom and more honourable for the Queen than the present one. But the Council, considering the conduct of Essex in coming to England in person to explain his action without leave given, persuaded the Queen to put him in the Tower, whence followed all those events which led to his decapitation on the first day of Lent 1601.
>
> So deeply does Her Majesty feel this that on the first day of Lent this year, which in the English calendar was the 19th of this month, she recalled the anniversary of so piteous a spectacle and burst into tears and dolorous lamentations as though for some deadly sin she had committed, and then fell ill of a sickness which the doctors immediately judged to be fatal ...
>
> The Queen's illness is want of sleep, want of appetite, labour of the lungs and the heart, cessation of the natural motions, irresponsiveness to remedies. There is but little fever, but also little strength.[89]

It was probably the death of the Countess of Nottingham which brought her brother, Robert Carey, Warden of the Middle March on the Scottish border, to Richmond. Robert, the Countess, their sister Lady Scrope (another of the Queen's ladies) and their eldest brother George, Lord Hunsdon, the Lord Chamberlain, were all the Queen's cousins. Their father's mother had been Mary Boleyn, sister of Anne Boleyn, Elizabeth's mother. Their father, the first Lord Hunsdon, the Queen's first cousin, had served as Lord Chamberlain from 1583 until his death in 1596. The Carey family were the Queen's closest blood relations, and she treated them with an intimacy which she allowed to few members of her Court.

Robert Carey wrote in his memoirs a graphic and moving account of the last three weeks of the Queen's life.[90]

> When I came to court, I found the Queen ill disposed, and she kept her inner lodging; yet she, hearing of my arrival, sent for me. I found her in one of her withdrawing chambers sitting low upon her cushions. She called me to her; I kissed her hand, and told her, it was my chiefest happiness to see her in safety and in health, which I wished might long continue. She took me by the hand, and wrung it hard; and said "No, Robin, I am not well!" and then discoursed with me of her indisposition, and that her heart had been sad and heavy for ten or twelve days; and, in her discourse, she fetched not so few as forty or fifty great sighs. I was grieved, at the first, to see her in this plight: for, in all my lifetime before, I never knew her fetch a sigh, but when the Queen of Scots was beheaded; then, upon my knowledge, she shed many tears and sighs, manifesting her innocence that she never gave consent to the death of that Queen. I used the best

words I could to persuade her from this melancholy humour; but I found by her it was too deep rooted in her heart, and hardly to be removed. This was upon a Saturday night: and she gave command that the great closet should be prepared for her to go to chapel the next morning.

The next day, all things being in a readiness, we long expected her coming; After eleven o'clock, one of the grooms came out, and bade make ready for the private closet; she would not go to the great. There we stayed long for her coming: but at last she had cushions laid for her in the privy chamber, hard by the closet door; and there she heard service. From that day forwards she grew worse and worse. She remained upon her cushions four days and nights, at the least. All about her could not persuade her, either to take any sustenance or go to bed. I, hearing that neither the physicians, nor none about her, could persuade her to take any course for her safety, feared her death would soon after ensue. I could not but think in what a wretched estate I should be left, most of my livelihood depending on her life. And hereupon I bethought myself with what grace and favour I was ever received by the King of Scots, whensoever I was sent to him. I did assure myself it was neither unjust nor unhonest for me to do for myself, if God at that time should call her to his mercy. Hereupon I wrote to the King of Scots, knowing him to be the right heir to the crown of England and certified him in what state her Majesty was. I desired him not to stir from Edinburgh: if of that sickness she should die, I would be the first man that should bring him news of it.

The Queen grew worse and worse, because she would be so: none about her being able to persuade her to go to bed. My Lord Admiral was sent for, who, by reason of my sister's death that was his wife, had absented himself some fortnight from court. What by fair means, what by force, he gat her to bed. There was no hope of her recovery, because she refused all remedies. On Wednesday, the 23rd of March, she grew speechless. That afternoon, by signs, she called for her Council: and by putting her hand to her head, when the King of Scots was named to succeed her, they all knew he was the man she desired should reign after her. About six at night, she made signs for the Archbishop, and her chaplains to come to her; at which time, I went in with them, and sat upon my knees full of tears to see that heavy sight. Her Majesty lay upon her back, with one hand in the bed and the other without. The bishop kneeled down by her, and examined her first of her faith: and she so punctually answered all his several questions by lifting up her eyes and holding up her hand, as it was a comfort to all beholders. Then the good man told her plainly, what she was and what she was to come to, and though she had been long a great Queen here upon earth, yet shortly she was to yield an accompt of her stewardship to the King of Kings. After this he began to pray, and all that were by did answer him. After he had continued long in prayer, till the old man's knees were weary, he blessed her, and meant to rise and leave her. The Queen made a sign with her hand. My sister Scroop, knowing her meaning, told the bishop, the Queen desired he would pray still. He did so for a long half-hour after, and then thought to leave her. The second time she made sign to have him continue in prayer. He did so for half an hour more, with earnest cries to God for her soul's health, which he uttered with that fervency of spirit as the Queen, to all our sight, much rejoiced thereat, and gave testimony to us all of her Christian and comfortable end. By this time, it grew late, and every one departed, all but her women that attended her. This that I heard with my ears and did see with my eyes, I thought it my duty to set down, and to affirm it for a truth upon the faith of a Christian; because I know there have been many false lies reported of the end and death of that good lady.

There is another legend, colourful but quite inaccurate, that the Queen died in the chamber above the palace gateway and that her ring was dropped from the window by Lady Scrope to her brother Robert Carey who was waiting below on his horse to carry it to King James in Scotland. The idea that the Queen would have died in the gatehouse rather than in the royal apartments is of course preposterous. For the rest of the story the best witness is Carey himself; and his account, if less romantic than the legend, is no less colourful. But he never explained how he got the ring which he showed to King James, nor precisely whose ring it was, so one cannot entirely rule out the possibility that Lady Scrope played some part in the story. Carey's narrative resumes:

I went to my lodging, and left word with one in the cofferer's chamber to call me, if that night it was thought she would die; and gave the porter an angel to let me in at any time, when I called. Between one and two of the clock on Thursday morning, he that I left in the cofferer's chamber, brought me word the Queen was dead. I rose and made all haste to the gate, to get in. There I was answered, I could not enter: the Lords of the Council having been with him and commanded him that none should go in or out, but by warrant from them. At the very instant, one of the Council, the Comptroller, asked whether I was at the gate. I said "Yes." He said, if I pleased, he would let me in. I desired to know how the Queen was. He answered, "Pretty well." I bade him good night. He replied and said, "Sir, if you will come in, I will give you my word and credit you shall go out again at your own pleasure." Upon his word, I entered the gate, and came up to the cofferer's chamber: where I found all the ladies weeping bitterly. He led me from thence to the privy chamber, where all the Council was assembled. There I was caught hold of; and assured I should not go for Scotland till their pleasures were further known. I told them I came of purpose to that end. From thence, they all went to the secretary's chamber: and, as they went, they gave a special command to the porters, that none should go out at the gates but such servants as they should send to prepare their coaches and horses for London.

There was I left, in the midst of the court, to think my own thoughts till they had done counsel. I went to my brother's chamber, who was in bed, having been overwatched many nights before. I got him up with all speed; and when the Council's men were going out of the gate, my brother thrust to the gate. The porter, knowing him to be a great officer, let him out. I pressed after him, and was stayed by the porter. My brother said angrily to the porter, "Let him out, I will answer for him!" Whereupon I was suffered to pass; which I was not a little glad of. I got to horse, and rode to the Knight Marshal's lodging by Charing Cross; and there stayed till the Lords came to Whitehall Garden. I stayed there till it was nine o'clock in the morning; and hearing that all the Lords were in the old orchard at Whitehall, I sent the Marshal to tell them that I had stayed all that while to know their pleasures; and that I would attend them, if they would command me any service. They were very glad when they heard I was not gone: and desired the Marshal to send for me; and I should, with all speed, be despatched for Scotland. The Marshal believed them; and sent Sir Arthur Savage for me. I made haste to them: One of the Council, my Lord of Banbury that now is, whispered the Marshal in the ear, and told him, if I came they would stay me and send some other in my stead. The Marshal got from them and met me coming to them, between the two gates. He bade me be gone, for he had learned, for certain, that if I came to them, they would betray me.

I returned, and took horse between nine and ten o'clock; and that night rode to Doncaster. The Friday night I came to my own house at Witherington, and presently took order with my deputies to see the Borders kept in quiet; which they had much to do: and gave order the next morning, the King of Scotland should be proclaimed King of England, and at Morpeth and

86 The funeral of Queen Elizabeth: (far left) the funeral bier; (left) Helena, Countess of Northampton, following the bier as principal mourner, escorted by Lord Buckhurst and the Lord Admiral. (British Museum)

Alnwick. Very early, on Saturday, I took horse for Edinburgh, and came to Norham about twelve at noon, so that I might well have been with the King at supper time. But I got a great fall by the way; and my horse, with one of his heels, gave me a great blow on the head, that made me shed much blood. It made me so weak, that I was forced to ride a soft pace after: so that the King was newly gone to bed by the time I knocked at the gate. I was quickly let in; and carried up to the King's Chamber. I kneeled by him, and saluted him by his title of "England, Scotland, France and Ireland." He gave me his hand to kiss, and bade me welcome. After he had long discoursed of the manner of the Queen's sickness, and of her death, he asked what letters I had from the Council. I told him, none: and acquainted him how narrowly I escaped from them. And yet I brought him a blue ring from a fair lady, that I hoped would give him assurance of the truth that I had reported. He took it, and looked upon it, and said, "It is enough. I know by this you are a true messenger." Then he committed me to the charge of my Lord Hume, and gave straight command that I should want nothing. He sent for his chirurgeons to attend me; and when I kissed his hand, at my departure, he said to me these gracious words: "I know you have lost a near kinswoman and a loving mistress: but take here my hand, I will be as good a master to you, and will requite you this service with honour and reward." So I left him that night, and went with my Lord Hume to my lodging: where I had all things fitting for so weary a man as I was. After my head was dressed, I took leave of my Lord and many others that attended me, and went to my rest.

The French ambassador wrote to his colleague in Madrid that 'the King of Scotland was at once proclaimed in the court at Richmond and the same day was proclaimed in the city by the King-at-Arms on horseback surrounded by all the Lords of the Council, the Archbishops, the Bishops, earls, barons and knights to the number of three hundred'.[91]

While King James hastened south to claim his new kingdom, the late great Queen was buried on 28 April with great ceremony in her grandfather's chapel in Westminster Abbey. Her last progress was by river from Richmond to Whitehall, where she lay in state for a month, before the funeral procession bore her to the Abbey. The sight of her effigy lying above the coffin moved the Londoners to tears and lamentation. Behind the funeral bier walked sixteen hundred mourners led by Helena Marchioness of Northampton escorted by the Lord Admiral on one side and by Lord Buckhurst, the Lord Treasurer, on the other.

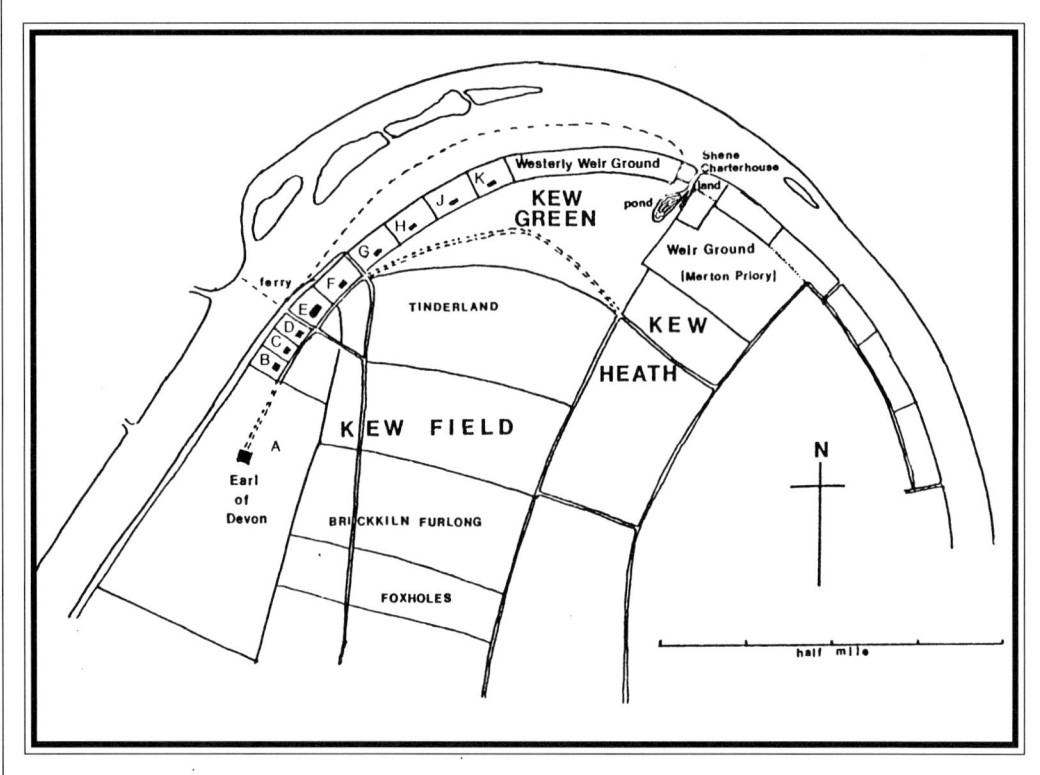

87 *Kew, c.1500*

Chapter XI

Princesses and Potentates at Kew

The tiny hamlet of Kew, from the early 16th century onwards, became the home of a series of extremely important people. It was not until the late 18th century that Kew could actually boast a royal palace, but in the 16th and early 17th centuries it was the home of princesses of the royal blood and some of the most powerful nobles in the land.

It is not easy to disentangle the story of the houses of these early residents, and to identify their sites. However, there is a guiding principle which does help a little: the clear distinction to be drawn between property which was either freehold or held on direct grant from the Crown and property which was 'copyhold' – that is to say held from the lord of the manor by a title deed which was itself a copy of an entry in the manorial rolls. Save in exceptional circumstances, such as a forfeiture due to neglect or the grant of a licence for a long-term lease, the manorial rolls were not concerned with freehold property, references to which will be found in separate deeds and state papers.

At the end of the 15th century, the map of Kew was roughly as shown in Figure 87.[1] The ferry to Brentford, which was the main reason for the development of this hamlet, crossed the river a little to the north of the site of the ancient ford. Kew Green, much larger than it is today, had a long narrow 'panhandle' stretching down almost to the ferry. From the ferry and the end of the Green two paths converged into one which then led southwards to Shene. Another path ran southwards from the ferry by the river-bank. In the north the river-bank was bordered by the manorial meadows. East of the Green were closes belonging to Merton Priory and Shene Charterhouse, and south of these lay Kew Heath across which ran the lane to Mortlake. From the south-east corner of the Green another track ran southwards to Shene, beside the Kew Field.

Kew Field was small – about ninety acres – and the holdings in it were mainly those of five copyhold tenants whose cottages lay between the western end of the Green and the river. Even so, the Field was then larger than it was later to be, for it then included the West Dene, on the western side of the lane from the ferry to Shene, and the whole of the northern furlong known as Tinderland. There were three main furlongs or 'shotts', in which the land was divided into narrow north-south strips; in the much smaller section called 'Foxholes' were some half-dozen shorter, broader holdings. To the west of the Field, between it and the river, lay a large parcel of freehold land; and a small group of freehold cottages and houses stood near the ferry.

The freehold houses (B, C, D and E on the plan) were in the hands of Thomas Byrkes. The ownership of the copyhold cottage (F) is uncertain, but it may have belonged to Richard Blacket. The other copyhold cottages belonged to Robert Lydgold (G), Robert Makyn (H), Thomas

Byrkes (J) and Stephen at Were (K). The Lydgold, Makyn and at Were ('at the weir') families can all be traced back in the manorial records to the mid-14th century.

The origin of the large plot of freehold land (A) may lie in the marriage dowries of the 12th and 13th century heiresses mentioned in Chapter 1, or it may have remained demesne land until a much later date. But by the end of the 15th century it had come into the hands of the Courtenay Earls of Devon. On it a mansion had been built. An account dated 1535 refers to the estate as 'lands descended to Edward late Earl of Devon from his father Hugh Courtenay once Earl of Devon'.[2] If this is correct it must refer to Edward who was created Earl of Devonshire in 1485 by Henry VII, and his father Sir Hugh Courtenay, who does not however appear to have borne the title of Earl. (The title had descended in the 15th century in another branch of the Courtenay family which died out in 1471. Sir Hugh was the nearest heir, so he might have been considered to be the titular Earl.)

In 1495 Earl Edward's son William, Lord Courtenay, married Edward IV's daughter Katherine, sister of Henry VII's Queen Elizabeth of York. She thus became the first of the many princesses to have a home at Kew. As long as Queen Elizabeth lived her sister and William Courtenay were in high favour. But after the Queen's death in 1503 Henry VII began to fear the possibilities of intrigue. In 1504 William Courtenay was imprisoned and attainted.

An automatic consequence of attainder was the forfeit of goods and estates to the Crown. So 'Devonshire House' (as we may call it for convenience) was available for official use. Archbishop Warham, the Chancellor, may have used it for a while; a document is endorsed as having been delivered to him 'at Kiow' on 6 August 1506.[3]

It was probably in this house that the young widow Catherine of Aragon and her sister-in-law, the 10-year-old Princess Mary, were staying in February 1508/9 when the dying King Henry VII summoned them to visit him at Richmond. The episode is related in a long letter from the Spanish ambassador to King Ferdinand.[4] Poor Catherine, left a widow in 1502, betrothed to her late husband's brother Henry in 1503 – but still not married by him – had led a miserable life in England for the last six years. She had fallen under the baneful influence of her confessor, a young Spanish friar, Diego Fernandez. On the day in question, just as she and Princess Mary were ready to set out for Richmond, the friar openly forbade Catherine to go that day. She had been ill the night before, but protested that she now felt perfectly well and able to travel to Richmond as the King had commanded. The friar persisted, telling her that she would commit mortal sin if she disobeyed her confessor. She gave way; and sent word by Mary, waiting impatiently outside with the attendants that were to accompany them, that she was ill. Mary went alone, and the King, hearing the whole story from her, was 'very much vexed'. When Catherine appeared at Richmond the following day, the King would not receive her; and, said the Spanish ambassador inveighing against the friar's influence, 'it is now more than twenty days since the King has seen the Princess'. The ambassador had set the scene by saying that the two princesses were 'staying in a lonely house which is in a park' and that the distance from Richmond Palace 'was at the utmost less than a league'. This must refer to Kew – and 'Devonshire house' was the only one at Kew at that time with grounds sufficient to be called a park.

The King died at Richmond Palace a month later, and two months after his death Catherine was finally married to her betrothed, the new King, Henry VIII.

88 *The Grandees of Kew and Sheen.*

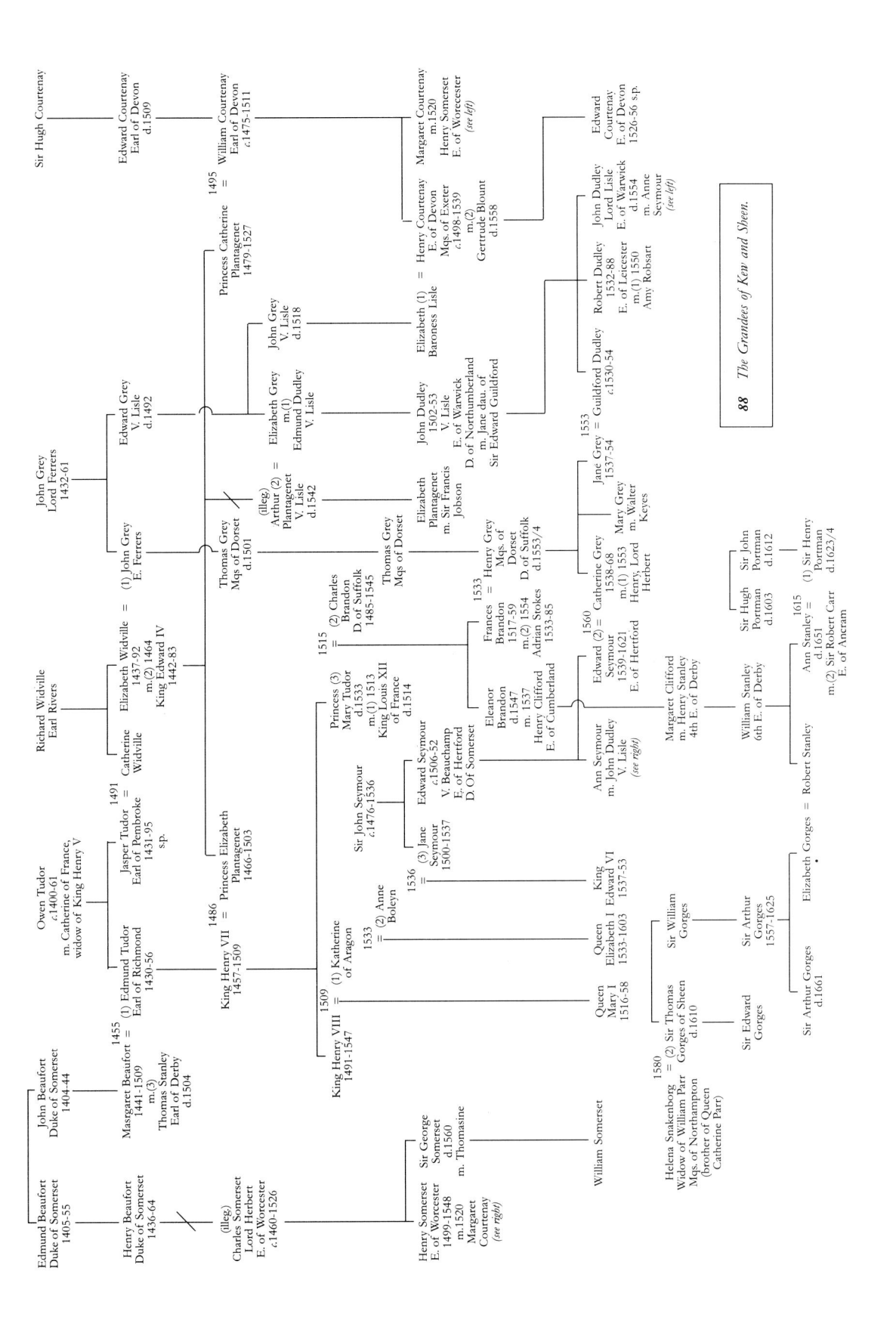

By this time another grandee had made his appearance at Kew. Sir Charles Somerset was a contemporary by age, a kinsman and a close associate of Henry VII. An illegitimate son of Henry Beaufort, 3rd Duke of Somerset, he had Plantagenet blood. His father and King Henry were first cousins, but his bastardy meant that he presented no threat to the throne. In the year after his accession Henry VII made Somerset the Captain of his bodyguard, and bestowed estates on him. He rose in favour; he became an Admiral, a Knight of the Garter, Vice-Chamberlain of the Household, an Ambassador; his estates were enlarged by more royal grants. In 1504 he became Baron Herbert in right of his wife, and two years later he was given the title in his own right.

In 1505 Somerset purchased from Thomas Byrkes of Kew the copyhold house with a 19-acre virgate of land in the field and one acre of meadow 'lying behind the house' (J on the plan).[5] From Richard Blacket he acquired at the same time another 'two acres of land in Keyhowe and a parcel of land in Keyhowe Field containing three roods'.[6] (The implication is that the two acres were not in the Field, but as they were copyhold, they were probably an extra holding of meadow adjacent to the 'acre behind the house'.) This property remained copyhold, and can be traced as such in the subsequent manorial records.

Just before Henry VII's death Somerset (or Lord Herbert as he then was) became Chamberlain of the King's Household. He was confirmed in this appointment by Henry VIII, who in 1513/4 created him Earl of Worcester. Then in 1517 he was granted by the King another house and 19-acre virgate at Kew with an acre of meadow behind the house.[7] It is possible that Worcester was already in occupation of this holding, and the description is identical with that of the land purchased from Byrkes, but the terms of the grant state clearly that the holding, which had previously been copyhold of the manor of Richmond (F), was henceforth to be held by Worcester in socage (i.e. as a freehold). With this grant went an additional 3¾ acres of land in the Kew Field – also to be held as freehold.

Worcester died in 1526. In his will he left his estates in Kew to his wife, with remainder to his youngest son George.[8] Sir George Somerset acquired some more land in Kew, buying the copyhold holding (G) from Thomas Staynford, grandson of Robert Lydgold. This had, apart from the cottage, a full 20-acre virgate with an acre of meadow and also an island in the river. This purchase may have enabled Somerset to consolidate a holding of 19 acres, all contiguous, at the western end of the northern furlong, Tinderland, in the Kew Field. He made it into a small park and built a lodge in it – probably the first house to be built on the south side of the Green. He then appears to have sold off the house (J) on the north side of the Green, together with the land immediately adjacent to it. These transactions have to be deduced from later entries in the manor rolls, as those from 1521-7 inclusive are missing.

The principal Somerset house at Kew however remained the freehold one (F). Here the Earl of Worcester had built a new mansion. Leland, the antiquarian, describes it as 'a new house built by the Lord Chamberlain or Lord High Steward in the reign of Henry VII'.[9]

In 1514 Worcester had been employed, as proxy for Princess Mary, Henry VIII's sister, to complete the negotiations for the contract for her marriage to the elderly King Louis XII of France. Mary was only 18, and was in love with Charles Brandon, Duke of Suffolk, who had recently been widowed for the second time. She had been induced to agree to the dynastic marriage with the promise that, if she survived her royal husband, she should be free to remarry at her own choice. Within a few months of the marriage and of her coronation as Queen of France, King Louis died. Charles Brandon, having promised the King not to pursue his suit with Mary, was sent as ambassador to congratulate King Francis I on his accession. Mary, who was fighting off the advances of Francis himself and others, induced Brandon to break his promise and to marry her at once in France. Henry VIII was furious, but when his wrath had abated – and been bought off – the Suffolks were able to return to England. A few years later they rented Worcester's new house at Kew. They resided there from time to time in the 1520s, but in 1533 Mary died and Suffolk married yet again.

In 1538 Suffolk decided to buy the house. Sir George Somerset, who lived at Bedmundsfield in Suffolk, was perhaps reluctant to sell. At all events, Thomas Cromwell was brought into the act. He wrote to Somerset, asking him to sell the house. Somerset did not have the influence at court which his father had enjoyed; he complied, hoping to get his reward later (in 1540 he reminded Cromwell of this obligation).[10] On 7 June 1538 Cromwell purchased the house from Somerset for £200,[11] and six days later he sold it for the same sum to Suffolk, who was charged an extra £10 'for the costs of th'assurance in the law'.[12]

At the same time Somerset sold the copyhold house (G) to a John Becke, who obtained a mortgage from a rich London merchant and alderman, Augustine Hynde.[13] In the summer of 1539 Becke and Hynde sold this property to the Duke of Suffolk,[14] and Hynde, who had also

89 Wedding portrait of Mary Tudor, Dowager Queen of France, and Charles Brandon, Duke of Suffolk, 1515.

acquired from Becke the former Makyn tenement (H) and a further five acres in the Kew Field, sold these to Suffolk as well.[15] Suffolk had thus become the principal landowner in Kew; but he was neighboured by the small park with the lodge which Sir George Somerset retained, by the freehold Devon lands, and by another large freehold house which has not yet been considered.

✠

This freehold house (E) had been Thomas Byrkes's own mansion. Of its history before his ownership nothing has yet been traced. It may have been a house attached to one of the original freeholds within the manor, or it may have been built on land sold by the Earls of Devon. One way or the other, the house and its owner were of sufficient importance to have Kew's first chapel as part of the premises. In 1522 Richard Fox, the Bishop of Winchester, within whose diocese Richmond and Kew lay, granted 'at the request of Thomas Byrkis Esquire a licence for Divine Service and Eucharist in a chapel erected in the hamlet of Kew, during the lives of the said Thomas Byrkis and his wife Ann'.[16]

Byrkes did not live much longer. His will, made in January 1522/3, was proved on 9 March 1525/6. In it he left his 'house in Keyo' and all lands to his wife Ann, with remainder to his son Anthony.[17] As mentioned above, Byrkes had owned other houses or cottages in Kew, all freehold, which may be presumed to have been on adjacent property (B, C and D). One of these was sold, together with a half-acre in Kew Field, by Ann Byrkes to Henry Courtenay, Earl of Devon (and now Marquess of Exeter) in 1528.[18] In 1533/4, Ann having died, Anthony Byrkes sold the remaining property. Two houses and six acres of pasture in Kew, together with properties in Drayton and Harlington in Middlesex were sold to a Robert Hammond;[19] the main house (E) with barn, stable, garden and orchard was purchased for 200 marks by Henry Norris, 'Esquire to the Body' to the King, one of Henry VIII's closest courtiers.[20]

That closeness proved his undoing. Two years later he was one of those accused of adultery with the Queen, Anne Boleyn. He was found guilty and executed on 14 May 1536. The Queen was beheaded on 19 May and on the following day Henry VIII married her successor, Jane Seymour. Almost as expeditiously Norris's house at Kew, escheated to the Crown on his attainder, was now granted to the new Queen's brother, Sir Edward Seymour, and his wife. The grant was confirmed by statute on 8 June, by which date Seymour had already been advanced to the title of Viscount Beauchamp.[21]

It may have been this house in which Princess Mary, eldest daughter of Henry VIII, stayed later that year. Virtually a prisoner and in disgrace since her mother's divorce, Mary had made her peace with her father after the death of Anne

90   Sir Edward Seymour, brother of Queen Jane, who became Viscount Beauchamp, then Earl of Hertford, and eventually Duke of Somerset. (Hulton-Deutsch Collection)

Boleyn. On 8 December 1536 she was allowed to visit the King at Richmond. 'My daughter,' he is alleged to have said, 'she who did you so much harm and prevented me from seeing you for so long, has paid the penalty.'[22] After a few days the King moved from Richmond Palace, and Mary was sent to Kew, and thence to Greenwich.[23] She was back again at Kew in the following spring, when her cook was accused of having been involved in a robbery.[24]

Although we have no firm evidence which house at Kew was at this time being used briefly as a sort of annexe to Richmond Palace, it seems quite probable that it was the one just granted to Lord Beauchamp, for he was evidently not desirous of keeping the house. He wanted to exchange it for one in the Strand, between London and Westminster, that was owned by the Bishop of Chichester, Lord President of the Council of the Marches of Wales. Cromwell was again brought in to negotiate. He wrote to the bishop, evidently suggesting that the exchange was the King's wish. Nothing daunted, the bishop wrote directly to the King on 2 April 1537, pointing out that he had no other house in London to use when in attendance on the King and that if he were to take 'the house at Cewe foranempst Braynford, at that distance it should be tedious for me to seek my lodging'.[25] A friend of the bishop's wrote to Cromwell, saying that the Lord President was 'very sad and in heaviness' at this request, and begging Cromwell to remind the

King of the bishop's faithful services.[26] The bishop was allowed to keep his house.

In the following year, however, Cromwell was able to arrange a deal on behalf of Beauchamp, who had meanwhile become Earl of Hertford. Cromwell himself purchased the house, with garden and eight acres of land and 12d. in rents, from Hertford for £80,[27] and sold it to one William Byrche (who seems to have paid only £50). Byrche was either acting on behalf of Sir John Dudley or had already arranged to let the house to him. In April 1538 Dudley and his wife, and his half-sister Elizabeth Plantagenet, moved into the house at Kew.[28] (Cromwell's accounts show the receipt of Byrche's £50 'for the house at Queo' only on 1 July.)[29] Four years later, in 1542, John Dudley, who had been made Viscount Lisle after the death of his Plantagenet stepfather who had borne that title, purchased the house from Byrche for £80.[30]

The fact that the house in 1538 had eight acres of land attached to it suggests that the other two houses sold by Anthony Byrkes to Robert Hamond, with six acres attached, had by then returned into the same ownership – although no document confirming this has been traced. Indeed, there seems to be no other way of accounting for the fate of these two houses.

91 Princess Mary (later Queen Mary I). Painting by Master John, 1544. (National Portrait Gallery)

In the mid-1540s came a series of rapid changes of ownership. Viscount Lisle sold the house to Sir William Paget in October 1545.[31] A letter which he sent to Paget on 22 September confirms that this is indeed the same house that was granted to Seymour – and shows that the problems of conveyancing and title searches are nothing new!

> I send the indenture of purchase of Kyeo with the King's licence of alienation and an obligation of 500 marks to me by Byrche. The rest of the Conveyance as the fine and other assurances shall be looked up and sent but these are sufficient to devise your assurances upon. The conveyance between the Earl of Hertforde and the late Lord Cromwell I have found, also the conveyance from Lord Cromwell to Byrche and the gift of the house from the King to the Earl of Hertforde and his wife.[32]

Hardly had Paget acquired the property than he obtained a licence to resell it to John Machell of London, a cloth-worker.[33] The sale was not completed however until January 1547/8.[34] In May 1549 Machell obtained a further licence to sell it to Sir Miles Partridge.[35] In all these documents the description remains the same '– a messuage, garden, 8 acres of land and 12d of rents in Kayo'. Miles Partridge was a notorious gambler. He was a follower of Seymour, Duke of Somerset and Lord Protector from the time of his nephew's accession as Edward VI in 1547. He had fought

92 Robert Dudley, Earl of Leicester. Miniature by Nicholas Hilliard. (National Portrait Gallery)

under John Dudley's command at the battle of Pinkie in Scotland in 1547 and had been knighted for his services.

In the meantime John Dudley had risen to become the one power in the land that could challenge Somerset's ascendancy. In 1549 he overthrew Somerset and took over power himself. In 1551 he was made Duke of Northumberland. Toward the end of the year he accused Somerset, who had been restored to the Council, but not to power, of plotting against his life. Sir Miles Partridge was implicated (probably quite untruthfully). Somerset was executed in January 1551/2 and Partridge was hanged a month later. Again the house at Kew escheated to the Crown. It was regranted in April 1552 to Sir Henry Gates.[36]

The grant to Gates is of interest because it gives much more information about the house and lands than any of the previous documents (and incidentally confirms that it was the house to which the chapel had been attached). The property is described as follows:

A capital messuage in Kew, and two gardens, and an orchard, a barn and a stable (lately a chapel). And a messuage called the Dayre [dairy] House, adjoining the capital messuage. And 1 acre of land on the south side of the Dayre House, and 4 acres of land in Allen's Close, and 3 acres and one rood of land in the common field called the Deane. At a yearly value of £4 9s 8d.

There is also an inventory of all Partridge's silver and household goods that were seized in the house at the time of his arrest.

Gates was a loyal supporter of Northumberland. His brother John had been appointed keeper of Syon Monastery after the Dissolution, and had become Captain of the Guard and then Chancellor of the Duchy of Lancaster when Northumberland took power. On the death of Edward VI, Northumberland made his ill-fated attempt to put Lady Jane Grey on the throne in place of Princess Mary. The two Gates brothers were implicated in the conspiracy, attainted and sentenced to death. Sir John Gates was executed in August 1553, but Sir Henry was reprieved, and was pardoned in November 1553.[37] His forfeited goods and chattels were returned, but his lands remained confiscated, so once more the house at Kew was escheated.

A new grant was not made until after Queen Elizabeth's accession. On 29 December 1558 Sir Robert Dudley, Lord Dudley, Queen Elizabeth's favourite, was granted, among other estates, the 'capital messuage and lands in Kewe of yearly value £4 9s. 8d.'.[38]

✠

Together with the lands forfeited by Partridge and then by Gates, the grant made to Dudley in December 1558 included the Devonshire lands at Kew, which had returned to the Courtenays.

On Henry VIII's accession, William Courtenay had been released from prison, and in 1511 he was allowed to inherit the earldom, his father having died two years before. Proceedings to restore his full rights were not completed when he himself died in June 1511, but were carried forward in favour of his son Henry who not only succeeded to the earldom but had a full restoration in blood in 1512. He remained in favour at court for the next twenty-five years, and was made Marquess of Exeter in 1525. As his power and possessions grew he became more independently-minded, and developed an antagonistic relationship with Cromwell.

Cromwell began to intrigue against the haughty Marquess and was helped to do so by the behaviour of the Marchioness, Gertrude, who was a devout Roman Catholic and a close friend of Catherine of Aragon. The Marchioness had been godmother to Princess Elizabeth and had carried Prince Edward to his baptism, but she had continued to correspond with Catherine after the divorce and she had come under the influence of Elizabeth Barton, the 'Nun of Kent', who had claimed the authority of divine visions for her outright denunciations of the royal divorce and of the breach with Rome.[39] Finally in 1538 Cromwell reckoned he had enough evidence, real or spurious, to justify a charge of treason against the Marquess. Courtenay and his wife were imprisoned, he was quickly tried and convicted and on 9 December 1538 he was executed. He was of course attainted, as were his wife and son, who were kept in prison. Again the Kew lands, with other property, were escheated. The Marchioness was pardoned and released not long after, but the son Edward Courtenay, the heir, was held in prison until Queen Mary's accession. Then the attainder on both was removed, and Edward was re-created Earl of Devonshire. The house and lands at Kew were formally regranted to him.[40] He was egged on by Bishop Gardiner to expect the Queen's hand in marriage, but when these hopes were dashed by Mary's marriage to Philip of Spain, the further possibility of a match with Princess Elizabeth and of placing her on the throne in Mary's stead led to his involvement in Wyatt's rebellion of 1554. He was imprisoned, then released on parole and exiled. He died in Padua, unmarried and without heirs, in 1556.

The old Marchioness of Exeter outlived her son by two years. Whether she continued to use the house at Kew is uncertain. In 1554 the Duchess of Somerset was asked by the Privy Council to move temporarily from Syon 'to the house of the Earl of Denshire at Kew' in order to leave Syon for the ambassadors while the Queen was in residence at Richmond,[41] which suggests that the house was then empty. But in 1555 the Marchioness wrote to her son, then in Brussels, about 'an examination of the household stuff at Kew and in London, with the inventories he had left',[42] which suggests that, if unoccupied, the house was certainly not aban-

93 Thomas Cromwell, 1st Earl of Essex, 1485?-1540. Painting after Hans Holbein. (National Portrait Gallery)

doned. And it was not until after the death of the Marchioness in September 1558 that a grant was made of 'the lands which reverted to the Crown on the death without heirs of Edward Courtenay Earl of Devon'. The recipient was Robert Dudley.[43]

The only clue to the extent of the Devonshire property in Kew lies in the account of 1535 already mentioned and in an accounting of 1539 of the lands which had been escheated from Henry former Marquess of Exeter on his attainder 'which he owned by right of inheritance'.[44] In both the annual value of Kew is given as 26s. 8d. If we compare this with the value placed on the Charterhouse lands at the same period (3s. 4d. an acre for meadow, 12d. an acre for the gardens and pastures within the walls, 8d. an acre for arable land and other pasture) we have a figure which, disregarding the house, could be as much as forty acres at 8d. an acre. The area shown in the plan at Fig. A is about thirty-four acres, which would allow a 4s. valuation for the house.

94 Edward Courtenay, Earl of Devon. (British Museum)

Dudley now held all the free land west of the lane from Richmond to the ferry except for that which belonged to the house now known as Suffolk Place. Charles Brandon, Duke of Suffolk, died in 1545. He had left his property in Kew to his wife for the rest of her life:

> I will that my saied wief shall also have it my gifte by thes presenties my house of Keyhu in the countie of Surrey and all my houses landes tenements and hereditamentes in Keyhu aforesaid for the term of her lyfe.[45]

Brandon's widow was his fourth wife, Katherine, in her own right Baroness Willoughby d'Eresby. She lived until 1580, but in 1552 she married Richard Bertie, ancestor of the Dukes of Ancaster and Earls of Lindsey. What then happened to the house at Kew is uncertain. A docquet for a grant of 'the house at Kew, Surrey' to Mr. Kempe of the Privy Council, dated 29 October 1558,[46] may refer to this house as it is a grant in freehold, and all the other freehold property in Kew was about to go to Dudley. According to Folkestone Williams, Suffolk's former house was occupied for a time by 'Wolsey's gentleman-usher (after he had been Treasurer of the Chamber to Edward VI and Queen Mary) who commenced Chatsworth …'.[47] This reference (which gives no source) confuses the two Cavendish brothers: William, who was the Treasurer and ancestor of the Cavendish Dukes of Devonshire, and George, who was Wolsey's gentleman-usher and biographer. But George Cavendish married a Margery Kemp, so perhaps there is a link there. On the other hand the grant to Mr. Kempe may have been abortive and replaced by the grant to Dudley.

What is certain is that by 1564 Suffolk Place was owned by Lord Mordaunt. John, the first Lord Mordaunt, a courtier of the reign of Henry VIII, died at the age of 72 in 1562. He was

VI *The young Queen Elizabeth, by an unknown artist.*
(National Portrait Gallery, London)

VII *Robert Dudley, Earl of Leicester, by an unknown artist.*
(National Portrait Gallery, London)

VIII *A dance at Queen Elizabeth's Court, detail from a painting by an unknown artist. (Penshurst Place)*

IX *Queen Elizabeth in procession, 1600. Detail from a painting attributed to Robert Peake the Elder. (Private Collection)*

95 Charles Brandon, Duke of Suffolk, towards the end of his life. Painting by an unknown artist. (National Portrait Gallery)

96 Katherine, Baroness Willoughby d'Eresby, the fourth wife of Charles Brandon, who inherited his house at Kew. Drawing by Hans Holbein. (The Royal Collection © Her Majesty the Queen)

succeeded by his eldest son John, who died in 1570. Suffolk Place had been neglected – perhaps even demolished – by the Mordaunts. In April 1564 the Manor Court of Richmond declared that 'the former messuage called Suffolk Place in Keyo in the hands of Lord Mordaunt is devastated and destroyed by the said Mordaunt, and is seized into the hands of the Lord'.[48] There is no trace of any subsequent grant or other disposal of the site, and one can only assume that it was given, with the freehold land which belonged to it, to Dudley or one of his successors in title of the adjoining properties. 'Devonshire House' must be assumed to have been demolished by Dudley, for there remained only one large house on the estate, which now got the name of Kew Farm.

The copyhold lands in the fields which Suffolk bought from Augustine Hynde, and the cottages pertaining to them, appear to have been restored to Hynde, who perhaps held a mortgage on them. There is no record of this transaction, so it must be assumed to have taken place early in Queen Mary's reign (for which the manor rolls are missing). There was however one exception. Some 7½ acres in Tinderland, part of the former Lydgold holding, appear to have been inherited by Suffolk's daughter Eleanor and her husband Henry Clifford, Earl of Cumberland. (The Manor Court roll for 25 April 1551 lists among the 'defaulters' who did not attend the Court 'the Earl of Westmorland in right of his wife'.[49] No property in Richmond or Kew appears to have belonged to the Earl of Westmorland or any of his three wives; but Henry Clifford had the title of *Baron* Westmorland, by which he would have been known before succeeding to the earldom in 1542, so this reference is probably to him.) This land then appears to have passed to the

Cumberlands' daughter Margaret, who married Henry Stanley, Lord Strange, later 4th Earl of Derby. Though Lord Strange's title to this land was contested by Lydgold heirs in the 1560s,[50] it was still in the hands of the 6th Earl of Derby in 1603. By then a cottage had been built adjacent to part of the land, on the south side of the Green – probably on a grant of land from the Green made in the last 15 years of Elizabeth's reign.

✠

When Augustine Hynde died in 1554 he left all his copyhold land in Kew and in 'Shene als Richmond' to his youngest son John Hynde.[51] It became the subject of a number of legal suits in the 1560s, but John Hynde was successful in retaining the property.[52] By the end of Queen Elizabeth's reign it had come into the possession of Sir Hugh Portman (but the loss of the manor rolls from 1589 to 1602 makes it impossible to trace the precise descent of the title).

Augustine Hynde also had a freehold estate at Kew. This was land that had belonged to Merton Priory. After the monastery's dissolution the Merton lands at Kew, described as 'a meadow called Keyomede and 16 acres of pasture', had been granted (together with land at Hartington and in the Richmond fields) to Ralph Annesley for life in 1539.[53] In 1544 a reversionary grant, to take effect from Annesley's death, was made to Richard Taverner,[54] and two years later Taverner sold the Kew and Richmond lands to Augustine Hynde.[55] Hynde left these freehold lands to his eldest son Rowland,[56] who sold them in 1594 to Hugh Portman.[57] The meadow was in three separate fields by the riverside, divided by manorial common meadows; the '16 acres of pasture', later known as the Ware (weir) Ground, lay directly behind two of these meadows, on the north side of Kew Heath.

Portman also acquired the Dudley estate at Kew. Dudley had sold this to Thomas Gardiner, a London goldsmith who was also a teller of the Exchequer. Gardiner lived in the house for a while,[58] then in April 1564 he granted a six-year lease to Richard Putto of Highgate. Within weeks Putto had assigned the lease to John Parkyns and two days later the latter reassigned it to two gentlemen from Essex. In the deed recording this last transaction we have a new description of the property:

> The lease of a messuage called Kewe Farm, with appurtenances of six closes of pasture, three lying together near the highway from Kewe to Richmond and the rest near certain closes called Richmond Fields; and of certain acres of arable in the common fields of Kewe and Richmond, late in the occupation of one Clayton and after in the occupation of one Chambers, which lease he had by assignment of the said Richard Putto on 16 June at £6.13.4 per annum.[59]

Gardiner, however, got into debt with the Crown. He was found to be £24,000 in arrears in his Exchequer accounts, and in September 1575 he surrendered the Kew property.[60] It was regranted to Thomas Handforde and Kenard Delaber as sureties for him.[61] They must then have sold the property – probably to Thomas Sackville, Lord Buckhurst.

Lord Buckhurst, the future Earl of Dorset and builder of Knole, had made his first recorded appearance as a householder in the area as tenant with his mother of the house on the monastery site at Shene, from which he was abruptly evicted in 1568.[62] The date of his acquisition of the house at Kew has not yet been traced, but it may have been about the same time as his purchase of some copyhold land in the Richmond fields in 1578.[63] In 1582 he sold this land to Anthony Mason, alias Wickes,[64] and in 1592 he sold the Kew property to Mason. It was described as '3 messuages, 3 cottages, 3 tofts, 1 dovecote, 2 gardens, 2 orchards, 6 acres of land and 6 closes of pasture'.[65]

Mason was the nephew of Sir John Mason, an important servant of the Crown in the later years of Henry VIII's reign and in those of Edward VI and Mary. Ambassador, Clerk of the Parliament, Member of Parliament, Treasurer of the Chamber, Chancellor of Oxford University, he had built up a large estate. Being childless he adopted as his heir his sister's son Anthony Wickes, who then took the name of Mason. Sir John died in 1566. Anthony, who himself became Clerk of Parliament in 1574, did not hold on to Kew Farm for long. A Chancery suit dated 12 June 1600 records that he had sold the property to Sir Hugh Portman 'for a very great sum of money about eight years ago'.[66]

Portman was married to a daughter of John Puckering, Speaker of the House of Commons. Puckering was probably already leasing Kew Farm from Buckhurst, for he entertained Queen Elizabeth 'at his house in Kew' on 11 December 1591. The following April Puckering was knighted and made Keeper of the Great Seal. The recipe for success was obvious, if expensive. He entertained the Queen at Kew again on 14 August 1594 and on 13 December 1595.

A memorandum apparently written by Puckering's steward shows the careful preparation that helped to ensure the success of these visits:

Remembrances for furnyture at Kew, and for her majestie's entertainment, 14 Aug. 1594.

A memorial of things to be considered of, if her majestie should come to my lord's house.
1. The maner of receyvynge bothe without the house and within, as well by my lord as my ladye.
2. What present shall be given by my lord, when and by whome it shall be presented, and whether any more than one.
3. The like for my ladye.
4. What presents my lord shall bestowe of the ladyes of the privye chamber or bedchamber, the grooms of the privye chamber, and gentlemen ushers and other officers, clerks of the kitchen or otherwise.
5. What rewards shall be given to the footemen, gardes, and other officers.
6. The purveyed diet for the queen, wherein are to be used her own cooks, and other officers for that purpose.
7. The diet for the lords and ladies, and some fit place for that purpose specially appoynted.
8. The allowance for diet for the footemen and gardes.
9. The appoyntment of my lords officers, to attend on their several offices, with sufficient assistants unto them for that time.
10. The orderinge of all my lords servants for their waiting, both gentlemen and yeomen, and how they shall be sorted to their several offices and places.
11. The proporcyon of the dietd fitted to eche place of service; plate, linen, and silver vessels.
12. To furnish how there will be, upon a soddeyne, provision of all things for that dietd made and of the best kinds, and what several persons shall undertake it.
13. As it must be for metes, so in like sorte for bread, ale, and wines of all sortes.
14. The lyke for bankettynge stuffs.
15. The swetynynge of the howse in all places by any means.
16. Grete care to be had, and conference with the gentlemen ushers, how her majestie would be lodged for best ease and likinge, far from heate or noyse of any office near her lodgyng, and how her bedchamber maye be kept free from anye noyse near it.
17. My lords attendance at her departure from his howse and his companye.
Ladies diet for bedchamber.
Ladies some lodged besydes ordinarie.
Lord Chamberlayne, in the howse.
Lord of Essex nere, and all his plate from me, and dyett for his servants at his lodgyngs.[67]

Of the visit in 1595, when Hugh Portman, now owner of his father-in-law's house, was himself knighted, we have a graphic firsthand account. It shows how much Puckering must have invested in this entertainment of his sovereign. Rowland White, writing to Sir Robert Sydney on 13 December 1595, relates:

> On Thursday her Majestie dined at Kew, my lord keaper's howse (who lately obtained of her Majestie his sute for 100 £ a yeare land, in fee-farm). Her interteinment for that meale was great and exceedingly costly; at her first lighting, she had a fine fanne with a handle garnisht with diamonds. When she was in the middle way, between the garden-gate and the howse, there came running towards her, one with a nosegay in his hand, delivered yt unto her with a short well pened speach; it had in yt a very rich jewell, with many pendants of unfirld diamonds, valewed at 400 £ at least; after dinner, in her privy chamber, he gave her a faire paire of virginals. In her bed-chamber he presented her with a fine gown and juppin, which things were pleasing to her highnes; and to grace his lordship the more, she, of herself, tooke from him a salt, a spoone, and a forke of faire agate.[68]

Sir John Puckering died at the house at Kew on 30 April 1596, and was buried in Westminster Abbey. Portman may have used the house for a while, but in June 1603 he obtained a licence at the Manor Court to let for 21 years to George Hudson, gent, 'one messuage with stable and garden adjoining, late in the occupation of William Bene … in Kew … commonly called the Farm House or Place'.[69]

✠

We must now revert to the other copyhold properties. Sir George Somerset and then his widow Thomasine retained the Park in the north-west corner of Kew Field until the latter's death in 1560, when it was inherited by their youngest son William.[70] (It was the custom of the manor of Richmond that the youngest son should inherit copyhold property – an ancient system known as 'Borough English'.) In 1566 William Somerset sold the Park and the lodge therein to William Awberry, a Doctor of Laws.[71]

The house on the opposite side of the Green (J), which had originally been part of the same property, with its acre of meadow in the rear and the extra two acres purchased from Richard Blacket, had passed through the hands of one Thomas Barnes and then of two successive Hugh Popes (father and son).[72] In May 1574 William Awberry bought it from Hugh Pope the younger, thus reuniting the properties.[73] It was quite possibly a more imposing house than the lodge in the Park; it is referred to as 'a capital mansion house'.

William Aubrey or Awberry (in the Richmond records he is always spelled in the latter way), while not such a great potentate as some

97   The tomb of Sir John Puckering and his wife in St Paul's Chapel, Westminster Abbey. (Dean & Chapter of Westminster)

of the other 16th-century residents of Kew, was a person of importance and considerable influence in Queen Elizabeth's reign. Born in Brecknockshire in Wales in 1529, he was educated in the law at Oxford, where he became the Principal of New Inn Hall in 1550 and Professor of Civil Law in 1553 at the age of 24, before he had even acquired his doctorate (1554). He then became an advocate in the Court of Arches, and was auditor and vicar-general of the province of Canterbury under Archbishop Grindal and Chancellor to Archbishop Whitgift. He subsequently became Master in Chancery and Master of Requests in Ordinary, in which capacity he was involved in some of the dynastic cases concerning the legitimacy of the Seymour and Grey heirs. He was a member of the Council of Marches for Wales, and a Member of Parliament from 1554, representing five different constituencies before he died on 23 July 1595. He left three sons and six daughters. His son Richard was the father of the famous antiquary John Aubrey, who wrote of his grandfather's effigy in St Paul's Cathedral: 'I have his originall picture. He had a delicate, quick, piercing and lively black eie, a severe eie browe, and a fresh complexion. The figure in his monument at St Paules is not like him – it is too big.'[74]

98 An engraving of the monument to Dr. William Awberry in St Paul's Cathedral. (From William Dugdale's History of St Paul's*)*

In 1587 Dr William Awberry and his wife Winifred made over all their property in Kew to their son Morgan Awberry and his wife Joan (it was perhaps a wedding present for the young couple).[75] William Awberry, in a series of small transactions over the years 1578-87 also acquired most of the remaining copyhold tenement in Kew (K) which had belonged for well over 200 years to the At Were family.[76] James Ware (as the name had become) owned only half a 'whole tenement' – 10 acres instead of the usual 20. He sold one half-acre to John Hynde; everything else including his cottage went to the Awberrys (though eventually Morgan Awberry sold one acre back to James Ware who then sold it to Hynde).[77]

In 1605 Morgan Awberry and his wife sold their estate at Kew to Sir Arthur Gorges and his wife Elizabeth.[78] Sir Arthur was the nephew of Sir Thomas of Shene Place. Sir Arthur, a man of letters and a poet, but also a Devon seaman whose mother was a cousin of Sir Walter Raleigh, was to become one of the companions and counsellors of Henry, Prince of Wales. He had gone on Raleigh's expedition to the Azores in 1597, as commander of Raleigh's ship, and he wrote an account of it in 1607 for the Prince, to whom with his great interest in ships and the sea Raleigh was a hero figure. In 1611 Gorges was made a Gentleman of Prince Henry's Privy Chamber. His poem mourning the Prince's untimely death in November 1612 reads, says Sir Roy Strong, 'like

99   Memorial brass from the tomb of Sir Arthur Gorges in the More Chapel, Chelsea Church. (From the Survey of London VIII – Chelsea part 2 – *plate 58.)*

a handbook to the ideas and attitudes that motivated those who made up the Prince's household during the years 1610-1612'.[79]

By the early 17th century therefore we have a new map of Kew. Devonshire House and Suffolk Place have disappeared, together with the smaller houses that had belonged to Thomas Byrkes. Everything to the west of the lane up to the tip of Kew Green was now freehold and in the hands of Sir Hugh Portman, including his great house of Kew Farm and also the 'Dairy House'. Adjoining this property, on the north side of the Green, Portman owned two of the original copyhold cottages, which may possibly have been rebuilt as one house by this time. Then, next to Portman along the riverside, Gorges owned the 'mansion house' and another cottage, and some extra meadowland. In front of part of the Portman and Gorges properties there were by now a number of small cottages built on parcels of land granted from the edge of the Green; a similar ribbon development was also taking place on the south side of the Green, to the east of the park. Kew Park, with its Lodge, also belonged to Gorges. In what was left of Kew Field, some 8½ acres were held by Gorges and 7½ by the Earl of Derby. With the exception of a single acre acquired from Anthony Mason by Stephen Pearce and 1½ acres which were owned by Richmond Church, all the rest was owned by Portman – 17¼ acres as freehold and 26 acres of copyhold land.

Although we know the owners of the houses and the land, we do not always know their tenants – and the houses were often let. There is a problem in placing some early residents of Kew whom one would dearly love to locate with certainty. One is Dr. William Turner, the clergyman and botanist, who served as physician and chaplain to the Duke of Somerset while the latter resided at Syon. Turner had lived abroad from 1542-7, but then he returned and settled at Kew for three years. A letter of his to William Cecil dated 11 June 1549 was written from 'Kewe'.[80]

100 Kew, c.1600.

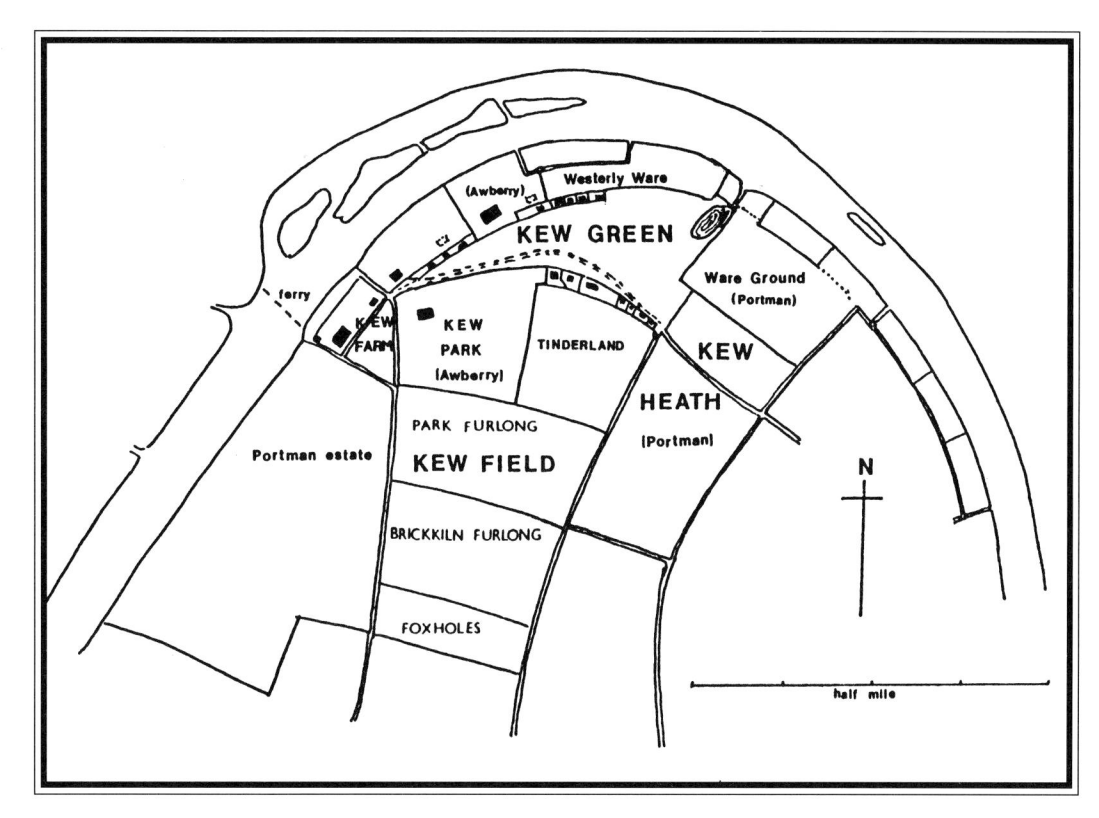

And in his famous *Herbal* he says of the plant *cicer* (or chick pea) that it 'is muche in Italy and Germany. I have seen them in the gardine of the barbican in London, and I have it in my garden at Kew.'[81] But where was Kew's first botanical garden? The likeliest guess – but it is only a guess – is that Turner occupied one of the small freehold houses. This would be close to the ferry, and extremely convenient for access to Syon.

One would also like to place Sir John Hele, Queen's Sergeant, and chief prosecutor at Raleigh's trial, who wrote in 1601 to Lord Cobham 'I am come to my house at Kewe, according to your letter.'[82] Hele's principal home was at Wimsbury near Plymouth, where he died in 1608.

Another puzzle arises over the identity of the mansion that was granted to James I's daughter, the Princess Elizabeth, in 1608 when she was first given her own establishment. It must have been one of the three major houses – either Portman's Kew Farm, Gorges's Kew Park or the latter's mansion house. It was possibly rented in the name of John Lord Harington, who had been the Princess's guardian and was now to be the first gentleman of her household. In May 1609 the Venetian ambassador wrote of 'Baron Harington who lives eight miles out of London and has been given charge of the Princess'.[83] In September of that year he reported: 'Yesterday I went to Richmond to visit the Duke of York [Prince Charles] and to Cheu to kiss the Princess's hand.'[84]

The Princess and Prince Henry were very close, and the closeness of their homes, when the Prince was established in Richmond Palace, was an evident source of delight for them, if of some inconvenience for Lord Harington. He wrote from Kew in October 1609 to Lord Salisbury: 'I cannot wait in person with the book of accounts for Princess Elizabeth, the Prince often calling

101 (above) John, 1st Lord Harington of Exton, guardian of Princess Elizabeth Stuart. (Victoria Art Gallery, Bath Museums)

102 (right) Princess Elizabeth, c.1611, by Marcus Gheeraerts the Younger.

for her to ride with him necessitates my own constant attendance.'[85] Princess Elizabeth remained at Kew until her marriage in 1613. In 1612 we have another glimpse of her when she had visited her father's palace at Nonsuch and been hunting there. She killed a doe and paid 20d. to the keeper of the park, and five shillings to the man who brought the doe back to Kew.[86]

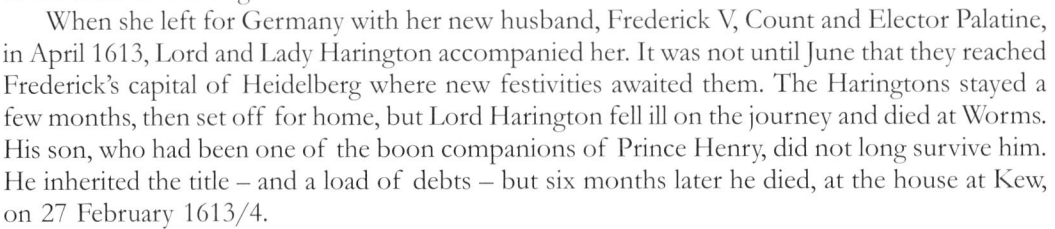

When she left for Germany with her new husband, Frederick V, Count and Elector Palatine, in April 1613, Lord and Lady Harington accompanied her. It was not until June that they reached Frederick's capital of Heidelberg where new festivities awaited them. The Haringtons stayed a few months, then set off for home, but Lord Harington fell ill on the journey and died at Worms. His son, who had been one of the boon companions of Prince Henry, did not long survive him. He inherited the title – and a load of debts – but six months later he died, at the house at Kew, on 27 February 1613/4.

It would seem therefore that 'the house at Kew' was occupied by the Haringtons and the Princess for at least six years – and this fact provides the only real clue as to which house it may have been. To lease a house for more than five years required a licence from the lord of the manor – even if the house were freehold. There is no record of any such licence being granted to Sir Arthur Gorges. But after the death of Sir Hugh Portman in March 1603/04 his brother John, who inherited the whole estate, obtained a licence to let all the premises 'descended to him on the death of his brother Hugh'.[87] So the likeliest conclusion is that Princess Elizabeth's establishment was Kew Farm.

Chapter XII

James I's New Park

Since 1584 Sir Thomas Gorges and his wife Helena, Marchioness of Northampton, had been the tenants of Shene Place – the old Charterhouse – and of its adjacent lands. Helena, daughter of a Swedish knight, Ulf Henriksson, had arrived in London in the autumn of 1565 as a maid of honour to the Swedish Princess Cecilia. The Princess, sister of King Eric, who had been one of Queen Elizabeth's ardent suitors, was paying a visit to the Queen.[1] The party had been met at Dover and escorted to London by William Parr, Marquess of Northampton, brother of Queen Catherine Parr, and regarded by Queen Elizabeth as her 'uncle'. Northampton had recently lost his second wife. Within a month or so of the Swedish party's arrival, Northampton confided to Princess Cecilia that he had fallen in love with the beautiful 16-year-old Helena. Helena accepted his proposal of marriage – but there was a major impediment. Northampton's first wife was still living and his divorce from her had been legally annulled during the reign of Queen Mary. The marriage would have to wait. Queen Elizabeth took Helena under her own protection and appointed her a maid of honour and Lady of the Bedchamber. She became not only a protégée, but a favourite and close friend of the Queen.

In 1571 the Marquess's first wife died and he was free to conclude a third marriage. With the Queen's full approval, and active encouragement, the elderly Marquess married his young Helena. Six weeks later, aged 58, he died. Elizabeth granted the widowed Marchioness a couple of manors to provide her with an independ-

103 Portrait of a young lady, 1569 (believed to be Helena Snakenborg, later Marchioness of Northampton). (Tate Gallery, London)

ent income, and an apartment at Hampton Court. By virtue of her late husband's position and relationship to the Queen, young Helena was the first lady of the Queen's court.

Five years later she married Thomas Gorges, a Groom of the Privy Chamber. They married without the Queen's consent; Gorges was at once imprisoned and Helena was banished from court. But they were soon forgiven. The Queen stood godmother to their first child, a daughter Elizabeth, born in 1578. Gorges now became a confidential courier to the Queen. He was made a Gentleman of the Robes and was knighted for his services. Then in 1584 he was granted Shene.

Thirteen years later, on 16 August 1597, the Queen granted him the keeperships of Richmond Palace, the wardrobe, the garden, and the New Park of Shene, which had fallen vacant through the death of Gregory Lovell.[2] Gorges also obtained the lease of the manors of Richmond, Petersham and Ham, which Lovell had held.[3] King James I confirmed these grants on his accession.[4]

Gorges's estate was bordered on the south by the New Park of Shene, on the east by other royal land. Towards the southern end of this land were the remains of the demesne farm; towards the north what was left of the hunting warren. From late in Henry VIII's reign the warren seems to have been abandoned as a hunting ground – perhaps because the new facilities available at Hampton Court were so much more spacious. It, and the demesne farmland, had been split up to be leased to various individuals.

There appear to have been two or three sections of the warren; the records are somewhat contradictory. There was the King's Lease (or Leas) and the Slaughterhouse Ground. These may have been alternative names for the same 50-acre parcel of land, or they may have been separate but adjacent. There was also an 18-acre parcel called the Great Piece. To the south of that lay the demesne farm lands which were still reckoned to be part of the Lower Field of Richmond, divided into two closes containing 46 (or 36) acres called the Lord's Pieces. Adjacent to the southern end of the Lord's Pieces was a smaller close of royal land adjoining the northern corner of Richmond Green. It was called Crane's Croft and was first granted to Sir William Tyler, former comptroller of the King's works, by Henry VII as early as 1499.[5]

The first recorded grant of the King's Lease was made on 12 July 1534 to John Hales, for his lifetime and without rent. Hales was also

104   Lands lying to the west of the Kew road, c.1550.

appointed proprietor of Kew Ferry – the first time that a monopoly of the ferry there had been sanctioned (which gave rise to protests by the Brentford watermen and the inhabitants of Kew and Brentford).[6] In 1547 a reversionary grant was made to the Marquess of Northampton of 'the pasture called the King's Lease containing by estimation 50 acres of land as granted to John Hales' to be held in socage (i.e. freehold), and of the right of 'free warren of the coneys, hares and other game within the King's Leas'.[7] Northampton immediately sold his reversionary right to the Duke of Somerset.[8]

John Hales appears to have died by 1566, but by then Somerset had long since been executed and attainted, so his reversionary right was extinguished. On 28 February 1566/7 a new grant, both of the ferry and of the land, was made to Morgan Lewes, Groom of the King's Chamber (whether this referred to Henry VIII's or Edward VI's household is not clear). In the particulars for this grant it is said that John Hales had held 'a close of land and pasture called the Slaughter-house Ground *als* the King's Lees … which contained by estimation [?]* acres of [arable] land and pasture and woodland'. The premises, it was noted, had been 'reserved to the use of the Queen's Majesty and her father and brother and late sister for the pasturing of their cattle [horses?] at such times as they shall lie at Richmond'. Lewes was granted, with the same reservation, a 21-year lease at 66s. 8d. a year for the land and a further 13s. 4d. for the ferry.[9]

Then on 11 December 1579 a further 21-year lease, from the expiry of that to Lewes [i.e. from February 1587/8] was granted to Dr. William Awbery, the proprietor of Kew Park. In this the land is described as 'the Slaughterhouse Ground *and* King's Leas in Kew, containing 100 acres of pasture'.[10] The same reservation of the right of pasturage was maintained, and the rent was unchanged at £4 for land and ferry together.

Considering the land on the map, rather than as described in the documents, it seems that 100 acres is much more likely to be a correct figure than 50 acres. It may be therefore that there were two closes, each of some fifty acres, one called the King's Lease and one the Slaughterhouse Ground, and that both had been granted to Hales, Lewes and Awbery, but only the King's Lease to Northampton. In the terrier of land owned by Sir John Raynford (1559) they are referred to as 'the King's Leases', which may support the theory that there was more than one parcel of land involved.

Only one grant relating to the Great Piece has been traced; it was made in 1538 to John Narbonne in the Manor Court.[11] It was described as 'a parcel of demesne land containing 18 acres which remained in the hands of the King, lying next to the pasture called the King's Lease on the east, the lands of the Charterhouse on the north, and Richmond fields on the west and south'. (This is one of the occasions when north-east is described in the records as east rather than north.) Here we have an indication that the 'Lord's Pieces' were considered as part of the Richmond Fields.

John Narbonne died without direct heirs about 1549 and the large holding of land, both freehold and copyhold, that he owned in Richmond escheated to the lord of the manor (the King) and was regranted to David Vincent. There is however no record of a regrant of the Great Piece.

David Vincent, keeper of the royal wardrobes at Richmond, Greenwich and Hampton Court, has already been mentioned. In the lease of property on the north side of Richmond Green granted to him by Anne of Cleves in 1546 were included Crane's Croft of seven acres and 'two closes of land lying together called the Lord's Piece and containing 46 acres'.[12] In the particulars for the confirmatory grant made by Edward VI in 1550, Crane's Croft was said to have been 'lately in the tenure of Walter Blackwell who paid yearly for the same 26s 8d' and the Lord's Piece to have been 'in the tenure of Walter Blackwell and Edmond Pygeon who paid an annual rent of

---

* The Roman numeral given in the particulars might be read either as L (50) or C (100). The compiler of *CPR* read it as 'L'; the present author believes it is a capital 'C'.

66s 8d'.[13] Whether these two were sub-tenants of Vincent between 1546 and 1550 or tenants in their own right before Vincent is not clear.

After Vincent had surrendered the formal lease in 1552, a new lease for 21 years was granted in 1555 to Thomas Palmer. This time the 'two pieces of pasture called the Lord's Pieces' were only said to contain 36 acres; they were described as 'in the tenure of Hugh Hynde, in the common fields'. Hynde paid a rent of 24s. Vincent remained as sub-tenant of Crane's Croft.[14]

Further leases of this entire property, with no change in the description save the insertion of 'late' before the names of the occupants, were granted to Bartholomew Yorke and his wife Joan for 21 years in 1569,[15] to Anthony Martin and Joan Yorke widow for 21 years in 1580,[16] to Anthony Martin alone in 1593,[17] and then to Edmund Beck for life, with remainder to Henry Brimming and then to Anthony Hungerford, in 1597.[18]

✠

Shortly after his accession to the English throne, King James I, whose greatest passion was hunting, determined to make a new park for Richmond Palace. Though Hampton Court was not far away, in James's eyes any palace must have an adequate deer park. The old 'New Park of Shene', of under fifty acres, was far too small. To its north however were those wide stretches of land described above, royal property but under lease to various people. There were the Charterhouse lands in the hands of Gorges and his wife, the Lord's Pieces and Crane's Croft in the hands of Edmund Beck, the Great Piece, the King's Lease and the Slaughterhouse Ground (possibly untenanted at this time, as no lease has been found since the 21-year grant to William Awberry in 1579.)

With Gorges and the Marchioness the King made a deal. They were to keep the monastery site itself, with their mansion, and the riverside meadows adjacent to it on the north side but would surrender the rest of the Charterhouse lands to the King for his new park, of which they were to be made keepers. In exchange, Gorges was to get a pension and an improved grant of all the other lands owned by him and the Marchioness.

The King's promises were duly delivered in a series of grants. On 21 February 1605 Gorges and his wife were appointed jointly and in survivorship as keepers of Richmond New Park.[19] On 22 May of that year Gorges was given a reversionary grant of all the Marchioness's property and a pension of £200 a year for life.[20] The King wrote to the Lord Treasurer:

> In recognition of services to Queen Elizabeth and ourself, and as some offices which he [Gorges] held under her have been otherwise disposed of by us, and some ground taken from him to be enclosed in our new park of Richmond, we grant him a lease in reversion for 40 years of all manors, tenements, etc, now in the tenure of Helena Marchioness of Northampton, his wife.[21]

Finally, on 10 April 1607, Gorges' own lease of the manors of Richmond, Petersham and Ham was also extended to 40 years.[22]

The King made a similar sort of deal with Edmund Beck; he bought in the existing lease for a compensatory payment of £80. He then enclosed the Lord's Pieces and Crane's Croft into his park, and granted Beck a new lease for 40 years of the rest of the property – the house on the Green called the Queen's Stable and the adjacent garden and orchard.[23] All these properties were of course added to the nucleus of the old 'New Park of Shene' which was merged into the New Park of Richmond.

Crane's Croft abutted on its north side on part of the Lower Richmond Field which was in the hands of manor tenants. The eastern boundary of the New Park therefore ran alongside Crane

105 King James I, portrait by Daniel Mytens, 1621. (National Portrait Gallery)

106 (above) Helena, Marchioness of Northampton, between her two husbands, William Parr, Marquess of Northampton (left) and Sir Thomas Gorges (right). (British Library, Lansdowne Roll 9)

107 (left) The effigies of Helena, Marchioness of Northampton and Sir Thomas Gorges from their tomb in Salisbury Cathedral.

Piece and the Green and the eastern edge of Crane's Croft in a neat straight line, but it then turned back westward for some 200 yards before continuing to the north along the edge of the field. As an afterthought the King considered straightening out this boundary. A line continued northward from the corner of Crane's Croft would soon reach the lane from Richmond Green to Kew Ferry which meandered up through the southern part of the field. So James decided to buy from the owners of strips in the field all those parts to the westward of this line and then of the lane itself. The original assessment of the land required was some twenty-five acres, and James was prepared to pay the quite fair price of £5 an acre.[24] The negotiations were entrusted to Gorges, and the manor records for 1605-7 list the precise amount of land sold by the several manorial tenants involved and the sums paid to them.[25] All but one agreed to sell outright; the other seems to have sold some, but leased another part, of his land to the King until it was sold by his heirs nearly thirty years later.[26]

The King also purchased, to add to the park, a 1½-acre strip of meadow which lay between the river and the old New Park of Shene.[27] This had probably had its origin in the 16th-century reclamation work along the river-bank; it had first been granted as 'one acre of waste ground' in the reign of Edward VI.[28] In all the King eventually purchased (or leased) about thirty-three acres from the inhabitants.

James I's New Park

Work had already begun on the formation of the new park by the summer of 1604, and an estimate was prepared in July for the construction of a new hunting lodge to be situated at its centre. Gorges was in charge of the main works at Richmond; but John Taverner, the surveyor of His Majesty's woods south of the Trent, was responsible for supplying timber. Trees were felled in the royal forests at Pamber in Hampshire and Sonning in Berkshire to provide timber for the lodge and for paling the park. Taverner's account from 21 July 1604 to 31 December 1605 shows that he spent £282 16s. 3d. on the cutting of this timber and its transport to Richmond by land and water. The timber was carted from both forests to Reading and sent on from there by boat.[29]

The account which Gorges submitted, covering the period from 8 February 1605 to 18 May 1606,[30] is of great interest for it gives full details of measurements and quantities, both for paling the park and for all the materials used for the lodge. It confirms that the acquisition of land from the field was an afterthought, as 92 loads of 'paling, posts, rails and shores' had to be moved from the position in which they had already been erected 'when the ground was taken in out of the field that the pale was new sett at'. One item in the account is 'for paling 1,195 rods in the park and meadows at 18d the rod',

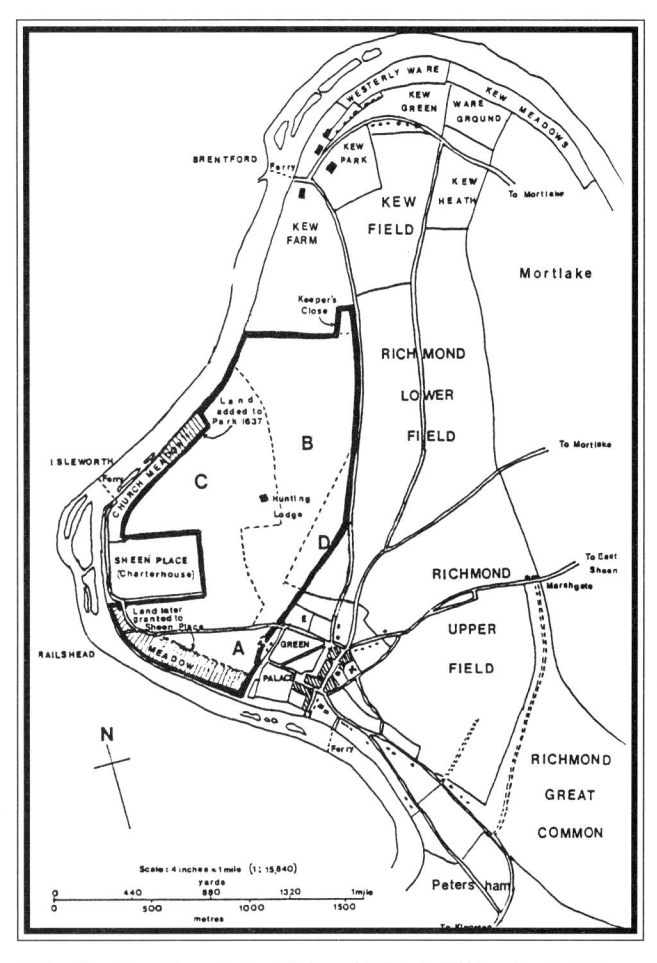

108 King James I's new park at Richmond 1605. A. Old Royal park; B. Former warren; C. Former lands of Charterhouse; D. Lands purchased from Richmond inhabitants; E. Royal stables.

the next is for 'the new setting of 182½ rods of pale when the ground was taken out of the field, at 6d the rod'. The total circuit of 1195 rods amounts to just under 3¾ miles; the section of pale that had to be reset was half a mile and 124 yards. Other work done in the park was the filling in of almost five miles of ditches, while new ditches were made round part of the perimeter. Five gates and stiles were provided.

The details of the materials used for building the lodge are so precise that they would almost in themselves suffice to reconstruct the plan and elevation. For instance, 143,600 bricks were used (at 11s. a hundred), 20,000 tiles (at 10s. 6d. a thousand) and 300 feet of glass at 6d. a foot. And so on, down to two wicker baskets at 6d. each. However, what appears to be a contemporary plan of the building has survived. In John Thorpe's book of plans there is one showing a small house, inscribed in pencil 'Richmond Lodg – Sticles'.[31] This plan can without difficulty be transposed onto a later plan of Richmond Lodge and is then seen to constitute the nucleus around which the later building grew by successive alterations and enlargements. Robert Stickles had been a member of the royal works organisation since at least 1583. A mason by trade, he was a versatile man, turning his hand not only to architecture but also to ship-designing. He became a clerk of works in 1597-8 and a year later was appointed as clerk of works for Richmond, a post which he then held until his death in 1620.[32] The design and building of the lodge would be a normal part of his duties.

The house was of brick, with stone dressings and a tiled roof. The plan shows a main block, containing on the ground floor a large hall, a pantry, a kitchen and a passageway. Two wings project in front at each end, each containing a ground-floor parlour. A porch stood in a small projecting bay midway between the wings; and at the back the staircase projected in a square central tower. Gorges's accounts show that there were five gables, each surmounted by a stone pyramid – presumably one at each end of the main block, one on each wing, and one on the porch. The staircase tower was roofed with lead. A further external adornment was a weather vane 'for the top of the lodge'. Stonework for '26 full lights' and '18 half lights' gives an idea of the mullioned fenestration. A glimpse of the internal decoration is afforded by the purchase of 27-dozen pounds of black and red ochre, one and a half gallons of oil and 24 pounds of size; and by the payment to a painter for 'colouring the staircase and painting and colouring the mantletres of all chimneys'.

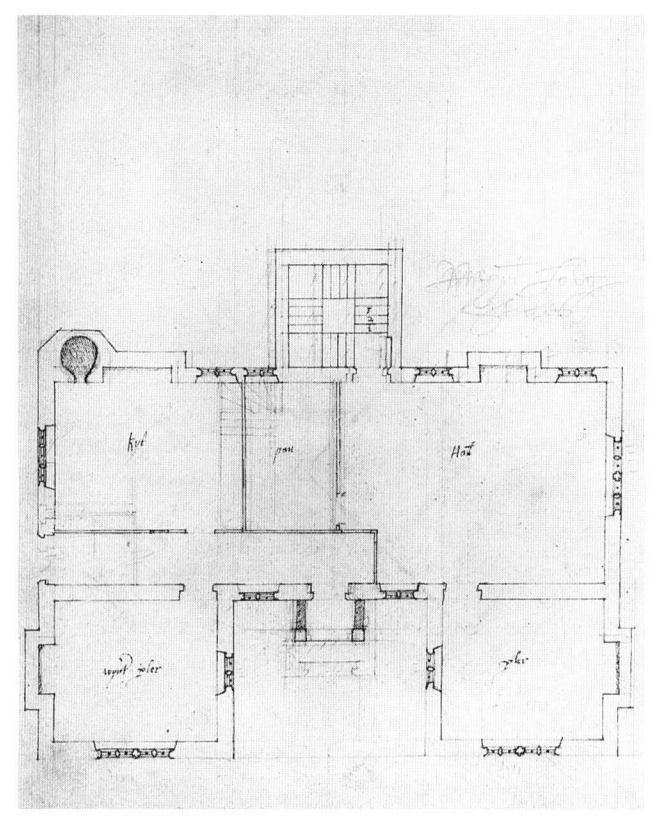

109 The plan of the lodge in James I's Richmond Park, designed by the Richmond Clerk of Works, Robert Stickles, from John Thorpe's Book of Architecture. (The rooms are marked, clockwise from top left, Kyt, pan, Hall, pler, wynt' pler.) (Sir John Soane's Museum)

The whole work of enclosing the new park, filling in old ditches and making new ones, and building the lodge took 456 days and cost (excluding the timber and the purchase of land) £686 7s. 7½d., some three-quarters of which was expended on the lodge. It was completed in May 1606, but the lodge must have been nearly finished a year earlier. On 13 May 1605 Lord Stanhope wrote to the Earl of Salisbury: 'His Majesty came to Richmond by 6 o'clock … He walked from Kew to Richmond through the park and shows to be in great liking of the house.'[33]

During the next 40 years some extra building appears to have been done, and some changes were made to the boundaries of the park. A new range of brick buildings containing kitchen premises allowed the original kitchen to be converted into two bedrooms; another range contained stabling, of which there is no mention in Gorges's accounts. Gorges carried out some repairs to the park pale 'carried away by the water' in 1608, and built two new hay barns in that year.[34] In the summer of 1617 Lord Hay (later Earl of Carlisle), the master of the wardrobe, was occupying the house.[35] Gorges's successor as keeper of the park, Sir Robert Douglas (later Viscount Belhaven) carried out more repairs and planted a new orchard in 1619.[36]

The main change in the park boundary was the splitting off of a wide belt of meadow, stretching from the Crane wharf by the palace right up to the Charterhouse lands. Precisely when this happened has not been traced. This ground was evidently part of the park when King James added in the thin strip of 1½ acres of meadow in 1605. By 1649, under the name of the 'Great Meadow' and containing some 27½ acres, it was reckoned as part of the Charterhouse holding and was said to have been included in the grant of the Charterhouse to the Duke of Lennox of 2 May 1638. In partial compensation, in 1637 a parcel of ground called 'Sheen Grove' containing seven acres, which had been part of the Charterhouse lands, was surrendered to the King by Viscount Belhaven for £20 paid in compensation, and was enclosed in the park.[37] This was probably the strip of meadow which lay at the northern end of the 64-acre grant, and which had formerly been a part of the meadow on the north side of the Charterhouse.

Also in 1637 the small enclave of six acres at the extreme northern end of the park was leased separately to Sir Selwyn Parker at 6s. 8d. a year under the description of 'the Slaughterhouse Ground or the King's Lease' – of which much larger area it had originally been a part.[38] It now became detached from the park and acquired a new name; the Keeper's Close. By 1649 it was held by the Earl of Ancram,[39] and it was sold in 1650 as an appendage to the palace rather than as an integral part of the park.[40]

When Parliament decided to sell off most of the royal estates after the execution of King Charles I, the park was included in the detailed survey made of the palace and manor.[41] This gives a very clear word-picture of the lodge as it stood at that time.

> All that messuage, dwelling house or lodge with the appurtenances, situate, lying and being in or near the midst or middle part of the said park, consisting of:
>
> - One handsome brick building, tiled and guttered with lead, containing a hall paved with square tile, a parlour floored with boards and wainscotted round, a buttery and two cellars under it, two ground chambers, two closets, and a passage, also floored with boards, one handsome dining room well floored, lighted and ceiled, a withdrawing room wainscotted round, three chambers and three closets all floored with boards well lighted and ceiled, and seven garrets all floored with boards and very well lighted and ceiled, and very fit for present use; also consisting of:-
>
> - one other range of brick building well lighted and ceiled containing a kitchen paved with free stone, a wash house and a dairy house paved with square tile, a woodroom, and three rooms overhead; and also consisting of:-
>
> - one other range or pile of brick building, containing a fair stable well planked, paved and ordered for ten horses to stand abreast, with a boarded loft over the same for hay, a pigeon house, and a coach house in the end thereof; and also of:-
>
> - one barn of four bays of building well tiled and billeted on two sides and one end thereof; and also consisting of:-
>
> - one garden called the House Garden, containing threescore and eight perches of land, fenced part with brick and part with deal boards; in the east corner whereof is one little garden house and within which are planted 28 wall fruit trees, 76 fruit trees and 2 cypress trees in a very decent manner; and also of:-
>
> - one other little garden called the Kitchen Garden, containing 30 perches of land, in which garden there are 44 fruit trees planted; and also of:-
>
> - one little court lying before the said lodge, walled on each side thereof with brick, in the end

whereof into the Park stands a fair gate of good ornament to the house; and of:-

- one other court or yard lying between the said lodge and the kitchen garden, in which yard there is a water pump very useful to the said lodge;

containing by admeasurement in the whole 3 roods and 5 perches of land.

With the park of 349 acres, one rood and ten perches, containing 1,946 trees (291 of them marked to be felled for the Navy) and an open barn or deer house, but no deer 'for the game were some years since destroyed', the whole estate constituted – in the words of Hugh Hindley, the Parliamentary surveyor – 'a very pleasant seat and a fit habitation for any private gentleman, and very commodious for all receptions'.[42]

On 6 April 1650 one William Brome 'on behalf of divers original creditors' agreed to purchase the estate, to be held in fee simple (i.e. freehold) for a total of £7,884 10s. 11½d.[43] The sale was completed on 20 May 1650.[44] The estate was then divided; the Lodge, with only a relatively small amount of land, came into the possession of Sir Thomas Jervase (or Gervoise) who had been steward of the manor of Richmond from 1644 to 1649; while most of the park was taken over by Sir John Trevor.[45] Trevor was a leading, but moderate, Parliamentarian who played an important part in the councils and committees of the Commonwealth. He was of those who favoured the restoration of King Charles II in 1660; but that restoration meant that he forfeited all his rights to the park, as the sales of royal property were immediately declared invalid.

At the southern end of the park were some twenty acres lying between the Great Meadow (by then attached to Sheen Place) and Sheen Lane. This remnant of the former 'New Park of Shene' was behind the houses that now stood on the north-west side of Richmond Green, the chief of which in 1650 was the large mansion of John Bentley, at the corner of Old Palace Lane (on the site where 'Cedar Grove' is today). John Bentley, a leading figure and Justice of the Peace in Richmond under the Commonwealth, acquired these 20 acres as a park for his own house. The origin of his wealth is somewhat suspect. According to information lodged against him by Elizabeth Mollett in June 1660, he had been 'woodmonger' to Charles I. Taking advantage of that position he had 'destroyed and made havoc of the timber and woods in the aforesaid forests in the time of the King's absence and since his late Majesty's death, to the value of £20,000'.[46]

John Bentley survived the restoration only briefly, dying at the age of 65 on 26 February 1660/1, with his reputation still apparently untarnished. He and his family were commemorated by a once magnificent (now sadly damaged) monument in Richmond Church. He appears to have been allowed to retain 'Bentley Park', as the 20 acres were then called, on a leased basis. Subsequently attached to the even grander mansion on the edge of the Green which was to become Fitzwilliam House, Bentley Park was not recovered into royal use until 1772 (*see* Chapter 23).

Chapter XIII

Richmond as the Seat of the Prince of Wales

The English coronation of King James I and his Queen Anne took place on 25 July 1603. It was followed by the arrival of the usual congratulatory embassies from fellow rulers, most prominent among them now the one from the Queen's brother, King Christian IV of Denmark. The resident secretary of the Venetian embassy commented on the pecking order:

> The Danish Ambassador who has upwards of 140 persons in his train is lodged at the palace of Richmond. The Ambassador of Brunswick with upwards of twenty is lodged and entertained at Kingston. The Ambassador of Brandenburg and the Ambassador of Wirtemburg are merely lodged and fed.[1]

Later in the year a renewed outbreak of the plague in London compelled the evacuation of the Law Courts, some of which came to Richmond. Some expense was incurred in providing fittings for the Court of Wards.[2]

Despite his creation of the new park, and his pleasure in it, King James made less use of Richmond than had Queen Elizabeth. He seems to have regarded it more as a convenient stopping-off place to spend a night or two on the way to Oatlands or to Hampton Court, which still boasted the better facilities for hunting. James's passion for the chase was unbounded and he was in no way deterred by the Gunpowder Plot of November 1605. On 8 December the Venetian ambassador wrote to the Doge:

> On Monday the King went to Richmond intending to go on to Hampton Court where he proposed to stay six or eight days for his

110 Charles, Duke of York, aged five, attributed to Robert Peake, 1605. (Bristol Museum and Art Gallery)

usual amusement of the chase. This journey is disapproved by the Queen and by all who have the King's interests at heart, for it seems unwise in a time of such turbulence and commotion that the King should go into the country attended by a few persons, and, as often happens, when lured on by the pleasure of the chase should stay out late into the evening thus offering an easy occasion to any who desires to injure him to do so. These and similar considerations have been laid before His Majesty but he, though he recognizes their truth, is resolved to rely on the divine mercy and to place his pleasure above his peril.[3]

Richmond Palace was not however neglected. Late in 1604 or early in 1605 the King seems to have decided that it should be used primarily as a home for his children. Three had survived infancy to be brought south into England: Henry, the eldest, born in February 1593/4; Elizabeth, born in 1596; and Charles, to whom was given the title of Duke of York, born in 1600. (A son and a daughter had already died in Scotland. Two younger daughters born in 1605 and 1606 both died in infancy.) The Princes Henry and Charles were established at Richmond with their tutors; Elizabeth was given into the charge of Lord and Lady Harington at Kew.

In September and October 1606, the King was touring around several royal houses and other estates, to hunt at each in turn. He was, said Thomas Birch, Prince Henry's 18th-century biographer, 'extremely out of humour with the sky for not raining and thereby weakening the scent of his dogs. The Prince remained at Richmond, where the French Ambassador who had been obliged to quit London on account of the plague, and could not follow the King because he made so little stay in any place, was a frequent visitor at his Highness's Court.'[4]

Some new works were carried out at Richmond Palace. In 1604-5 a pheasant house was built in the 'Green Garden', by which was meant presumably that part of the gardens nearest the Green, and into which new steps were made from the Privy Garden. Sundry repairs were effected, including releading of the chapel roof

111 Henry, Prince of Wales, at Richmond Palace. Portrait by Robert Peake, c.1610. (National Portrait Gallery)

and restoring the steps and paving round the fountain in what was now named 'Conduit Court'.[5] The little ship *Disdain* presented to Prince Henry by the Earl of Nottingham in 1604 was brought up to Richmond and moored there. In 1606-7 various alterations were made to it by the joiners of the King's works.[6] Phineas Pett, who had built the *Disdain*, presented the Prince in 1607 with a model ship which he had made, which was placed in a room off the Galleries.[7] A room in the palace was refloored for 'the Prince's Artillery'.[8]

Young Henry was interested in all things martial and naval, but also in history and the arts. His heroes were Sir Walter Raleigh, King Henry IV of France and Maurice of Nassau. From early in 1610 he began to build up an art collection, and once he had his own establishment he sent far and wide to acquire paintings, sculptures and bronzes to adorn the palaces at St James's and Richmond, his two principal residences.

The Prince was obviously fond of Richmond and its situation by the river. He learned to swim, and though warned that it was unwise to do so, he often used to swim in the river after his dinner. He also 'took a great delight in walking by the side of the Thames in moonlight, to hear the sound and echo of the trumpets; both the situation and the season exposing him too much to the evening dews'.[9]

Although he was a keen horseman and a skilful exponent of all the martial arts, hunting bored him. In October 1606 the French ambassador wrote of the 12-year-old Prince:

> None of his pleasures savour the least of a child. He is a particular lover of horses and what belongs to them; but is not fond of hunting; and when he goes to it, it is rather for the pleasure of galloping than that which the dogs give him.[10]

'The Prince will return to Richmond; he does not care for such assiduity at the chase' echoed the Venetian ambassador in 1611.[11] This attitude led to a clash with his father who told him, 'You are no sportsman'. There is an anecdote of the Prince at Richmond which illustrates both the character gap between him and his father and shows how dear he must have been to the local inhabitants. It relates to an occasion when he was actually out hunting. The dog of a local butcher sprang at the stag which was the royal quarry and killed it before the hunt arrived. The butcher tried to make off with the carcass but was caught. The Prince's companions were furious, but the Prince said, 'What if the butcher's dog killed the stag? How could the butcher help it?' When one of the party remarked that the King 'would have sworn so as no man could have endured' Henry replied, 'Away! All the pleasure in the world is not worth an oath.'[12]

Around the Prince at Richmond was gathered a group of young, well-travelled, intelligent and artistic courtiers, some of whom figure in their own right in the story of Kew. Foremost of these was John, the son of Lord Harington of Exton, who was Princess Elizabeth's guardian. Just a year older than the Prince young John Harington was one of his closest companions. Sir Robert Ker (or Carr) of Ancrum and Sir Arthur Gorges, poet and seaman, were both Gentlemen of the Prince's Bedchamber.

Early in 1610 Prince Henry was granted his own household establishment. At his court, at St James's and Richmond, he had his own companies of players and musicians, the latter led by Dr. John Bull. In addition to all the suite of gentlemen, grooms, pages and household officers, were a music teacher and a dancing teacher, a librarian, a riding master, a master of the Prince's ship and a master gunner, as well as an architect, a surveyor and a paymaster of the Prince's works.[13]

Prince Henry was formally invested as Prince of Wales in London in June 1610. He went down to Richmond before the event; then on Thursday 31 May he returned from Richmond to Whitehall by river. He was met by the King at the Whitehall steps – but many nobles and merchants had taken to their barges to escort the Prince for the last part of his journey. King James, who was already somewhat jealous of his son's popularity, was careful to see that Henry should not steal even the show in his honour. He had given the City companies only a week's notice of the event; he accompanied Henry on the river journey from Whitehall to the Court of Requests for the actual creation ceremony on 4 June. But the festivities were not stinted: they went on for a week, with investitures, a masque, a tournament, fireworks and a mock sea battle on the Thames.[14]

112   *Henry, Prince of Wales, with John Harington, by Robert Peake, 1603. (Metropolitan Museum of Art, New York)*

Three months after his investiture as Prince of Wales, Henry was given a formal grant of Richmond Palace, with the manors of Richmond, Petersham and Ham.[15] At once he started to think of major works. The grant was dated 1 September; by the end of September he had approached the representative in London of the Grand Duke of Tuscany to ask the Duke to make available to him the services of the brothers Francini, well-known court artists of the polymath kind who could paint, sculpt, design buildings and gardens and masques. The Duke replied that unfortunately the Francinis were already engaged on works for the King of France and could not be spared. He offered instead Constantino de'Servi who could be available to come to England from France after April 1611. De'Servi, a Florentine by origin, had worked in Rome, Innsbruck, Prague, Naples, Florence and most recently in France. He was a versatile all-purpose court artist of the description Prince Henry was seeking. The Prince accepted the offer.[16]

113 The Thames at Richmond, seen through a window of the palace. Detail from the Peake portrait of Henry, Prince of Wales. (National Portrait Gallery)

While awaiting de'Servi's arrival, Prince Henry pressed ahead with preliminary work and with plans for garden works with the assistance of Inigo Jones, his surveyor, and Solomon de Caus, his architect.

Both Jones and de Caus had already worked for the Prince's mother Anne of Denmark, Jones as a designer of masques, de Caus on garden works. The latter was a Huguenot hydraulic engineer, who had family connections in London and had visited England about 1588. After working in Italy and then for the Archduke Albert (son of the Emperor Maximilian II) he came back to England in 1607-8. Queen Anne gave him commissions both at Somerset House and at Greenwich. He had been particularly strongly influenced by the fountains, cascades, grottoes, automata and giant statues of the Italian gardens at Villa d'Este, Frascati and Pratolino; he now adorned Somerset House and Greenwich with fountains in this style (though modest in scale). At the same time he started to give Prince Henry lessons in perspective drawing.

On the establishment of Prince Henry's household in 1610, de Caus had been appointed 'Architect' with the salary of £100 a year, and Inigo Jones surveyor at £50 a year. With these two Henry planned his new gardens. Some assistance was also sought from Mountain Jennings, the gardener of Theobalds House, which Robert Cecil, Earl of Salisbury, had exchanged with the Crown in 1607 for Hatfield. De Caus and Jennings were also working together on the new gardens at Hatfield.

Exactly what plans were made for Richmond we do not know. It is however clear that the works included three elements. The first was a considerable reclamation of the river-bank, from Crane Wharf past the palace and the 'Friars' up to Water Lane. This involved the incorporation into the reclaimed lands of three small islands (probably little more than bullrush beds) which lay immediately offshore from the palace and Friars. Mountain Jennings was paid for 'drawinge sundrye plattes of the orcharde, howse, Friers and the three Islandes' with his charges for travelling to and from Hatfield.[17] The work was carried out by Inigo Jones, in whose hand is a very rough sketch of the project which still survives.[18]

It has been suggested[19] that the 'three islands' were something created by Jones for the project, but it is clear that they had existed long before the project, and that three islands ceased to exist about this time. They were probably the same three islands granted by Edward II to the Carmelites in 1316 along with the manor house of Shene. In 1542 they were granted to John Lovell, keeper of the orchard and garden at Richmond Palace, as 'three aytes in the Thames against the Fryars'.[20] In 1572 they were regranted to John Hopkins and his wife as 'three aytes formerly in the tenure of George Lovell' (a son of John), and in 1578 Hopkins surrendered them to John Hynde.[21] Hynde's property all went to Sir Hugh Portman; and in December 1604 the Manor Court recorded that the heirs of Sir Hugh Portman had failed to produce copies [of court roll entries] 'to entitle him to the three aytes lying in the River of Thames near unto His Majesty's Mansion House ... other than one copy showed in Court to the Steward, which we think to be no sufficient proof for the maintenance of his title thereunto'.[22] The aytes would therefore revert to the lord of the manor, i.e. the Crown. This is the last mention of these three islands in the manorial rolls. They do not appear in Inigo Jones's sketch plan, which shows a single large island offshore and a substantial reclamation of the river-bank westwards of the inlet at the end of Water Lane.*

The surviving accounts for this work are themselves somewhat ambiguous. On 17 May 1611 Inigo Jones submitted 'an estimate of the charges of the pyling and planking and brickwork for the three Islands at Richmont' which is worth quoting in full.

114 Anne of Denmark, Queen of James I, c.1612. Portrait attributed to W. Larkin. (National Portrait Gallery)

Item: tymber for pyling and planks and working of the same, with the wharf before ye Howse	£887
Item: the brickwork upon the said pyles being laid with taces [?overlapping courses] and some part with ashler as occasion shall require, with the brick wall and the wharf before the Howse	£1774
Item: the cesternehowse for the conveyance of all the water to those islands	£504

---

* Today there are three islands in the Thames west of Richmond Bridge. The large one, 'Corporation Island', has a title which can be traced in the manor rolls back to 1602. The two small ones, opposite the Palace, are the remains of another large one, the title to which is traceable back to 1580. This was divided into two by the Duke of Queensbury in the late 18th century and the two parts have since been much eroded by the river. These existing islands are quite distinct from the 'three islands' mentioned above.

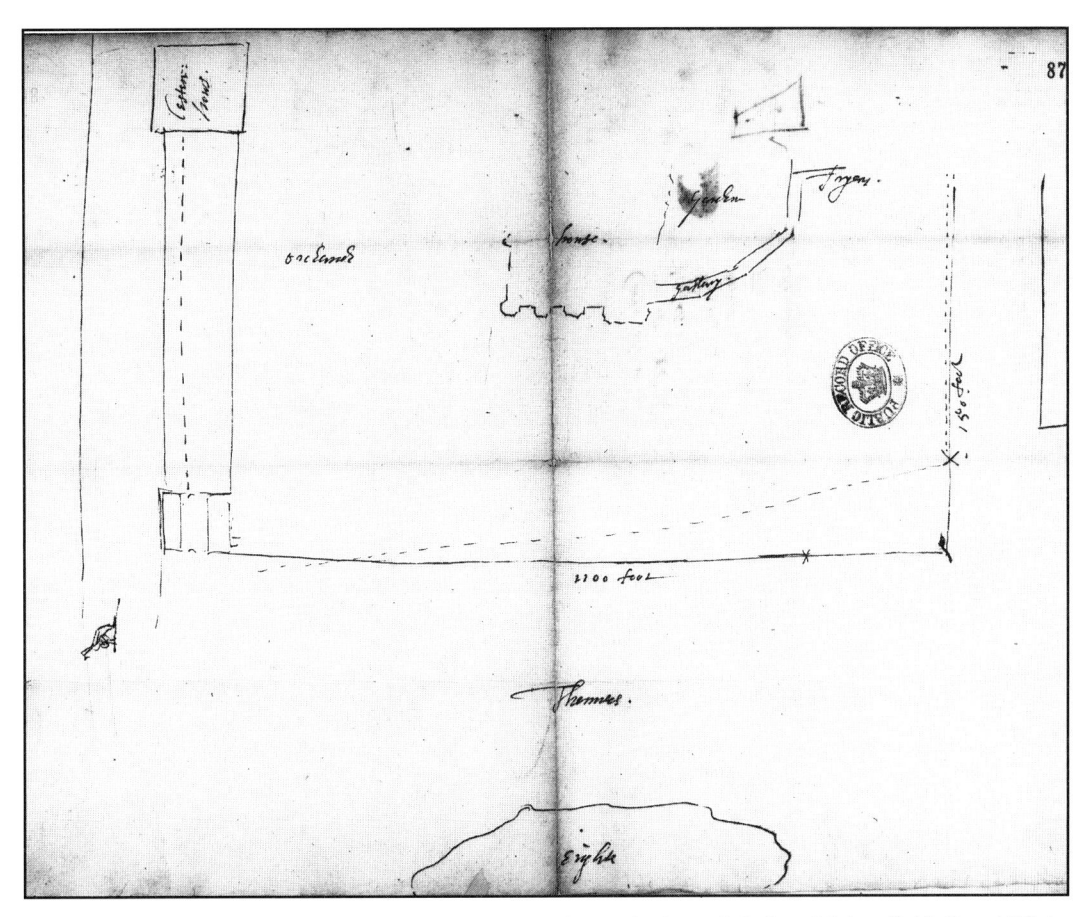

115 Inigo Jones's sketch plan showing the reclamation work on the river bank outside Richmond Palace. (Public Record Office)

Some totall of the estimate	£3175
whereof the Middle Isle with pyling, planking and brickwork	£1092

Besides the leveling and raising of those islands higher with earth, inlaying the wharf on either side of the Howse and the wharfing between the Islands and the Thames, laying of the pipe from the cesterne to those three Islands, the making of staires or bridges to passe into ye Islands and the devices of the frenchman which cannot be valued because unknown.[23]

This was followed by an account for 'the charge of digging and levelling the ground of the Fryers, the workes about the Aightes with the cesterne howse, pyling of the wharfe, and other provisions from the first of November 1610 to the last of June 1611'. The monthly expenditure is recorded. The total for the period was £1,662 4s. 1d., of which a quarter was spent in May and a half in June.[24] There are more detailed accounts for June and July 1611, with extra expenditure of £1,026 19s. 9d. in the latter month, but these do not specify the work being done 'at the Fryers'. They break down the expenditure into wages and materials. 'Labourers and carts' (and in July barges), 'the digging out and carrying of earth and levelling the ground' figure in both months' costs along with the wages of carpenters, bricklayers, masons and smiths and the provision of timber, stone, bricks (and 'Flemish bricks'), tiles, lime, sand and chalk.[25]

116 Wenceslaus Hollar's engraving of Richmond Palace, 1638. (Ashmolean Museum)

A separate set of accounts from 1 June 1610 to 31 May 1611 shows work on the 'cesterne' in April and May 1611.[26]

So what was going on? It seems clear that Jones was not making three new islands where none existed before. Rather he is 'raising' the three existing ones. He is digging out a lot of earth and levelling the Fryers. ('The Fryers' in local Richmond usage was a name given not only to the actual grounds of the old friary, but also to the whole of the waste ground between the palace and the friary and the river-bank.) There are new wharfs 'inlaid' on each side of the house, and also 'between the Islands and the Thames'. The islands are to be supplied with water from the cistern house and are to be made accessible by 'stairs' and bridges.

117 Designs by Solomon de Caus for Richmond Palace gardens. (left: from Les Raisons des Forces Mouvantes; *right: from:* Les Perspectives.*)*

My suggestion – and it can be only a hypothesis – is that the project was, at least in origin, to construct a rectangular pool around the three small islands near the river-bank, between 'the wharf on either side of the Howse' and the wharf 'between the Islands and the Thames'. Within this the islands, linked by bridges to each other and the poolside,* were to be built up with mounds and adorned with fountains or waterfalls as part of the 'Frenchman's devices'. When the project was eventually abandoned, incompleted, the pool was simply filled in again behind the new outer wharf – and the three islands disappeared for ever. Jones's plan (which is not itself dated) simply shows the line of the outer wharf, and so reflects this final stage.

The second feature of the works was the filling in of the old moat and the creation of a new canal and a cistern house. There is no positive evidence that the moat was filled in at this time, but it had clearly ceased to exist by the time of the Parliamentary Survey of 1649, and the suppression of the moat would be an inevitable consequence of the land reclamation. An excavation made on the site of new houses being built in Old Palace Lane in 1972 revealed a moat wall considered to be of early 17th-century construction.[27] This was approximately at the point where Inigo Jones's plan shows the 'Cestern hows' – which is linked in some undefined way with a building on the river-bank (two straight lines and one dotted one on the plan). These lines may indicate one arm of the former moat, or new channels for water from the river to the cistern house, from which a new canal may have been run off at right angles (crossing Crane Piece in a culvert), into the adjacent park.

The building on the river-bank linked to the cistern house can be seen, still uncompleted, in Hollar's engraving of the palace. Its purpose is expressly stated in the survey of Crane Piece made in 1653, after one Edward Bushell had drawn attention to the fact that this piece of royal property had been omitted from the 1649 survey and the particulars of sale. It is described as 'that modell of building intended for a waterhouse called the Rockhouse but never finished, situate and

118   *Giant figures designed by Solomon de Caus for Richmond Palace. From* Les Raisons des Forces Mouvantes.

---

* Compare the Solomon de Caus project illustrated at figure 118 (lower).

being on the aforesaid parcel of ground called the Wharf, being raised with a brick wall one storey high and not covered'.[28]

This is probably the foundation work for one of Solomon de Caus' proposed constructions. For if no complete plan of the intended garden works survives, there are at least several drawings by de Caus of individual features that may have been designed for Richmond. In his book *Les Raisons des Forces Mouvantes*, published in 1624, de Caus said that he had included several designs for Prince Henry, 'some to serve as ornament to his house at Richmond and others to satisfy his gentle curiosity which always wanted to see and to know something new'. Among these designs are a fountain decorated with Tudor roses, and one for a rectangular artificial mountain with a ramp leading to a terrace at the top, as well as one for a reclining giant river god and one for a seated giant, both atop artificial craggy mountains of rock with cascades and grottoes. One of these may well be the project that was begun by the riverside. Although de'Servi, after his arrival on the scene, claimed that all de Caus' plans were abandoned in favour of his own, there is evidence in the accounts that de Caus' works went on; an undated letter from de Caus to Lord Salisbury's secretary asked if 'the rock' had arrived in London, and requested the return of shells and drawings provided for the Lord Treasurer's inspection.[29]

By the time that Constantino de'Servi arrived in England, in June 1611, these works were already well under way. On 9 June de'Servi wrote that he was at Richmond where the Prince intended to lay out a garden with grottoes and fountains, but there was a great shortage of money.[30] He was to make 'fountains, summer houses, galleries and other things'. By 23 June de'Servi reported to Florence that *his* designs for the palace grounds had delighted the Prince, in comparison to those of 'that Frenchman'.[31] By the end of July not only, he said, were his designs approved over the others and authorised to go ahead, but he was to make a giant three times the size of the one at Pratolino, with many rooms in it, a dovecote in the head and two grottoes in the base.[32] De'Servi makes frequent reference to the interference of his rivals, and it is clear that his influence and success was much resented by de Caus and Jones. He was granted a salary double that of de Caus and four times that of Jones. But by 22 August the Prince had shown his designs to the King, and he was preparing to make models of the statues and fountains.[33]

The lack of funds however now began to tell. By December de'Servi would 'bring forth no models' without further payment.[34] He was critical of the works organisation and wrote a long memorandum to the Prince setting out how the accounts ought to be handled, with

119 Henry, Prince of Wales, c.1612. Miniature by Isaac Oliver. (The Royal Collection © Her Majesty the Queen)

himself in total charge 'in the way that these things are done in Florence and other places in Italy'.[35]

Then in the summer of 1612, despite the lack of funds, the Prince grew more ambitious. He was expecting to be married to Maria, the daughter of the Duke of Savoy. He wanted to greet his bride with a new palace in the latest Italian style. On 24 July the Tuscan representative in London reported that de'Servi was spending all his time at Richmond where the Prince 'undertakes to the designs of Signor Constantino de'Servi the great work of a new palace saying he wished to begin as soon as possible so that his wife would find it built'.[36] He referred to the project again in a further letter five days later.[37]

In August, in a letter in which de'Servi asked to be recalled to Florence for various reasons, including the persecution of Catholics in England and the fact that there was 'a scarcity of money at this court' – he had not been paid for a year – he himself referred to Henry's project for a palace,[38] and we know from a later letter of a plan that he should return to Italy to gather materials in Florence and Livorno for the construction of the palace.[39]

Then suddenly the cloud-capped towers vanished into thin air. At the beginning of October the strong, athletic, 18-year-old Prince had a fever. He ignored it; he was deeply involved with the preparations for his sister Elizabeth's marriage to the Elector Palatine, who arrived in London on 18 October. On 25 October the Prince took to his bed, but on the next day he got up to play cards. From the 27th he wasted fast – his disease has subsequently been diagnosed as typhoid. On 6 November he died.

The family were distraught with grief, as was the whole court; and, we may be sure, the people of Richmond. At the palace all work stopped. At the end of December the Prince's household was dissolved. Of de'Servi's projects and de Caus' little perhaps had been achieved except the foundations of the uncompleted 'rockhouse', the building of the cistern house and some basic water works. Of Jones's the reclaimed river-bank at least remained. It is perhaps sad that one of England's greatest architects should have left to Richmond only such an earthy monument – but Inigo Jones had yet to bring his architectural skills to a peak by a prolonged visit to Italy. It has been suggested that he built a picture gallery at Richmond for Prince Henry, on the strength of a promise made by the Prince to the sculptor Abraham Vanderdoort that his work would be displayed in the gallery being built by Inigo Jones[40] – but this gallery was almost certainly at St James's.

Nevertheless, considerable sums had been spent at Richmond during the two years 1610-12, both by the Prince and by the King's works organisation. The total was over £10,000.[41] An account by the paymaster of the Prince's works for the period August 1611-November 1612 shows £2,422 18s. 3d. paid for works at Richmond House and Shene, and an extra £303 13s. 6d. for 'Mouns^r de Caus' works'[42] – a clear indication that de Caus was still carrying on with some projects after de'Servi's appearance on the scene.

Though the accounts are not very detailed, some of the improvements made to the palace at this time can be identified. Repair work was necessitated by floods in 1610-11.[43] A 'closet or library' was made for the Prince.[44] A new tennis court was built (its site is unknown, and it was demolished six years later; perhaps it was a closed court to supplement the old open one).[45] At Shene, the stables were repaired and enlarged, for Henry was importing fine horses from many countries. A riding school, similar to that at St James's, was built. (The 1649 Parliamentary Survey mentions the 'Riding House' – a 'barn heretofore used for riding of the King's great horses, containing five bays of building, well tiled and ordered'.)[46] A German visitor in the summer of 1611 recorded that he had seen Prince Henry and Prince Charles receiving instruction in the riding school 'in an old monastery called Sheen'.[47]

120   Charles, Prince of Wales. Portrait attributed to A. van Blijenberch. (National Portrait Gallery)

It appears that Prince Henry at some point prevailed on the Marchioness of Northampton to lease Shene House to him. Perhaps he intended it for use as a base while the palace was rebuilt. After the Prince's death King James continued the lease and paid the Marchioness compensation 'for better providing for herself a convenient dwelling place elsewhere'.[48] In 1618 the Exchequer accounts, in paying the quarterly rent of £61 6s. 3d., note that 'His Majesty is thinking fit to retain [Shene House]'.[49] In December-January 1621/2 payments were made for 'repairs to the Prince's house at Sheen'.[50]

For the next four years Richmond Palace remained nominally in the King's hands. Prince Charles, the Duke of York, was not quite twelve when he became heir to the throne, and although he had been given a separate establishment in 1611, he was still too young to be set up with a full princely household and his own court. When the wedding of his sister Elizabeth, postponed because of Henry's death, was finally celebrated in February 1612/3 and she set off for her new home at Heidelberg, Charles was left as the only royal child remaining in England.

Richmond continued to be his principal home, but for a year or two the King and Queen again used it more frequently. That summer de Caus was back at Richmond for two months, but for what purpose is unknown. Perhaps he was just tidying up the uncompleted projects.[51] By the end of the year the King had decided to approve a new household establishment for Charles, to be effective from 1 July 1614.

Several of Prince Henry's companions were transferred to the new household, including Sir Robert Carr of Ancrum and Sir Arthur Gorges. Robin Carey, who had ridden to Edinburgh in 1603, became keeper of the Prince's privy purse. Thomas Murray remained as the Prince's tutor; his nephew William, who was the same age as the Prince and had been educated with him, was the 'whipping boy' who was punished when Charles did something naughty. William was later to become owner of Ham House, lord of the manors of Ham and Petersham and eventually Earl of Dysart, so perhaps the close relationship that he had with Charles throughout his life provided compensation for his early pains.

In June 1615 King James stayed at Richmond before setting off on a royal progress round the country; he returned there for a visit from the King of Denmark. He was now actively considering the marriage of Charles as a stroke of foreign policy. Feelers had been put out in 1613 for a match with Louis XIII's sister Christina, but James was more interested in pursuing the prospect of a Spanish alliance to be sealed with the marriage of Charles to the Infanta Maria, and the French negotiations were broken off.

Two weeks before his 16th birthday, on 4 November 1616, Charles was invested as Prince of Wales. A reorganisation of his household resulted in Thomas Murray changing his rôle from tutor to secretary, with Sir Robert Carr as keeper of the privy purse and Sir Robert Douglas as treasurer. On 10 January 1616/7 the palace of Richmond and the manors of Richmond, Petersham and Ham were granted to Sir Francis Bacon and other trustees for the Prince;[52] but in the following month, on 19 February, a regrant was made directly to Charles, Prince of Wales.[53]

Charles had no architectural ambitions. He shared his brother's love of art and continued actively to build up the collection of pictures, but he was pretty well content to leave Richmond Palace the way it was. Apart from some repairs and the demolition of Henry's new tennis court, almost the only works carried out at the palace during Charles's time were the conversion of the cistern house into a 'munition house' or armoury, the provision of a shuffleboard room and the construction of a new pheasant house.[54]

The pheasantry aroused much interest in foreign visitors. Two Italians gave detailed accounts of it in 1618,[55] from a combination of which emerges the following description.

> They are placed in a small orchard beneath the palace windows with a few cherry and plum trees, the grass being allowed to grow as pasture for the birds ... No one could enter except by the gate, which was always shut, so that the animals might not be disturbed by the traffic or curiosity of people. The place is divided by compartments ... with wooden partitions ... about five feet high into eight sections or squares each with its own door. They might be about 18 feet long by 12 broad. All have turf, and they think this necessary as the birds can take exercise and feed there as well as lay their eggs ... They all have the tip of one of their wings clipped to prevent them from flying away, the site not being roofed in ... Trees protect them from the sun and each place has its little wooden house, similar to and no larger than those used for watch dogs. Each house has straw on the floor and a hatch at the side besides the door and the birds retire thither at night, probably to protect them from being found by beasts of prey ... Some are pied red and all the rest white, very handsome to look at ... There are five females and one male for each place, the white being separated from the speckled, and the common ones from the rest ... Their food varies. Some have wild peas, a very common vegetable here, found in great quantities. They give them in season handfuls of these, grain, etc. They are fond of mustard seed and earth worms. But the best thing is to give them what is most abundant and costs least, as they will readily eat lettuce, chopped cabbage and all manner of greens ...
>
> The hens lay their eggs in the grass, and they are carefully collected and placed in due time under clucking hens, who hatch them. Last month we saw eighty chicks already hatched under several brood hens, being reared in coops with two partitions, the hen being in the one and the food of the young pheasants in the other, to which they have access at pleasure. The food consists of ants' eggs; clean water is placed for them in shallow pans ... I have seen them cover the young birds with netting to protect them from birds of prey and prevent them from escaping, as their wings are not clipped.

✠

Charles became King on his father's death at Theobalds on 27 March 1625. Six weeks later he married Henrietta Maria, daughter of King Henry IV and sister of Louis XIII of France. The expulsion of Charles's brother-in-law from Bohemia and the Palatinate had finally put paid to the idea of a Spanish alliance, though on his ill-fated trip to Madrid with Buckingham in 1623 he had still hoped to secure Frederick's restoration to the Palatinate as a condition of the marriage. With the Spanish alliance degenerating rapidly into war with Spain, the French made overtures. The French demanded, no less than the Spaniards, a guarantee of religious liberty for English Catholics as a condition of the marriage treaty, and although Charles had himself made a solemn promise to the House of Commons that no such clause would be acceptable in any marriage treaty, the negotiations for Charles's betrothal to Henrietta Maria had been concluded by the end of 1624.

Again in 1625 the post-coronation congratulatory embassy from the new Queen's country was accommodated at Richmond Palace. This time it was of course the French who had the honour. They brought their ladies, two of them pregnant. 'The Duchess of Chevreux and the Countess of Tillières have given birth at Richmond to a daughter and a son respectively,' commented the Venetian ambassador on 31 July.[56]

In the same despatch the ambassador reported that the plague in London was becoming most serious and that people were dying by thousands. Again some of the Courts were moved to Richmond, as soon as the French had departed. Already at the beginning of June the Great

X *Henry, Prince of Wales, at Richmond Palace*, portrait by Robert Peake, c.1610. (National Portrait Gallery, London)

XI *A stag hunt in Richmond Park. A painting attributed to Joan Carlile. (Lamport Hall Trustees)*

Wardrobe had been removed from London to Sheen House.[57] An attempt was made to isolate Richmond from contagion, though it was far from successful. On 5 August the Privy Council wrote to Surrey Justices of the Peace:

> Since His Majesty's proclamation to the contrary divers citizens have settled in the town of Richmond and others continue intercourse with servants and friends in London. Divers of His Majesty's servants are already there and others are going, especially of His Majesty's Exchequer as the Office of Requests is to be at Richmond during the contagion in London and Westminster.[58]

The Richmond parish registers bear gloomy witness that the precautions were in vain. The usual average was three or four burials a month. In the second half of 1625 the figures were 22 in July, 44 in August, 37 in September, 21 in October, 18 in November, 7 in December. One of the victims was Sir Edward Gorges, son of Sir Thomas and the Marchioness Helena.

It was in 1622 that King James had finally decided to grant a new long lease of Sheen House. The recipient was Sir Robert Douglas, Prince Charles's treasurer, who had already been appointed keeper of the palace and park. The lease was for 20 years from Michaelmas 1622, and renewed the covenant reserving use of all but the Prior's Lodging to the Court when required.[59] This clause was called into operation when the Great Wardrobe was evacuated to Sheen.[60]

On 15 February 1626/7 the King settled Richmond Palace with the manors of Richmond, Petersham and Ham on Queen Henrietta Maria.[61] For some years the inhabitants of Richmond had been agitating for a final separation from the jurisdiction of Kingston (though they remained in the same vicarage) by the establishment of a separate Court Leet. This was a court that had its origins in the feudal system as the 'View of Frank Pledge', primarily concerned with ensuring that all those who owed duty of service and were taxable should be duly sworn and inscribed. But the Court Leet had powers of regulation and of levying fines that went beyond those of the manor court (or Court Baron); and in particular it had the task of appointing the local officials – the constables, tithing men and ale-conners. That the Kingston Court Leet and the bailiffs of that town should have any jurisdiction in Richmond rankled, and Prince Charles's own Council had supported the inhabitants' petitions in 1622 and 1624, but nothing had been done. Now that Charles was King another petition was forwarded in 1626: 'Kingston skimmeth away the cream from your Majesty,' it claimed. At the same time, coincidentally but conveniently, Kingston was seeking a confirmation of its charter, for Hampton was claiming the right to a market. The King ordered a full investigation; two committees were set up, one to consider Richmond's petition, and one to consider Kingston's charter. The first of these reported in favour of Richmond, and the second in favour of Kingston. A compromise was worked out. Richmond was to be freed from the jurisdiction of Kingston and was to have its own Court Leet. Kingston was to have a new Charter in which its jurisdiction over Richmond, Kew, Petersham and Ham would be surrendered, but by which Kingston's rights to hold the only market for seven miles and to hold three annual fairs would be confirmed. On 15 September 1628 the Attorney General was instructed to set up a Court Leet for the manors of Richmond, Petersham and Ham, of which Sir Robert Douglas was to be steward.[62] On 13 October Sir Robert was formally appointed as steward for life of the new Court Leet.[63] It held its first meeting at Richmond Palace on 15 April 1629.[64]

Though Charles I would, like his father, use Richmond as a base for the royal children, it was some years yet before even the eldest was ready to be left. The first-born child of Charles and Henrietta Maria, a son Charles, died on the day he was born in May 1629. A year later another boy, the future Charles II, was born on 29 May 1630. He was followed by a daughter Mary in November 1631 and a son James, Duke of York, in October 1633. Then came three more girls, only one of whom (Elizabeth) survived early childhood, another son Henry, Duke of Gloucester, born in 1640 and finally a daughter Henrietta Anne born in 1644.

In 1634, when Prince Charles was just four years old, the Rev. Brian Duppa was appointed his tutor. From then on these two spent much time together at Richmond, for Duppa remained the Prince's tutor even when made Bishop of Chichester in June 1638, until appointed Bishop of Salisbury in the summer of 1641.

The works carried out at the palace during this period were generally of a minor character: a new planked wharf 116 feet long in 1628,[65] in 1631-2 the construction of a new gallery 24-feet long 'for Lady Mary to pass through the lodgings'[66] (this must have been some kind of short cut for the baby princess's nurse – perhaps from the Queen's apartments to the nurs-

121 Brian Duppa, Bishop of Winchester (and previously of Chichester and Salisbury). Engraving by R. Reading.

ery, for the Lady Mary cannot yet have been even crawling). In 1636-7 an ornamental 'bird-house' was built in the orchard; it was a 12-foot wide octagon, with eight pillars each 13-feet high – how it was roofed or screened is unknown, but it was painted green.[67] Three years later a pigeon house with slated roof was built in the Green Garden.[68] A new clock was made by David Ramsey and installed in the clock tower, where the dial was regilded and the 'pyramid' (roof?) re-leaded.[69] A lot of repair work was also carried out on the stables at Sheen.[70]

The major activity at Richmond in the mid-1630s was the construction of the King's great new park, described in the next chapter. But the second half of the decade saw also a revival of the custom of putting on plays in Richmond Palace for the entertainment of the court. The first such dramatic event seems to have been a masque staged at Richmond on 12 September 1636 to celebrate the arrival of the King and Queen from a visit to Oxford. It was billed (and later printed) as 'presented by the most illustrious Prince Charles' – but was in fact put on by the Earl of Dorset's sons, Lord Buckhurst and Edward Sackville. It was staged 'in the galleries around the first court' and Edward Pearce painted the scenery.[71]

In the winter of 1638-9 the court made a long stay at Richmond. A company from London put on plays on 6 November and 28 December to celebrate the birthdays of Princess Mary and Princess Elizabeth. (One hopes that Elizabeth, aged three, enjoyed *The Northern Lass* as much as the eight-year-old Mary must have chortled over *The Merry Devil of Edmonton*.) Further performances were given on New Year's Day (*Beggar's Bush*) and on 7 January (*The Spanish Curate*).[72] These performances were presumably given in the guardroom, where 'new stages and degrees for acting plays' had been built in 1637-8.[73] The following winter five plays were presented at Richmond: three by the Prince's Company and two by the King's Company. £20 was paid for each performance – to cover also travelling expenses and the loss of a night's earnings at the company's London playhouse.[74]

About the end of 1637 the Prince's treasurer Sir Robert Douglas, who had been given the title of Viscount Belhaven in 1633, having been stricken with blindness, surrendered the lease of Shene and all his offices in the palace, park and manor of Richmond, to retire to Scotland. Before this, in May 1637, he had put in a curious petition to the King. He claimed that in the reign of King James he had spent £763 of his own money on the lodge and a keeper's lodge in Richmond Park. In recompense the King 'gave him the making of a baronet by way of payment, but because he could not have at that time above £250 for that dignity the late King referred him for satisfaction to his present Majesty, then Prince, on his return from Spain; this sum he has not yet received'. Sir Robert Pye, Remembrancer of the Exchequer, minuted wryly:

> The moneys received by Sir Robert Douglas, now Lord Belhaven, since the beginning of the reign, apart from his pension of £666 13s 4d and his fee for the keeping of His Majesty's house and park at Richmond, were £7000 in two grants. These facts were referred to the King and the matter was left to his wisdom.[75]

In February 1637/8 the Attorney General informed Secretary Windebank that he had now received Lord Belhaven's surrender of the grants of the late monastery of Shene, of the keepership

122   The children of Charles I, 1637. Painting after Sir Anthony van Dyck. (National Portrait Gallery)

of Richmond House and Park and of the stewardship of the courts leet and baron of Richmond. He enquired which of these were to be granted to the Duke of Lennox.[76]

James Stuart, fourth Duke of Lennox, had been a legal ward of King James I who was the nearest heir male of the family after the third Duke died when the boy was 12 years old. He had been brought up at the English court and was a close companion of his distant cousin, King Charles I. On 2 May 1638 he was given the grant of 'Sheen Priory' for life[77] and was appointed as keeper of the palace and the Little Park. He was created Duke of Richmond on 8 August 1641.

It was in 1638, at the age of eight, that Prince Charles was given his own household establishment as Prince of Wales. This was not, as in the cases of his uncle and father, followed by a grant of Richmond Manor and Palace. They remained in the hands of the Queen, and at the age of eight Charles was hardly yet independent of his mother. He and the other younger children remained for much of the time at Richmond, with the Earl of Newcastle acting as the Prince's 'governor' and Bishop Duppa still as his tutor. But in the Bishop's words, written in September 1639, 'The Prince … hastens apace out of his childhood'.[78]

Chapter XIV

Charles I's New Park of Richmond

About 1631-2 King Charles I conceived the idea of making a new 'great park' at Richmond.[*] Edward Hyde, Earl of Clarendon, in his *History of the Rebellion*, wrote:

> The King, who was excessively affected to Hunting, and the Sports of the Field, had a great desire to make a great Park for Red, as well as Fallow Deer, between Richmond and Hampton Court, where he had large Wasts of his own, and great parcels of Wood, which made it very fit for the use he designed it to: but as some Parishes had Commons in those Wasts, so, many Gentlemen, and Farmers, had good Houses, and good Farms intermingled with those Wasts of their own Inheritance, or for their Lives, or Years; and without taking of Them into the Park, it would not be of the largeness, or for the use proposed. His Majesty desired to purchase those Lands, and was very willing to buy them upon higher terms, than the People could sell them at to any body else, if they had occasion to part with them, and thought it no unreasonable thing, upon those terms, to expect this from his subjects; and so he employ'd his own Surveyor, and other of his Officers, to treat with the Owners, many whereof were his own Tenants, whose farms would at last expire.
>
> The major part of the People were in a short time prevailed with, but many very obstinately refused; and a Gentleman, who had the best Estate, with a convenient House, and Gardens, would by no means part with it; and the King being as earnest to compass it, it made a great noise, as if the King would take away mens Estates at his own pleasure.[1]

The Lord Treasurer, Bishop Juxon of London, and the Chancellor of the Exchequer, Lord Cottington, were opposed to the scheme from the outset, not only, says Clarendon, because of the popular discontent it was arousing, but also because of the cost, both of the land and of the brick wall to enclose it. Clarendon expounds at some length on their attempts and those of Archbishop Laud to dissuade the King, and the latter's determination to go ahead regardless. Cottington, as the owner at this time of Twickenham Park,[2] no doubt received a good many complaints from his near neighbours, but finally gave way when the King said he was already having the bricks made and was starting to build the wall on parts of his own land. Bishop Juxon also may have had pressures on him from his cousins in Mortlake, where John Juxon was lord of the small manor of East Sheen.

Clarendon's account suggests that, as in the case of James I's park-making at Richmond, a lot of the land which King Charles intended to enclose was already his to dispose of. This was not in fact the case, although the King may have persuaded himself that it was. The map of the 'New Park' drawn by Nicholas Lane about 1632[3] shows what the ownership of the enclosed lands had been. The proposed park boundary drawn on it was revised several times before the final line was inserted in January 1637/8.

[*] This date is based on the presumed date of Nicholas Lane's survey — see note 3.

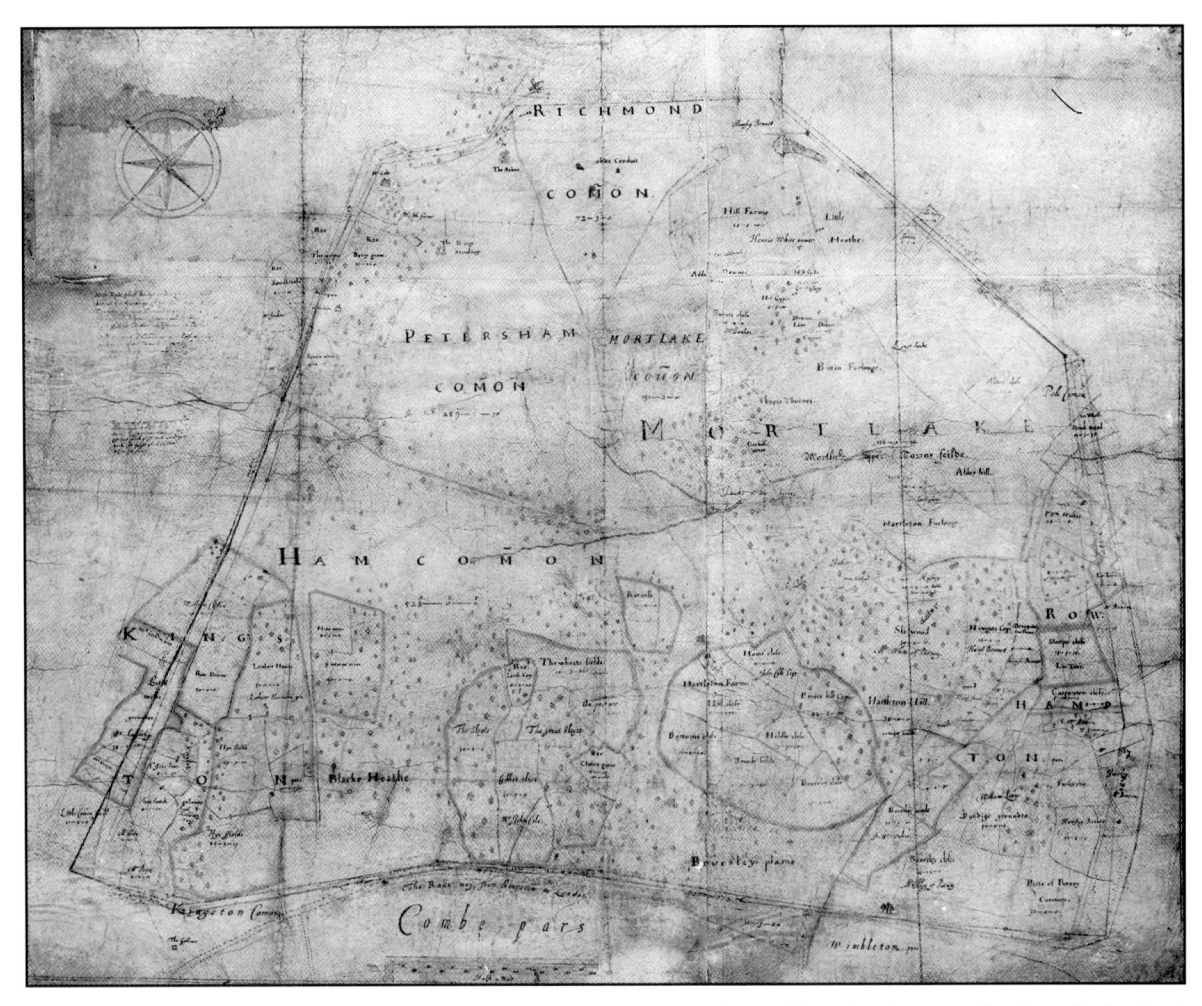

123 The making of Richmond Park. Nicholas Lane's map shows several projected lines of enclosure as well as the one finally adopted. (Museum of London)

The site on the hill overlooking Richmond, Kingston, Mortlake and Roehampton was no doubt chosen in the first place because there were large areas of wasteland or commons. The boundaries of these were tortuous however, and within them were many large closes of privately owned land. While the manors of Richmond, Petersham and Ham were royal manors, so that in a sense their substantial commons were at the disposal of the King as the ultimate lord of the manor, the situation was far more complicated. All three manors had been granted to the Queen, Henrietta Maria, and Ham and Petersham were in lease to the Cole family, the head of which was now Gregory Cole. A reversionary lease had already been granted by the Queen's trustees to William Murray of Ham House. So the Coles and the Murrays had rights in the commons, which had to be considered, as did the old-established common rights (of pasture, wood-gathering, etc.) of the manorial tenants.

Even the four areas of land marked on Lane's map as 'Rex' (i.e. the King's own land) were in fact demesne lands of the manors of Petersham and Ham, and formed part of Gregory Cole's leasehold estate. It was no doubt Cole to whom Clarendon referred as the 'gentleman who had the best estate, with a convenient house and gardens', for he not only owned (as leaseholder) the old Petersham manor house – later to become Petersham Lodge – but also Hartleton Farm with its farmhouse and some 235 acres of land, divided into two large (and one small) separate holdings, in the south-eastern corner of Ham Common. Hartleton Farm was not however part of Ham. It was the remains of the old manor of Hartington Combe which had belonged to Merton Priory. George Cole had acquired the freehold of it in 1605.

There were a few other houses in the area which was eventually enclosed for the park. A small cottage in Petersham to the east of the manor house had belonged to John Garrett. On the southern edge of Ham Common were two houses and other buildings on the ground called 'Loanes' which had belonged to William Clifton. His main house was enclosed, the other was left outside the park and inherited the name. To the north-east of Mortlake Great Common lay Hill Farm with a farmhouse, owned by Henry White.

Another map of the same period as Lane's was drawn by Elias Allen.[4] This gives more detail of the roads in the enclosed area, but shows less detail of the landholdings (and the Kingston corner has been torn off). From this one can see that there were two main highways crossing the park: one from Richmond running south to Coombe, and one from Mortlake running south-west to Ham. These intersected at what is now called Ham Cross. Another road led down from Mortlake to Hartleton Hill (and presumably on to the farm), but seems to have ended there. The main London-Portsmouth road through Kingston was left outside the boundaries of the park.

The area eventually enclosed was some four square miles. Its shape on the map, with a flat base formed by the Portsmouth Road, may be compared to that of a haycock, the sides sloping gradually inwards to a flat top formed by the wall across Richmond Common and a part of the Mortlake lands. About 45 per cent had been common land, but the King drew his new boundaries in such a way as to leave at least a little common land to all the affected communities.

Mortlake was the community most adversely affected by the King's plans. The manor of Wimbledon, which included Mortlake, Roehampton and Putney, belonged to Edward Cecil, Viscount Wimbledon, and the King had no claim at all on land there. Yet from Mortlake Charles wanted not only more than 200 acres of common but a similar amount of the town field, and another 300 or so acres of closes belonging to individual tenants, chief among whom were the Juxons. Moreover, some land in East Sheen had recently been bequeathed to the parish as an endowment for maintenance of the church, and although only an acre and a half of this fell within the area to be enclosed, the Vestry were naturally loth to consider parting with it.

From Putney some 36 acres of common were wanted; from Roehampton some 225 acres, all in individually owned closes. One of the owners was Jerome Weston, second Earl of Portland, whose father had been Lord Treasurer until his death in March 1634/5. The Westons owned Putney Park as a freehold, and in May 1635 the Earl was granted a licence to enclose an additional 450 acres into his park.[5] The date of this licence was however after the King had started the process of forming his own park, and although it appears that Portland played an important part in the negotiations over land in Roehampton and gathered most of it into his own hands before selling it on to the King, his role in most of these transactions was probably that of a middleman rather than a principal. (Some small parts of the land which he sold to the King had however been his father's or were described in the deed of sale as 'impaled within the new park of the said Earl of Portland at Rowhampton'.) It would also seem that much of the land in two of the estates ostensibly acquired for the King's park lay outside the park wall and probably remained in Portland's hands.

Viscount Wimbledon also seems to have played a middleman's part (beyond that of lord of the manor) in the acquisition of land. All the copyhold land in Mortlake and Roehampton which was to be enclosed in the park was surrendered directly to his use. (By contrast, the surrenders of copyhold land in Petersham were to the use of the King's Commissioners.) This even included much of the land conveyed to the King by the Earl of Portland. There must have been a subsequent grant by Lord Wimbledon to the King or to the Commissioners, but this has not been traced.

Another, fairly small, contribution to the park was required from Kingston. This land was mostly in private hands but it included also 17 acres of common and about 30 acres of land in fields belonging to the town.

※

On 12 December 1634 the King appointed a Commission to negotiate with the local people and landowners over purchase of the lands, compensation for common rights, etc. It included a number of local dignitaries, among them Lord Cottington himself, Sir Francis Crane of Mortlake, Sir Robert Pye of Richmond, and William Murray of Ham House, Groom of the Bedchamber and a well-known figure at Richmond Palace. The Attorney-General, the Surveyor-General (Charles Harbord) and three auditors of the revenue were the other members.[6] By April 1635 they had only succeeded in acquiring five acres, though the Kingston inhabitants had agreed to part with the common land at Gallows Hill, provided they received quick payment. Mortlake's obstinacy was reported.[7]

Already by April 1635, however, the process of enclosure had begun. On 12 February the King had empowered Lord Cottington to contract for the construction of a brick wall with an estimated compass of eight miles. Cottington employed one Edward Manning 'to take the care and oversight of the said work and the payment of the workmen'.[8]

Meanwhile the Commission pressed on with its negotiations. The inhabitants of Richmond agreed in January 1635/6 to give up their rights in 92 acres of common,[9] though in the event they lost only some 70 acres. A deal was struck with William Murray, Gregory Cole, and the freeholders and copyholders of Petersham and Ham whereby, for £4,000 compensation, they agreed to relinquish 265 acres of common land in Petersham and 483 acres in Ham.[10]

In 1636 Viscount Wimbledon and his tenants of Mortlake and Putney agreed to surrender 185 acres of commons in Mortlake (as well as a further 23½ acres which were 'in difference [i.e. dispute] between Richmond and Mortlake') and 36 acres of Putney Common.[11]

Gradually, too, the individual owners agreed to sell. There are in fact extant records which cover, in one way or another and in greater or less detail, virtually all the land acquired for the park. Few of these transactions have previously been identified or published. The records now traced, ranging from original copies of contracts of sale to drafts of surrender records in manorial courts, are reviewed in Appendix 8. In some cases the compensation paid is noted; these cover about 75-80 per cent of the land, and include even sub-tenants.

The King probably anticipated expenditure of £20,000 in buying the land, for in November 1635 payment was authorised to Edward Manning and Thomas Young of £10,900 'in part of £20,000 for lands to be taken into the New Park at Richmond'.[12] However the final expenditure clearly exceeded this estimate – if all the compensatory payments were in fact made.

The total of compensation payments so far traced amounts to just over £19,200. A rough estimate, on a comparative basis, can be attempted of the payments that would probably have been made for the other properties. This suggests that the total outlay on the acquisition of land was likely to have been in the region of £25,000. The prices per acre varied considerably – they may have been affected not only by the quality and usage of the land but also by the reluctance or bargaining power of the sellers. The highest price seems to have been £32 per acre for the 1½ acres purchased from Edward Hurst and family in Kingston, and Henry Perkins got over £25 an acre for his nine acres in Petersham. These were small holdings; but some of the major landowners were also able to command high prices. Gregory Cole received more than £22 an acre for Hartleton Farm, and the Juxons in Mortlake averaged almost £20 per acre for their holdings of which a third were woodland. The more normal price for agricultural land seems to have been about £15 an acre – but this was an excellent price in the 1630s. It may be compared with the £5 an acre paid by James I 30 years earlier or with a price of £13 10s. 0d. an acre for four acres of prime land adjacent to Richmond Green in 1631.[13]

Cole sold Hartleton Farm to the King in November 1636,[14] and shortly afterwards sold the Petersham manor house and land, the surrender of which to the Park Commissioners was recorded in the manor rolls in January 1636/7.[15] Whether out of dudgeon at having lost his house, as Clarendon's account would lead one to expect, or whether to invest his gains elsewhere, he promptly left the area. He assigned his rights in the lease of Petersham and Ham manors (which his father had acquired from Sir Thomas Gorges in 1608) to William Murray of Ham House, who already held the reversionary lease granted to him in 1631.[16] Murray's first court as Lord (*pro tempore*) of the manor of Petersham was held on 20 January 1636/7; the first at Ham on 21 April 1637.

Despite the favourable terms offered, the initial opposition of some of the inhabitants of Mortlake was resolute. They appear to have been supported in their protest by the steward of Wimbledon manor. Two notes made by members of the Privy Council record the proceedings of a meeting held on 16 December 1635 when the matter was discussed. Edward Nicholas, clerk of the Council, noted:

> The poor men of Moreclack to be referred to Mr Attorney General to examine and give order. Lord Belhaven to have notice to take such security for them as he thinks fit. Mr Baker, steward of Lord Wimbledon, to be enjoined to deliver the Court Rolls by this day sennight or else to be committed.[17]

Sir Francis Windebank, the Secretary of State, provides the missing detail of the form taken by the Mortlake protest:

> Complaint of Lord Belhaven against certain inhabitants of Mortlake for cutting down bushes and young trees in the ground near Richmond and Mortlake which His Majesty designed to enclose for a park, referred to the Attorney-General.[18]

It may be noted that Mr. Baker was no longer steward of Wimbledon by March 1637.

Whether the King eventually paid compensation to all the individual inhabitants of Mortlake whose land he enclosed is uncertain; but it seems clear that the Mortlake Vestry were never compensated for their 1½ acres of 'church lands'. In February 1636/7 the Vestry did agree that the trustees of the lands should contract with the Commissioners to sell the lands taken into the park,[19] but perhaps the trustees still held out for too high a price. In 1647 the Vestry had to agree to reduce the rent paid by their tenant for the church lands since part of them 'were taken in by his Majesty into the great Park and yet unpaid for'.[20] They were still trying in vain to recover something in 1653 and in 1676.[21]

Edward Manning, perhaps as a result of popular resentment about the park, had some evident difficulty in getting the labour and equipment he needed to complete the enclosure. On 28 March 1636 instructions were sent to 'all Mayors and others the King's officers' to assist him 'in taking up the required bricklayers, labourers, carts and carriages'.[22]

Manning's accounts for the works which he supervised in the park are in four parts, divided not by periods but by tasks. The completion of the brick enclosure wall took almost three years: the first payment was authorised on 26 February 1634/5 and the certificate of completion was signed by the Surveyor-General on 17 December 1637. The wall, originally estimated at only eight miles, was when completed a little over eleven miles in length; at an agreed cost of 45 shillings per rod of 16½ feet for a nine-foot-high wall the total price, including gates and locks and some extra foundations on soft ground, amounted to £8,122 7s. 6d.[23]

The second task, authorised in April 1635, was to make a paddock for deer, enclosed by wooden paling, in the corner of the park near Beverly Bridge. This was quite rapidly accomplished at a cost of £338 5s. 2d. In all nearly a mile and a half of paling was erected, but some of this may have been internal partitioning.[24] This work was followed by the building of a lodge, a deerhouse and a barn, all in the deer paddock, and some further enlargement of the paddock itself. This job, started at the end of May 1635, was not finished until the beginning of March 1636/7. The cost was £874 8s. 7d.[25]

Manning's fourth task, from August 1636 to November 1637, had more of a landscaping nature. It was described as 'railing in coppices, the making of a pond, the cutting of lawns, etc, in the New Park of Richmond, and for bringing in a river'. It was accomplished, at £100 under the estimate, for £1,400 18s. 3½d.[26] The phrase 'bringing in a river' is interesting; it obviously does not refer to Beverly Brook, and is probably to be explained by a harnessing of the springs by what is now White Ash Lodge and in the Sidmouth plantation to feed and supplement the two streams which now run into the Upper Pen pond. This pond may have been the one created at this time; a pond of sufficient size to require a punt existed by 1650.[27] The lawns which were cut may have been in the flat ground between this pond and Hartleton Farm, which now began a new existence as a lodge for a park-keeper.

On 15 June 1637 the King appointed Jerome Weston, Earl of Portland, to be keeper of the New Park of Richmond, Surrey, for life with a fee of 12d. a day. The Earl's appointment was largely an honorary sinecure; the actual work of keeping the park had already been entrusted to two deputies, Ludowick Carlile and Humphrey Rogers. Both were gentlemen, not 'gamekeepers' in the later sense, and had salaries of £50 a year, the payment of which, authorised in November 1637, was backdated to Lady Day 1636.[28] The park was divided into two 'Walks', and each deputy was assigned responsibility for one walk and a lodging in one of Gregory Cole's main houses. To Carlile, keeper of Petersham Lodge and Walk, was allotted the house by the Petersham Road. To Rogers, keeper of Hartleton Lodge and Walk, went the old house at Hartleton Farm. It needed rebuilding, and apparently Rogers organised this himself, for a warrant of 6 July 1637 to pay the Earl of Portland £290 'or as much thereof as shall be expedient' in building a lodge for Rogers was superseded four months later by one to pay the same sum directly to Rogers 'for building a lodge for himself'.[29] Rogers in fact spent £554 5s. 7d. in building this lodge and in a few other small tasks such as the demolition of Loanes house.[30] The new Hartleton Lodge was completed in April 1638.

Once Portland and his deputies had been appointed, and the initial works completed, the responsibility of Lord Cottington and Edward Manning for expenditure on the park ceased. But there was still more work to be done. Lord Portland appears to have submitted a series of accounts of which only one (for 30 June 1638 to 1 February 1638/9 has survived.[31] In this a new contractor, John Cooke, appears; he was paid over £200 in this period for repairs to a lodge and to the paddocks, for building a barn, a deer-house and a boathouse, for making a new paddock, for making bridges, fencing lands, turfing a pond head and 'grubbing up Rydeings' [clearing bridle paths?]. Ludowick Carlile's expenses of £30 'for making a garden about the Greate Lodge' (this must have been Petersham Lodge at this time) were another item in this account. There was also a payment to the widow of one Henry West for his expenses when, 'by his Majesty's special command' he had 'looked into' the woods in the park. Evidently the King had wanted some forestry expertise.

Red deer were already being brought into the park. A payment of £100 was made to Carlile and Rogers in February 1637/8 for 'pease, tares and hay, for the red and fallow deer in the Great Park at Richmond'.[32] In 1640 over £2,000 was paid for the costs of catching red deer in Windsor Forest and transporting them to the New Park in Richmond.[33]

The landowners had lost their lands, but for generous compensation. Manorial tenants suffered from a restriction in grazing rights due to the loss of commons. The manor rolls of Ham laid down new rules. Before the enclosure every tenant had had the right to keep four oxen, three kine, two horses and 63 sheep. This was now sharply reduced to four cows or two horses for houses without land, and six sheep and two oxen or two cows for every 21 acres of land held.[34] Though we have no similar details, the inhabitants of Mortlake, at least, must have suffered a similar reduction in grazing rights. However, we know that monetary compensation was paid to the Ham tenants; and it would appear that the effects of the creation of the New Park on the other inhabitants of the villages around it were not too oppressive. The rights of the people to enter the park to gather firewood and their rights of way across the park were preserved, and gates and ladder-stiles were placed to allow access, at least for those on foot, from each of the surrounding communities.

The inhabitants of Mortlake claimed that their economy was seriously affected by the enclosure of a large area of common field. In January 1637 they petitioned the King for relief from the ship-money assessment 'in regard His Majesty has taken into his park at Richmond one half their lands'.[35] The sheriff of Surrey was told to 'ease them in such proportion as should be just' and to make up the shortfall by getting something extra from 'another part of the county that could more easily bear it'. But the analysis in Appendix 8 shows that an overwhelming proportion of the land that was taken from the Mortlake field was in fact in the hands of just one family – the Juxons, who held the lordship of the sub-manor of East Sheen and West Hall.

In March 1639 William Murray, now lord of the manors of Petersham and Ham by lease, petitioned the King to grant him what was left of those manors outside the park in freehold. He stated that the Queen had directed that a surrender [of her rights therein] should be made to the King. The King agreed, and instructed the Lord Treasurer and the Chancellor to 'compound with

124 A stag hunt in Richmond Park. A painting attributed to Joan Carlile, wife of Ludowick Carlile, keeper of Petersham Walk and Lodge. (Trustees of Lamport Hall)

the petitioner for such valuable consideration for these manors and lands above the rent as they shall find fit, and then give order to the Attorney-General that when the surrender is passed from the Queen to His Majesty he prepare a grant to the petitioner according to his desire'.[36] The grant seems never to have materialised; the Queen did not surrender her rights. Murray repeated his petition in July 1641,[37] but the Civil War intervened and it was not until 1 May 1671 that the Earl (later Duke) of Lauderdale was finally granted the manors in freehold.

The King made good use of his park in the few years that remained before the outbreak of the Civil War. His last visits to the park must have been in August 1647 when he was held prisoner at Hampton Court, while three of his children were at Syon. In addition to the visits which were permitted between the two houses in both directions, the King and the Duke of York – Prince James – were allowed to relax with a little hunting. On 28 August 'the King was a hunting ... in New Park, killed a Stag and a Buck: afterwards dined at Syon'. And a few days later 'the Duke of York, with the Lords, were hunting in the New Parke at Richmond, where was good sport – the King chearefull and much company there'.[38]

After the execution of the King in January 1648/9, the Parliament prepared to sell off the royal lands. As has been related above, Richmond Palace and the Old Park were both sold to private purchasers. But a different fate was reserved for the New Park of Richmond, which – together with Somerset House, Hampton Court, Greenwich, the Tower of London, Windsor Castle and Hyde Park – was excepted from the act providing for the sale of crown lands. On 30 June 1649 the House of Commons (which now was Parliament, the House of Lords having been abolished) resolved 'that the City of London have the New Park, in the County of Surrey, settled upon them and their Successors, as an Act of Favour from this House, for the Use of the City, and their Successors; and that an Act be brought in to that Purpose'.[39]

The Act was passed on 17 July, with an added proviso excepting 'timber trees' (i.e. for the Navy) from the grant, and with a recommendation to the Lord Mayor and Corporation 'that the Keepers in the New Park be continued in their respective Places, and enjoy the Profits thereunto belonging: they continuing faithful to their Trust'.[40] The City Corporation, having set up a committee to handle various matters including the park with terms of reference that looked as though commercial exploitation of the park might be envisaged, was reminded by the House of Commons in February 1649/50 that 'it was the intention of Parliament … that the same should be preserved as a Park still, without Destruction; and to remain as an Ornament to the City, and a Mark of Favour from the Parliament unto the said City'.[41]

Almost at once the City found itself facing bills for repair of the park wall. Perhaps the haste with which the 11 miles of wall had been built – and the difficulties in getting bricklayers – now began to tell. £90 was paid out for repairs in 1650, £60 in 1651, £60 13s. 6d. in 1653, £20 in 1654 and 1655, £26 1s. 6d. in 1656, £2 12s. 8d. in 1657.[42] These and other charges were more than defrayed by the sale of timber; and the fees paid to Carlile and Rogers as keepers were more than doubly offset by renting to them in farm the profits to be made from the use of the park (excepting the deer).[43] A special committee to manage the park was established by the Common Council in 1653.[44]

Despite the annual repairs, the Common Council of the City was informed in November 1659 by the Committee for the New Parke that the wall 'is very much broken downe and decayed and that they had agreed with twoe persons for the makeinge of such a number of Brickes as should be needful for the repairing and amending of the same wall'.[45] The committee was given *carte blanche* and was told to fell and cut as many trees as might be necessary to raise the cost of the repair by the sale of timber.

The City Corporation also took pains to keep up the stock of deer in the park, while enjoying the privilege of being able to order up from time to time 'a brase of fatt Staggs' as a present to the Parliament,[46] or venison 'for entertainment of the Lord Protector and the Common Council'.[47] The keepers appear to have had some initial difficulty in adjusting to the new regime. When the Lord Mayor ordered 'a Bucke for the Commissioners of the monthly Assessment in the County of Surrey' – an assessment the Corporation was trying to get reduced in respect of the park – the keepers refused to provide it. The Lord Mayor had to 'declare the sense of the Court to them personally that they shall obey his Lordship's warrant for deer, and shall give an account from time to time of what deer they shall deliver thereupon'.[48]

When Charles II was about to return to England in 1660 he wrote a long letter from Breda in Holland to the Lord Mayor and Aldermen of London. The City Corporation, who had some natural apprehension about the restoration in view of the City's strong support of Parliament against Charles I, were quick to grasp this olive branch. They sent a deputation of 14 members to the Hague to wait upon the King, and equipped its members not only with a gift of £12,000 (£10,000 for the King, £1,000 each for the Dukes of York and Gloucester), but with the news of instructions that 'the Lord Mayor doe at the first opportunity of His Majesty's comeinge to this City in the name thereof and of this Court, present the newe Parke to His Majesty and inform His Majesty that this Citty hath beene only his Majestyes stewards for the same'.[49] The Lord Mayor and Aldermen waited upon the King on 2 June to congratulate him on his restoration and to make the formal act of restitution of the park. The Lord Mayor took the opportunity in his speech to point out 'that it was well it was in the City's hands for that they had preserved the wood, vert and game'.

King Charles II had the tact to reply 'that he looked upon the said Parke to be kept for him and that hee accepted it not as restored but as freely given unto him by the Citty and thanked them for the same'.[50]

Chapter XV

Richmond in the Civil War

The menace of plague had loomed large again in 1636 when there were further orders to the magistrates to allow no strangers into Richmond – with greater success than in 1625. But in 1640 there was a real scare in the household of the royal children. The plague struck Richmond suddenly in June. Cornelius Holland, paymaster for the royal children, wrote to Sir Henry Vane, Treasurer of the Household, seeking instructions as to whether to move the children from Richmond. 'It has pleased God to visit the town of Richmond with the plague in two houses near to the pond at the entrance to the town. Two died this forenoon full of the tokens out of one house and two more out of another house this afternoon since Dr Chambers was with the King.'[1] Fifty-nine people were buried in Richmond that year in June, July and August.

Cornelius Holland went on to say that he believed the source of the infection in the town was 'a barber's man of the tent who died in one of these houses when Tuesday was sennight'. The 'tent' was probably a tented camp for men of the Surrey trained bands (militia), two hundred of whom had been called out on 15 May 'to guard the House at Richmond to care for the Prince and Their Majesties' other children'.[2]

The country was now moving inexorably towards the breakdown that led to civil war. Already at war with the rebellious Scottish Covenanters, the King lacked money to pay his own troops, who were increasingly discontented. He had dissolved Parliament in 1629 and for 11 years had been trying to rule without one. In April 1640 he finally had to call a new Parliament to ask for money to pursue the Scottish war. Parliament wanted a general redress of grievances and refused to grant money until peace was made with the Scots. On 5 May the 'Short Parliament' was again dissolved by the King. There had been riots in London on May Day. With the country disaffected and his army near to mutiny, the stationing of 200 men of the trained bands to guard Richmond Palace must have seemed a necessary precaution.

This is not the place to chronicle the constitutional victory which the 'Long Parliament', summoned in November 1640, had achieved over the King by the end of 1641, nor the blunders that then plunged the country into a needless civil war. Suffice it to say that in February 1641/2 Queen Henrietta Maria and the Princess Mary (who had been married the previous May, aged nine, to the son of the Prince of Orange) were despatched to the safety of Holland. Likewise the Marquess of Hertford, who had just taken over the post of governor to Prince Charles, got his charge and the Duke of York safely away from Richmond to join the King at Greenwich. From there they set off to the north, and remained together for the next three years of civil war.

So far as is known, no fighting took place within the manor of Richmond during the civil wars, but a number of skirmishes were close enough to cause the inhabitants some alarm. Already in February 1641/2 Sir Richard Onslow, the Deputy Lieutenant of Surrey, had taken action to raise the trained bands and secure for the Parliamentary cause the important arms magazine at Kingston, dispersing the small royalist force which had attempted to seize it. In November 1642 the King was advancing on London from the west on the north side of the river, while Prince Rupert moved up south of the river with a force of cavalry. Rupert's thrust was blocked at Kingston Bridge. He turned back, crossed the river at Staines and joined the King's army in time to defeat the Parliamentary regiments stationed at Brentford. His cavalry then rampaged through the town, causing a lot of damage though no loss of civilian life. Syon House was occupied by the royalist forces, who fired on the ammunition ships being sent down the Thames by the Earl of Essex, the Parliamentary commander, and sank several of them in the river between Syon and Sheen. The royalist advance was however blocked successfully at Turnham Green where Essex had managed to muster a greatly superior force including all the London trained bands. The King withdrew his army, first to Kingston, then to Reading and finally to Oxford.

The fighting did not come near to Richmond again for some years, and though the town had a strong royalist community, it was firmly under Parliamentary control. On 18 September 1643 Parliament moved to protect the park – which park is not certain, but it is probable that Charles I's New Park of Richmond was the one intended. Sir John Dingley, Mr. Doaker and Sir Matthew Brent were appointed 'to care for the preservation of the park, deer and woods within the Park of Richmond, and to depute such persons for the preservation of the said place as they shall think fit'. The 'trained bands and all other persons' were required to assist in preserving the park.[3] Several of the local royalists, including the Duke of Lennox at Sheen, William Murray of Ham House and Richard Bennett of Kew Park, were charged as 'delinquents', their lands were declared sequestrated, and they had to 'compound' for the release of the properties by the payment of large fines.[4]

By 1647 the King was a virtual prisoner in the hands of Parliament, which was however beginning to fall out with its victorious, but independently-minded army. Charles was held at Holmby (or Holdenby) House in Northamptonshire, a country mansion which James I had acquired from Sir Christopher Hatton in 1608. Although kept under guard, he was treated with dignity and respect; he was still the King and, though at a considerable disadvantage, was negotiating with Parliament rather than being dictated to by it. Charles let drop a hint that he might be allowed to take up residence at Richmond. This was approved by a vote in Parliament and a message was sent to the King to seek his confirmation of the arrangement.

However, on 3 June Charles was taken away from Holmby by Cornet Joyce and brought to the army headquarters at Newmarket. His acknowledgement 'well approving that his Parliament have sent their votes to him concerning his removal to Richmond' was received in London on 24 June, but on the previous day General Fairfax had delivered his 'remonstrance' to Parliament and was now moving on London. Where the army went, the King had to follow. An almost contemporary newspaper account says that Fairfax and the army 'also importune the Parliament as they tender the peace and safety of the country that they reassume the consideration of their voting His Majesty's person to Richmond, the army being commanded to withdraw forty miles from London'.[5]

As the dispute between the army and the Parliament grew sharper, and as Parliament was relying on the support of London, Fairfax marshalled the army on Hounslow Heath. On 6 August he advanced into London; and the army became the effective rulers of the country. On 24 August the King was sent to Hampton Court. Although Richmond Palace had been made ready to receive him, the extra distance of Hampton Court from London made it seem a somewhat safer place to keep him securely under the army's aegis.

At Hampton Court Charles was once again installed in relative comfort in a royal palace. He was allowed to visit the Duke of York, Princess Elizabeth and Prince Henry at Syon, where they were held in the care of the Earl of Northumberland. The children were allowed also to visit their father at Hampton Court; and even some hunting together in Richmond Park was permitted to the King and the Duke of York.

Then, on 11 November 1647, Charles made a bid for freedom. He escaped from Hampton Court and made his way to the Isle of Wight where he had hoped that the governor would help him flee the country. Although he was disappointed in this, and his status at Carisbrooke Castle soon deteriorated from royal guest to captive, he was able at the end of December to conclude the secret treaty with Scottish representatives which precipitated the Second Civil War of 1648.

The attack of the Scots in the north was supported by various uprisings of the Cavaliers in England. Among these was one in May-June 1648 led by the Earl of Holland. He set out from Kingston to Reigate but was forced to retreat. On 4 July the Committee of Both Houses, meeting at Derby House, sent instructions to the governor of Windsor Castle to send out cavalry scouts to intercept any threatened surprise attack on Oatlands, Hampton Court, Richmond or Nonsuch.[6] Three days later another instruction went out appointing senior officers to have an especial care of the Thames ferries from Chelsea to Shepperton. Richmond and Kew ferries were put under the charge of Sir Thomas Jervois.[7] A further instruction on the same day was that all ferry boats were to be secured from sunset to sunrise on the Middlesex bank of the river, and that guards were to be posted by day to ensure that none should cross 'except market people and those on state business with passes'.[8] But on that very day, 7 July, a brisk engagement on Kingston Common put an end to the Earl of Holland's uprising.

Charles I never saw Richmond again. From Carisbrooke he was taken to Hurst Castle in Hampshire and from there to Windsor and on to St James's where he was held in close confinement, leaving only to go to his trial in Westminster Hall and his execution in Whitehall.

✠

Following the execution of the King and the formal abolition of the monarchy, Parliament proceeded to the sale of the royal estates, from which much money could be brought into the Treasury. A few palaces, Hampton Court among them, were reserved for Cromwell's use. Richmond New Park was given to the City of London. Richmond Palace and the Little Park with its lodge, and Sheen House (the former Charterhouse) were among those to be sold. Detailed surveys were made of each property; and, though they were unfortunately not accompanied by plans, they contain a great deal of information helping to reconstruct the buildings and lands as they were in 1650. All have been printed elsewhere.[9] Those dealing with the palace and the Little Park have been considered in chapters VI and XII.

The description of the old Charterhouse in the 1650 survey shows that the buildings had by that time been divided up to make a little hamlet of some dozen householders. The Duke of Richmond and Lennox had been assessed by the Committee for Compounding in December 1646 for a vast sum on all his estates, with '£40 added for the site of West Shene Monastery'. He had paid his fine and been discharged in May 1647.[10] Whether it was before or after that time that the dividing up into separate sub-tenancies had taken place is unknown.

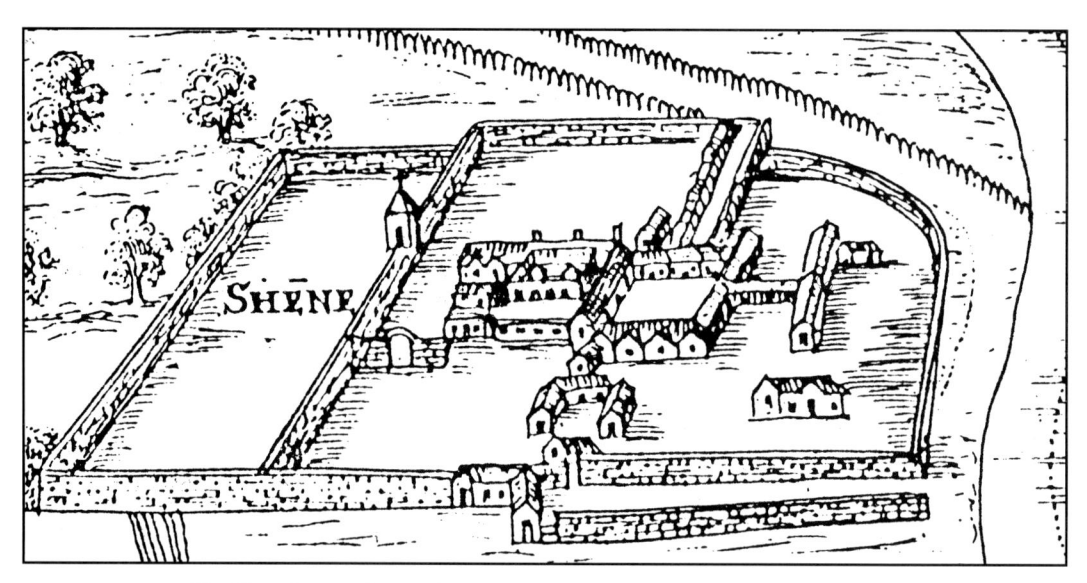

125 The Charterhouse as shown in Moses Glover's map of Isleworth hundred, 1635 (at Syon House).

The main house, formerly the 'Prior's Lodging', was in the occupation of one Humphrey Parke. Of the great church only a part was 'yet standing but very ruinous and fit for nothing but to be demolished'. What may have been the former chapter-house had become 'Lady St John's lodging', then occupied by a George Cooke. (Although the Lady St John cannot be positively identified,[*] this name may suggest that the conversion had been made many years earlier.) The 'monks' hall' [i.e. refectory] was still standing, as were at least six of the former monks' houses. The lay brothers' cloister, though it formed the basis of the royal stables, had in part been turned into two large houses and one smaller one. In the largest of these lived Sir John Dingley of whom his memorial in Richmond Church says that 'he lived and died [in 1671] imperturbable, taking no part in the very turbulent affairs of state'.[11]

There is a comprehensive description of the royal stables, which consisted of the 'riding house', a stable for 16 'great horses', stables for six hunters and six coach horses, another range with a coach-house and stabling for a further 18 horses, a saddler's office, a smith's forge and a 'great barn', and four acres of stable yard called the 'Little Frayles'.

Sheen was sold on 29 May 1650 to Alexander Eaton for £2,233 11s. 9d.[12] The Little Park with the lodge went for nearly £8,000 to William Brome.[13] Richmond Palace, together with 'the Fryars', Richmond Green, the Keeper's Close at the north end of the Little Park, Stony Close in Kew, a meadow in Shepperton (originally attached to the park to provide hay for the deer), the Queen's Stable on the north side of Richmond Green, the proprietorship of Richmond Ferry, and the lordship of the manor, was sold to a three-man consortium, Thomas Rokeby, William Goodrick and Adam Baynes, for the sum of £13,562 0s. 6d. The contract of sale was agreed on 12 April,[14] and the sale completed on 10 July 1650.[15]

✠

What happened next is somewhat obscure. The original purchasers must have sold their interest very quickly, unless they were just front men. The lordship of the manor was acquired

---

[*] She was presumably the widoe of Oliver St John, first Lord St John of Bletsho (d.1582), for the latter was involved in the reception of Cardinal Chatillon at Shene in 1568 (see p.114).

by the regicide Sir Gregory Norton, Bart, a former member of the Parliamentary Committee for Revenues and of the Committee for Compounding. On his death (he was buried in Richmond on 26 March 1652), he disinherited his only surviving son Henry, who succeeded to the baronetcy, and made his friend Humphrey Edwards, another regicide, his heir in Richmond. Edwards, who is mentioned as 'Lord of the Manor' in January 1652/3,[16] lived in Richmond until his death in 1658 (buried 2 August); he seems, however, to have relinquished the lordship of the manor to Martha, Lady Norton, Sir Gregory's widow, in whose name the manor court was convened in April 1655.[17] Martha then married on 22 October 1655[18] Robert Gordon, 4th Viscount Kenmure, an active Scottish royalist who had taken part in Charles II's campaign in 1651, when he was taken prisoner at Worcester, and then in the Earl of Glencairn's rising in 1653, after which a price was put on his head. Quite how he then made his peace so rapidly and successfully that he could become, by marriage, lord of the manor of Richmond[19] within two years is a question that might repay further study.

Again, however, there seems to have been an abdication. Kenmure lived until February 1662/3 and Lady Martha until 1671, but by January 1657/8 the Richmond manor courts were being held in the name of Sir Henry Norton,[20] who then remained lord of the manor until the restoration of King Charles II.

The Nortons did not however use the palace as a splendid residence. Instead, it seems to have been turned into a stone quarry. It seems probable that the purchasers in 1650 sold it off in several parcels, and that the Nortons bought only the lordship and part of the brick buildings facing the Green and the outer court. One Henry Carter seems to have acquired title to the stone buildings – the Privy Lodgings, the Chapel, the Hall, etc. 'Henry Carter of Richmond was the first puller-down of the King's house there', reported an informant, Elizabeth Mollett, in June 1660, 'and sold the stone and material of the house to the value of £2000 and upwards … and was one of the good buyers himself … and raised forces within these last three months to oppose the Restoration'.[21]

The process of demolition had started almost at once. On 30 October 1651 William Leaver was fined 3s. 4d. by the manor court 'for driving his cart loaden with stones within ten days last past from the Great House cross Richmond Green out of the usual way to the prejudice thereof contrary to several orders in that behalf made'.[22]

The new owners were not very careful of the rights of the inhabitants. From 1651 the manor court records are full of 'presentments' made against 'the Owners of the Park' for closing 'the ancient highway leading to Sheen'; against Mr. Wilby for closing 'the ancient way to the Crane' (Old Palace Lane); against George Carter for attempting to enclose part of the Green; against Henry Carter for straitening (restricting) Friars Lane 'under pretence of a right thereunto'; against the lord of the manor himself for proposing to enclose with a brick wall part of the Green in front of the palace where there had formerly been merely a chequer rail for ornament; and so on.[23] The complaint about Old Palace Lane was repeated year after year without any apparent effect.

The separate survey made of Crane Piece in May 1653[24] may have been instigated by this dispute. The eventual outcome seems to have been the enclosure of all of Crane Piece except for a lane preserved as a right of way and a wider patch of ground by the river's edge. The enclosed land, which included the 'building intended for a Waterhouse called the Rockhouse, but never finished', became eventually the site of Asgill House and the major part of its grounds.

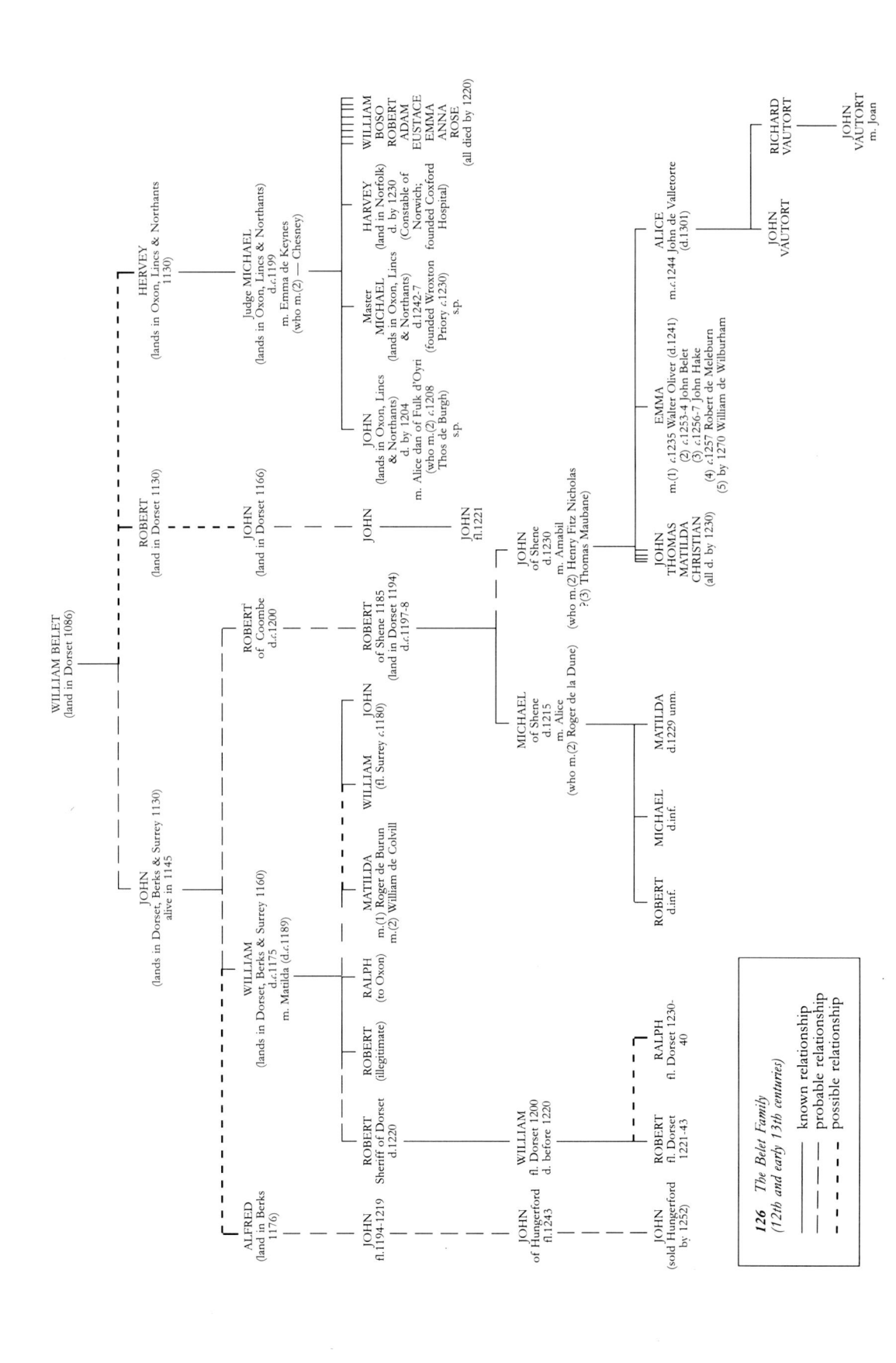

126 *The Belet Family*
(12th and early 13th centuries)

Appendix I

The Belet Family in the 12th and Early 13th Centuries

William Belet, whose name is in the Battle Abbey roll, was a landowner in Dorset at the time of the Domesday Survey, holding Frome [Belet], Woodsford, Nutsford, Lyme, and other land in the county.[1]

From him the two main branches of the family seem to have sprung: one (which divides in the next two generations) in Dorset and Surrey, and the other with lands chiefly in Oxfordshire, Northamptonshire and Lincolnshire. As explained below, the Revd. Owen Manning in his monumental *History of Surrey* confused these two branches. His error has been perpetuated by others who have used him as a source, including the author of the articles on the family in the *Dictionary of National Biography*.

The Pipe Roll for 31 Henry I (1130-1) lists two Belets: John with lands in Dorset, Berkshire and Surrey;[2] and Harvey with lands in Oxfordshire, Northamptonshire and Lincolnshire.[3] We may assume that John was the son (or at least the direct heir) of the original William, for his holdings in Dorset are identifiable with William's. Whether Harvey was also a son of William is uncertain, but a close relationship with the Dorset-Surrey branch seems probable.

Harvey's branch of the family is easier to trace and it will be convenient to deal with it first. His son and successor was Michael Belet who held land in the same three counties. In the reign of Henry II he was made a judge, and he also held the appointment of cupbearer to the King. This was a real job – in effect that of wine steward – not a titular one. Michael Belet's name appears in the Pipe Rolls from 2 Henry II (1155-6) onwards. In 1165-6 occurs a payment to him for sending the King's wine from Oxford to Woodstock.[4] In 1171-2 he is referred to for the first time as '*pincerna*' – cupbearer.[5] There are other references to his responsibility for the King's wine supply in various parts of the country.[6] He was Sheriff of Surrey in 1174-5 and in the following year became Sheriff of Worcester, an appointment which he held for 10 years before moving to be Sheriff of Warwickshire and Leicester. He figures in the accounts for many counties as a judge or as a tax assessor, but he never appears to have held any land (except temporarily in Worcester in his office as Sheriff) outside the three counties of Oxfordshire, Northamptonshire and Lincolnshire. He married Emma, daughter of John de Keynes, and had eight sons and three daughters. He died about 1199; and his widow subsequently married a Chesney.

The whole of this Michael's family is named in the foundation charter of the priory of Wroxton in Oxfordshire, founded and endowed about 1230 by his son, another Michael.[7] This second Michael was a canonist and a civil lawyer, and is nearly always referred to in the rolls as 'Master Michael Belet'. Of Master Michael's brothers we need note only two: John, the eldest, who died about 1204 leaving a widow Alice, daughter of Fulk d'Oyri, and Harvey. There were many claims for the right of giving – or taking – Alice's hand in marriage, but all the references to these occur in the counties of Northamptonshire, Lincolnshire and Norfolk (where the Belets had apparently acquired some land including the manor of Roudham).[8] A suit of dower brought by Alice in 1204 against her brother-in-law Master Michael, who had inherited John's lands, refers specifically to Wroxton in Oxfordshire, Thorpe Underwood in Northamptonshire and Syston in Lincolnshire.[9]

In 1206 Master Michael Belet applied for the post of King's cupbearer, as of his right 'as Michael, father of the aforesaid Master Michael, held it', and agreed to pay £100 for the King's charter granting the office.[10] After £60 of this sum had been paid, the King reneged on the grant. In 1212, when Master Michael still owed 60 marks (£40) it was noted that 'he should not be summoned to account because the King has kept that office in his own hands and still holds it'.[11] There had evidently been some trouble between King John and Master Michael, for in 1211 the latter had accounted for a debt of 500 marks 'for having the goodwill of the King, and for his lands and rents of which he was disseised on account of the King's displeasure with him'.[12]

All these references appear in the Pipe Rolls for Oxfordshire, and had nothing to do with Shene in Surrey. The regrant to Master Michael made in 1211 is presumably the charter of King John later mentioned in the Charter Rolls in 1252: 'The King [Henry III] has inspected the charter whereby King John confirmed to Master Michael Belet all the lands of Harvey his grandfather, with certain liberties, and [grants] confirmation of these liberties to the Prior and Canons of Wroxton who now hold the said lands by the gift of the said Michael, the founder of that house.'[13]

Master Michael, having bought his way back into the King's favour, appears to have finally succeeded in obtaining his appointment as cupbearer. At the banquet to celebrate the wedding of Henry III with Eleanor of Provence and the new Queen's coronation in 1236 he was listed as playing his part as cupbearer in the King's house by ancient right, at the side of the Earl of Arundel who was the King's Butler. Master Michael's role was described as being 'to pass the refilled cup to the Earl whenever the King asked the Earl for it'.[14]

Master Michael died in the mid-1240s. He appears to have given all his estates to his foundation of Wroxton Priory.[15] His brother Harvey, who was Constable of Norwich, gave the manor of Roudham in Norfolk to St Mary's Coxford to found a hospital there.[16]

The Pipe Roll of 1130-1 lists John Belet with three entries in Dorset (one of which links him with a holding of forest in Berkshire), one entry in Berkshire (which links him with Surrey) and three entries in Surrey.[17] Of the Surrey entries one concerns the debt which he owed 'for having back his lands of Sceanes'. A second entry is an assessment for 60 shillings owing for 'a long standing knight's fee', and the third discharges him of debts of 40 shillings and 22 shillings arising from unspecified holdings in Surrey. From the later evidence, these other holdings must be at Bagshot and Coombe, for there is no indication that the Belets ever held any other land in Surrey. It may well be that the Belet lands at Bagshot stretched over the county boundary to link up with a holding in the great forest of Windsor in Berkshire.

There are no more surviving Pipe Rolls until 1155. We may however reasonably assume that the John Belet who witnessed a charter of Robert de Newburgh in Dorset at some date between 1154 and 1159[18] was the John Belet of 1130-1.[19] Then a new generation of Belets appears. In 1160-1 Robert Belet paid a new debt of 40 shillings for 'forfeiture' of his lands in Surrey.[20] This was a voluntary forfeiture, and the lands in question appear to be Coombe and Bagshot.

In 1163-4 the Sheriff of Surrey accounted for £10 in respect of the escheated estate of Robert Belet,[21] and in the following year a breakdown of the accounts enables us to identify this estate as being made up as follows:[22]

Coombe, a member of Kingston	£7
Pasture in the park of Coombe	14s.
Another pasture [at Ham]	3s.
Another pasture in Kingston	3s.
Bagshot	£2
[Total]	£10 0s.

Bagshot disappeared from the list of escheats in the following year, and it was probably restored to the Belet family (though not to Robert). The sums for Coombe, etc., are shown year after year, though the value of the pasture in Kingston was increased from three shillings to seven shillings in 1165-6,[23] and then to 30 shillings in 1167-8.[24] That last amendment brought the total annual revenue due from the escheated Belet estate to £9 7s.; and that sum is then included in the Sheriff's accounting each year for more than twenty years. At the beginning of Richard I's reign, as will be described below, Robert Belet finally recovered the Coombe estate.

The voluntary surrender of Coombe may have been part of a deal in return for which Robert Belet was granted a valuable fishery. This was probably at Kew, and he paid for it a fine of 100 marks – by instalments over the next 18 years.[25]

Shene is never mentioned explicitly in the Pipe Rolls at this time. Obviously it was not a part of the lands surrendered by Robert Belet or it would have been specified in the accounts. This could be because he was never Lord of Shene, or it could be that he retained Shene. The grant of the fishery (which later became the fishery of the manor of Shene) would in itself suggest that Robert was the lord of the manor. However, there is good reason for doubting this, and for accepting the alternative explanation – that Shene was inherited by a brother of Robert, named William Belet.

In Dorset, John Belet appears to have been succeeded by a William Belet whose name occurs in the Red Book of the Exchequer (from 1160-1) and in the Pipe Rolls (from 1167).[26] The Red Book shows William as also liable in 1166 for two knight's fees in Surrey.[27] As Coombe is now excluded, these are presumably for Shene and Bagshot – and we may assume that it was William to whom Bagshot was regranted. William next appears as a witness to a Merton Priory deed concerning land in Fetcham in 1167.[28] He must also have inherited the forest holding in Berkshire, although this only becomes apparent at the time of his death. In 1175-6 he is recorded as owing 20 marks for a forest levy in that county – but with the annotation 'he is dead'.[29]

In that same year 1175-6 a Robert Belet appeared for the first time in the Dorset accounts, in succession to William,[30] but he did not take over the Berkshire debt, and this appears to mark the final separation of the Dorset estates from those in Surrey and Berkshire. In Surrey there are two more entries about the forest levy: 'Ralph Belet son of William owes half a mark for the same' and 'Robert, bastard son of William Belet, owes half a mark for the same'.[31] The Robert who succeeded to the Dorset estates was probably a legitimate son of William.

These debts for the forest levy in Berkshire took a long time to clear up, apart from the half mark owed by the bastard Robert, which he seems to have paid promptly. For the next three years William's debt is recorded each year, always with the 'but he is dead' note appended. Ralph's debt of half a mark is similarly recorded in Surrey, though in 1176-7 it is specifically noted as arising in Berkshire.[32] Then in 1179-80 the 20 marks owed by William is split up in the Berkshire accounts: 10 marks are to be paid by his widow (named in the following year as Matilda), and 10 marks are to be paid by their son Ralph, who has now moved to Oxfordshire.[33] Ralph settled this debt, and his original debt of one half mark, by 1182-3, in the Oxfordshire accounts.[34] In each of two years Matilda paid one mark in Berkshire towards the reduction of her debt, but she still owed £5 6s. 8d. when her name appears for the last time in 1188-9.[35] Presumably she then died also, for in the following year and thereafter until 1194 the outstanding debt of £5 6s. 8d. is noted under the old formula as due from William 'but he is dead'.[36] After 1194 the debt was apparently written off.

Ralph Belet, after his sojourn in Oxfordshire, appears to have been engaged on royal service. In 1195 he passed through Hampshire with a party escorting someone to the King.[37] In 1203 he was again noted on escort duty in Hampshire for which his expenses were paid;[38] and in the following year he was taking money overseas on the King's behalf.[39]

If the assumption made earlier that there is a direct connection between the forest holding in Berkshire and the holding at Bagshot is correct, this Ralph Belet may well be the Ralph mentioned in the report of jurors of Bagshot, in 1212, who had been dispossessed by Henry II because he was in arrears with his service.[40] The Belets however kept part of Bagshot, which suggests that the division of the debt between Ralph and his mother had resulted in a division of the lands, half of which went to another heir of William and Matilda.

To return to Surrey, Robert Belet continued year by year to pay off by instalments his debt for the fishery, which he finally cleared in 1182-3, and each year until 1189 the Sheriff continued to account for the escheated lands at Coombe. Shene is never mentioned. But in 1185-6 a Robert Belet starts to account in Surrey for a debt of 30 marks 'as a fine for his land'.[41] This cannot be Coombe which was not regranted until 1190. It must therefore be Shene and what was left of Bagshot.

A series of questions now present themselves. Who is this Robert Belet? Is he Robert, the once and future Lord of Coombe? Is he a son, a nephew, a grandson, of William? Is he Robert of Dorset? The available evidence does not enable a positive identification to be made, but it does suggest a plausible hypothesis.

In the first place it seems unlikely that Robert of Shene could be a son of William, unless he were either identical with Robert of Dorset or Robert the bastard. To have had a legitimate and an illegitimate son with the same name is at least possible; two legitimate sons and an illegitimate son with the same names stretches credulity too far.

It is also unlikely that Robert of Shene is the illegitimate son, for bastards could not inherit lands held in chief from the King. Such lands could perhaps be regranted, but in that case the lands would have had to have been escheated first – and there is no sign of that.

We can be certain that Robert of Shene was not Robert of Dorset, who obtained a large new estate in that county (half the honour of Powerstoke) in 1194.[42] In addition to the entries concerning this and the old knight's fee, the Dorset Pipe Roll for that year has another entry referring specifically to 'Robert Belet of Shene' who had a grant of land at Cnichteton (Knighton) for which he paid £4 as a fine.[43] He is thus clearly distinguished from the local Robert, who became Sheriff of Dorset and Somerset in 1199 and held that post until 1207, by which time Robert of Coombe and Robert of Shene were dead.[44]

Then there is the question why, if William died about 1175, it should be 10 years before this fine is levied from Robert 'for his lands'. They were, it would seem, neither escheated nor held in wardship, so they were presumably inherited directly by a son of William. Apart from the two Roberts considered above, and Ralph who seems to have disappeared from Surrey, we know of no other sons. But there were two other Belets, brothers, who were around in Surrey shortly after the death of William in 1175. They were 'John Belet and William his brother', witnesses to a Merton Priory deed during the time of Prior Robert (1177-86).[45] They might be sons of William. One of them might have inherited Shene and Bagshot, and then have died about 1185, without having a direct heir. So Robert then inherited, and not being a direct heir had to pay a fine for his lands.

It is of interest that two other Merton deeds were witnessed by 'Robert Belet', one during the same priorate, the other dating between 1186 and 1198.[46] Unfortunately these deeds, relating to land at Kingston, give no clue as to whether the Robert Belet is 'of Coombe' or 'of Shene'.

Were Robert of Coombe and Robert of Shene one and the same? This again seems unlikely, for two reasons. The records show quite clearly that the re-grant of Coombe was not made until 1190, and that the Robert to whom it was re-granted was the same man who had voluntarily forfeited the estate 30 years before. The entry concerning the annual rent reads: 'Robert Belet owes £9 7s in Coombe and Kingston by letter of the King in this year and henceforth'.[47] A further entry, concerning the fine, states that 'Robert Belet owes four score marks for having his heritage of Coombe with the park which is worth £9 7s, from which the King's father disseised him with his consent'.[48] Robert Belet of Coombe must therefore have been at least fifty years old – probably more – in 1190. But when Robert Belet of Shene died in 1197 or 1198 he left as his heir a son who was only about ten years old.

The fathering of a son at the age of 50 would not be impossible, but the argument is strengthened by a second point. The death of Robert of Shene is signalled by the Pipe Roll entry in 1198: 'Richard de Heriet accounts for £100 for having the wardship of the land and heir of Robert Belet, and the right of marrying him so that this be not to his disparagement'.[49] This is not however matched by any change in the accounting for the annual rent for Coombe. In 1198 and 1199 Robert Belet of Coombe is still shown as himself paying the rent of £9 7s.[50] It is only in 1200 that the rent for Coombe is shown as due from 'the heir of Robert Belet'.[51] So the elderly Robert of Coombe appears to have outlived by two years the younger Robert of Shene.

If we accept that the two Roberts are different people, the younger Robert could hardly have been the son of John or William (sons of the William who died in 1175) for the insertion of an extra generation here is almost impossible. A likelier hypothesis is that Robert of Shene was the son of Robert of Coombe. Whether Shene passed directly to Robert of Coombe on William's death in 1175 and was then surrendered by him to Robert the younger in 1185 (perhaps when he attained his majority) or whether it passed through the hands of a son of William who, dying childless in 1185, left it to his cousin Robert cannot be answered positively; but the fine levied in 1185 makes the second the more likely hypothesis. In any case a father-son relationship between Robert the elder and Robert the younger makes the generations fit appropriately and provides an easy explanation why the heir to both was the same young boy – the ward of Richard de Heriet.

In 1204 'the heir of Robert Belet' was assessed in Surrey for 100 shillings for a scutage levied at the rate of two and a half marks (33s. 4d.) per knight's fee.[52] This shows that he must have held three fees, which must include Coombe as well as Shene and Bagshot. Meanwhile, Richard de Heriet was paying off his debt for the wardship by instalments each year up to 1206. He then made over the remainder of the debt to Philip de Oxey.[53] In 1207 Oxey settled the debt and also cleared the outstanding sum still owing on the scutage.[54] With these debts settled, the Surrey Belets disappear from the Pipe Rolls for the next few years.

The Pipe Rolls up to 1207 do not give the name of the heir of Robert Belet (or of both Roberts). This is however revealed in the Book of Fees and in the Red Book of the Exchequer. An original list of serjeanties compiled about 1207 is probably the source for later lists in the Book of Fees dated 1244 and 1247-50.[55] A similar list dated 1210-12 is in the Red Book.[56] In these it is stated that Shene was held by Michael Belet by serjeanty of cupbearer. Though the dates of these lists may be open to question, there is a list compiled in 1212 which is exactly dateable, and is also more informative. It was drawn up with a view to considering the commutation of serjeanties into a money rent. Local juries were appointed, and the returns were delivered to the Exchequer on 30 June 1212.

For Shene the jurors reported: 'Syenes was demesne of the King. The old King Henry [Henry I] gave the manor of Syenes to the forebears of Michael Belet who now holds it by serjeanty of cupbearer.'[57]

The report by the Bagshot jurors was more complicated: 'Bacshet was the King's demesne and Ralph held the farm of 40 shillings and King Henry the father of our King [i.e. Henry II], because the service was in arrears, gave it to Hoppescourt by serjeanty of veltrary [the service of slipping the hounds when the King was hunting], and Robert de Basing purchased the same part of it and paid the King 40 shillings and had a charter of the King, and Robert de Basing his heir now holds it. The old King Henry [Henry I] gave another part of Bacsiet to John Belet but the service for it is not known. And Michael Belet his heir now holds it.'[58]

Michael Belet disposed of the Bagshot holding before his death in 1215.[59] After his death Coombe (not mentioned in the 1212 report because it was not a serjeanty) came into the hands of the Nevill family. So the Belet estate in Surrey was reduced to Shene only – still held in theory by serjeanty of cupbearer; but the serjeanty had been commuted 'in the time of King John' to an annual rent of four shillings.[60]

The serjeanty of cupbearer was a duty only performed at the coronation – and was something different from the post held by the Oxfordshire Belets. But it was of course the fact that Shene was held by a Michael Belet by serjeanty of cupbearer at the very time that Master Michael was claiming his hereditary right to the office of cupbearer that led both the indexer of one of the earliest published collections of rolls and the Revd. Owen Manning to confuse the two Michaels and the two branches of the family.[61] But Master Michael outlived Michael of Shene by some thirty years.

From the time of Michael Belet onwards the descent of Shene is quite clear and the genealogy of the other branches of the Belet family ceases to be of direct concern. There is however one question remaining – the identity of the John Belet, lay brother, who married Emma Oliver (née Belet) of Shene in 1253 or 1254.

On the identity of this John Belet we can only speculate, but it seems likely that he was a distant cousin. There are two cadet branches of the family which can be traced but which have not yet been considered. One is in Dorset, holding a small amount of land which is not identifiable. The first reference to this may be the 1130-1 entry which shows a Robert Belet (?brother of John) owing five shillings.[62] In 1166 a John Belet held one-fifth of a knight's fee.[63] This holding reappears in a Fine Roll in 1221 when John Belet, son of John Belet, paid 20 shillings for a relief of his one-fifth of a fee in Dorset 'which John Senior held in chief and to whom John Junior is the next heir'.[64] The John (Senior) of 1221 was probably the son of the John of 1166. The John (Junior) might be the husband, or father of the husband, of Emma Oliver.

Another, and perhaps somewhat likelier, source for Emma's husband is a family in Hungerford. In 1186-7 an Alfred Belet had a holding in Berkshire on which he was assessed for four shillings.[65] Perhaps he was a brother of William and Robert. In 1194 a John Belet paid four shillings scutage.[66] By 1203 this holding of John Belet is clearly identified as one-fifth of a knight's fee;[67] and in 1219 it is shown as being for one hide in Hungerford.[68] In 1242-3 the one-fifth fee is held by John Belet of 'Ingleford' (Hungerford).[69] By 1252 John Belet of Ingleford had disposed of his land to Nicholas Yatingden who was granted a confirmatory charter.[70] Is it possible that John Belet had disposed of this land prior to becoming a lay brother?

Appendix 2

The Sites of the Old Manor House and the 14th- and 15th-Century Palaces

It is clear that the 14th-century palace was, like its successors, by the riverside, that it was moated, and that it had two courts: the inner, lower or 'Douncourt' (later corrupted to 'Touncourt') and the outer, upper or 'Overcourt'. Douncourt was where the bulk of the living accommodation was situated; Overcourt contained the farm buildings. As the Douncourt is mentioned in Queen Isabella's time,[1] it is safe to assume that the old manor house already had these two courts before Edward III reconstructed it as a palace.

That there was already a moat is evident from the expenditure of £28 as early as 1361-2 for 'cleaning out the moat'.[2] Richard II's instructions for demolition referred to 'the houses and buildings in the court within the moat and the court without the moat';[3] so the moat must have been between the two courts. It surrounded the Douncourt; Overcourt was outside it.

The documents referring to the works on the Lancastrian palace clearly distinguish between three areas; 'the site of the old manor of Shene', 'the new manor of Shene' and 'the manor of Byfleet at Shene'; it is equally clear that these were adjacent to each other. New moats were dug to separate them. In 1414 £14 3s. 4d. was paid for a 'ditch between the manor of Shene and the new timber building called Byfleet'.[4] In 1436-9 a great moat 25-feet wide and eight-feet deep was dug between 'the old site of the manor of Shene' and 'the new building of the manor of Shene'.[5] These references show that neither the new building nor Byfleet was on the site of the old manor house and the 14th-century palace.

'Byfleet' can with reasonable certainty be equated with the site of the friary founded by Henry VII. Having its own chapel, it would have been an obvious choice for a complex in which to house the friars. The cost of the new foundation would be limited to the necessary alterations – and there is certainly no indication in the accounts of major expenditure on the friars' new home. The building, presumably the friary chapel, drawn by Wyngaerde in 1562, appears by its style far more likely to have been constructed in the early 15th century than in the early 16th century. Byfleet, then, was at the south-east end of the palace group.

That means in turn that the site of the main building of the Lancastrian palace, started by Henry V but not finished until Henry VI's reign, was central, with 'the old site of the manor of Shene' on its north-western side. It has already been remarked (p.33) that the plan of the Privy Lodgings block of the Tudor palace resembled that of a 15th-century castle, and that Henry VII's work probably used the foundations, at least, of the Lancastrian building. It is thus possible to equate the site of 'the new building of the manor of Shene' with that of the Tudor Privy Lodgings – in what is now the lawn of Trumpeters' House. Between this and the Byfleet site was empty ground, developed as a garden. At the south-east side of this garden would have been the ditch dug in 1414 between 'the manor of Shene' and 'Byfleet'.

The site of the original manor house and of the Plantagenet palace must therefore have been to the north-west again: in the area which was the great orchard of the Tudor palace and which is now the gardens of Trumpeters' Lodge (and part of the grounds of Asgill House).

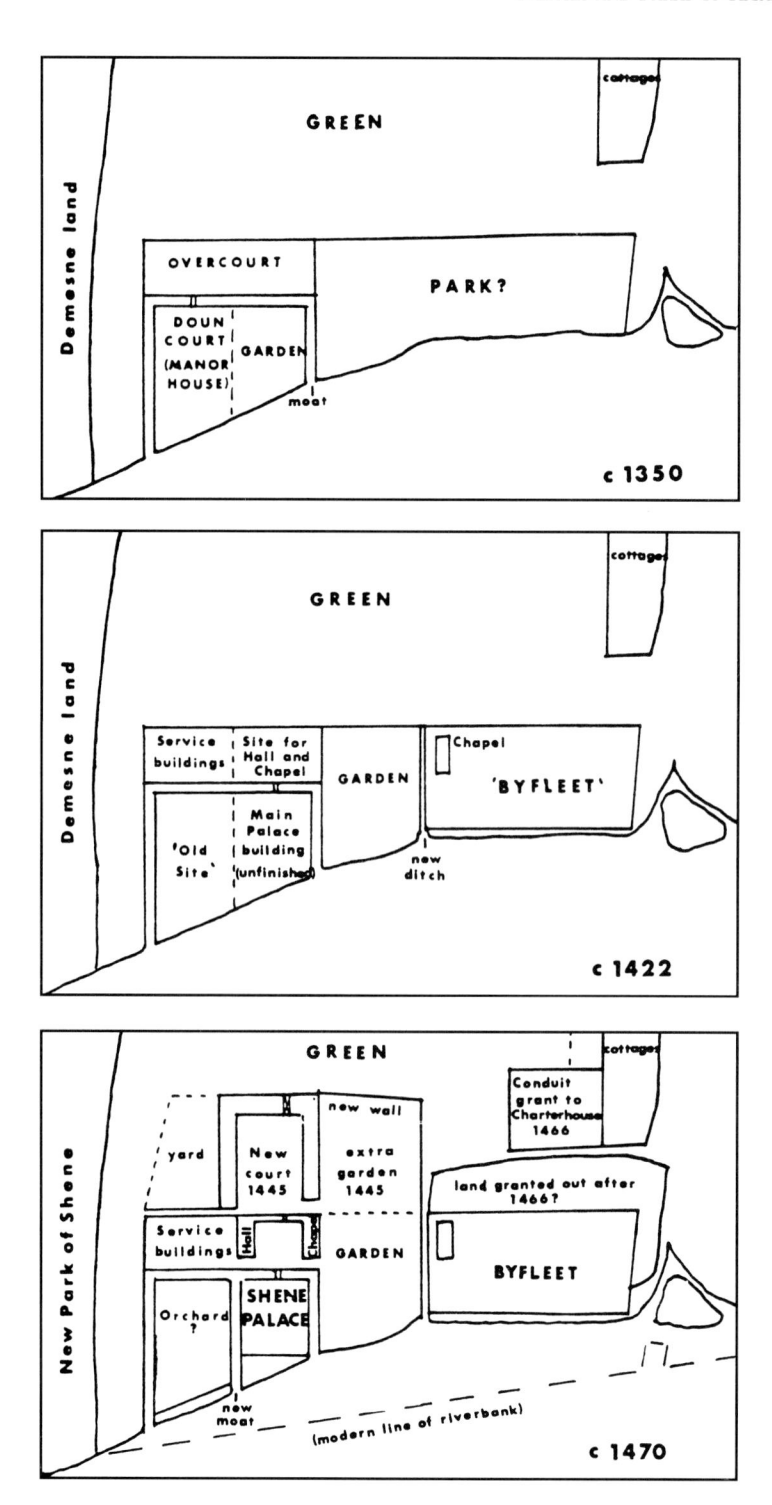

127 The sites of the 14th- and 15th-century palaces (diagrammatic and not to scale).

How much of this complex was enclosed by the original moat? It cannot have been the manor house Douncourt only, or it would not have been necessary to dig the new section of moat in 1436-9. The dimensions quoted in the context of cleaning operations in 1371[6] and 1376[7] are useful, but anomalous. An exact measurement is given on each occasion for the length of moat cleaned; but the figures are significantly different – 874 feet 6 inches in 1371; only 738 feet in 1376. Why was this, and why were two relatively expensive cleaning operations necessary within five years? The answer must be that the building works of the 1370s had choked the moat with debris, but that not all of it needed to be cleaned out in 1376.

Looking at the reconstructed plan of the Tudor palace, it is possible to fit these dimensions very neatly. The river at that time widened considerably from the 'Crane Wharf' eastwards. Its line can be seen in the riverside wall of the great orchard, which runs back at an angle from the present riverside wall of the Trumpeters' Lodge garden. That there was only a narrow bank between this wall and then the Privy Lodgings and the river is evident from the Wyngaerde drawings. The inside measurements of a moat running from Crane Wharf along the north-western side of the great orchard, then turning at right angles to separate the orchard from the kitchens area, and the Privy Lodgings from the buildings in Fountain Court, then turning again at right angles back to the river immediately outside the south-eastern façade of the Privy Lodgings would be approximately 350 feet plus 400 feet plus 150 feet. These give a total of 900 feet, and a figure of 750 feet if the short arm is omitted – which almost fit the 1370s figures. One has only to assume that by Tudor times the building-up of wharves by the ends of the moat may have pushed the river-bank some ten to twelve feet further out into the river to claim that the fit could be exact.

There is other evidence for the moat on this line. Some excavations in 1972 revealed an early 17th-century moat wall near the northern corner of the moat postulated above – in alignment with the suggested north-eastern arm of the moat.[8] Though this may be attributed to the works undertaken in 1610-12, and may have been an extension of the original moat rather than a reconstruction of it (as the old moat was itself probably filled in at this time), the alignment is significant. Wyngaerde's drawings, though not showing the end of a moat by Crane Wharf, do show conduit arches and overflow pipes in the wall of the kitchen quarters, which suggest the existence of a moat at that end of the great orchard. That a moat separated the Tudor Privy Lodgings and the palace gardens is evident from the construction of a bridge 'going over the moat into the garden' in 1517[9] and from the repair of 'the privy bridge out of the King's lodging into the garden' in 1534.[10]

The conclusion must be therefore that the Tudor Privy Lodgings (and therefore the main building of the Lancastrian palace) were built within the original moat. As they were not on the site of the original manor house and palace, the area where they were built was probably the original garden. This in turn explains why there was no need to clear out the short arm of the moat in 1376 – it was remote from the scene of the recent building work.

To summarise: along the river-bank in the mid-15th century would have been, from west to east:

the Crane wharf,
the western arm of the original moat,
the site of the manor house and the Plantagenet palace,
the new moat dug in 1436-9,
the main building of the Lancastrian palace,
the eastern arm of the original moat,
the gardens,
the ditch dug in 1414,
the Byfleet buildings.

On the landward side of these sites there is another apparent anomaly. The north-eastern boundary of the friary (and so of Byfleet) lay on a line (behind the present King Street buildings) that was approximately that of the front of Trumpeters' House and the lane leading from the main court of the palace out into Old Palace Lane (anciently Crane Piece). Today, and certainly since Tudor times, the palace area protrudes a couple of hundred feet north-eastwards beyond this line. It is inherently probable that, as long as the manor house and the palace in the early days had only two courts, the boundary was in a continuous line with that of Byfleet. The 14th-century 'Overcourt' would thus have been in the area where the kitchen buildings, woodyard, etc., of the Tudor palace stood – and perhaps covered the whole area north of the moat, taking in also the site of Trumpeters' House.

There are no clear references to courts in the building accounts of 1413-22 or of the 1430s, but the references therein to the 'great chapel' (apparently in distinction from the Byfleet chapel) and to the 'great hall' suggest the possibility that these were built, detached from the main building, in a separate court outside the moat. The likeliest hypothesis is that this was the origin of the 'Fountain Court' of the Tudor plan, which at this point also echoed its 15th-century predecessor. There is, for instance, a reference to a closet built for the King on the south (i.e. the south-east) side of the chapel – where the 'Queen's closet' was located in the 1649 inventory. A new range of buildings was erected to the north (i.e. north-west) of the great hall – where the Tudor kitchens were.[11]

The instructions given to the clerk of works in 1445 to 'new make a great quadrangle with a gatehouse all of new' and a new brick wall to enclose the garden[12] may well mark the decision to enclose part of the Green in order to extend the palace. On this hypothesis the new 'great quadrangle' was the predecessor of the great outer court of Tudor times – now Old Palace Yard – and the new wall enclosing an enlarged garden would have stood where the Tudor palace had its range of lodgings overlooking the Green, on the sites of Maids of Honour Row, etc.

The measurements given by William of Worcester when he visited Shene in 1480[13] – a courtyard of 120 paces by 100 paces (by John Harvey's reckoning, 210 feet by 175 feet) – fit closely enough with the Tudor plan. So one is drawn back to the conclusion that, at least in its essential elements, the plan of the Lancastrian palace, when completed in the 1450s, was very similar to that of its Tudor successor.

Appendix 3

Priors of Shene Charterhouse

1414-1422   John Wydrington
Named as 'Prior' in the foundation charter, but not appointed by the General Chapter of the Order until 1417. Subsequently Procurator of London Charterhouse. Died 1431 [Lambeth MS 413].

1422-(1453)*   John Bokyngham
Instituted 1422 [Lambeth MS 413].
Signed receipt as Prior 9 November 1430 [E 213/39].
Signed indenture as Prior 1444.
Signed grant as Prior 1453 [doc. at Coughton Court, Warks].

1461*   John Ives
Signed as Prior (undated) petition to King asking for confirmation charter [SC8/28, no.1396].
Mentioned as Prior in confirmation charter 1461.
[Pat 1 Edward IV, vi, mm 15-18].

(1474)*-1477   William Wildy
Mentioned in four grants 1474-7:
   [Pat 14 Edward IV, i, mm 25-26]
   [Pat 14 Edward IV, ii, m 23]
   [Pat 16 Edward IV, i, m 26]
   [Pat 17 Edward IV, ii, m 31].

1478-1496   John Ingleby
 Chief Visitor of the English Province.
Visited Perth Charterhouse as Prior of Shene 1478.
Mentioned in three grants 1479 and 1485:
   [Pat 19 Edward IV, m 25]
   [Pat 26 Edward IV, mm 2, 10].
Executor of the will of Queen Elizabeth (Woodville)1492.
Bishop of Llandaff 1496.
In charge of works at Shene Palace 1498-9 and died at Shene 1499.

---

* The dates of John Ives's priorate are not established; it seems likely that he was the only Prior in office between John Bokyngham and William Wildy.

1496-1502/3	Ralph Tracy Visitor of the English Province. Prior in 1496 [SC 12/25/55]. Visitor in 16 Henry VII. Intervened on behalf of Perkin Warbeck 1498. Murdered at Shene 21 March 1502/3. (He was a cousin of Constantine Browne, who was Abbess of Syon 1518-31.)

1503-1534	John Jonbourne (or Jobourn)
	Chief Visitor of the English Province.
	Mentioned in various grants:
	    [*CLPFD* IV, 4221, 6264, 6711]
	    [*CLPFD* V, 403, 627(22)]
	    [E 40/4758].
	Retired 1534.

1534-1535	John Michell Formerly Procurator, appointed Prior 1534, [*CLPFD* V, 1749]. Transferred to Witham as Prior 1535. Visitor of the English Province 1535. Returned to Shene after refoundation 1555-9.
1535-1538	Henry Man Visitor of the English Province. Procurator of Shene 1534, then appointed Prior of Witham 1535. Transferred to Shene as Prior 1535. Prior at the Dissolution 1538. Subsequently Bishop of Sodor and Man 1546. Died 1556.
1555-1559	Maurice Chauncey Acting Prior 1555 on restoration of monks to Shene. Appointment as Prior confirmed by Cardinal Pole 3 December 1556 and by General Chapter 1557. Subsequently Prior of Val de Grace Charterhouse, Bruges 1561-8 and of 'Shene Anglorum' 1568-81. Died at Paris 1581.

Appendix 4

The Demesne Lands of the Charterhouse

The various documents dealing with the disposal of Shene Charterhouse after the Dissolution include some widely differing lists of the demesne lands. The original list (A), which with only minor variations was also used for the grant to the Earl of Hertford in 1541, for the refoundation grant in 1555/6, and for the grant to Sir Thomas Gorges in 1583, is clearly incomplete, for the total acreage listed outside the walls (88½ acres) falls far short of the amount of land in Shene granted to the Charterhouse. The grant of 1415, even allowing for the fact that additional land was subsequently reclaimed from the river, must have covered something like eighty acres, of which the monastery site itself accounted for some twenty-five. To the fifty-five or so acres of demesne land outside the walls must be added the 64 acres granted in 1442 and the 48 acres granted in 1479, making a total of, say, 167 acres.

The other two lists, one (B) compiled when Somerset surrendered his grant on 1 July 1547, and the other (C) at the time of the grant to Suffolk in 1551/2, are both of them more detailed and more accurate, and they agree much more closely with the total acreage. List B adds up to some 160½ acres, list C to 168½. It is surprising, therefore, how different they are in detail. Few of the names of fields and closes are the same, and the acreages given for those fields whose identities can be equated often differ by a significant amount.

The 1547 list (B) is unique in giving acreages which seem to have been accurately measured rather than estimated. It also notes the lanes or tracks which border each field. List C contains a number of indications as to which fields adjoined each other or their location in relation to other features. It is possible therefore from these two lists to draw up a pair of plans which (allowing for some shifting of boundary pales) at least do not appear irreconcilable.

List A presents a quite different problem. A clue to the reason for its incompleteness may lie in the Augmentation Office roll of 1539 in which there are two entries: one for the 'site and demesne land of Shene' valued at £5 6s. 0d., and one for 'the farm of meadows at Richmond' valued at £3 13s. 4d. The sum of £5 6s. 0d. is that given for the lands on list A; so it can be taken that list A excludes this additional leased-out land and relates only to the land actually being used directly by the monastic community. Although at a rate of 3s. 4d. an acre for meadowland (as in list A) £3 13s. 4d. would only account for an extra 22 acres, it may be that the farmed-out land was in fact a mixture of true meadow and of pasture to be valued only at 8d. an acre. For instance, 65 acres of pasture at 8d. and 9 acres of meadow at 3s. 4d. would produce the sum of £3 13s. 4d. and would bring the total acreage, when added to the 88½ acres of list A to 162½, in line with the totals in lists B and C.[*]

A possible scenario might therefore be that a clerk, unfamiliar with the local situation, dug list A out of the archives when the grant to Hertford was to be made, and assumed, incorrectly, that it covered the entire property in question. Hertford, and everyone else concerned, knew that he was supposed to be

---

[*] Another possible combination would be 70 acres of pasture and 8 acres of meadow.

getting the entire estate – and there is no trace of any separate additional grant of the extra land. When Hertford discovered that the list was defective, he may not have worried that he was being under-charged, but he may have had a proper survey of the land made in order to protect his interest – and this may be the origin of the very precise measurements for some of the fields in list B.

One might then further hypothesise that a few years' development of the farm, including perhaps the reclamation of a few acres of extra land by the river-bank, had rendered the detailed survey out of date by 1551/2. A new list (C), with the acreages once again merely estimated, was therefore drawn up, with the changes in field names substituted.

This is of course sheer speculation, but it seems plausible. Equally speculative must be the answer to the question as to why the two later and more accurate lists were ignored when the refoundation grant was made in 1555/6. The clerk then responsible may have thought that, as what was being given back to the monks was what had been granted to Hertford in 1541, he need look no further than that grant for a description of the property. A similar economy of clerical effort could have resulted in the grant to Gorges being based on the 1556 description, so that list A was used in all these cases.

There is little point in trying to draw a plan based on list A, for the identity of the farmed-out land can only be guessed at. Perhaps it included some of Lammas Mead and the Great Meadow. Perhaps, since it is described as 'meadows' it included the 'New Mead' and the 'meadow next to Richmond' of list B – neither of which were true water meadows. Alternatively, it may have included the two large broom-fields which were the most distant part of the estate and which are hard to equate with anything in list A.

One minor, but intriguing, problem common to all three lists is the identity of 'Robin Hood Walk'. The suggestion in the plans that it might have been the area at the east side of the monastic site is but one possibility. By the 1730s this area was an espaliered fruit garden; and the name of Robin Hood's Walk was given to the avenue which continued on the north side of it (i.e. the part between Horse Close and New Mead in the 1547 plan).

Note. These lists do not include some other small properties belonging to the Charterhouse in, or adjacent to, the manor of Shene, which were disposed of separately. These were the 'Church Hawe' at Petersham, five cottages by the conduit head on Richmond Green, the land by the conduit head in Church Shott (see Appendix 5), and Croft Mead (later called Stony Close) by the fishery at Kew. There were also some small properties in Ham, Mortlake, East Sheen and Chiswick, and the Isleworth Ferry.

LIST A

(i) Ministers' accounts, 1540-1 [SC6/3464, m 53]
(ii) Particulars of grant to Earl of Hertford, 28 January 1540/1 [E318/572, f 15]
(iii) Refoundation grant, 26 January 1555/6 [*CPR* 1555-7, pp.354-5]
(iv) Particulars of grant to Sir Thomas Gorges, 27 November 1583 [E310/25/142, p 49]

Site of the late Priory etc.

in (i)	containing 24 acres, 1 rood, 6 perches			
in (ii)	including –			
(iii)	the Cloyster Garden	1½ acres		15 acres at
and	the Little Prayle	3½ acres		12d. the acre
(iv)	the Great Prayle	10 acres		= 15s. 0d.

Pasture

Stony Close	2 acres		
Brome Close	2 acres		
Whete Close	10 acres		39½ acres at
Robynhoode Walke	1½ acres		8d. the acre
Limekylnefelde	12 acres		= 26s. 4d.
Cowley	12 acres		

[In iii and iv the last two items are merged together as Lymkyln Field 24 acres.]

Arable

Little Sheney	1 acre		
Whete Close	10 acres		
Brykekyln Felde	8 acres		37 acres at
Oxeclose	10 acres		8d. the acre
another adjacent to the same	8 acres		= 24s. 8d.

Meadows

Rokeless Mede	1 acre		12 acres at
Lamas Mede	3 acres		3s. 4d. the acre
meadow next by the Thames	8 acres		= 40s. 0d.

Total acreage (excluding site)   88½ acres   Total £5 6s. 0d.

Plus (in ii only) Land at conduit head   4d.

LIST B

Surrender by Edward Duke of Somerset, 1 July 1547 [E305/G33].

Site, etc. of capital messuage called Shene, and buildings, gardens etc.

Meadow	- Rocless Mead, containing 7½ acres and 4 rods
Close	- Shotyng Close with lane to the Park pale and lane to the north, containing 11½ acres and 10 rods
Meadow	- next to Richmond with two lanes to the Park pale and one to the north, containing 17½ acres
Close	- Wheate Close at end of the brick wall, with a lane to the north, containing 14 acres and 55 rods
Close	- Brome Close next to Richmond, with two lanes west and north, containing 17 acres and 45 rods
Close	- Bromefield next to Kayo, with two lanes to the west, containing 20 acres
Meadow	- New Mead, with two lanes to the west, containing 17½ acres and 15 rods
Close	- Horse Lease, with a lane, containing 10 acres and 3 rods
Close	- Robynhood Walke, with one way, containing 3 acres and 3 rods
Meadow	- Lamass Mead, with a lane and a way against the water, containing 7½ acres
Meadow	- Great Mead, against the Thames, containing 13 acres
Close	- Horse Close, with lane adjacent to the Shepehouse, containing 21 acres

[Total acreage (excluding site) – 160 acres, 1 rood, 15 rods.]

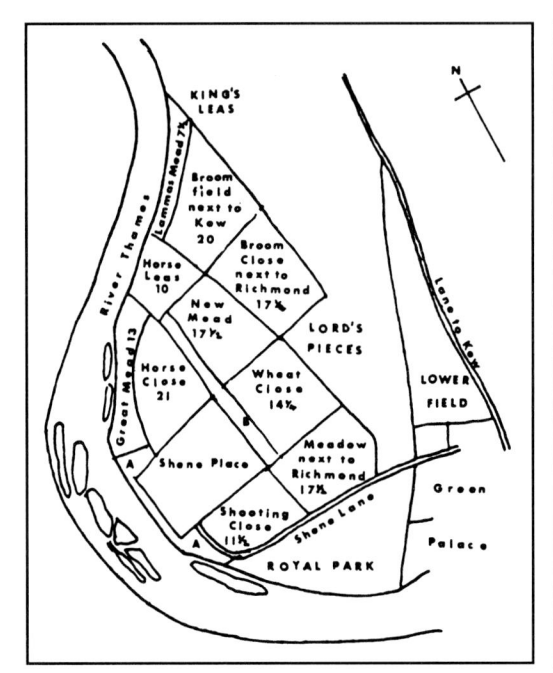

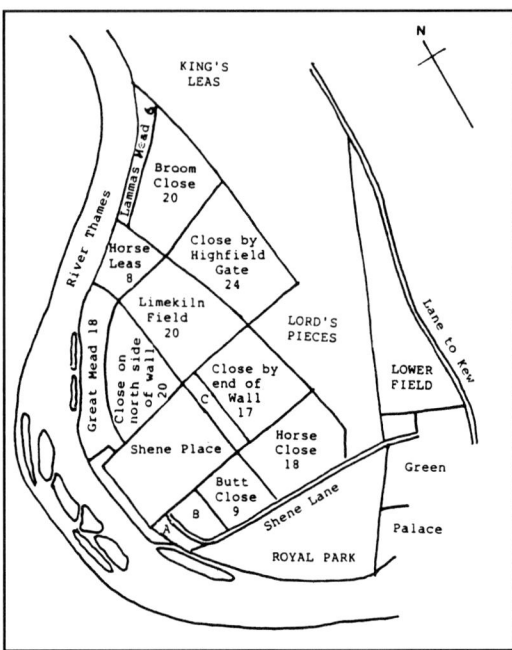

128 Left: *The Duke of Somerset's estate 1547 (list B) – A. Rockless Mead 7½, B. Robin Hood Walk 3; Right: The Duke of Somerset's estate 1551/2 (list C) – A. Rockless Mead 1½, B. Close by Crown Gate 4, C. ?Robin Hood's Walk 1½*

LIST C

Survey made 4 January 1551/2 of lands held by Edward Duke of Somerset from year to year at the King's pleasure [LR2/90, p.100].

Site
Mansion house called Shene Place, and:–	
Land called the Pray	8 acres
Land on east of the tower	½ acre
Land called the Churchyard	4 acres
Land next the slawterhous	2 acres
Land next the flesshehall	1 acre
	rent £8 1s. 2d.

Meadows
Lammass Mede (against the Kinges Lease)	6 acres
Great Mede (by the Ferry)	18 acres
Rokleys Mede (next Richemount Park)	1½ acres
[total 25½ acres at 5s. per acre]	rent £6 7s. 6d.

Pasture
Horse Close (next to Butt Close)	18 acres
Close by the wall end	17 acres
Lymekilclose	20 acres
[total 55 acres at 2s. per acre]	rent £5 10s. 0d.

Pasture and arable
Close by Highfield Gate	24 acres
Close on north side of the wall	20 acres
Close called Horse Lease (next to Lammass Mead)	8 acres
[total 52 acres at 1s. 8d. per acre]	rent £4 6s. 8d.

Divers parcels of demesne land
Close outside the Crowne Gate	4 acres
Butt Close (next to the last close)	9 acres
Brome Close (next to the Horse Lease)	20 acres
Close called Robynhodes Walke	3 acres
[total 36 acres at 1s. 4d. per acre]	rent £2 8s. 0d.
[Total acreage (excluding site) 168½ acres]	total rent £26 13s. 4d.

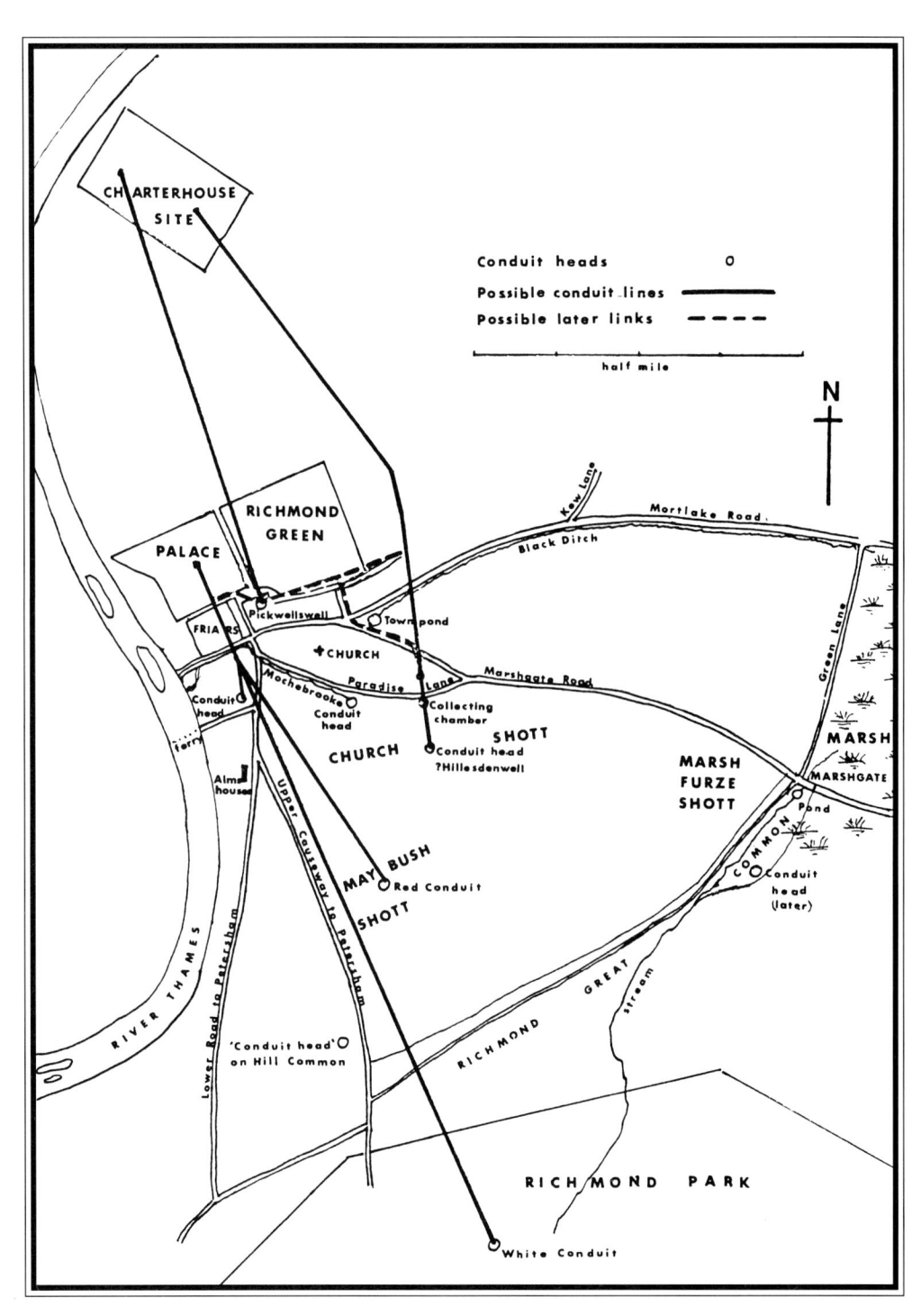

129 Richmond Palace and Shene Charterhouse – water supplies in the 17th century

Appendix 5

The Water Supply of the Palace and Charterhouse

The Parliamentary Survey of 1649 gives the following information about the palace water supply:

> There are two Cesternes of lead set in frames of wood standing on the backside of the sayd privie kitchen unto which cesternes belong three severall pipes of lead comming from three severall cunduit heads; to wit one of them comming from the cunduit in Newparke in Surrey called the whyte cunduit one other comming from a cunduit in Richmond townefeild called the red cunduit and the other comming from a cunduit or spring near the alms houses in Richmond, close upon the River of Thames, the water comming into these two cesternes is by severall smale branches conveyed into all the principall offices and roomes of Richmond Court and is of singular use thereunto.[1]

The survey of the former Charterhouse site similarly relates that:

> ... the tenements before mentioned are very well accommodated with water which is brought and conveyed unto them through several small pipes of lead branched from one great pipe of lead from the stopcock or conduit head on Richmond Green into a great cistern of stone placed within the said wall of Shene.[2]

From the grant made to the Charterhouse in 1466 we know that it had had two sources of supply: an original conduit from a spring called 'Hillesdenwell', and then – because that proved inadequate – a new conduit from the spring called 'Welway' or 'Pickwelleswell'.[3]

There should therefore be at least five conduit heads to be found in Richmond. In fact there are eight locations which have had such a description, though in one case at least it seems to be a misnomer.

The three conduit heads serving the palace are readily identifiable.

White Conduit still survives. The name has endured and the much repaired conduit head, now covered in concrete, can be seen on the edge of 'Conduit Wood' in Richmond Park. If the pipes from here to the palace took a straight path they would have passed across what was still in Tudor times Richmond Great Common, through the corner of the upper field and down the side of the hill (or upper causeway). It may be that the 'running streams' recorded by Alfred Barkas as having been found below the basements of shops in Upper Hill Rise (now Richmond Hill) a few years before 1918 were relics of this watercourse. Barkas also records a similar stream in 'the north corner of the Cardigan House grounds'.[4] It is of course possible that the pipes, instead of running straight, crossed to the west side of the hill.

Red Conduit was in the upper field in the Maybush Shott (which was sometimes called 'Red Conduit Shott'). Maybush Shott was bounded (in modern terms) by Mount Ararat Road, Friars Stile Road, Richmond Hill, and on the north by a line which follows the southern boundaries of Richmond Hill Court, 18 and 32 Montague Road, 25 Onslow Road, 1-9 Chislehurst Road and 79 Mount Ararat Road. The shott was divided into strips running north-south, parallel with the hill.

The manorial records enable an accurate identification to be made of the particular strip in which the conduit head stood. On 2 May 1614 John Jewett surrendered to the use of Helen Bun widow 'half an acre in the Upper Field on part of which the Red Conduit long before this hath stood'.[5] On 11 April 1656 Dr. William Turner, who then owned the strip adjoining this half-acre on the east side, was presented in the manor court for 'taking away three foot in breadth from the ground of John Gregory called the Red Conduit Half Acre'.[6] The title of the half-acre can be traced from Helen Bun to John Gregory, and on from there. It lay where Onslow Road is today, and its southern end was opposite the Friars' Stile (at the top end of Marlborough Road). At what point in the half-acre the conduit head stood is uncertain.

If the pipes from here ran in a straight line to the palace, they would have crossed the Vineyard in the vicinity of Clarence House and would perhaps have joined up with the White Conduit pipes in the Friars.

The *riverside conduit* was, it would seem, not exactly 'near the almshouses', as described in the 1650 survey. (This would put it in the ground of the later Northumberland House, south of Ferry Hill – now Bridge Street, for these were the old Queen Elizabeth almshouses in Petersham Road.) There is however clear evidence that the King's conduit head stood on the north side of Ferry Hill, in the grounds of the large mansion that occupied what is now the southern end of the Riverside Development site. This mansion was owned, from 1657 onwards, by Thomas Weld (or Wilde) Esq. In 1664 he became involved in a controversy over the conduit head which was of sufficient importance to be considered, and acted on, by the Privy Council.[7]

'Before the late wars', reads the Council's warrant, 'His Majesty had a conduit house in the grounds of Thomas Wilde of Richmond, Esq, from which through his garden and other grounds water was conveyed by lead pipes to His Majesty's palace of Richmond, but during the late usurpation the pipes being taken up severally by the soldiers the water was by consent of Mr. Wilde and at the charge of the inhabitants brought in an arch of brick from the King's conduit house into the highway and there received in a cistern, whereby His Majesty's Palace and several houses of the inhabitants there are with more conveniency and less charge served with water than by laying new pipes where the old ones were.' It would seem however that Mr. Weld was overcharging – 'he would sell the water to the inhabitants at a great price'. Perhaps (though the document is not clear on this point) he was also charging the palace for water, which the King felt should be provided free. The dispute had escalated, and Weld had stopped up the new watercourse. While granting that the King might if he wished lay new pipes to replace the old ones, he was refusing access to his grounds to His Majesty's officers for any other purpose; and moreover he was getting 'workmen to dig sewers in his backside to drain the springs' (an indication that the actual source of the water was indeed in this property), and to break down 'the King's vaults which are in his backside'. The Privy Council threatened prosecution by the Attorney General if the efforts of two local JPs did not suffice to bring Mr. Weld to heel.

There is no indication in the Parliamentary Survey compiled only 15 years earlier – and after 'the late wars' – of any fourth source, so it seems certain that this spring and conduit head was indeed the one there described – somewhat loosely – as 'near the almshouses'.

The pipes from this conduit head* had been the subject of earlier problems, for the occupants of the houses between the conduit head and the palace were tempted to tap them for their own use. Both in the manorial records[8] and in those of the Privy Council,[9] this problem is noted in the 1620s. The names of the offending inhabitants show that the pipes took a straight course, crossing below Water Lane and through 'the Friars' to run through the back gardens of some of the houses along King Street.

The Charterhouse conduit heads are somewhat less easy to identify. The 1649 survey refers only to one 'on Richmond Green'. The area where Old Palace Terrace and Paved Court now stand was formerly Charterhouse land – but there is no grant other than those of the conduits to account for Charterhouse ownership. The Pickwell family figure in the manorial records in the reigns of Henry V, Henry VI and

---

* Or, perhaps, from all three, as they may have joined into one main pipe south of Water Lane.

Henry VII. An obscure reference in 1446 may indicate that they held land adjacent to this parcel of Charterhouse land.[10] Tentatively, therefore, one may suggest that '*Pickwell's Well*' was on this corner of the Green. It would at least be reasonable that the later source of supply should be the one still used in 1649.*

Where then was '*Hillesden Well*'? There are four other so-called 'conduit heads' in Richmond: one by Mount Ararat Road, one 'behind the Churchyard', one on Pesthouse Common, and one on Hill Common.

The documentary evidence appears to point to the first of these. In the earliest post-Dissolution grant of the Charterhouse demesne lands, to the Earl of Hertford in 1541, an extra item is added on, at a rent of 4d. per annum, for 'one parcel of land lying at the Conduit Head'.[11] There were separate leases to various people for the several cottages on the site by the Green, none of which refer to the conduit head there. Eventually these all came into a single ownership, and a new grant of that property in 1635 includes also 'a parcel of land of one rood lying at the head of the conduit, parcel of the demesne land of the late Monastery of Shene, formerly in the occupation of Anthony Lynton, at a rent of 4d per annum'.[12] This parcel of land at the conduit head then passes in title with the Green-side property, including the purchase as freehold by John Thorpe in 1650[13] and its sale by him in 1669.[14] However, it does not appear to be the conduit by the Green.

The terrier of the Richmond fields, compiled about 1620, includes an entry in Church Shott for a half-acre of land owned by the Crown 'in the use of A. Lynton'.[15] The manorial records, referring to the purchase and sale by William Stobart of the adjacent strip, show this same parcel of land as 'late the King's' in 1654[16] and as owned by John Thorpe in 1664.[17] Lynton owned no other property in the Richmond fields, and Thorpe only one other quarter-acre in Heath Shott. Despite the discrepancy in description between 'one rood' and a 'half-acre', there must be a strong presumption that this land in Church Shott was the land at the conduit head.

There is a further entry to support this conclusion. In 1656 the manor court presented that 'the great stone conduit standing near the east end of Richmond Town which time out of mind hath conveyed water to Richmond Palace, the Priory of East [*sic*] Sheen and other places to them belonging hath anciently and in the year 1654 stood within the Common Field of Richmond upon the head of a land then anciently the King's land so that those which have had right and interest to the water thither coming and running from thence might at any time freely go and pass to and from the same without interruption but was in the year 1655 inclosed within the farm yard of Dr Wm Turner by what right we know not.'[18] Turner occupied the land on the east side of the strip in question, which is now represented by Mount Ararat Road. He may have leased the freehold land with the conduit head from John Thorpe.

At the junction of Mount Ararat Road and Paradise Road was the best-known feature of these early waterworks, but it appears to have been an underground collecting chamber rather than a conduit head. It was known in the mid-19th century to the inhabitants of the area who drew water from it; and during the Richmond water crisis of 1877 (when the Southwark and Vauxhall Water Co. shut off its supplies before the new municipal system was ready) it was officially used as an emergency source, with a pump installed. In 1909 it was opened up when workmen were widening the road, and was investigated, recorded and photographed, but was wrongly

130 The Tudor collecting chamber at the foot of Mount Ararat Road, when opened up in 1909.

---

* It should however be noted that in the 1490s Nicholas Pykwell owned a house and land in the area which later formed part of the grounds of Mr. Weld's house, mentioned above. This might suggest a possibility that Pickwell's Well was the third palace conduit head, the water from which might at some date before 1649 have been diverted from the Charterhouse to the Palace. There are two arguments which seem to negate this possibility. In the first place a conduit head in this location would be an obvious source of supply for the Palace, but an unlikely one for the Charterhouse. Secondly, there are clear links between the Charterhouse and the two conduit heads on the Green and in Church Shott.

identified as the 'Red Conduit'. The main chamber was about six yards long, by six feet wide and eight feet high. It lay parallel to Paradise Road, and there was a conduit leading into it from the hill above, and another leading out on the other side, beneath Paradise Road. It had a brick vault and a stone lower tank, and could be entered by a stone arch at one end which had evidently once had a wooden door with bolts.[19]

In 1990 the chamber was investigated by Per, Marquis du Saint Empire, an archaeologist specialising in underground water supplies. He found also a further narrow vaulted passage, running west-south-west from this chamber, which was apparently an additional collecting source. He was able to follow it to the point where it ran into the modern brickwork of the lower floor of the multi-storey car park in Paradise Road.

It seems likely that the main source and conduit head itself was a spring further up Mount Ararat Road, possibly at the top end of the strip, by the corner of the path which is now the Vineyard. A report compiled in 1834 says that the houses in Spring Terrace were supplied with water from 'a spring in the field at the back'.[20]

Where did the outflow conduit lead? A similar chamber was found in the grounds of the former Carrington Lodge (which was between Sheen Road and Paradise Road – across from the chamber just described). This could well lie on a more or less direct line to the Charterhouse site. If the manorial record of 1656 quoted above is correct, there may have been also a pipe leading to the palace. This might account for the oft-quoted reference to an inscription on a stone found in the wall of No.1 The Green: '... on this stone ... foot to ye pipe ... foot deep. July 24, 1739'.

Alternatively, the conduit from the chamber mentioned above might have run down the present Sheen Road and up Duke Street to the Green – and thence to the Charterhouse, with a later branch to the palace.

There must however remain some doubt as to the accuracy of the manorial record on this historical point, for if the conduit were still in use to supply either the palace or the Charterhouse site, it is odd that it was not mentioned in the Parliamentary inventories. But the former royal ownership of the land and its use by Anthony Lynton with the 4d. per annum rent demonstrate a clear connection with the Charterhouse.

※

Three other conduits or conduit heads should be mentioned, though they have no claim to be considered as supply sources for palace or Charterhouse.

The *Conduit behind the Churchyard* gave its name to Conduit Field, so marked on the manor map of 1771,[21] and probably to Conduit Shott, an alternative (though less frequently used) name for Church Shott. The conduit is well documented in the manorial records. Conduit Field was in 1771 in the same ownership as Halford House and its grounds, which it adjoined on the east side. This little estate, extending as far east as Vineyard Passage, had been put together from three one-acre holdings and a 'cove' of a quarter-acre. (The ownership of the cove can be traced back far enough to demonstrate that it was not the land 'in the use of A. Lynton'.) The manorial records for 1657 locate the easternmost of the three acres as 'abutting the conduit there on the north part';[22] and entries for 1672 and 1679 place the quarter-acre as 'near the conduit'.[23] In 1607 and again in 1627 and 1629 the inhabitants were forbidden to wash clothes within 40 feet of the 'conduit lying behind Richmond Church',[24] so it is apparent that this was not an enclosed conduit head, but an open well. It may indeed have been the spring from which flowed the stream (anciently called Mochebrooke)[25] which ran along the course of Red Lion Street and Water Lane into the Thames. As this was described as early as 1535 as a 'common sewer' it was evidently not a piped watercourse of pure water. The spring itself may have been enclosed within a 'conduit head' to provide a dipping well for the inhabitants, but by the 18th century both it and the overflow stream were proving something of a nuisance, for it was evidently close to the roadside. In 1734 Thomas Sayer sought leave 'to arch over the common sewer leading from the conduit to the churchyard and to set posts to make the highway more commodious and to hinder misfortunes that may happen now lying open'.[26] And in 1744 the manor court 'having examined the Conduit at the backside of the Castle commonly called Paradise

Row' [the grounds of the old *Castle Inn* in the main street stretched up to Paradise Road] 'do find it to be a dangerous place unless railed round otherwise it will be dangerous to both man and horse'.[27] By 1775 it had been closed altogether and was referred to as 'the late conduit'.[28]

The *Conduit Head on Pesthouse Common* confined one of the springs which gave Spring Grove its name. The marsh by the border with Mortlake (remembered in the names Marshgate, Marsh Furze Shott, etc.) extended some way south of the road from Richmond to East Sheen, onto the northern end of the Great Common (later Pesthouse Common). Apart from these springs the marsh was fed by two streams. One rose near the White Conduit and formed the manorial and parish boundary for much of its course through what is now Richmond Park and beside Grove Road onto the common and across the road to East Sheen. The other was a 'Black Ditch' running from the Richmond Town Pond (on the site of Dome Buildings at the end of George Street) along the Quadrant and the Lower Mortlake Road. The town pond was probably fed originally by a spring; but by the mid-19th century the Black Ditch had become stagnant and was filled in. Part of the stream from the park was enclosed in an 18-inch underground pipe in 1869-70. In 1870 the dipping well at the conduit head was domed over.[29] (The open stream in the park, which has now inherited the name of Black Ditch, runs on the surface only between its source and the park wall.)

The age of the Pesthouse Common conduit head is unknown. It certainly existed before the stream went underground, but it is not mentioned in the early manorial records and no reference was made to it in 1656 when the manor court was considering enclosure to reduce the danger to cattle of the bogs in the area.[30] Its use as a pure water source was probably limited to the houses in the Marshgate area,* until 1846 when a pipe was run from it to supply the royal laundry which had recently been set up at the edge of the Old Deer Park.[31]

There was for a while another so-called 'conduit head' at the northern corner of *Hill Common* (now Terrace Field), though it seems clear that this was simply a dipping well. There is no indication that any piped conduit was ever led off from it, though it may later have had a hand pump installed. It was used principally by the inmates of Bishop Duppa's almshouses for as long as they remained in their original location on the hill by the end of Friars Stile Road. It was probably fed by one of the several springs in this part of the hillside, the most famous of which was the chalybeate spring, a bit lower down the hill, which was developed in the late 17th century as 'Richmond Wells'.

---

* In the early 19th century the Manor Court issued licences for pipes to be laid from this conduit head to the main houses at Marshgate.

Appendix 6

The Richmond Friary 1534-8

After the dissolution and dispersal of the order of Observant Friars in 1534 one of their houses (Greenwich) is known to have been handed over to the Franciscan Conventuals and two at least (Southampton and Newark) to the Austin (Augustinian) Friars. The chronicler John Stow makes a broader statement: 'The 11 of August [1534] were all the places of the Observant Fryers at Greenwich, Canterbury, Richmond, Newark and Newcastle put downe, and Augustine Fryers set in their place for the time ...'[1] Though this statement is certainly incorrect in respect of Greenwich, and probably also in respect of Canterbury and Newcastle, it may be true that Richmond, as well as Newark and Southampton, became an Austin Friary. The evidence is thin, but not negligible.

It seems clear that there were friars of some kind established in Richmond during the years 1537 and 1538. Princess Mary's privy purse accounts contain several entries for alms given to the 'freres' at Richmond at various times between November 1537 and May 1538, and also record other contacts between the friary and the palace such as two shillings paid 'to one of the freres of Richmount bringing apples to my lades grace' in April 1538 and twenty pence paid in May to 'freres bringing strawberes'.[2]

Such regular contacts make it most unlikely that these friars were merely displaced individuals; there was almost certainly a community occupying the former Observant Friary. (And it seems inherently probable that the King would not have wished the friary, which had such close links with the palace, to have remained empty.) But were they Austin Friars?

Late in 1534 a list was drawn up of 'Observant Friars remaining in the Kingdom'.[3] There were also lists of those who had died, those who had gone overseas, and a few categorised as 'exempt'. The qualification for this last status may be implied from the fact that it contained the name of John Lawrence, who had been Cromwell's agent and secret correspondent in the Richmond Friary.[4] The list of those 'remaining in the Kingdom' shows a wide dispersion to houses of other orders throughout the country, but it includes the names of three friars 'at Richmond' (John Bakare, William Penrith and Thomas Packe). It is extremely improbable that Observant Friars would, so soon after their dissolution, have been allowed to return to their former house unless it had been put under new management and they were in effect prisoners there.

Apart from the assertion in Stow's *Annales*, there are two scraps of evidence pointing to occupation of the Richmond Friary by Austin Friars. One is the 'capacity' – or licence to receive a benefice and to change his habit for that of a secular priest – granted by Archbishop Cranmer on 10 January 1536 to John Marbury, 'friar of Richmond, of the Augustinian order'.[5] It is not certain that the Richmond referred to was in Surrey rather than Yorkshire, but it is very probable. Other references to Richmond, Yorkshire, in the Faculty Office Register are clearly noted as 'in the diocese of York'. There was no Austin house in Richmond, Yorkshire. Moreover, the capacity was granted gratis, which suggests that Marbury had good contacts – perhaps more likely in Richmond, Surrey.

The second item is the drawing of a seal, made in the early 19th century by Benjamin Howlett and now in the library of the Society of Antiquaries.[6] It is an oval seal, apparently depicting a scourging post between two scourges, and bearing the inscription: *Sigillū Prior et Convent' Augustinor' de Observantia Richmonde*. It is described as the seal of 'William Fraunceys Prior and the Convent of the Observance, Richmond' and its provenance is said to be 'on a paper receipt in the Augmentation Office'. No date is given.

So far the Augmentation Office paper has eluded identification. A possible candidate for Prior William Fraunceys is however traceable. Among the recipients of dispensations to hold benefices listed in the Faculty Office registers is the name of 'William Ponde *als* Francis, B.Th., Austin Friar', who received his capacity 'with complete change of habit' on 16 May 1536[7] – just four months after John Marbury. Unfortunately no locality is stated. The dispensation was again granted gratis and is annotated 'warrant shown'. If this was Prior William Fraunceys (and there is no other dispensation listed for such a name), the document from which the seal was copied must have been dated between 1534 and 1536 and would indeed indicate that the Richmond Friary had been taken over by Austin Friars.

It would in any case have been dissolved by 1538, for by the end of that year all friaries in the country had been suppressed. The Faculty Office registers contain 'mass dispensations' for all the members of many dissolved religious houses, but there were also many houses not so covered – and the registers contain no such clue as to the dissolution of an Austin Friary in Richmond in 1538. (They do contain the names of John Lawrence and of two other former Observants of Richmond who were granted dispensations in 1535, 1537 and 1539 respectively.)

Returning to the seal, there are peculiarities about the alleged inscription. Certainly there were no 'Observant Austin Friars', so one might perhaps suggest that the inscription on the seal of the Franciscan Observants had merely been amended to show the change of order. This supposition may be strengthened by the fact that a somewhat similar design of seal (in this case a cross between a scourge and a scourging pillar) was used by the reformed Franciscans' province of Hungary.[8] But the head of a Franciscan friary was normally styled 'Warden' not 'Prior'. A G Little says that 'the title Prior was not used in the Franciscan Order',[9] but there are four instances in the Faculty Office registers of its use in connection with the heads of dissolved Conventual houses in 1538,[10] so its use at a late date at Richmond cannot be wholly excluded. 'Prior' was certainly a title in use at some Austin friaries.

While far from conclusive, the evidence reviewed here does suggest that Richmond may well have been occupied by Austin Friars between 1534 and 1538. If the Augmentation Office paper can eventually be traced, it may settle the question.

131 The alleged seal of the Richmond Friary (from Brayley's A History of Surrey*, based on the drawing by Benjamin Howlett).*

Appendix 7

Plays Performed at Richmond Palace, February 1574/5 to March 1602/3

Date	Company and Director	Title of Play (when known)
13 Feb 1574/5 (Shrove Sunday)	Children of the Queen's Chapel (William Hunnys)	
15 Feb 1574/5 (Shrove Tuesday)	Earl of Warwick's servants	
22 Feb 1574/5	Merchant Taylor's School (Richard Mulcaster)	
26 Dec 1578	Earl of Warwick's servants	Three Sisters of Mantua
27 Dec 1578	Children of the Queen's Chapel	The Historie of …
28 Dec 1578	Lord Chamberlain's servants	The Cruelty of a Stepmother
1 Jan 1578/9	Children of St Paul's (?Master Sebastian)	A Moral of the Marriage of Mind and Measure
4 Jan 1578/9	Earl of Leicester's servants	A Pastoral of a Greek Maid
6 Jan 1578/9 (Twelfth Night)	Lord Chamberlain's servants	The Rape of the Second Helen
10 Feb 1582/3 (Shrove Sunday)	Earl of Leicester's servants	A History of Telomo
12 Feb 1582/3 (Shrove Tuesday)	Merchant Taylors' School (Richard Mulcaster)	A History of Ariodante and Genevora
26 Dec 1588	The Queen's Company	
27 Dec 1588	Children of St Paul's (Thomas Gyles)	
29 Dec 1588	The Lord Admiral's Company (Wm. Gascoigne & Wm. Spencer)	
1 Jan 1588/9	Children of St Paul's	
12 Jan 1588/9	Children of St Paul's	?Midas
26 Dec 1589	The Queen's Company (John Dutton & John Lanham)	

PLAYS PERFORMED AT RICHMOND PALACE, FEBRUARY 1574/5 TO MARCH 1602/3   239

28 Dec 1589	Children of St Paul's (Thomas Gyles)	
1 Jan 1589/90	Children of St Paul's	
6 Jan 1589/90	Children of St Paul's	?Midas
26 Dec 1590	The Queen's Company (Lawrence Dutton & John Dutton)	
27 Dec 1590	Lord Strange's Company* (George Ottewell)	
1 Jan 1590/1	The Queen's Company (John Laneham)	
3 Jan 1590/1	The Queen's Company	
6 Jan 1590/1	The Queen's Company	
26 Dec 1595	Lord Hunsdon's Company* (John Hemynge & Geo Bryan)	
27 Dec 1595	Lord Hunsdon's Company*	
1 Jan 1595/6	Lord Admiral's Company	
4 Jan 1595/6	Lord Admiral's Company	
6 Jan 1595/6	Lord Hunsdon's Company*	
18 Feb 1598/9 (Shrove Sunday)	Earl of Nottingham's Company (i.e. Lord Admiral's) (Rbt. Shawe & Thos. Downton)	
20 Feb 1598/9 (Shrove Tuesday)	Lord Chamberlain's Company* (John Hemyng & Thos. Pope)	
26 Dec 1599	Lord Chamberlain's Company* (John Hemyng)	
27 Dec 1599 (Robert Shawe)	Earl of Nottingham's Company	The Pleasant Comedy of Old Fortunatus
1 Jan 1599/1600	Earl of Nottingham's Company	The Shoemaker's Holiday
6 Jan 1599/1600	Lord Chamberlain's Company*	
3 Feb 1599/1600 (Shrove Sunday)	Lord Chamberlain's Company*	
5 Feb 1599/1600 (Shrove Tuesday)	Earl of Derby's Company (Robert Browne)	
2 Feb 1602/3 (Candlemas)	Lord Chamberlain's Company*	
6 Mar 1602/3 (Shrove Sunday)	Lord Admiral's Company	
?('night last before the date aforesaid')	Lord Admiral's Company	

* The Company of which Shakespeare was a member.

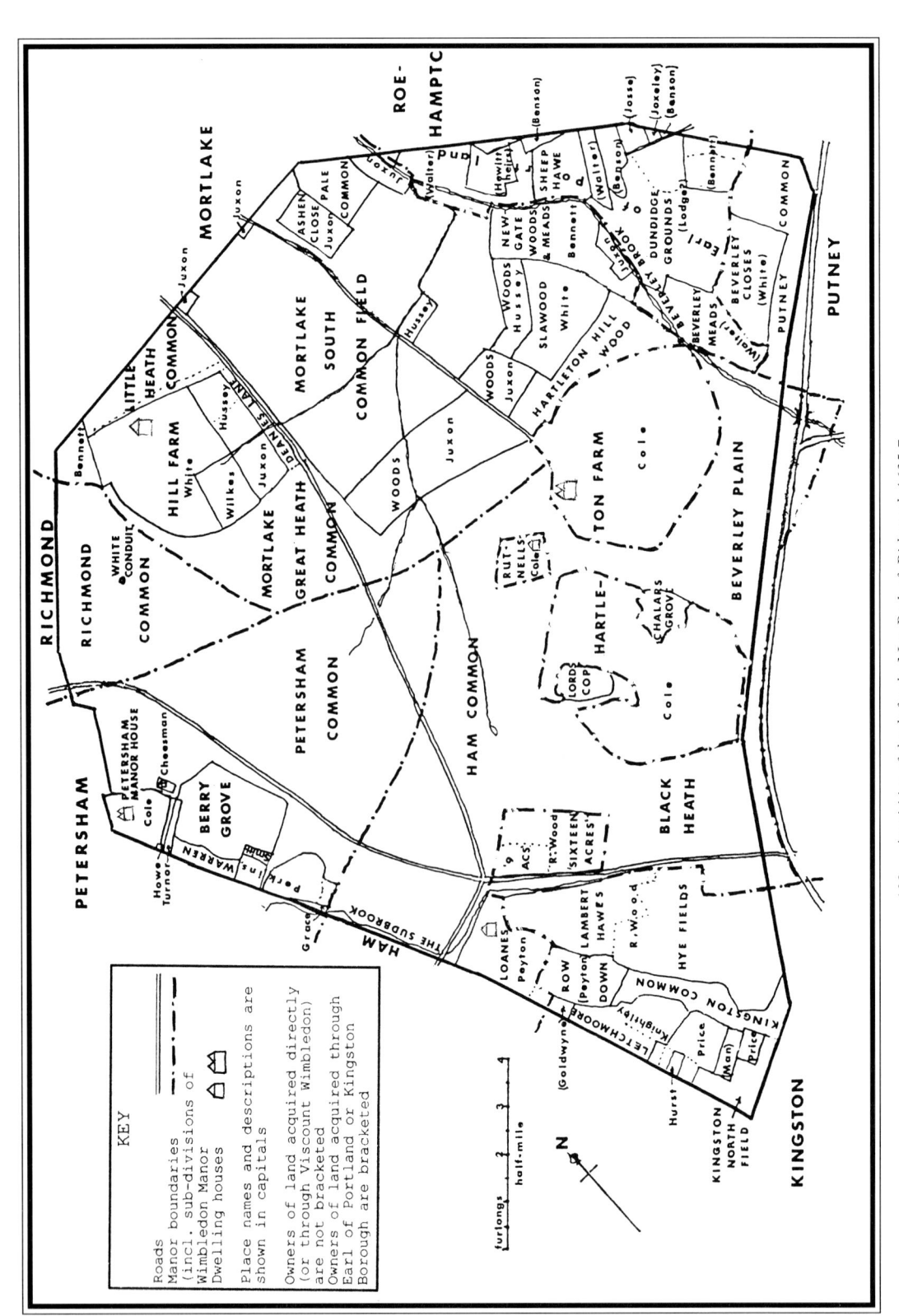

132 *Acquisition of lands for the New Park of Richmond, 1635-7.*

Appendix 8

The Acquisition of Land for Charles I's New Park at Richmond

Introduction

Contrary to the impression given by previous publications, there are extant records covering – in some way and to a greater or lesser extent of detail – virtually all the deals made by the King or his Commissioners in acquiring the land for the New Park.

The principal sources are:

(i) an undated document (probably, judging by its handwriting, of the first half of the 19th century) entitled 'Richmond Park: abstract of contracts for the purchase of land there, 1635 and 1636'. (Public Record Office, reference WORK16/5/1) The original documents on which this abstract was based have not so far been traced;

(ii) the 'modern deeds' series of Exchequer papers in the PRO (E214);

(iii) enrolments in the Chancery close rolls (PRO C54);

(iv) the rolls of the manor court of Petersham (Surrey Record Office 58/4/1 series);

(v) a warrant issued under the privy seal on 25 March 1637, addressed to the stewards of the manors of Petersham and Wimbledon, concerning the admission of several minor children to lands in Petersham, Mortlake and Roehampton which the children's legal guardians had contracted to surrender for enclosure in the park. (Surrey Record Office reference 58/3/3/1);

(vi) the court rolls of the manor of Wimbledon (which included Mortlake, Roehampton and Putney) for the period 1630-40 are missing. There is, however, among the Spencer papers deposited in the Northamptonshire Record Office, a book in which were collected the drafts of manor roll entries from 1635 to 1637 (and one from 1639). These are not always easy to decipher, and the entries concerning land enclosed in the park sometimes appear at variance with details recorded in other documents dealing with the same land or landowners. They are however reconcilable with a little ingenuity – and they serve to cover all the gaps left by the other documentation. It will be noted that all the surrenders made by manorial tenants of land in Mortlake and Roehampton enclosed in the King's Park were to the lord of the manor, Viscount Wimbledon, and not directly to the King's Commissioners. Some of the other documents however point to direct deals.

A potential source of great interest, if it could be traced, would be an accounting by Edward Manning and Thomas Young of their disbursement of the sum paid to them on 13 November 1635: '£10,900 in part of £20,000 for lands to be taken into the New Park at Richmond' (CSP Dom 1635, p.479). No such account has survived in the Pipe Office (E351) or Audit Office (AO1) papers.

Of great value for identifying landowners before the enclosure of the park is the map drawn by Nicholas Lane.*(The original is in the Museum of London, where there is also a photographic copy for study in the library; a much more legible later copy in the PRO – MR295 – contains a number of errors.) Lane's map was however surveyed and drawn some years before the enclosure – the note on it dated January 1637 [i.e. 1637/8] which identified the final line of the boundary wall, out of five variants shown, states that it was made 'Certayne yeares before the Erectinge of his Majesties New park wall'; and several of the landowners named were dead by 1635. One of those shown, John Garrett of Petersham, had died by April 1632, which suggests that the survey was made before that date. So the map often does not show those persons from whom the land was actually purchased. There are two other problems in using the map. There are many discrepancies in area between those shown on the map and those given in the documents, which may well result from the documents dealing in 'nominal' acres, of which the measured area might be anything from ½ acre to 1½ acres. Secondly, there is difficulty in determining, in some peripheral cases, what area is meant to be included in the figure shown on the map. Elias Allen's map (PRO – MPE986) adds nothing on the issue of land ownership to the fuller detail supplied by Lane.

In interpreting the entries concerning Mortlake and Roehampton, recourse has been had to the detailed survey of the whole manor of Wimbledon made in 1617 by Ralph Treswell for Thomas Cecil, Earl of Exeter, then lord of the manor. This is also in the Northamptonshire Record Office. It helps to identify the location of closes named in the Court Book records but not on Lane's map, and to compare the acreages given in sales and surrenders with the Lane calculations. It may be noted here that there were no common fields left in Roehampton by 1617; all the land had been enclosed.

I should like to acknowledge the help I have received both from Tom Greeves in making many useful comments on my first draft and from Raymond Gill, historian of Mortlake, in providing me with a transcript of that part of the 1617 survey dealing with Mortlake, in drawing my attention to the existence of the Wimbledon Manor Court Book and also to the document noted at E2c (iii) below, and in providing background information on Lady Hussey and on the Juxon family. He also first suggested to me the comparison of acreages in the Mortlake field (as given in 1617 and in recorded sales and surrenders) which will be found at E2. I have however made my own estimate of the area covered in the 1617 survey which was enclosed in the park; it differs slightly from his, but only to the extent of a few acres.

The land taken into the park is considered below in five categories, subdivided into localities:

A. Common lands
B. The demesne lands of Petersham and Ham
C. Hartleton Farm
D. Privately-owned closes
E. Lands in the common fields of Kingston and Mortlake.

A. COMMON LANDS

1. Richmond
The royal manor had been granted to Queen Henrietta Maria in 1627; it was leased in farm to Sir Richard Douglas (Lord Belhaven) who was also steward of the manor for the King and Queen, and so was virtually still in royal hands. According to the abstract of contracts (WORK16/5/1) an agreement was made with the manorial tenants of Richmond on 18 January 1635/6 for the enclosure of 92 acres of common into the park. (The agreement is not however mentioned in the Richmond manor rolls.)

The area shown on Lane's map is only 72 acres, 3 roods. The discrepancy here may be due to the boundary dispute with Mortlake (see at 4 below).

2. Petersham and Ham
The two royal manors, also granted in 1627 to Queen Henrietta Maria, were in lease to Gregory Cole (with a reversionary lease already granted to William Murray). On 22 December 1635 Murray, Cole and all the tenants (listed) of the two manors agreed with the King to give up for the new park 265 acres of common

---
* See p.198.

belonging to Petersham and 483 acres belonging to Ham, for a compensatory sum of £4,000 to be distributed 'to each severall person according to his severall interest'. The King further agreed that neither he nor his successors nor any farmers of the manors should henceforward take any profit from the residue of the manorial commons, which should be for the sole benefit and profit of the manorial tenants (C54/3430 m. 26).

Lane's map gives the areas as: Petersham 289ac. 3r. 30p.*, and Ham 528 acres. The large discrepancy in these figures suggests that Lane may have been calculating to an earlier enclosure line than that adopted by December 1635.

3. Kingston
The agreement of 2 June 1636 between the King and the bailiffs and freemen of Kingston (see E1 below) included the sale of 'a parcel of waste called the Slades containing 17 acres, near the North Field' (E214/882 and C54/3433 m. 3).

Lane's map shows 20 acres of common in a long narrow strip, called 'Gallowes', apparently in the tenure of a Ralph Richbell.

4. Mortlake and Putney
The abstract (WORK16/5/1) cites two agreements relating to the commons within Lord Wimbledon's manor.

(a) On 21 December 1635 Lord Wimbledon 'and his tenants of Mortlake' agreed to sell 213 acres of common and waste ground within the manor.

(b) By a second agreement (which presumably cancelled the first) made on 12 May 1636 Lord Wimbledon 'and his tenants of the manors of Wimbledon, Mortlake and Putney' agreed to sell '220½ acres, viz: in Mortlake 185 acres besides 23½ in difference between Richmond and Mortlake, and in Wimbledon, Putney and Rowhampton 36 acres, discharged of all Common and claims to common'.

If the 23½ acres of disputed land is added, Mortlake's total of 208½ acres is reasonably close to that given in the first agreement. Changes of boundary line may have left a little more common outside the park by May 1636.

Lane's map shows six pieces of common in Mortlake and one in Putney, but he gives areas only for four of these (estimates are shown in brackets for the others):

Mortlake [Great Heath] Common	131ac. 2r.
Little Heathe (part)	(25ac.)
Land adjoining Little Heathe	3ac. 3r. 10p.**
Deanes Lane	(6ac.)**
Pale Common (part)	(12ac.)
Hartleton Hill Wood	38ac.
total for Mortlake (approx.)	216ac. 1r. 10p.
Putney Common (part)	30ac.
total for entire manor (approx.)	246ac. 1r. 10p.

B. DEMESNE LAND OF PETERSHAM AND HAM

1. By an indenture of 21 December 1635 (C54/3430 m 25) Gregory Cole agreed to convey to the King not only the 748 acres of common land in the two manors, but also: (a) the wood called Berry Grove and a parcel of the adjoining close called the Warren, together containing 30 acres, and (b) the coppice wood called the Lord's Grove containing 7 acres, both being parcels of the demesne lands of Petersham and Ham. No compensation figure is mentioned.

---
* The PRO copy gives 259ac. 3r. 30p.
** The area 3ac. 3r. 10p. is marked on a thin strip of land on the south-western side of Little Heathe, just outside the boundary of Hill Farm. On the PRO copy this strip runs into Deanes Lane, but on the original map there is a separation. The area which Lane marks as Deanes Lane appears to be about six acres; but as he gives no separate acreage it is possible that he included this in the total for Mortlake [Great Heath] Common.

Berry Grove and the Warren are shown on Lane's map (and Allen's) as 'Rex' (i.e. the King's own property) but they were obviously part of Cole's leased estate. Lane gives an area for Berry Grove of 27ac. 2r. and shows the line of wall as cutting off about a quarter of the Warren (total area 10ac. 1r. 30p.). So there is no problem in matching these Petersham demesne lands to the indenture.

On the edges of Hartleton Farm in Ham Common, Lane however shows *two* parcels of 'Rex' land: the 'Lord's Cop' (4ac. 2r. 20p.) and 'Chalar's Grove' (6ac. 1r. 35p.). Chalar's Grove is noted on the map as 'now arable', so it does not suit the description of a 'coppice wood'. While it is possible that Chalar's Grove was included as part of Hartleton Farm, rather than the Ham demesne, another possibility is that there was an error in the enrolment and that some words of the original indenture, which should have come between 'Lord's' and 'Grove' were omitted (e.g. 'Lord's Cop containing 5 acres and a parcel of arable land called Chalar's Grove containing 7 acres').

2. At the Petersham Manor Court on 20 January 1636/7 Gregory Cole and his wife Jane, Thomas Cole and John Yates surrendered to three of the Park Commissioners (Sir Robert Pye, Sir Edmund Sawyer and Sir Charles Harbord) for the King's use, 'his capital messuage containing a whole tenement and a dovecote, barn, stables, etc., in Petersham, now or lately occupied by Gregory Cole'. No compensatory payment is stated. This was the old Petersham manor house, about to become Petersham Lodge (Surrey Record Office 58/4/1/7).

Lane shows the house and its adjacent land as Cole's, but does not give an area. It would appear to be about ten acres.

C. HARTLETON FARM

This was what remained of the old Merton Priory manor of Hartingdon Combe, which had been purchased by George Cole (Gregory's father) from John Evelyn in 1605. It was held in chief from the King by one quarter of a knight's fee.

On 18 November 1636 Gregory Cole and his wife Jane sold to the King for £5,517 17s. 6d. 'all his manor or farm or grange at Hartington *als* Hartleton and Rutnells, containing 250 acres' (E214/1398).

Lane's map shows the holding as being in three blocks, separated by narrow stretches of Ham Common. Excluding the demesne lands mentioned at B1 above, these contained:

(a) the easterly block, where the farmhouse and other farm buildings were located, totalling	109ac. 3r. 05p.
(b) the westerly block, with no buildings, totalling	111ac.
(c) the small northerly block, (Rutnell's), with a cottage and another building	13ac.
total	233ac. 3r. 05p.

All were subdivided into a number of closes, some of them wooded, of which Lane records the separate names and acreages. He gave the owner's name, incorrectly, as John Cole.

D. PRIVATE CLOSES

1. *Petersham* (N.B. The manor rolls record no compensatory payments.)

(a) At the Petersham Manor Court of 20 January 1636/7 James Grace and his wife Elizabeth surrendered to the Park Commissioners, for the King, two parcels of closes each containing a half-acre in Sudbrook (Surrey RO 58/4/1/7). Lane shows land belonging to a Mr Gr..e,[*] of which only a small part was enclosed in the park.

---

[*] Not fully legible in the original. The PRO copy has 'Grove'.

(b) At the Petersham Manor Court on 21 April 1637 John Cheesman and his wife Lydia (formerly wife of John Garrett who had died between 21 October 1631 and the Court held on 1 April 1632) and Lydia's daughter Elizabeth Garrett surrendered to the Park Commissioners, a cottage and orchard formerly occupied by John Cheesman but now enclosed in the New Park (Surrey RO 58/4/1/8).

This holding is shown by Lane as lying next to the manor house grounds, on the north side of Berry Grove, and as belonging to John Garrett. It appears to be about one acre.

(c) The warrant of 25 March 1637 (Surrey RO 58/3/3/1) records that on 13 July 1636 Henry Perkins of Petersham had agreed with the Park Commissioners to grant them two closes in Petersham containing 9 acres, for a compensatory payment of £240. (This land was part of a tenement and 31½ acres which had belonged to Henry's wife Thomazine and to which their son Henry, then aged 12, was the heir – see the Court record for 19 April 1636.)

At the Petersham Manor Court on 21 April 1637 Henry Perkins Senior surrendered the 9 acres to his son, to enable a recovery process to be undertaken to break the entail. At the end of the process the 9 acres had been conveyed to Sir Robert Pye and Sir Charles Harbord, for the King (Surrey RO 58/4/1/8).

The Lane map actually shows three closes: one south of the Warren with a total area of 2ac. 2r., of which only half was enclosed in the park. The second close lay on the eastern side of Sudbrook, and had an area of 7 acres. The third, immediately adjacent to this on the south side, had an area of 2ac. 1r. 10p., of which again only about half was enclosed in the park.

(d) At the Petersham Manor Court of 2 June 1637 Simon Howe and his wife Anne surrendered to the Park Commissioners a parcel of orchard containing one acre (Surrey RO 58/4/1/8). This, not identified by Lane, appears to be between the Manor House and Berry Grove.

(e) At the Petersham Manor Court of 26 March 1638 Thomas Smith and his wife Mary surrendered to the Park Commissioners a tenement and a close of pasture containing 1½ acres (Surrey RO 58/4/1/8). Lane shows this as John Smith's, containing 1ac. 0r. 35p., by the south-west corner of Berry Grove.

(f) A surrender made out of court on 19 February 1638/9 by Richard Turnor to the Park Commissioners was recorded at the Petersham Manor Court on 6 April 1639. It was of a parcel of land containing one acre, adjoining the land late of Gregory Cole east and the orchard late of Simon Howe north (Surrey RO 58/4/1/8). This is another part of the neck of land between the manor house and Berry Grove, not identified by Lane.

2. Ham

By indenture of 27 March 1637 (E214/129) Henry Peyton (who was William Clifton's executor) sold to the King for £370 'the messuage called Lones in the Manor of Ham, and 12 acres of pasture adjacent to it called Lone's Ground, and 6 acres of meadow near adjoining called Coose Eight', which had all been leased by Clifton to Robert Lea for 21 years from June 1633, and also 'part of a close containing 8 acres lately in the occupation of Richard Cavard lying near the Lones Ground in Ham'.

No assignment of Lea's lease has been traced. On 7 November 1637 Richard Cavard assigned to the King for £17 10s. his interest in the remaining term (about 4 years) of his lease of 'two closes containing 8 acres lying together within Ham' (E214/461).

Clifton's property at Lones (of which only about three-fifths was taken into the park) is shown by Lane as containing in all 28ac. 0r. 5p. There were four buildings on the property, three of which, including the main house, were enclosed in the park. The demolition of 'Loanes house and the walls before it' at a cost of £7 5s. 0d. is noted in Humphry Rogers' accounts for July 1637 – April 1638. The name was subsequently transferred to the one remaining house, just outside the Ham Gate. Cavard's holding was probably the close to the south, of which about one-quarter was enclosed in the park, the area and the ownership of which is not identified on Lane's map. The map shows the 20 acres of 'Row Downe' as being also in Clifton's ownership, but this was only a leasehold from the town of Kingston, and is dealt with separately (see at E 1 a (i) and E 1 b below).

(N.B. Lane shows Clifton's property as being in Kingston, but it is clear from the above deeds that it was in the manor of Ham.)

3. Kingston

(a) On 24 May 1636 William Knightley and his wife Susan sold to the King for £280 part of 'Latchmore Grounds in the parish of Kingston', containing 20 acres (E214/372 and C54/3433 m. 1).

Lane's map shows 'Letchmoore groundes' belonging to Mr. Knightley as containing a total of 38ac. 1r. 10p. The name of Knightley is also written across two closes (containing 8ac. 2r. 30p.) on the east side of Latchmore Grounds and shown as occupied by John Price. As the area enclosed in the park of what is clearly marked as Latchmore Grounds would not be more than about twelve acres, it seems that these other two closes were part of the land sold by Knightley and that Price was his tenant. (The area of 38ac. 1r. 10p. given by Lane for 'Letchmoore groundes' may also include the lands at (b) and some of those at (c) below.)

(b) On 24 May 1636 Edward Hurst of Kingston and Henry Baldwyn of Guildford and his wife Mary (who was Hurst's daughter and heir) sold to the King for £48 'so much of a close of 3 acres in the North Field of Kingston near Latchmore, between land of John Price north and south, as is to be enclosed in his Majesty's New Park, containing about 1½ acres' (E214/215 and C54/3433 m. 2).

Hurst's holding, bisected by the New Park wall, is shown by Lane, with no area stated, but evidently about three acres in extent.

(c) On 28 May 1636 John Price of Kingston sold to the King for £352 a close of pasture on Noke's Hill or the Slades, lately occupied by John Hollys, containing 9 acres, also parts (as enclosed by the park wall) of three other closes: one of 5 acres on Noke's Hill lately occupied by Sir Anthony Browne; another of 5 acres near Noke's Hill also lately occupied by Hollys; and the third of 3 acres near Noke's Hill lately occupied by William Colchester (E214/881 and C54/3433 m. 6).

The three closes cut by the park wall are easily identifiable as the one marked 'Mr Brown'[*] on Lane's map and the two (unnamed) north of Mr Hurst's. The 9-acre close presents a problem. If it is not Price's 8ac. 2r. 30p. (which it is suggested above was probably part of Knightley's land) it could perhaps be 'Tare Snatch'[*] (shown by Lane as in Price's occupation but as containing only 6ac. 1r. 20p.) or it might be the whole area south of 'Mr Man', of which Lane shows Price as in occupation of only a part, containing 4ac. 2r. 10p.

(d) By indenture of 15 June 1636 (E214/1091) Sir Robert Wood of Islington, as guardian of Robert Wood (heir of Roger Wood) undertook to arrange for the acquisition by the King, for a consideration of £914 16s. 0d., of '70 acres of land and 12 acres of pasture and 53 acres of woods in Kingston'. The actual conveyance has not been traced.

This appears to be Robert Harrison's property as shown on Lane's map (including the two closes called 16 acres[**] and 9 acres lying to the east of the road from Richmond to Coombe). These total some 68 acres of fields and 54 acres of woodland. (Old freeholds were often stated to contain a larger acreage than that given by accurate computation.) Though Lane does not identify the 16-acre and 9-acre closes as Harrison's, he does show them as being both in the same ownership, and (f) below demonstrates that the 16-acre close was indeed Harrison's.

(e) On 17 June 1636 William Hambleton of Kingston, Agnes Evans widow of Westminster and Francis and William Evans watermen of London jointly sold to the King for £106 'ten small parcels of meadow and pasture containing 7 acres in White Slade and Noke's Hill' (E214/10 and C54/3433 m. 3).

These were probably strips or small holdings in the part of what Lane called the 'Little Common Field' (i.e. the Kingston North Field), enclosed by the park wall.

(f) On 28 April 1637 Edward Chapman assigned to the King for a consideration of £80 his interest in a lease from Robert Harrison (for 21 years from Michaelmas 1629 – see E214/514) of a parcel of wood

---

[*] 'Brown' is the reading on the PRO copy; the name is difficult to decipher on the original. The PRO copy is inaccurate in naming Tare Snatch as 'Hare Snatch'.

[**] The PRO copy omits the area (23 acres) given by Lane for the Sixteen Acre Close. The original Sixteen Acres was probably just the southern half of this whole enclosure; the extra 7 acres representing the northern quarter.

ground called Postell's Grove, containing 16 acres, being part of Chappell Farm in Kingston (E214/9). This has to be the wooded close called 'Sixteen Acres' on Lane's map, but was perhaps just the original 16 acres.

Other land in this south-western corner of the park belonged to the town of Kingston and is noted at E 1 below.

4. Putney and Roehampton

With the exceptions of Putney Common and the holdings mentioned at (c) and (d) below, all the land to be enclosed in the New Park from the Putney and Roehampton sections of Wimbledon Manor appears to have been first gathered up into the ownership of Jerome, Earl of Portland. Some of this land may have been acquired in implementation of the licence granted to him on 5 May 1635 to enclose an extra 450 acres to enlarge his existing Putney Park (Patent 10 Charles I pt 8). However that licence was granted after the King had already started the process of forming his own new park and some of Portland's acquisitions must have been made on the King's behalf or in the full knowledge that they were to be sold on to the King. Only item (vii) is explicitly linked to Putney Park, and item (v) appears to have been the subject of a contract with the Park Commissioners before it came into Portland's possession. The surrender by the Earl of Portland to Viscount Wimbledon (see (b) below) does not cover all the land listed at (a).

(a) On 16 February 1636/7 the Earl, together with his mother Frances, Dowager Countess of Portland, Sir Richard Tichburne, and John Pinchon of Whittle in Essex, sold to the King for £2,100 (E214/884):

(i) Dundidge Grounds containing 50 acres (so shown by Lane, who gives the owner as William Lodge – this name should be 'Edge' according to the 1617 survey).

(ii) Two closes near and adjoining to Dundidge Grounds called Carpenter's Close and the Sheep Hawe, together containing 22 acres. Lane shows these as Carpenters Close (8 acres) belonging to Sir William Walter and Sheepe Close (13ac. 3r. 30p.) belonging to the Lord Treasurer (father of Jerome, Earl of Portland).

(iii) Beverly Meads adjoining Dundidge Grounds containing 30 acres. Lane gives an area of 29ac. 1r. and the owner as Sir William Walter.

The three items above are described as 'lately enclosed in his Majesty's New Park'.

(iv) A close of pasture containing 10½ acres to the east of Dundidge Grounds. This is presumably the close of 10ac. 2r. 05p. shown by Lane as Humfrey Bennett's.

(v) Part of another close of pasture lying east of Dundidge Grounds containing 7 acres. Comparison with (b) (i) below suggests that this is probably the parts of two other closes belonging to Humfrey Bennett, which Lane's map shows to the east of the one above and as cut across by the new park wall.

(vi) Three closes lying east of Dundidge Grounds containing 16 acres. These are probably 'Fursey Close' as marked by Lane and parts of the closes to the east of the lane marked as Mr. Ofley's.

(vii) 'Several yards and closes lying impaled within the new park of the said Earl of Portland at Rowhampton, containing 6 acres'. It seems likely that these were the remaining small parcels by the park wall, and cut by it, shown by Lane as belonging to the Lord Treasurer, Mr. Joxeley* and Mr. Benson, and possibly the northern part of Sir William Walker's land (marked by a dotted line on the map).

(b) A surrender by the Earl of Portland to Edward Viscount Wimbledon on 16 February 1636/7 recorded in the Wimbledon Manor Court Book (p.57) mentions the following properties:

(i) A close called Stubfield containing 10 acres and a part of two other closes called Stubfield containing 7 acres.

The 1617 survey identifies these closes as 'Stubble Fields', then belonging to Thomas Bennett and containing altogether 25 acres. They lay to the east of Dundidge Wood and can be equated with a (iv) and (v) above.

(ii) A close called Carpenter's containing 8 acres, and

(iii) Two closes called Sheepgape containing 30 acres.

* 'Poverley' on the PRO copy.

These items equate with a (ii) above (though the Sheep Hawe there mentioned is only some 14 acres).

(iv) A close called Stroudes containing 15 acres.

The 1617 survey shows Sir William Walter as holding Little Stroud Close of 15 acres. It was to the north of Sheepgape Close and separated from it by Great Stroud Wood (12 acres), Great Stroud Meadow (4½ acres) and a smaller Sheepgape Close of 4 acres, all then belonging to William Wood. It seems probable therefore that this item, together with the extra 16 acres or so from (iii) above, account for most of the land at the north end of the Roehampton section of the park, shown by Lane's map as 28ac. 1r. 5p. belonging to Sir William Walter (some of which area may be outside the park wall) plus 8ac. 2r. 35p. of woodland belonging to Mr. Hewitt's heirs.

(c) (i) The warrant of 25 March 1637 (Surrey RO 58/3/3/1) records two separate transactions negotiated with Timothy Benson and his wife Katherine. (Benson had since died, leaving a 10-year-old son as his heir.) On 14 December 1636 the Bensons had agreed with the Park Commissioners to surrender for £14 'four closes containing 5 acres called Le Copps and Fursey Close lying together in Rowhampton adjoining Carpenter's Close on the north and Dundidge Grounds on the south'. This can only be the close shown on Lane's map as Benson's, containing 5ac. 0r. 10p. (rather than the Fursey Close named on the map).

In the other transaction Jerome Earl of Portland had agreed an exchange of lands with the Bensons. The latter were to grant him 'two closes of arable and meadow called Great Steete and Little Steete in Rowhampton containing 14 acres' in exchange for '30 acres called Oatelands and a rood of land part of Davis's grant and a tenement thereon'.

The 1617 survey places five closes called Steetes on the north-east side of Carpenter's, Sheepgape and Stroud Closes. Three of these (with an area given as 13 acres) belonged to Timothy Benson. Only a relatively small part of them was enclosed in the park: the area marked on Lane's map as bisected by the wall and containing 3ac. 2r. 15p. It is likely that the remainder of this land was eventually surrendered to, and retained by, the Earl of Portland. The evident imbalance of values in the Portland exchange may account for the very low compensation figure paid for the 5-acre close.

(ii) The Wimbledon Manor Court Book (p.80) records a recovery process (for breaking the entail) at the court held on 12 April 1637 in respect of 19 acres in Roehampton formerly of Katherine Benson. This appears to cover the full 14 acres of Steetes and the 5-acre close. At the end of the process the recovery was to the use of Lord Wimbledon.

(d) The warrant of 25 March 1637 (Surrey RO 58/3/3/1) records an agreement of 16 February 1636/7 between the Park Commissioners and James Josse and his wife Elizabeth (and on behalf of the four-year-old Edward Josse) whereby they were to grant to the Commissioners for compensation of £1,378 12s. 0d.:

(i) a close in Little Clay Shott *als* Balding Lane in Rowhampton containing 6 acres and a messuage newly built and barns and stables;
(ii) a parcel of land called Upper Neyland containing 7ac. 3r. and two messuages;
(iii) all but one acre of a field called Newfield Close [area unstated];
(iv) 8 acres called Coleman's Pit;
(v) a yard and 5 acres called Mylde Lands in Rowhampton.

The Josses had on 3 May 1636 been granted in the Wimbledon Manor Court (Court Book p.40) a licence to let for 18 years to Sir James Cunningham 'a messuage and several closes called Upper Noylands, Newfield and Coleman's Pit', containing altogether 25 acres. This suggests that their Newfield Close was about 9 acres.

Very little of this estate actually fell within the boundaries of the new park. Coleman's Pit (owned in 1617 by John Juxon), Upper Neylands (owned by Robert Broke) and Little Clay Shott (owned by Margaret Harris) were all at the northern end of Roehampton, near Barnes Common. There were many closes in the area called 'Newfield' in the south near Putney Common and the lane to Dundidge. The two closes shown by Lane in this area as belonging to Mr. Offley had been in 1617 the property of Ralph Crewe and contained 8 acres; they are the likeliest identification for Josse's Newfield Close. (South of them was a

5-acre Newfield Close belonging to Mr. Cole of Petersham – Mr. Joxeley's on Lane's map – of which only about one acre was enclosed in the park.) As with the Benson property, much of the Josse estate may have been retained by the Earl of Portland.

(e) A surrender by William Offley and his wife Susan to Henry White is recorded in the Wimbledon Manor Court Book (p.20) on 25 September 1635. It appears to cover all Offley's property (including *inter alia* four 'Newfield' closes and two called 'Newfield Ditch', none of which seem to fit the description of the Josse close). This surrender also included 'six closes adjacent to Beverly and to the Common containing 30 acres'. On 3 May 1636 the Court recorded (pp.48-9) the surrender by Henry White to Edward Viscount Wimbledon of land in Mortlake (see D5g and E2d below) and of '30 acres of land by Beverly Bridge in the parish of Putney'.

These are the Beverley Closes shown by Lane as belonging to 'Mr Offley of Putney' and as containing 25ac. 2r.

5. Mortlake

As noted in the introduction, most of the property enclosed in the park from Mortlake appears to have been surrendered to the lord of the manor (Edward Viscount Wimbledon) by his tenants. There may then have been a general grant (not traced) to the King or his Commissioners by Lord Wimbledon. However there are also many documents which suggest direct transactions between the inhabitants of Mortlake and the King or the Commissioners.

(a) (i) In a document of which the original is in the Richmond Public Library (document no. 123 – the text of which is printed in C.L. Collenette's *A History of Richmond Park*, pp.68-9) Richard Wilkes agreed on 14 March 1635/6 to sell to the Park Commissioners for £135 Adder's Down Close containing 10 acres and 2 acres in the Common Field.

(ii) On 3 May 1636 the surrender by Richard Wilkes to Viscount Wimbledon was recorded (Wimbledon Manor Court Book p.48) of 'a close called Adder's Down containing 12 acres in the common fields of Mortlake' (*sic*). Adder's Down was not in the Common Field; but the '12 acres' in the draft has been substituted for a passage, illegibly crossed out, which would be just about the right length to read '10 acres and two acres'.

Adder's Down Close, in the Hill Farm area, is shown by Lane as belonging to Wilkes and as containing 10ac. 3r. 10p.

(b) (i) The abstract (WORK16/5/1) refers to the sale by Humfrey Bennett on 12 May 1636 of Hill Close containing 9 acres.

(ii) The Wimbledon Manor Court Book (p.45) records on 3 May 1636 the surrender by Humphry Bennet to Edward Viscount Wimbledon of:

8 acres and a rood of land in the Upper Field of Mortlake 'now enclosed in the new park called the King's Park near Richmond'; and
15 acres of mead called New Gate meadow; and
18½ acres of woodland called New Gate woods; and
9 acres of land called Hill Close.

Hill Close was the land north-west of Hill Farm, adjoining Richmond Common. Lane shows Bennett as the owner, but gives no area. 'Newgate Cop' (18 acres) and 'Newgate Medowe' (11ac. 0r. 10p.) are both shown by Lane on the west bank of Beverley Brook, as owned by Humphry Bennett.

(c) The Wimbledon Manor Court Book (pp.45-6) records on 3 May 1636 the surrender by Patience Lady Hussey and Lancelot Symonds and his wife Jane to Lord Wimbledon of 36½ acres of arable land in the Upper Field of Mortlake (see at E2c below) and of 22 acres of woodland and coppices.

Lane's map shows Lady Hussey as owning Hill Coppice (5ac. 3r. 30p.), Hill Feilde (6ac. 1r. 20p.), 'Newe Close' in the Common Field (4ac.), and a woodland of 14ac. 2r. 10p. Omitting the 4-acre close in the Common Field, the total is 26ac. 3r. 20p.

(d) The warrant of 25 March 1637 (Surrey RO 58/3/3/1) records an agreement made on 20 May 1636 between the Park Commissioners and members of the Juxon family: John Juxon, Thomas Juxon, Maurice Gething and his wife Elizabeth, William Wagstaff and his wife Sarah, and Thomas Ferrer and his wife Judith (this last couple acting as guardians for Judith's 14-year-old son Joseph Juxon). Elizabeth Gething and Sarah Wagstaff were sisters of John and Thomas Juxon and half-sisters of young Joseph. Judith Ferrer(s) had been the second wife (married 1621) of John Juxon Senior, who died in 1626.

For compensation of £3,180 13s. 4d. the Juxons agreed to grant for enclosure in the park:
 (i) a close containing 11 acres (probably 'Ashen Close' shown on Lane's map as containing 12 acres);
 (ii) Burnt Close containing 10 acres. This was in the Hill Farm area, shown on the map as belonging to 'Mr Juckes' and as containing 10ac. 2r.;
 (iii) 4 acres of woodland in Fernhills and Howsell [Hazel] Pitts.

The 1617 survey shows that Hazel Pits Shott contained only 5½ acres, and was apparently all woodland. All but one acre was in the hands of owners whose property was acquired by the Juxons. This property is not marked on Lane's map; it was to the north of Lady Hussey's woodland. 'Fernhills' – not identified – was presumably a part of the shott.
 (iv) five coppices containing 62ac. 2r. These are the three parcels of woodland shown by Lane as: 'Thos Juxon – Five halfe acres – 6ac. 1r. 20p.'; 'Thos Juckes his heyres – 46ac. 1r. 30p.'; and 'Juckes – 11ac. 3r. 10p.'. The total of these by Lane's computation is 64ac. 2r. 20p.
 (v) from William Wagstaff in right of his wife 27½ acres and 2 roods in the Common Field;
 (vi) from Joseph Juxon 47 acres in the Common Field.

(e) The abstract (WORK16/5/1) refers to the sale on 23 May 1636 by 'John and Thomas Juxon and others' of other land in the Common Field (see E2d below) and of:
 (i) 3 acres called Newgate Meadow; and
 (ii) a part of Pond Mead containing 4 acres.

The smallholding in Newgate Meadow is probably that shown by Lane as held by Mr. Gittin containing 2ac. 3r. 10p. Lane shows Lord Wimbledon in occupation of 6ac. 3r. 35p. of Pond Mead, of which the portion enclosed would have been about 4 acres. This was in fact an error, as the 1617 survey shows that Lord Wimbledon held the northern part of Pond Mead, whereas the southernmost 7 acres were held by William Childe, whose property was acquired by John Juxon Senior.

(f) The Wimbledon Manor Court Book records three surrenders (pp.46-7) and two recoveries (pp.71 and 76) relating to Juxon family properties:
 (i) 3 May 1636 Maurice Gething and wife Elizabeth to Edward Viscount Wimbledon
 Close containing 4 acres, and
 All title and interest in five coppices containing 58 acres 2 roods in Mortlake and now enclosed in the new park of the King near Richmond.
 (The 4-acre close is possibly the woodland at Fernhills and Hazel Pits as at d(iii) above.)
 (ii) 3 May 1636 John Juxon to Edward Viscount Wimbledon 30½ acres of arable in Mortlake, and all title ... in five coppices ... etc. [as above]
 (iii) 3 May 1636 William Wagstaffe and wife Sara to Edward Viscount Wimbledon
 38 acres of arable in the common fields, and
 all title ... in five coppices ... etc. [as above]
 (The arable perhaps includes Ashen Close – see E2g (iii) below)
 (iv) 12 April 1637 Recovery to Edward Viscount Wimbledon of 30½ acres of arable and title in five coppices as surrendered by John Juxon
 (v) 12 April 1637 Recovery to Edward Viscount Wimbledon of 52 acres of land, 10 acres of pasture and 26 acres of woods, part of the inheritance of Joseph Juxon.

(The 52 acres of land may include the two small Juxon closes (3 acres and 3 roods), shown by Lane on the northern edge of the park, in addition to the 47 acres mentioned at d (vi) above.)

It is not clear why most of the Juxon woodland required surrender of title by several members of the family, as it was divided up between them in John Juxon's will of 1626 (PCC 112Hele – PROB11/150). In this two copses containing 21 acres at Short Thorns and two containing 34½ acres by Hartleton Lane are clearly identifiable – 22½ acres going in trust for Joseph (if Juxon's wife produced no further posthumous child for him). Presumably there was another 3½ acres of woodland among the other bequests to Joseph. This would bring the total to 59 acres in five parcels (compare the 58½ acres in the three surrenders above). These are evidently the equivalent of the 62½ acres in five coppices at d (iv) above, but the four acre discrepancy cannot readily be explained.

(g) The Wimbledon Manor Court Book (pp.48-9) records on 3 May 1636 the surrender by Henry White, yeoman, to Edward Viscount Wimbledon, of:

A copse of woodland, containing 30 acres,
12 acres of arable, and
All of Hill Farm containing 56 acres in Mortlake,
[and the 30 acres by Beverley Bridge already mentioned].

The first and third of these items are shown on Lane's map as belonging to White, with areas of 30ac. 2r. 10p. (Slawood – north of the Hartleton Hill Woods) and 53ac. 2r. 20p. (Hill Farm) respectively. The 12 acres of arable were in the Common Field (see E2d below).

E. COMMON FIELDS

1. *Kingston*

(a) By indenture of 2 June 1636 (E214/882 and C54/3433 m. 3) Robert Harwood and Thomas Bishopp, bailiffs of the town of Kingston upon Thames, and the freemen of the town, agreed to sell to the King for £346 eight parcels of land. One of these was the 17 acres of waste called the Slades, already noted at A 3 above. The others were:

(i) a parcel of land called Rough Downes, containing 20 acres, near the common called 'Slades', in the occupation of William Clifton decd by lease for 27 years yet to come at a rent of £3 10s. 0d. a year. (For the assignment of the lease see (b) below.) This is shown by Lane as 'Row Downe' (20 acres) in the occupation of William Clifton.

(ii) a parcel of land containing one acre in Whyte Slade in the North Field of Kingston, occupied by John Price.

(iii) a parcel of one acre in Whyte Slade occupied by Robert Tylt.

(iv) a close of 5 acres in Whyte Slade occupied by Hannah Man, widow. (This is shown as 'Mr Man' on Lane's map.)

(v) a parcel of 29 perches in Noke's Hill Furlong in North Field, being part of a half-acre occupied by John Price.

(vi) a parcel of 5 roods in the North Field, being part of a close of 4 acres occupied by John Goldwyne (shown by Lane as lying to the north of the Latchmore Grounds).

(vii) a parcel of 3 roods in Noke's Hill, being part of 5 roods occupied by Sir Robert Wood.

Nos (ii) and (iii) above are presumably to the south of the holdings of Mr. Man and Mr. Price as shown on Lane's map. Nos (v) and (vii) must be on the west side, cut by the park wall.

(b) On 27 March 1637 Henry Peyton, as administrator of the estate of William Clifton, decd, assigned to the King for a consideration of £13 his interest in the land formerly granted to John London by the bailiffs of Kingston (and subsequently acquired by William Clifton) being 'a coppice or woodland called Rough Downes, containing 20 acres, lying between the lands of Robert Harrison on the east, the land late of John London called the Loanes on the north, the land of John Price on the west, and the common called Rough Downes on the south' (E214/640).

2. Mortlake

The following transactions involving land in the Mortlake Upper (or South) Common Field have been recorded, many of them already mentioned above.

(a) Sale by Richard Wilkes 14 March 1635/6 (see D5a above). 2ac.

(b) Surrender by Humphrey Bennett 3 May 1636 (see D5b above). 8¼ac.

(c) (i) The surrender by Patience Lady Hussey and Lancelot and Jane Symonds of 36½ acres in the Upper Fields (see D5c above) states that 'part is now inclosed in the new park ... and part is not inclosed'. There are however two additional transactions relating to this land. It should be explained that Patience married four times. Her second husband, William Symon(d)s, the father of Lancelot, died in 1622. Sir James Hussey, her third husband, died in 1625; but she seems to have reverted to her title of Lady Hussey after her fourth husband, Richard Budd, died in 1630.

(ii) A contract dated 9 March [1635]* between the Park Commissioners and Henry Lyford, butcher of Mortlake, provides for the assignment to the Commissioners of Lyford's interest in a lease granted by Richard Budd Esq. and Dame Patience his wife and Lancelot Symons, for a term of 31 years from Michaelmas 1630, of a messuage and 70 acres of land. Of these 70 acres, 41ac. 1r. had been subleased by Lyford to John Poole 'for 14 years yet to come'. Of this land, 23ac. 1r. occupied by Poole and 12ac. 1r. still in the tenure of Lyford were being enclosed in the park. Lyford's compensation was to be £110. 12¼ac.

(iii) By an agreement of 9 March 1635 with the Commissioners, John Poole contracted to assign to the King his interest in the 23 acres and 1 rood of land 'lying in the upper fields of Mortlake', being parcel of 41 acres and 1 rood demised to him by Henry Lyford 'for 14 years yet to come' at an annual rent of £40. Poole's compensation was to be £35, but it was also written into the agreement that his rent for the remaining 18 acres should be reduced to only £8 17s. a year. [*Historical MSS Commission, 15th Report* (1897) Appx. Part II (Manuscripts of J. Eliot Hodgkin Esq. FSA of Richmond, Surrey), p.294.] 23¼ac.

(d) The surrender by Henry White to Lord Wimbledon on 3 May 1636 (see D5g above) included 12 acres of arable, presumably in the common fields. 12ac.

(e) The Wimbledon Manor Court Book (p.48) records on 3 May 1636 the surrender by Timothy Jackson to Edward Viscount Wimbledon of 8 acres of arable and 4 acres of woods in Mortlake, now enclosed in the King's new park. These were probably all in the common fields; the woodland is not identified as a close, and the 1617 survey does show some small patches of wood within the fields. 12ac.

(f) In 1608 Thomas Whitfield had given a house and some land to the parish of Mortlake for the maintenance of the church. This had been let in 1632 to William and Margery Crabbe. Of the land, a half-acre at the northern end of Pond (Ashen) Close and an acre in Long Furlong were enclosed in the park. On 26 February 1636/7 the Vestry agreed that the trustees should contract with Sir Charles Harbert (*sic* – ?Harbord) to sell 'for the King's Majesty's use' the lands 'now taken into his Majesty's New Park'. If a contract was agreed, it has not been traced; but neither the Vestry nor the trustees were paid for the land. In 1647 the Vestry agreed to reduce Crabbe's rent since part of his lands 'were taken in by his Majesty into the great Park and yet unpaid for'. As late as 1676 the Vestry were still claiming compensation. (See Raymond Gill, *Richmond Park in the Seventeenth Century*, pp.4-5; J.E. Anderson, *A History of Mortlake* (1886, reissued 1983), p.22; and Mortlake Vestry Book I, pp.66, 71-2, 74v.) 1½ac.

The Juxon holdings

(g) (i) Sale by William and Sarah Wagstaff on 20 May 1636 (see D5d (v) above) of 27½ acres and 2 roods in the common field.

(ii) Surrender by the Wagstaffs to Lord Wimbledon on 3 May 1636 (see D5f (iii) above) of 38 acres in the common field. The apparent discrepancy here may possibly be explained by the inclusion in the surrender

---

* There is a typed transcript of this document in the Richmond Public Library; it omits the year, which has been supplied from c(iii). The original, stated in a note on the transcript to be in the Barnes Public Library, cannot now be traced.

of Ashen Close, which could be counted as part of the Common Field and which is not otherwise mentioned in the surrenders recorded in the Manor Court Book. 38ac.

(h) (i) Sale on behalf of Joseph Juxon on 20 May 1636 (see D5d (vi) above) of 47 acres in the common field.
(ii) Recovery to Edward Viscount Wimbledon on 12 April 1637 of 52 acres of land (see D5f (v)). The discrepancy here may result from the inclusion of the two small closes shown by Lane as Juxon land on the northern edge of the park, one of 3 acres and the other of three roods, which were not part of the common field. 47ac.

(i) (i) The abstract (WORK16/5/1) records the sale on 23 May 1636 of 30 acres of John Juxon's land in the common fields.
(ii) The Manor Court Book (see D5f (ii)) records the surrender by John Juxon of 30½ acres of arable; and this figure is repeated in the recovery of 12 April 1637 (D5f (iv)). 30½ac.

(j) The abstract (WORK16/5/1) records the sale on 23 May 1636 of 39½ acres of Thomas Juxon's land in the common fields. 39½ac.

The above figures give a total of 226¼ acres enclosed in the park from the Mortlake Field for which some form of documentation can be traced. Of this total no less than 155 acres had belonged to members of the Juxon family.

Were there other manorial tenants whose land in the field was enclosed? From the 1617 survey it is possible to construct a plan and so an estimate of the lands then listed which later fell within the park boundaries. This can be only an approximation, as the precise relationship of the park wall to the old shott boundaries in the field is not known. Lane's map, while not entirely accurate – it misplaces Hartleton Furlong for instance – is still helpful in drawing up the detailed plan of the enclosed area. In my calculation I have included as within the park the whole of the following shotts (omitting however the main woodlands): Great Whitting, Rowting, Long Furlong, Bitton, Hartleton Furlong, Short Thorns, Wheatcroft, Newgate, Hazel Pits, Fouldridge, Little Yalder, Great Yalder and Pond Close. I have also added the southernmost 3 acres of Smallingdon Shott.* The following table gives the comparison of the 1617 holdings as thus computed and the known sales and surrenders in 1636-7. The results are strikingly close – even serendipitously producing the same total! It can therefore be asserted with some confidence that all the land enclosed in the park from the Mortlake Field has indeed been identified in the documents recited above.

---

* Lane's map shows the park boundary as passing a little to the north of the northern edge of Ashen Close. This sets it within Smallingdon Shott.

Land Enclosed in Richmond Park from the Mortlake Common Field

1617 Survey			1635-37 Sales and Surrenders	
Landowners	Holdings (ac.)		Landowners	Land enclosed (ac.)
Thos Whitfield	23¼	⎤		
Wm Childe	74¼	├ 155¼	Juxon family	155
Heirs of Thos Husdon	57¾	⎦		
Wm Symonds	28		Lady Hussey	35½
Wm Jeffreys	4¼			
Robt Glascock	1¼			
Miles Holland	12¼		Timothy Jackson	12
Thos Perpoynt	6¼	⎤		
Mary and Sara Perpoynt	5	├ 11¼	Henry White	12
Thos Bennett	10½		Humphry Bennett	8¼
Simon Wilkes	2		Richard Wilkes	2
Mortlake Church	1½		Mortlake Church	1½
TOTAL	226¼		TOTAL	226¼

Lane's figure of 174ac. 2r. 34p. for the acreage enclosed from the field must be increased by the 12 acres of Ashen Close and the 4 acres of New Close, which are both included in the holdings counted above. But his total remains only 190ac. 2r. 34p. – far short of the 226ac. 1r. produced by either of the above calculations. It is evident that many, if not all, of the holdings in the field were in fact smaller than the traditional areas expressed in 'notional acres'.

Appendix 9

Lords, Farmers and Stewards of the Manor up to 1660

1. Lords of the Manor

Lords of Shene

c.1120s	John Belet
c.1166	?William Belet
c.1185	Robert Belet
1198	Michael Belet infant (guardian Richard de Heriet)
c.1207	Michael Belet
1215	Matilda Belet infant (guardian Wymund de Ralegh)
1229	John Belet
1231	Emma Belet infant (guardian Henry FitzNicholas)
1238	Walter Oliver & wife Emma
1253	John Belet & wife Emma
1255	John Hake & wife Emma
1256	Robert de Meleburn & wife Emma
1264	Gilbert de Clare, Earl of Gloucester and Hereford
?	Hugh de Wyndsor
c.1270	Hugh de Wyndsor (son)
1271	Robert Burnell
c.1275	Sir Otto de Grandison
1290	Bishop Robert Burnell (in trust)
1293	Sir Otto de Grandison (reversion – Edward Burnell)
1312	(reversion – Hugh le Despenser)
1313	Edward II
1326	Queen Isabella (d.1358)
1358	Edward III
1377	Richard II

Farmers (ie. lessees) of the manor

1253	William de Kilkenny
1254	Artaldus de St Romano (1 year)
1255	Guy de Lezign
1258	John Maunsel (to 1263)
1296	Edward Prince of Wales
1313-1326	John de Boseham
1361	Ralph Thurbarn (10 years)
?	Edward Thurbarn
1382	Robert de Dyneleye (10 years)

255

Lords of Shene		*Farmers (ie. lessees) of the manor*	
		1385	John Swanton (10 years)
		1393	Wm Swanton & Richard Goion (10 years)
		1395	John Goion (8 years)
1399	Henry IV	1400	Wm Loveney (10 years)
		1404	Adam Symond (10 years)
		1409	Wm Kynwolmersh & Richard Maydeston (7 years)
		1410	Thos Arundel, Archbishop of Canterbury (10 years)
		1412	Thos Holgill (10 years)
1412/13	Henry V		
1422	Henry VI	1425	John Ardene (10 years)
		1438	John Ardene (10 years)
		1444	John Somersett
		1450	John Somersett (life)
		1451	Wm Hulyn & Thos Barton (20 years)
1461	Edward IV	1461	Edmund Glase (20 years)
1466	Queen Elizabeth (Woodville)	1470	Thos Barton (12 years)
		1484	Henry Davy (20 years)
1485/6	Henry VII	1485	Thomas Fysshe & Richard Brampton (12 years)
		1496	do (20 years)
	Lords of Richmond		
1501	Henry VII		
1509	Henry VIII	1511	Richard Brampton
		1522	Massie Villyard & Thos Brampton (d.1538) (30 years)
1540	Anne of Cleves	1547	David Vincent (80 years)
1548	Edward VI		
1553	Queen Mary I		
1558	Queen Elizabeth I	1564	Gregory Lovell (d.1596) (by assignment)
		1596	Sir Thomas Gorges & Helena Marchioness of Northampton
1603	James I	1603	the same (confirmed)
		1607	the same (40 years)
1610	Henry Prince of Wales	1611-19	Sir Edward Gorges
1612	James I		
1616/7	Charles Prince of Wales (succ as Charles I 1625)	1626	Sir Robert Douglas (cr Lord Belhaven 1633)
1627	Queen Henrietta Maria	1638-49	James Duke of Lennox (d.1655)
1650	Sir Gregory Norton Bt		
1653	Humphrey Edwards		
1655	Dame Martha Norton		
1656	Viscount Kenmure & wife Martha		
1657	Sir Henry Norton Bt		

2. Stewards and Keepers of the Manor

Until the late 15th century the manor was usually entrusted to 'keepers', whose rôle appears to have been essentially that of a steward.

The entries below are in some cases derived from grants recorded in the patent rolls or the fine rolls; others are identified from the rolls of the manor court over which the steward normally presided.

1313-20 John de Boseham, keeper
1320-4 Humphrey de Walden, steward
1324 Humphrey de Walden and Richard de Ikerne, joint stewards
1324-6 Richard de Ikerne and Richard de Wynfarthing, joint stewards
(from 1326 to 1358 the manor was in the hands of Queen Isabella)
1358-90 John de Swanton, keeper
1390-5 Thomas de Swanton, keeper
(1395-1429. The palace was demolished in 1395 and presumably the responsibility for management of the manor then remained in the hands of the 'farmers' until Henry V resumed an active interest in it. The next recorded appointment of a keeper was not, however, until 1429.)
1429-31 John de Bury, keeper
1431-7 Robert Mansfield, keeper
1437-52 John de Bury, Junior, keeper
1452-61 John de Bury and Thomas Barton, joint keepers
1461-?1485 William Norborough, keeper
1485-? Thomas Fysshe and Richard Brampton, joint keepers
From 1494 onwards, the appointment was always as 'steward'
fl.1497 Thomas Weyman
fl.1498 Thomas Vernon
1500-33 Hugh Stevenson
fl.1535 Geoffrey Chamber
fl.1554 Sir Anthony Browne
1566-88 William Fleetwood

From 1589 to 1602 the manor rolls are missing. In 1621 the manor court noted that 'divers writings belonging to this Manor remain in the hands of Sir Richard Grobham, Knt., formerly Steward of the Manor'. However, one later reference gives the name of Christopher Rithe as steward in March 1600.

1603-19 Robert Clarke

The office of deputy steward seems to date from 1620. From then until 1770 the stewardship (save during the Commonwealth period) was generally held by a peer or a royal favourite.

	Stewards		Deputy Stewards
1620-5	not traced*	1620-7	Edward Hurst
1626-38	Sir Robert Douglas	1628-49	Robert Lewis
	(cr. Lord Belhaven 1633)	(1631	Edward Lewis)
1638-44	Duke of Lennox		
1644-9	Sir Thomas Jervoise	1649	Richard Crabe
1650-5	Richard Graves	(1650-60	no appointment)
1655-60	Nathaniel Snape		

---

* Possibly Sir Robert Douglas – see footnote at Appendix 10 (1).

Appendix 10

Palace Officials and Gardeners up to 1660

1. **Keepers of the Mansion House, Wardrobe, Vessels and Victuals, Gardens and New Park**
28 Sept. 1484	Henry Davy
23 Sept. 1485	Robert Skerne
29 Nov. 1486	Thomas Fysshe and Richard Brampton
29 Nov. 1522	Massie Villyard and Thomas Brampton (performing duties since 8 August 1520)
16 Sept. 1546	David Vincent (surrendered 1 February 1554/5)
1553?	Sir Henry Sidney (Keeper of House, Garden and Park)
12 March 1555	Gregory Lovell
16 Aug. 1597	Sir Thomas Gorges
1603	Sir Thomas Gorges and Helena Marchioness of Northampton (grant for life 20 March 1604/5; surrendered by Lady Helena 10 July 1627)
(10 Jan. 1608	Sir Edward Gorges – grant in reversion after Sir Thomas and Lady Helena – never effective)
17 Jan. 1625/6	Sir Robert Douglas;[*] later Viscount Belhaven (surrendered 28 Feb. 1638)
2 May 1638	James Stuart, Duke of Lennox

2. **Under-Keepers of the Mansion House**
1557	Lyonel Redman
1595	Stephen Peirce
1605	William Risbrooke (d.1627/8)
20 July 1616	Nicholas Bird (grant in reversion after William Risbrooke)
3 July 1641	George Barker
1649	Robert Roane (claimed assignment from Barker)

3. **Keepers of the Wardrobe at Richmond**
   (N.B. There seems to have been two holders of the post at a time for part of the 16th century.)
(1511)	John Staunton		
Jan. 1525/6	John Pate	?	Roger Bryne
6 Feb. 1537	Rbt. Smith (vice Pate)	22 Dec. 1530	David Vincent (vice Bryne)
28 March 1553	William Griffith	?	Henry Pleasington

---

[*] Douglas was probably appointed before the grant of 1625/6, the earliest traced. A receipt for money for planting an orchard and repairing the Park pale was signed on 4 May 1619 by Sir Robert Douglas as 'Treasurer of the Prince's Household and Keeper of His Highness' House and Park of Richmond' (orignal in Richmond public library).

18 July 1559	Nicholas Snow
	(d.1583 [vice Griffith and Pleasington])
1595	Stephen Peirce (d. Aug. 1630)
c.1630	Theobald Peirce

4. Keepers of the King's Library at Richmond

7 April 1492-1506	Quentin Paulet
20 Sept. 1509	Giles Duwes
11 March 1534	Will Tyldesley

5. Keepers of the Gardens at Shene and Richmond Palaces, before 1650

(to 1387)	Robert Gardyner ('Gardener of the King's Garden at Shene')
3 June 1387	William Rockyngham ('Gardener of the King's Garden at Shene', in successsion to Robert Gardyner; confirmed in appointment for life in 1391 and 1399)
(by 17 July 1419)	John du Pont ('Governor and Surveyor of the King's Garden at Shene')
8 June 1457	Thomas Barton ('Gardener of Shene')
12 July 1461	Edmund Glase ('Gardener of Shene'; reappointed 1463)

Note: From the appointment of Henry Davy in 1484 to that of Edward Villiers in 1660, the 'Keepers of the Mansion House and Wardrobe' were also appointed as 'Gardeners of Shene' or 'Keepers of the Orchard and Gardens', and drew the old salary of 3d. a day for this post. But separate appointments were also made of persons who were actually in charge of the gardens.

1503-6	'Lovell gardener at Richmond'
in 1509	John Ryan and Thomas Swyft were the gardeners at Richmond
9 May 1528	John Lovell (d.c.1550) 'Surveyor of the Orchard and Garden'
	(He had previously been gardener at Greenwich; described as 'King's Gardener' 1536)
27 Aug. 1550	John Lovell II (his son; d.1590) 'Overseer and Keeper of the Orchard and Garden'
16 July 1591	Joan Lovell (widow of John II, d.1603/4) 'Overseer and Keeper of the Orchard and Keeper of the Garden'
? 1603/4	Edward Lovell (probably son of John II; d.1619) 'Overseer and Keeper of the Orchard and Garden'
11 March 1609	Walter Meek granted reversion after the death of Edward Lovell as 'Overseer and Keeper of the Orchard and Garden'
27 Nov. 1635	James Martin 'Keeper of Richmond Garden'

Appendix 11

Keepers of the Parks up to 1660

1. Keepers of the Warren of Shene and of the New Park of Shene

(a) Warren only:

    (before 1361)   William Dalle
    28 July 1361   John de Swanton (retired 1390)
    23 May 1390   Thomas de Swanton (d.1395; son of last)
    28 June 1395   William Hervy
    7 Oct. 1430   John Benet (vacated 1437)
    3 May 1437   Richard Merston (vacated 1456)

(b) New Park only:

    29 May 1440   John de Bury
    17 June 1452   Thomas Barton

(c) Warren and New Park:

    9 April 1456   Thomas Barton
    20 July 1461   Edmund Glase
    28 Sept. 1484   Henry Davy
    23 Sept. 1485   Robert Skerne
    29 Nov. 1486   Thomas Fysshe and Richard Brampton

(d) New Park only:

    29 Oct. 1518   Thomas Brampton
    29 Nov. 1522   Massie Villyard and Thomas Brampton
    16 Sept. 1546   David Vincent (surrendered 9 Feb. 1554/5)
    1553?   Sir Henry Sidney
    12 March 1555   Gregory Lovell
    16 Aug. 1597   Sir Thomas Gorges
    (1604 – incorporated in James I's New Park)

2. Keepers of Henry VIII's 'New Park of Richmond, Co. Middlesex'
(otherwise Isleworth Park or Twickenham Park)

    23 June 1521   Sir William Tyler (d.1529)
    13 Dec. 1529   Sir Francis Bryan (vacated 1546)
    12 July 1546   Robert Bourchier (or Bocher)
    2 July 1556   Sir Henry Jernegan
    (3 March 1574   Park leased to Edward Bacon)

3. **Keepers of James I's 'New Park'**
(became the 'Old' or 'Little' Park in 1637)

1604	Sir Thomas Gorges
by 1619	Sir Robert Douglas (later Lord Belhaven) (regrant 1625/6)
2 May 1638	James Stuart, Duke of Lennox
22 May 1650	Park sold to William Brome 'in behalf of divers original creditors'. The Lodge and some grounds were occupied by Sir Thomas Gervoise (or Jarvis); 20 acres adjoining the Green by John Bentley; the rest by Sir John Trevor.

4. **Keepers and Under-Keepers of Charles I's New Park of Richmond**

Keeper of the Park: 15 June 1637	Jerome Weston, Earl of Portland
Keeper of Hartleton Walk: 1637	Humphrey Rogers
Keeper of Petersham Walk: 1637	Ludowick Carlile

(The appointments of Rogers and Carlile were confirmed by the Commonwealth and the City of London.)

Glossary

Measurements of length and land

Acre
: by statute the area contained by the length of a furlong and the breadth of a chain (640 acres = 1 square mile). 'Acres' in the fields often varied from a half to one and a half times this size.

Carucate
: the quantity of land considered ploughable by one ox team – normally four virgates.

Chain
: one tenth of a furlong – 22 yards (from a surveyor's chain).

Furlong
: originally the length of a plough furrow – one-eighth of a mile (220 yards). Also used for a major division of a common field, notionally one furlong in width (compare shott).

Hide
: originally a tax assessment on land; later virtually synonymous with a carucate.

Perch / Rod
: one quarter of a chain's length – 5½ yards (but sometimes a rod of 6 yards length was used as a unit of measurement); also used as a measure of area – one perch or rod square.

Rood
: an area of 40 perches or rods – one quarter of an acre. (N.B. occasionally 'yard' was also used in this sense.)

Shot(t)
: a major division of a common field (from the length of a bowshot).

Virgate
: the quantity of arable land considered tillable by one man – an amount which varied in different areas, but in Richmond was 20 acres.

Land tenure

Capital messuage
: the main house of a tenement; later just a large house.

Copyhold
: land held from the lord of the manor, any transfer of which had to be effected by its 'surrender' to the lord for regrant. It was therefore recorded in the manor court rolls, and a 'copy' of the entry of the 'admission' of a new tenant served as the title deed.

Customary tenant
: a tenant holding land in accordance with the customs of the manor; in origin a villein, but later a copyholder.

Farm
: the leasing of a property (or an office of profit) for a 'firm' (i.e. fixed) annual sum to a tenant or 'farmer' who was then entitled to whatever income he could make from the property or office.

Freehold
: land held by a freeman, who could dispose of it freely within certain limits (e.g. the lord's licence might be needed for a long lease or for sale to an inhabitant of another manor).

Freeman	a tenant not tied to the manor, who owed homage to the lord but paid only a quit rent for his land.
Messuage	a house, with its immediately adjacent garden, yards, etc.
Quit rent	an annual sum paid in quittance of any labour services.
Tenement	the holding of a tenant; the normal 'whole tenement' was a virgate of arable land, an entitlement to the use of meadow (in Richmond notionally one acre) and a capital messuage.
Villein	a bond tenant, tied to his manor of birth, who owed the lord of the manor labour services for his landholding.

Money and taxation

Aid	a tax for some civil purpose.
Angel	ten shillings.
Crown	five shillings.
Fine	a sum of money paid to 'finish' some transaction, such as the purchase of property or of an office; later, a sum paid to 'finish' a prosecution, hence a financial penalty.
Knight's fee	the holding of land for which, originally, one knight should be provided to serve in the King's army when required. Later used as a unit of taxation (e.g. 2 marks per knight's fee).
£ s. d.	pounds, shillings, pence. 12 pence (d) = 1 shilling; 20 shillings (s) = 1 pound (£).
Mark	two-thirds of a pound (13s. 4d.).
Scutage	a tax for a military purpose.

Miscellaneous

Almayn	a jacket in the German style.
Banquet	a collation of sweets, nuts and fruit, served either separately or after a main meal, often in a special 'banqueting house'.
Canted	with corners cut obliquely across the right angle.
Degree (or gree)	a pace, or yard; also a storey of a building.
Halepace	a stand for spectators.
Rehearsed	aforesaid.
Trapper	the trapping cloth of a horse.
Wanlace	a hunter's hide.
Warren	an unfenced hunting ground (as distinct from an enclosed park); a ground in which rabbits were bred.
Weir	a trap for fish erected across a river.

Bibliography

I ORIGINAL DOCUMENTS

i. Public Record Office, London, (PRO).
The classes of documents to which reference has been made are:

AO	Audit Office	1	Declared accounts
C	Chancery	54	Close rolls
		66	Patent rolls
		82	Privy Council signet rolls
CP	Common Pleas	25/2	Feet of fines
E	Exchequer	36	Treasury of Receipt – misc books
		40	do – ancient deeds
		101	King's Remembrancer – accounts various
		147	do – particulars for grants
		179	do – lay subsidy rolls
		214	do – modern deeds
		305	Augmentation Office – deeds of purchase
		310	do – particulars for leases
		315	do – misc charters
		317	do – parliamentary surveys
		318	do – particulars for grants
		320	do – particulars for sales
		326	do – ancient deeds
		351	Pipe Office – declared accounts
		364	do – foreign account rolls
		367	do – particulars for leases
LR	Land Revenue	2	Misc books and surveys
		3	Manor court rolls and books
		4	Accounts – woods
		13	Quit rolls
MPE, MPZ, MR		–	Maps and plans
PROB	Probate Registry	11	Enrolments of wills
SC	Special Collections	6	Ministers' accounts
		12	Rentals and surveys
SP	State Papers	–	(Vols in chronological sequence)
WORK	Board of Works	5	Accounts
		16	Royal parks

ii British Library (BL)

Cotton MSS	OthoB14 ff96, 100	Charterhouse of Shene
	VitellB11 f54	Burial of James IV
Harleian MSS	252	Court of Henry Prince of Wales
	6850 f90	Puckering's preparations for visit by Queen Elizabeth I
	7009	Constantine de' Servi at Richmond

265

Harleian Charter	45H45	Grant by Michael Belet
Add MSS	11291	Loan to Charles I
	11303	Shene – lay brothers' statutes
	24062 f145	Shene Charterhouse 1415
	32464	Constantine de' Servi at Richmond
	59899	Works accounts
Add Charters	49A46	Sale of house at Kew 1538
	13590	Grants to Duke of Lennox
	25512	Sale of house at Kew 1592

iii Bodleian Library, Oxford

Dodsworth MSS	35 f10	Exchange of Petersham with Chertsey Abbey
Rawlinson MSS	D318 f140v	Repairs to Shene Charterhouse
	D776-7	Works at Richmond 1530s

iv Ashmolean Museum, Oxford

Large Vol 4	ff10a, 11a, 11c	Drawings of Richmond
	12a, 12b, 54	Palace by Antonis van Wyngaerde

v Surrey County Record Office, Kingston upon Thames (SyRO)

3/3/44	Note about Ancram mortgage (at Muniment Room, Guildford)
13/6	New Park, Richmond
58/2	Ham manor court rolls
58/3/3/1	Warrant concerning land for Richmond Park
58/4	Petersham manor court rolls
2353/51/16/62	Water supply at Richmond

vi Royal Archives, Windsor (RA)

vii Museum of London
Nicholas Lane map of Richmond Park area c1632-7

viii Northamptonshire Record Office, Northampton
Wimbledon manor records

ix Archivo di Stato, Florence (ASF)

x Landesbibliothek, Kassel
MS Haas 18

II PUBLISHED DOCUMENTS

i Calendars and documents published by the Records Commission

Charter rolls	– *Calendarium rotulorum chartarum*, ed. R. Lemmed and J. Caley (1803)
	– *Rotuli chartarum*, ed. T.D. Hardy (1837)
Close rolls	– *Rotuli litterarum clausarum in Turri Londinensis* (2v), ed. T.D. Hardy (1833)
Fine rolls	– *Excerpta e rotulis finium in Turri Londinensis* (2v), ed. C. Roberts (1835-6)
	– *Rotuli de oblatis et finibus temp. Johannis Regis*, ed. T.D. Hardy (1835)
Inquisitions	– *Inquisitiones post mortem* (4v), ed. J. Caley (1806-28)
Original rolls	– *Abbreviated calendar of original rolls* (2v), ed. — Playford (1805-10)
Patent rolls	– *Calendarium rotulorum pat. in Turri Londinensis*, ed. T. Astle (1802)
	– *Patent rolls*, ed. T.D. Hardy (1835)
Pipe rolls	– *Magnum rotulum scaccarii* (great roll of the Pipe) 31 Henry I (*sic*), ed. Joseph Hunter (1833)
	– *Rotulus cancellarii*, 3 John (1833)
	– *The great roll of the Pipe for 2, 3, 4 Henry II*, ed. Joseph Hunter (1844)

	– The great roll of the Pipe for 1 Richard I, ed. Joseph Hunter (1844)
Plea rolls	*– Placitorum abbrevatio*, ed. W. Illingworth (1811)

State Papers of the Reign of King Henry VIII (1831-52)
Testa de Nevill, ed. J. Caley and W. Illingworth (1807)
Valor Ecclesiasticus (4v), ed. Joseph Hunter (1810-34)

ii Public Records Office Calendars, etc (showing abbreviations used in footnotes)

CCR	*Calendar of Close Rolls*
CChR	*Calendar of Charter Rolls*
CFR	*Calendar of Fine Rolls*
CIAQD	*Calendar of Inquisitions ad quod damnum*
CIMisc	*Calendar of Inquisitions, miscellaneous*
CIPM	*Calendar of Inquisitions post mortem*
CLPFD	*Calendar of Letters and Papers, Foreign and Domestic, Henry VIII*
CPR	*Calendar of Patent Rolls*
CSPDom	*Calendar of State Papers, Domestic*
CSPFor	*Calendar of State Papers, Foreign*
CSPMilan	*Calendar of State Papers, Milan*
CSPSpanish	*Calendar of State Papers, Spanish (Simancas)*
CSPVenetian	*Calendar of State Papers, Venetian*
CalPapR	*Calendar of Papal Registers*
CalChyW	*Calendar of Chancery Warrants*

Curia Regis Rolls
Feudal Aids, Inquisitions, etc
Privy Council Acts, Proceedings

iii Domesday Book
Surrey, trans. Sara Wood, ed. John Morris (Phillimore, Chichester, 1975).
Dorset, trans. Margaret Newman, ed. C. & F. Thorn (Phillimore, Chichester, 1983).

iv *Archaeologia*
XV (1806)	Payments for works at Richmond
XVII (1814)	Foundation of Syon Convent
XVIII (1817)	Betrothal of Charles of Castille and Princess Mary

v Historical Manuscripts Commission
15th Report Appx Part 2 MSS of J. Eliot Hodgkin (1897).
Calendar of Salisbury MSS Vol XVIII (HMSO, 1938).

vi Pipe Roll Society (one vol for each year – issued from 1884 onwards)
Pipe Rolls for 5-34 Henry II
Pipe Rolls for 2-10 Richard I
Pipe Rolls for 1-17 John
Praestite Rolls etc for 14-18 John
Pipe Rolls for 2-5 and 14 Henry III
Memorandum Roll 14 Henry III
Calendar of Exchequer Memorandum Rolls 1326-7
Lincolnshire Feet of Fines 1199-1215

vii Rolls Series
No.24	*Letters and Papers illustrating the Reigns of Richard III and Henry VII* (2v), ed. J. Gairdner (1861-3).
No.60	*Materials for a History of the Reign of Henry VII* (2v), ed. W. Campbell (1873)
No.76	*Chronicles, Edward I and II* (2v), ed. W. Stubbs (1882)
No.99	*The Red Book of the Exchequer* (3v), ed. H. Hall (1896)

viii **Surrey Archaeological Collections** (published by Surrey Archaeological Society)
Vol.5 includes Parliamentary Survey of Richmond Palace and Manor, 1871
Vol.17 includes Parliamentary Survey of Church lands, 1902
Vol.27 includes Parliamentary Survey of Crane Piece, Richmond, 1914
Vols.38-9 include Statutes of the Lay Brothers of Shene, 1930-1
Vol.71 includes Parliamentary Survey of Shene Charterhouse, 1977
Extra Vol.1 – *Surrey Feet of Fines in the Public Record Office*, 1894

ix **Surrey Record Society**
Vol.16 – nos. 35, 36 and 39 *Surrey Quarter Sessions Records (1658-66)*, 1934-8

x **Miscellaneous** (listed by editors: see also some items in Part III)
Anderson, J.E., *Mortlake Parish Vestry Book 1578-1652* (privately printed 1914).
Chambers, D.S., *Faculty Office Registers 1534-49* (Oxford U P, 1966).
Collins, A., *Sydney State Papers* (T. Osborne, London, 1746).
Devon, F., *Issues of the Exchequer* (John Murray, London, 1837).
Devon, F., *Issues of the Exchequer, James I* (John Rudwell, London, 1836).
Feuillerat, A., *Documents relating to the Office of Revels in the time of Queen Elizabeth* (Louvain, 1908).
Grose, Francis, *The Antiquarian Repertory* (orig. published 1775) (4v), ed. E. Jeffery (E. Jeffery, London, 1807-9).
Harington, Sir John, *Nugae Antiquae* (orig. published 1769) (2v), ed. Thomas Park (Vernon & Hood, London, 1804).
Harvey, J.H., *William Worcestre Itineraries* (Oxford U P, 1969).
Haynes, S., *Collection of State Papers ... left by William Cecil, Lord Burghley* (W. Bowyer, London, 1740).
Heales, Alfred, *The Records of Merton Priory* (H. Frowde, London, 1898).
Hotten, J.C., *Sarcastic Notices of the Long Parliament* ('The Mystery of the Good Old Cause' orig. published 1660) (London, 1863).
Hume, M.A., *Spanish Chronicle of Henry VIII* (London, 1889).
Ingram, James, trans. and ed., *The Anglo-Saxon Chronicle* (J.M. Dent [Everyman] London, 1912).
Kempe, A.J., *The Loseley Manuscripts* (1835).
Kingsford, C.L., *Chronicles of London* (Oxford U P, 1905 [reprint 1977]).
Leadam, I.S., *Select Cases from the Star Chamber* Selden Society (no.16) (London, 1903).
Leland, John, *Collecteana* (6v), ed. T. Hearne (Oxford, 1715).
Lodge, Edmund, *Illustrations of British History* (3v) (orig. published 1791) (Chidley, London, 1838).
Madden, F., *Privy Purse Expenses of the Princess Mary* (Pickering, London, 1831).
Nelson, Sir Thomas, London Corporation documents on Richmond Park 1650-60 in *Richmond Park* (Blades, London, 1883).
Nichols, J.G., *Wills from Doctors' Commons*, Camden Society (no.83) (London, 1863).
Nicolas, N.H., *Privy Purse Expenses of Elizabeth of York* (Pickering, London, 1830) (reprint F Muller, London, 1972).
Parkinson, A., *Collecteana Anglo-Minoritica* (1726).
(Public Record Office), *Book of Fees (Testa de Nevill)* (HMSO, London, 1920-3).
Rymer, Thomas, *Foedera* (20v) (Churchill, London, 1704-35).
Smith, J. Challenor, *Parish Registers of Richmond* (2v) (Surrey Parish Register Society, London, 1903-5).
Theiner, Augustin, *Vetera Monumenta Hibernorum et Scotorum* (Rome, 1864).
Thomas, A.H., and Thornley, I.D., *Great Chronicle of London* (City of London, 1938).
Walker, J., *Letters written by eminent persons ... from the Bodleian Library* (Longman, London, 1813).
Whitelock, Dorothy, *English Historical Documents, Vol 1, c500-1042* (Eyre & Spottiswoode, London, 1955).

III PUBLISHED BOOKS AND DOCUMENTS
– Contemporary diaries, letters, chronicles, etc.
Carey, Sir Robert, *Memoirs* (written before 1627), ed. Earl of Cork and Orrery (R & J Dodsley, London, 1759).
Cavendish, George, *The Life and Death of Cardinal Wolsey* (written 1554-8), ed. R.S. Sylvester (Early English Text Society, Oxford, 1959).

Chamberlain, John, *Letters written by John Chamberlain during the Reign of Queen Elizabeth*, ed. Sarah Williams, Camden Society (no.79) (London, 1861).
Coke, Roger, *A Detection of the Court and State of England during the last Four Reigns* (London, 1694).
Dee, Dr. John, *Privat Diary*, Camden Society (no.19) (London, 1842).
Dee, Dr. John, *The Compendious Rehearsal ... of his Life* (written 1592), published in *Johannis confratris et monachi Glastoniensis Chronica* (2v), 1726, and in *Autobiographical Tracts*, ed. James Crossley (Vol.24 of *Remains Historical and Literary connected with the Counties Palatine of Lancaster and Chester*) (1851).
Edward VI, King, *Literary Remains of Edward VI*, ed. J.G. Nichols (Roxburgh Club, 1857).
Elizabeth I, Queen, *Elizabeth I*, ed. Maria Perry (Folio Society, London, 1990).
Ellis, Henry (ed.), *Original Letters Illustrative of English History*, Series I (3v) (Triphook & Lepard, London, 1824).
Hall, Edward, *Chronicle* (*The Union of the Noble and Illustre Families of Lancastre and York*) (1542), ed. Sir Henry Ellis (London, 1809).
Harington, Sir John, *Letters and Epigrams of Sir John Harington*, ed. N.E. McClure (U of Pennsylvania, Philadelphia, 1930).
Harington, Sir John, *A New Discourse on a Stale Subject, called the Metamorphosis of Ajax*, ed. E.S. Downs (Routledge & Kegan Paul, London, 1962).
Leland, John, *Cygnea Cantio* (London, 1545).
[Lisle family & friends], *Lisle Letters*, ed. M. StC. Byrne (Penguin, London, 1985).
Machyn, Henry, *Diary 1550-63*, ed. J.G. Nichols, Camden Society (no.42) (London, 1848).
Margaret, Queen, *Letters of Queen Margaret of Anjou*, ed. C. Monro, Camden Society (no.86) (London, 1863).
Nichols, J.G. (ed.), *Chronicle of the Grey Friars of London*, Camden Society (no.53) (London, 1852).
Pasmore, Stephen (ed.), *The Life and Times of Queen Elizabeth I at Richmond Palace* (Richmond Local History Society, 1992)
[Paston family], *The Paston Letters*, ed. J.Gairdner (Chatto & Windus, London, 1904).
Rolle, Richard, *The Incendium Amoris of Richard Rolle of Hampole*, ed. M. Deansely (Manchester U P, 1915).
Skelton, John, *The Complete Poems of John Skelton*, ed. P. Henderson (Dent, London, 1931).
Stow, John, *A Survey of London* (1598), ed. C.L. Kingsford (Clarendon Press, Oxford, 1908).
Turner, William, *Herbal*, 1st part John Gybkyn (London, 1551).
    2nd & 3rd parts (Arnold Birckman, Cologne 1562-8).
Wright, Thomas (ed.), *Letters Relating to the Suppression of the Monasteries*, Camden Society (no.26) (London, 1843).

IV *PUBLISHED BOOKS ON THE HISTORY OF RICHMOND AND KEW

(listed in chronological order of publication. Note: some specialized monographs dealing with subjects outside the scope of this book have been omitted. See also articles at Part VI.)

Aubrey, John, *The Natural History and Antiquities of the County of Surrey* (5v) (E. Curll, London, 1719).
Anon (?John Lewis), *Two Historical Accounts of the Making of the New Forest in Hampshire ... and Richmond New Park in Surrey* (M. Cooper, London, 1751).
Anon (?John Lewis), *Merlin's Life and Prophecies* (M. Cooper & C. Sympson, London, 1755).
Anon (?John Lewis), *A Tract in the National Interest* (J. Sheppeard, London, 1757).
Chambers, Sir William, *Plans, Elevations, Sections and Perspective Views of the Gardens and Buildings at Kew* (published for the author 1763).
Lysons, Rev. Daniel, *The Environs of London, ... Vol 1, County of Surrey* (T. Cadell, London, 1792).
Manning, Rev. Owen, and Bray, William, *The History and Antiquities of the County of Surrey* (3v) (White, Cochrane, London, 1804-14).
Evans, John, *Richmond and its Vicinity* (Darnill, Richmond, 1824).
Hofland, Barbara, *Richmond and its Surrounding Scenery* (W.B. Cooke, London, 1832).
Brayley, Edward W., *A Topographical History of Surrey* (5v) (London & Dorking, 1841-8).
Simpson, Edwin, *The History of Kew* (privately published 1849).
Anon, *Wanderings through the Conservatories at Kew* (SPCK, London, c.1855).
Hiscoke & Son's *Richmond Notes* (a monthly magazine), March 1863-Sept 1868 (Hiscoke & Son, Richmond).
Crisp, Richard, *Richmond and its Inhabitants from the Olden Time* (Sampson Low, London, 1866).
'A Resident' (?John Lucas), *A History of Richmond New Park* (Nutting, London, 1877).

---

* As this section of the bibliography is in itself an essay in the historiography of the area, it is being printed in full in both Volumes 1 and 2. It therefore contains some works which are of relevance only to Volume 2.

Anon, *Round Richmond* (Marshall Japp, London, 1881).
Nelson, Sir Thomas J., *Richmond Park: Extracts from the Records of Parliament and of the Corporation of London* (Blades, London, 1883).
Walford, Edward, *Greater London: A Narrative of its History, its People and its Places* (2v) (Cassell, London, 1883-4).
Chancellor, E. Beresford, *Historical Richmond* (George Bell, London, 1885).
Simpson, R.W., *Simpson's Guide to Richmond and Kew Gardens* (R.W. Simpson, Richmond, 1884).
Goldney, S., *Kew: Our Village and its Associations* (privately printed 1892).
Chancellor, E. Beresford, *The History and Antiquities of Richmond, Kew, Petersham, Ham, etc* (Hiscock, Richmond, 1894).
Garnett, Richard, *Richmond on the Thames* (Seeley, London, 1896).
Gascoyne, Somers T., *Recollections of Richmond, its Institutions and their Development* (F.W. Dimbleby, Richmond, 1898).
Way, Thomas R., and Chapman, Frederick, *Architectural Remains of Richmond, Twickenham, Kew, Petersham and Mortlake* (John Lane, London, 1900).
Bell, Mrs. Arthur G., *The Royal Manor of Richmond with Petersham, Ham and Kew* (George Bell, London, 1907).
Bean, W.J., *The Royal Botanic Gardens, Kew* (Cassell, London, 1908).
De Vere, Coryn, *Handbook of Richmond Park* (Knapp, Drewet, London, 1909).
Sanders, Lloyd, *Old Kew, Chiswick and Kensington* (Methuen, London, 1910).
Hodgson, F.C., *Thames-side in the Past* (George Allen, London, 1913).
Cave, Estella, Lady, *Memories of Old Richmond* (John Murray, London, 1922).
Cundall, H.M., *Bygone Richmond* (John Lane, London, 1925).
Collenette, C.L., *A History of Richmond Park* (Sidgwick & Jackson, London, 1937).
Ommaney, F.D., *The House in the Park* (Longmans Green, London, 1944).
Piper, A.C., *History of Richmond Parish Church* (privately printed 1947).
Courlander, Kathleen, *Richmond* (Batsford, London, 1953).
Charlton, John, *Kew Palace* (HMSO, London, 1956).
Turrill, W.B., *The Royal Botanic Gardens, Kew: Past and Present* (H.Jenkins, London, 1959).
Dunbar, Janet, *A Prospect of Richmond* (Harrap, London, 1966).
Allan, Mea, *The Hookers of Kew*, (M.Joseph, London, 1967).
Fletcher Jones, Pamela, *Richmond Park: Portrait of a Royal Playground* (Phillimore, London & Chichester, 1972).
Bingham, Madeleine, *The Making of Kew* (M. Joseph, London, 1975).
King, Ronald, *The World of Kew* (Constable, London, 1976).
Richmond Society History Section, *Richmond, Surrey, As It Was* (Hendon Pub Co, Nelson, Lancs., 1976).
Wright, Mariateresa, *Vintage Richmond* (Hendon Pub Co, Nelson, Lancs., 1978).
Blunt, Wilfred, *In for a Penny* (H. Hamilton, London, 1978).
Gascoigne, Bamber, *Images of Richmond* (St Helena Press, Richmond, 1978).
Hepper, Nigel (ed.), *Kew Gardens for Science and Pleasure* (HMSO, London, 1982).
Cassidy, George E., *Kew As It Was* (Hendon Pub Co, Nelson, Lancs., 1982).
Cloake, John, *The Growth of Richmond* (Richmond Society History Section, 1982; new edition, Richmond Local History Society, 1992).
King, Ronald, *Royal Kew* (Constable, London, 1985).
Brown, M. Baxter, *Richmond Park, the History of a Royal Deer Park* (Robert Hale, London, 1985).
Cloake, John, *Richmond's Great Monastery: the Charterhouse of Jesus of Bethlehem of Shene* (Richmond Local History Society, 1990).
Gill, Raymond, *Richmond Park in the Seventeenth Century* (Barnes & Mortlake History Society, 1990).
Richmond Local History Society (ed. John Cloake), *Richmond in Old Photographs* (Alan Sutton, Stroud, 1990).
Cloake, John, *Richmond Past* (Historical Publications, London, 1991).
Cloake, John, *Royal Bounty: the Richmond Parish Lands Charity 1786-1991* (Trustees of the Richmond Parish Lands Charity, 1992).
Blomfield, David, *The Story of Kew* (Leybourne Publications, 1992).
Pasmore, Stephen, *The Life and Times of Queen Elizabeth I at Richmond Palace* (Richmond Local History Society, paper no.7, 1992)

Clark, Roger George, *Richmond Today* (Robert Hale, 1994)
Blomfield, David, *Kew Past* (Phillimore, 1994)

V   PUBLISHED BOOKS – GENERAL SECONDARY SOURCES

Aikin, Lucy, *Memoirs of the Court of Queen Elizabeth* (Longman, London, 1819).
Anderson, J.E., *History of Mortlake* (privately printed 1886, reprint 1983).
Aungier, George J., *The History and Antiquities of Syon Monastery, etc* (J.B. Nichols, London, 1840).
Banks, T.C., *Dormant and Extinct Baronage* (5v) (J. White, London, 1807-37).
Beaven, E.B., *Aldermen of the City of London* (2v) (City of London, 1913).
Beccatelli, Cardinal Ludovico, *The Life of Cardinal Reginald Pole*, trans. by Rev. B. Pye (C. Bathurst, London, 1766).
Birch, Thomas, *The Life of Henry Prince of Wales* (A. Miller, London, 1760).
Black, J.C., *The Reign of Elizabeth* (Oxford U P, 1936).
Bohun, Edmund, *The Character of Queen Elizabeth* (Rd Chiswell, London, 1693).
Burnet, Bishop Gilbert, *History of the Reformation in England* (orig. pub. 1679-1714), ed.. Rev. N. Pocock (3v) (Clarendon Press, Oxford. 1865).
Chambers, E.K., *The Elizabethan Stage* (Oxford U P, 1924).
Chapman, Hester W., *Two Tudor Portraits* (Jonathan Cape, London, 1960).
Clarendon, Earl of, *The History of the rebellion and the Civil Wars in England* (3v) (Oxford, 1702-3).
Colvin, Howard M. (gen. ed.), *The History of the King's Works* (6v) (HMSO, London, 1963-82).
Colvin, Howard M., *Biographical Dictionary of British Architects, 1600-1840* (John Murray, London, 1978).
Cook, G.H., *English Monasteries in the Middle Ages* (Phoenix House, London, 1961).
Davies, Godfrey, *The Early Stuarts*, 1603-1660 (Oxford U P, 1937).
Dugdale, Sir William, *Monasticon Anglicanum* (orig. pub. 1655-73) (6v in 8), ed. Henry Ellis *et al* (London, 1817-30).
Falkus, Christopher, *The Private Lives of the Tudor Monarchs* (Folio Society, London, 1974).
Farrer, W., *An Outline Itinerary of King Henry I* (Oxford U P, 1920).
Fletcher, Benton, *Royal Homes near London* (Bodley Head, London, 1930).
Froude, J.A., *History of England* (12v) (John W. Parker, London, 1856-70).
Gasquet, Cardinal F.N, *Henry VIII and the English Monasteries* (orig. pub. 1888-9), 5th edition (2v) (J. Hodges, London, 1893).
Grimble, Ian, *The Harington Family* (Jonathan Cape, London, 1957).
Grove, Joseph, *History of the Life and Times of Cardinal Wolsey* (4v) (London, 1742-4).
Hadfield, M., Harling, R., and Highton, L., *British Gardeners: a Biographical Dictionary* (Conde Nast and Zwemmer, London, 1980).
Hadley, Olwen, *Royal Palaces* (Robert Hale, 1972).
Harris, John, *The Artist and the Country House* (Sotheby Parke Bernet, London, 1979).
Harvey, John H., *Henry Yevele* (Batsford, London, 1944).
Harvey, John H., *The Plantagenets* (Batsford, London, 1948).
Harvey, John H., *English Mediaeval Architects* (Batsford, London, 1954).
Hendricks, Dom Lawrence, *The London Charterhouse, its Monks and its Martyrs* (Kegan Paul & Trench, London, 1889).
Holinshed, Raphael, *Chronicles of Englande, Scotlande and Irelande* (2v) (London, 1577).
Hore, J.P., *History of the Royal Buckhounds* (Remington, London, 1893).
Jenkins, Elizabeth, *Elizabeth the Great* (Gollancz, London, 1958).
Johnson, Paul, *The Life and Times of Edward III* (Weidenfeld & Nicolson, London, 1973).
Johnston, Robert, *Historia Rerum Britannicorum* (J. Ravesteyn, Amsterdam, 1655).
Kipling, Gordon, *The Triumph of Honour: Burgundian Origins of the Elizabethan Renaissance* (Leiden, 1977).
Knowles, Dom David and Grimes, W.F., *Charterhouse* (Longmans Green, London, 1954).
Knowles, Dom David, *The Religious Orders in England* (3v) (Cambridge U P, 1959).
Lettenhove, Baron K. de, *Relations Politiques des Pays Bas et de l'Angleterre sous la Règne de Philippe II* (Brussels, 1882).
Lingard, John, *History of England* (8v) (London, 1819-30).
Mackie, J.D., *The Early Tudors 1485-1558* (Oxford U P, 1952).
Mattingley, Garrett, *Catherine of Aragon* (Jonathan Cape, London, 1942).

Millar, Oliver, *Tudor, Stuart and Early Georgian Pictures in the Collection of HM the Queen* (Phaidon, London, 1963).
Oppé, A.P., *English Drawings of the Stuart and Georgian Periods ... at Windsor Castle* (Phaidon, London, 1950).
Pollard, A.F., *Wolsey* (Longmans Green, London, 1953).
Ridley, Jasper, *The Life and Times of Mary Tudor* (Weidenfeld & Nicolson, London, 1973).
Ridley, Jasper, *Elizabeth I* (Constable, London, 1987).
Robinson, John Martin, *Royal Residences* (Macdonald, London, 1982).
Sackville West, R.W., *Works of Thomas Sackville* (John Russell Smith, London, 1859).
Salzman, L.F., *Building in England down to 1540* (Clarendon Press, Oxford, 1952).
Schenk, W., *Reginald Pole, Cardinal of England* (Longmans Green, London, 1950).
Sharpe, Sir Montagu, *Middlesex in British, Roman and Saxon Times* (1919), 2nd revised edition (Methuen, London, 1932).
Senior, Michael, *The Life and Times of Richard II* (Weidenfeld & Nicolson, London, 1981).
Steele, M.S., *Plays and Masques at Court during the Reigns of Elizabeth, James and Charles* (Yale U P, 1926).
Stow, John, *The Annales or Generall Chronicle of England* (1592) (orig pub as 'Chronicles' 1580, as 'Annales' 1592), revised edn (R. Meighen, London, 1631).
Strickland, Agnes, *Lives of the Queens of England* (12v) (H. Colburn, London, 1840-8).
Strickland, Agnes, *Lives of the Queens of Scotland and English Princesses* (8v) (Edinburgh & London, 1859).
Strickland, Agnes, *Tudor and Stuart Princesses* (1868) (revised edition George Bell, London, 1907).
Strong, Sir Roy, *The Renaissance Garden in England* (Thames & Hudson, London, 1979).
Strong, Sir Roy, *Henry Prince of Wales and England's Lost Renaissance* (Thames & Hudson, London, 1986).
Tanner, Thomas, *Notitia Monastica* (Oxford, 1695).
Thompson, E. Margaret, *The Carthusian Order in England* (SPCK, London, 1930).
Thurley, Simon, *The Royal Palaces of Tudor England* (Yale U P, 1993).
Trevelyan, Sir G.M., *English Social History* (1942) (illustrated edition, Longmans Green, London, 1949-52).
Urwin, Alan, *Twicknam Park* (privately published 1965).
Williams, Folkstone, *Domestic Memoirs of the Royal Family* (3v) (Hurst & Blackett, London, 1860).
Williams, Neville, *The Royal Residences of Great Britain* (Barrie & Rockliffe, London, 1960).
Williams, Neville, *The Life and Times of Henry VII* (Weidenfeld & Nicolson, London, 1973).
Williams, Neville, *The Life and Times of Elizabeth I* (Weidenfeld & Nicolson, London, 1972).
Wrottesley, Maj. Gen. Hon. G., *Pedigrees from the Plea Rolls* (Harrison, London, 1905).
Wylie, J.H., *The Reign of Henry the Fifth* (Cambridge U P, 1914).

VI **ARTICLES** – to which reference is made in the text or which are of particular relevance to the subject of this book.
Aird, Prof. Ian, 'The Death of Amy Robsart', *English Historical Review*, vol.71 (1956).
Barkas, Dr. A.A., 'Our Ancient Springs', *Richmond and Twickenham Times* (3 April 1920).
Cloake, John, 'The Charterhouse of Sheen', *Surrey Archaeological Collections*, vol.71 (1977).
Cloake, John, 'The Existing Remains of Richmond Palace', *Richmond History*, no.2 (1981).
'C G G', 'Underground Richmond', *Richmond and Twickenham Times* (6 November 1909).
Dixon, Philip, 'Excavations at Richmond Palace, Surrey', *Post Mediaeval Archaeology*, vol.9 (1975).
Hope, W.H. St John, 'Mount Grace Charterhouse', *Yorkshire Archaeological Journal*, vol.18 (1905).
Hussey, Christopher, 'Richmond Palace, Surrey', *Country Life* (14 and 21 April 1944).
Kingsford, H.S., 'The Seals of the Franciscans', *Franciscan History and Legend in English Mediaeval Art*, ed. A.G. Little (Manchester, 1937).
Little, A.G., 'The Introduction of the Observant Friars into England', *Proceedings of the British Academy* (1921-3).
Scharf, George, 'On a Votive Painting of St George and the Dragon, with Kneeling Figures of Henry VII, his Queen and Children, formerly at Strawberry Hill and now in the Possession of Her Majesty the Queen', *Archaeologia* vol.49(2) (1886).
Sjogren, Gunnar, 'Helen, Marchioness of Northampton', *History Today* vol.28 (September 1978).
Summerson, John, 'The Book of Architecture of John Thorpe in Sir John Soane's Museum', *Walpole Society*, vol.40 (1966).

VII **PERIODICALS** to which reference is made in the text of the book.
Kingdom's Weekly Intelligencer 1647

Notes

Chapter I: The Manor of Shene, before the Palace, pp.1-15

1. *William of Malmesbury's Chronicle of the Kings of England*, trans. and ed. J.A. Giles (London, 1847), pp.128 and 132.
2. *English Historical Documents*, vol.I, *c.*500-1042, ed. Dorothy Whitelock (Eyre & Spottiswoode, London, 1955), pp.509-11. The will is recorded in an 11th-century cartulary of Bury St Edmunds, now in the Cambridge University Library.
3. The form Sceon is also found in another Anglo-Saxon will, that of the Thane Wulfric who in 1002 set up a founding endowment for Burton Abbey in Staffordshire, which included 'a hide at Sceon'. But this refers to Sheen in northern Staffordshire, not to the Surrey one.
4. Sir Montagu Sharpe, *Middlesex in British, Roman and Saxon Times* (Methuen, London, 1919, 2nd edition, revised, 1932), pp.42-63.
5. *Anglo-Saxon Chronicle*, trans. James Ingram. Everyman edition, p.116.
6. *Ibid.*
7. *Domesday Book: 3: Surrey*, ed. John Morris, trans. Sara Wood (Phillimore, Chichester, 1975), Section 1.8.
8. *Ibid.*, Section 1.8.
9. *Ibid.*, Section 22.4.
10. See W. Farrer, *An Outline Itinerary of King Henry I* (Oxford, 1920). It is clear from this that Henry I was never in England in 1125; he came over from Normandy in September 1126, but his subsequent movements prior to his return to Normandy the following summer do not include Shene. Richard Crisp in his *Richmond and its Inhabitants* (London, 1866) seems to have started the story.
11. *Pipe Roll 31 Henry I*, p.49.
12. *Book of Fees*, p.70.
13. *Pipe Roll 31 Henry I*, p.51.
14. *Ibid.*, pp.13, 15, 123.
15. Manning and Bray, *History of Surrey* I, p.xxx.
16. *Pipe Roll 7 Henry II*, p.43.
17. *Pipe Rolls 11 Henry II*, p.111; *12 Henry II*, p.107 etc.
18. *Pipe Roll 32 Henry II*, p.197.
19. *Pipe Roll 2 Richard I*, pp.152, 155.
20. *Pipe Roll 6 Richard I*, p.191.
21. *Pipe Roll 10 Richard I*, p.149.
22. *Pipe Roll 9 John*, p.65.
23. *Red Book* II, p.561. (The entry relating to Bagshot was in fact a partial error – see Appendix I.)
24. *Book of Fees*, p.70.
25. *Praestite Rolls etc 14-18 John*, p.101.
26. *Curia Regis Rolls* VII, p.168.
27. *Pipe Roll 16 John*, p.37.
28. *Curia Regis Rolls* I, p.153.
29. *Book of Fees* II, p.1153.
30. *Records of Merton Priory*, p.66.
31. BL Harl Charter 45H45. (The grant is undated.)
32. *Record Commission Calendar of Close Rolls* I, p.237.
33. *Book of Fees* I, p.273.
34. *Fine Rolls in the Tower of London, Henry III*, p.5.
35. *Records of Merton Priory*, Appx XLIX. See also Ped Fin Surrey 3 Henry III no.14.
36. *Curia Regis Rolls* VIII, p.352.
37. *CChR* I, p.43.
38. *Pipe Roll 14 Henry III*, p.10; *Memorandum Rolls*, 14 Henry III, p.5; *Fine Rolls in the Tower of London, Henry III*, p.190.
39. Ped Fin Surrey 14 Henry III, no.2.
40. *Curia Regis Rolls* XVI, no.439.
41. Maj Gen the Hon G. Wrottesley, *Pedigrees from the Plea Rolls* (London), p.495.
42. *Fine Rolls in the Tower of London, Henry III*, p.218.
43. *CCR* II, p.5.
44. *Ibid.*, p.166.
45. *Ibid.*, p.188.
46. *Curia Regis Rolls XVI*, p.439.
47. *Book of Fees*, p.1362.
48. *Ibid.*, p.1378.
49. Plac Co Surrey 25 Henry III, rot4d.
50. *CCR* V, p.118.
51. *Ibid.* IV, p.326.
52. *Records of Merton Priory*, p.148.
53. The date of the marriage is as given by Edward W. Brayley, *History of Surrey* (1850), p.60. He quotes no.reference but it seems highly probable.
54. Curia Regis 34 Henry III, m 13, no.139. (See Wrottesley, *Pedigrees from the Plea Rolls*, p.495.)
55. Ped Fin Cos Divers, Michaelmas 37/38 Henry III (CP2/25).
56. Rot Pip 38 Henry III.
57. *CCR* IX, p.21.
58. *Ibid.* XIII, p.220.
59. Rot Pip 7 Edward I; Rot Pip 15 Edward I.
60. *CPR 1247-58*, p.189: 19 April 37 Henry III.
61. *Fine Rolls in the Tower of London II*, p.195.
62. *CCR* IX, p.165.
63. *Ibid.* X, p.115.
64. *CPR 1247-58*, p.615. Also Ped Fin Surrey 42 Henry III, no.106.
65. Ped Fin Surrey 42 Henry III, no.105.
66. *CChR* II, p.50. See also *Calendar of Ancient Charters*, p.91b: Cart 48 Henry III, m l.
67. Ped Fin, Cos Divers 54 Henry III, no.471.
68. *CChR* II, p.243.
69. Ped Fin Surrey 56 Henry III, no.262.
70. *CChR* II, p.180 (Cart 56 Henry III, m 4.)
71. Plac Cor Surrey 3 Edward I, rot 39.
72. *CCR 1272-79*, p.520.
73. *CPR 1271-81*, p.357. (Pat Edward I, m 26.)
74. *CChR* II, p.221. (Cart 8 Edward I, m 72.)
75. *CFR 1272-1307*, p.220.
76. Manning and Bray, *History of Surrey* I, pp.360 and 408.
77. *CIPM* III, p.47. no.65. Esch 21 Edward I, no.50 (C133/63).

273

78 *Rot Claus* 1 Edward II, m 14.
79 *CPR* 1292-1301, p.188.
80 *Ibid.*, p.418.
81 *CIPM* IV, p.11, no.26. Esch 29 Edward I, no.35 (C133/100 m 3).
82 Ped Fin Surrey 2 Edward II, nos.21a and 37 (CP2/25/227/30).
83 *CPR* 1327-30, p.433.
84 *CPR* 1313-17, p.4.
85 Extent of the Manor of Shene (SC11/638).
86 Exchequer K R Subsidies 184/4; see *Surrey Record Society* vols.18 and 33.
87 Ped Fin Surrey 25 Edward III, no.31 (CP2/25/229/50).
88 *CPR* 1307-13, p.529.
89 *Feudal Aids, Inquisitions,* etc V, p.110.

Chapter II: The Plantagenet Palace, pp.17-27

1 *CFR* 1307-13, p.529.
2 *Chronicles Edward I & II*: Rolls Series II p.300.
3 SC6/1014/3 m 2.
4 *CPR* 1313-17, p.377.
5 *CPR* 1313-17, p.514.
6 *CPR* 1317-21, p.75 (Pat 11 EdII pt 1 m 3).
7 *CPR* 1317-21, p.103.
8 SC6/1014/6 m 2.
9 *CFR* 1319-27, p.20.
10 *HKW* I, p.508.
11 *CFR* 1319-27, p.259.
12 *CFR* 1319-27, pp.295-6.
13 E101/380/4 ff 18 and 29; Soc Antiq MS 122 f 32v.
14 *CPR* 1327-30, pp.66-9.
15 *CPR* 1330-34, pp.153, 195, 529-30; *CPR* 1343-45, p.447.
16 *CPR* 1330-34.
17 SC6/1014/10-13.
18 *CPR* 1350-54, p.519.
19 *CPR* 1354-58, p.118.
20 *CPR* 1354-58, p.375.
21 *CPR* 1358-61, p.107.
22 *CPR* 1358-61, p.243.
23 Pipe Roll 35 Edward III rot comp 1.
24 Pipe Roll 36 Edward III rot comp 6.
25 E101/493/18.
26 E101/493/18 mm 2, 3, 4.
27 E101/493/18 m 4; and /12 m 2.
28 E101/493/29 m 2.
29 E101/493/18 mm 3, 4.
30 E101/493/12 m 1.
31 E101/493/12 m 2.
32 For Ac Roll 42 Edward III rot Bd; E101/493/29.
33 E101/493/18 m 4.
34 E101/493/18 mm 2, 4; For Ac Roll 43 Edward III. rot Cd; E101/494/7 m 1-2.
35 E101/493/18 m 4.
36 *Ibid.*, mm 2, 4.
37 *Ibid.*, m 4.
38 E101/494/22 rot 4 m 2.
39 E101/545/37 m 1.
40 For Ac Roll 45 Edward III rot Dd m ii; E101/494/17.
41 *Ibid.*
42 E101/494/28, m 3.
43 For Ac Roll 45 Edward III rot Dd m ii; E101/494/17.
44 E101/494/28 mm 2-4.
45 E101/495/1 mm 1-2.
46 E101/494/28 mm 2-4.
47 E101/495/1 mm 1-2.
48 *CPR* 1367-70, p.437.
49 E101/493/12 and E101/493/29.
50 *CPR* 1364-67, p.417 and p.426.

51 *CPR* 1361-64, p.351.
52 John de Swanton was appointed (during pleasure) as keeper of the manor house on 10 October 1358 (*CPR* 1358-61, p.107); as keeper of the warren (for life) on 28 July 1361 (*CPR* 1361-64, p.108). He was appointed keeper of the manor house and the wardrobe for life in 1377 (*CPR* 1374-77, p.400) and this grant, together with the keepership of the warren, was confirmed by Richard II in 1378 (*CPR* 1377-81, p.236).
53 *CFR* 1356-68, p.175.
54 Mentioned in the grant to Dyneleye (next).
55 *CFR* 1377-83, p.317; and 1383-91, p.93.
56 *CFR* 1383-91, p.92 (twice) and p.102.
57 E101/495/1 mm 1, 2.
58 E101/473/2 mm 7-9, 22; E101/473/5 m 10.
59 *CPR* 1389-92, p.82.
60 *Rymer's Foedera. Syllabus*, p.526.
61 Foreign Account Roll 3 Henry IV rot H.
62 F. Devon, *Issues of the Exchequer* (1837), p.255 – Issue Roll, Easter, 17 Richard II.
63 *CPR* 1377-81, p.236 note; and 1389-92, p.249.
64 *CFR* 1391-99, p.105.
65 *Ibid.*, p.165.
66 *CPR* 1392-96, pp.595 and 643.
67 *CFR* 1399-1405, pp.56, 295; 1405-13, pp.142, 161, 239.
68 *CPR* 1399-1401, p.139. See also *CCR* 1402-05, p.79.
69 *CPR* 1385-89, p.314.
70 *CPR* 1389-92, p.466.

Chapter III: The Lancastrian Palace, pp.29-34

1 *CPR* 1413-16, p.346.
2 *Ibid.*, p.116.
3 *Ibid.*, p.11.
4 *Ibid.*, p.59.
5 *Ibid.*, p.99.
6 *Ibid.*, p.132.
7 E101/188/1 and 10.
8 E364/58 rot G.
9 *CPR* 1436-41, p.145; E101/503/9.
10 *CPR* 1413-16, p.346.
11 E364/58, rot G.
12 E364/58, rot G.
13 E101/502/28.
14 E364/58 rot B.
15 E364/68 rot H.
16 E365/70 rot G.
17 E364/56 rot B.
18 E101/502/28.
19 E364/56 rot B.
20 E364/70 rot G.
21 *CPR* 1429-36, p.2.
22 E364/70 rot H.
23 E101/479/7.
24 E101/496/8.
25 E101/503/15.
26 E101/479/7.
27 E101/503/15.
28 E101/479/7.
29 E101/503/12.
30 E364/83 rot E.
31 *Privy Council Proceedings* VI, p.32.
32 *CPR* 1461-67, p.525.
33 E101/503/19.
34 J.H. Harvey, *William Worcestre Itineraries* (Oxford, 1969), pp.270-1. Harvey calculates the length of one of William of Worcester's paces as about 21 inches, which would make the dimensions of the hall 77 feet by 42 feet and those of the Great Court 210 feet by 175 feet.
35 Bodleian Lib, Dodsworth MS 35, f 10.

36 *CCR Henry V*, i, p.217.
37 *CFR* 1422-30, p.97; 1437-45, pp.21 and 108.
38 *CFR* 1441-46, p.234; 1446-52, p.407.
39 *CFR* 1445-52, p.248; 1452-61, p.159.
40 *CFR* 1461-71, p.40.
41 *CFR* 1461-71, p.284.
42 *CFR* 1471-85, p.295; *CPR* 1476-85, p.408.
43 *CFR* 1485-1509, p.45; *CPR* 1485-95, p.154. Pat Henry VII, pt 1, m 8 (20).

Chapter IV: The Charterhouse of Shene, pp.35-48

1 M. Deansley, *The Incendium Amoris of Richard Rolle of Hampole* (1915), pp.99-105, 120.
2 *CChR* V, p.469.
3 *Ibid.*, p.479. The text is given in Dugdale's *Monasticon* VI, pp.31-32.
4 The foundation charter of 1414 grants 'the priories of Grenewych and Lewesham … and all other possessions formerly held by the Abbey of Fécamp in Normandy'; the charter of 1415 correctly attributes the previous ownership to Ghent. Some of the Shene land at East Greenwich, apparently including the manor house, was exchanged in 1433 for other land held by Humphrey Duke of Gloucester. The East Greenwich manor house, later fortified by the Duke, eventually evolved into Greenwich Palace.
5 A full list is given in *Manning and Bray* I, pp.418-19.
6 BL Cotton MS Otho BXIV, f 96.
7 *HKW* II, p.265; see also J. Harvey, *English Mediaeval Architects*, pp.277-8.
8 Lote's will was proved on 10 February 1417/8; Walton was one of his executors. Walton's will was made on 16 August and proved on 6 October 1418. (Harvey, *EMA*.)
9 BL Add MS 24062, f 145.
10 Tanner, *Notitiae Monastica*, p.544; and Rymer's *Foedera* IX, p.290.
11 Pat 5 Henry V, m 22 (*CPR* 1416-22, p.114).
12 BL Cotton MS Otho BXIV, f 100.
13 F. Devon, *Issues of the Exchequer* (1837), p.340. Details of some of the books in the library of the Shene Charterhouse are given in Thompson *COE*, pp.331-34.
14 *CPR* 1416-22, p.87 (Pat 4 Henry V, m 3v); BL Add MS 4601/93 (120).
15 *CPR* 1416-22, p.141 (Pat 5 Henry V, m 28v.).
16 Thompson *COE*, pp.240-1. (Though named as 'Prior' in the foundation charter, Wydrington was technically only 'Rector' until his confirmation by the General Chapter.)
17 *CPR* 1416-22, p.445 (Pat 10 Henry V, m 10v).
18 *CPR* 1416-22, p.397.
19 E364/58 rot G.
20 BL Add MS 11303; printed in *SAC*, vols 38 and 39.
21 Bodleian Liby: Rawlinson MS D318, f 140v.
22 BL Cotton MS, Otho BXIV, f 96.
23 *CPR* 1461-67, p.513 (Pat 6 Edward IV, i, m 17).
24 J.H. Harvey, *William Worcester Itineraries* (1969), pp.270-1. Worcester intended also to give a dimension for the 'width' of the cloister (presumably the distance between the outside wall and the cloister walk) but never filled in the figure.
25 See note 34 to Chapter 3.
26 For plans of the London Charterhouse see D. Knowles and W.F. Grimes, *Charterhouse* (1954), and for Mount Grace see the article by W.H. St John Hope in the *Yorkshire Archaeological Journal* XVIII (1905), pp.270 *seq*. The plan of Shene Charterhouse is discussed in my article 'The Charterhouse of Shene' in *SAC* LXXI (1977), pp.145-98, and in my monograph *Richmond's Great Monastery*, Richmond Local History Society (1990).
27 *CPR* 1422-29, p.222; 1461-67, pp.160-1 and p.513; *1467-77*, p.467; *1476-85*, p.210; *1494-1509*, p.510; as well as those quoted below.
28 *CPR* 1441-46, p.56.

29 *CPR* 1476-85, p.156.
30 *Manning and Bray* I, p.420.
31 *Mon Angl* I, p.974.
32 For a detailed account of these disputes see Thompson *COE*, pp.233, 242-5 and 301.
33 *CSP* (*Venetian*) I, p.567.
34 *CSP* (*Venetian*) IV (Appendix), p.462 no.1003.
35 Thompson *COE*, p.302, quoting Lambeth MS 413, year 1420.
36 Thompson *COE*, p.286, quoting Lambeth MS 413, f 64v.
37 *CSP* (*Milan*) I, p.348; and Thompson *COE*, p.371, quoting Le Vasseur, *Ephemerides*, p.355, and Polidore Vergil, *Historia Anglic*, lib 26.
38 *Chronicles of London*, ed. C.L. Kingsford (OUP, 1905 – reprint Alan Sutton, 1977), p.259; and Thompson *COE*, pp.297 and 371, quoting Le Vasseur, *Ephemerides* i, p.355.
39 The King's letter was printed in full in Augustin Theiner, *Vetera Monumenta Hibernorum et Scotorum* (Rome, 1864), pp.511-12. The Pope's reply is in the British Library (Cottonian MSS, Vitell BII, f 61) and is printed in Rymer's *Foedera* XIII, p.385.
40 John Stow, *Survey of London*, ed. C.L. Kingford (1908), I, p.298. See also Stow's *Annales* (1631 edition), p.494. Stow says he saw 'the body so lapped in lead, thrown into an old waste room amongst old timber, stone, lead and other rubble'. St Michael's, Wood Street, destroyed in the Great Fire in 1666, was rebuilt by Wren, but demolished in 1894. There was no marker or memorial to show the burial of King James's head.
41 *CLPFD* I, ii, p.1016, no.2268.
42 *CSP* (*Venetian*) IV, p.335, no.881.
43 *CLPFD* II, p.107, no.342 (Pat 6 Henry VIII, ii, m 32).
44 PCC 37 Horne (PROB 11/11).
45 *Paston Letters*, ed. James Gairdner (London, 1904), V, p.135.
46 *Ibid.*, VI, p.8.
47 *CLPFD* II, p.1449.
48 F. Madden, *Privy Purse Expenses of the Princess Mary* (London, 1831). In March 1537/8 a shilling tip was given to a servant of the Prior of the Charterhouse for bringing apples.
49 *CLPFD* III, p.105, no.303.
50 Ludovico Beccatelli, *The Life of Cardinal Reginald Pole*, trans. by Rev. Benjamin Pye (1766), p.14; W. Schenk, *Reginald Pole, Cardinal of England* (1950), p.1.
51 *CLPFD* II, ii, p.1455.
52 Beccatelli, *op. cit.*, pp.20-21; Schenk, *op. cit.*, pp.19-23.
53 George Cavendish, *The Life and Death of Cardinal Wolsey*, ed. R.S. Sylvester (Early English Text Society, 1959), p.130 (spelling modernised).
54 Beccatelli, *op. cit.*, p.23; Schenk, *op. cit.*, p.25.
55 Beccatelli, *op. cit.*, pp.23-9; Schenk, *op. cit.*, pp.26-30.
56 *SP Henry VIII*, XIII, i, no.42.

Chapter V: The 'New Park' of Shene, pp.49-53

1 *CPR* 1354-58, p.118.
2 *CPR* 1436-41, p.128.
3 *CPR* 1436-41, p.416.
4 *CPR* 1446-52, p.68; see also the warrant for payment of this allowance, dated 27 October 1447 at *CCR* 1447-54, p.2.
5 E101/496/10.
6 LR2/190, pp.101-2.
7 LR3/101/5 m 3 verso, m 4 verso; LR3/101/6 m 12, m 32; LR3/71, pp.15 and 27.
8 LR3/71, p.27.
9 *Letters of Queen Margaret of Anjou*, Camden Society, 1863.
10 J.H. Harvey, *William Worcestre Intineraries*, p.271.
11 F. Grose, *The Antiquarian Repertory* (1808), Vol.2, Book 3, p.*313.
12 George Cavendish, *op. cit.*, pp.123, 127, 130 (spelling, etc, modernised).
13 *CLPFD* Hy VIII, IV p.2811 no.6249 [BL Cott App XLVIII 22].
14 The assertion at plate XL in Angus's *Seats of the Nobility* (1787)

that Queen Elizabeth repaired the old house in the New Park in 1550 is not borne out by any accounts for that, or any other, year. And Elizabeth was not yet Queen in 1550.
15 LR3/101/6 m 30.
16 LR2/190, ff 100-102.

Chapter VI: The Building of Henry VII's Palace, pp.55-74

1 E101/414/6, f 3.
2 *Ibid.*, f 15.
3 *CSP (Milan)* I, p.347.
4 *The Great Chronicle of London*, ed. A.H. Thomas and I.D. Thornley (1938), p.286.
5 *CSP (Milan)* I, p.347.
6 *CSP (Spanish)* I, p.158, no.203.
7 N.H. Nicolas, *Privy Purse Expenses of Elizabeth of York* (1830), pp.18, 92.
8 *HKW* IV, p.223.
9 *The Great Chronicle of London*, p.295.
10 *Chronicles of London*, ed. C.L. Kingsford (OUP, 1905 – reprint 1977), p.233.
11 F. Grose, *The Antiquarian Repertory* (1808), Vol.2, book 3, p.*312.
12 *Ibid.*, pp.*314-316 (spelling and punctuation, etc, adapted by the present author).
13 Parliamentary Survey, E317 Surrey 46, printed in *SAC* V (1871), pp.76-85.
14 Article by George Scharf in *Archaeologia* XLIX (1886), pp.243-300.
15 *HKW* IV, p.225.
16 *HKW* IV, p.144. The Tudor tennis court at Hampton Court, built by Henry VIII, was on a different site, and looked much like a small chapel.
17 Simon Thurley, *The Royal Palaces of Tudor England* (Yale, 1993), p.31.
18 Gordon Kipling, *The Triumph of Honour, Burgundian Origins of the Elizabethan Renaissance* (Leiden, 1977).
19 It is likely that Henry Redman and Robert Nevill were involved (see p.73).
20 CLPFD I, p.1244; Patent 5 Henry VIII pt 2, m 25; C66/621. This property had nothing to do with the palace woodyard; it appears to have been on the south-east side of Water Lane.
21 BL Add MS 59899, 21 July 1505.
22 John Harvey, *English Mediaeval Architects*, p.35.
23 BL Add MS 59899, 26 July 1504 and 21 July 1505.
24 *Ibid.*, 21 July 1505; E36/214.
25 E36/214, ff 43v, 186.
26 *Great Chronicle of London*, p.330.
27 A. Parkinson, *Collectanea Anglo-Minoritica* (1726), I p.211.
28 A.G. Little, 'The Introduction of the Observant Friars into England', *Proceedings of the British Academy* (1921-3)
29 *HKW* III, p.195, quoting E101/415/3.
30 LR3/101/2, m 12.
31 E101/415/3, f 94v.
32 E101/415/3, f 101; Phillipps MS 4104.
33 E36/214, pp.55, 77.
34 Phillipps MS 4104; E36/214, pp.140, 170, 209, 295, 302.
35 Phillipps MS 4104.
36 LR3/101/2, m 25.
37 E36/214, p.328.

Chapter VII: Henry VII's 'New Park of Richmond, County Middlesex', pp.75-77

1 *CFR 1422-30*, p.97.
2 Rot Parl 9 Henry V, pt 1, m 7.
3 Rot Parl 2 Henry VI, pt 3, m 21.
4 *CPR 1422-29*, p.380.
5 M. Deanesley, *Incendium Amoris*, 129-30; William of Worcester, *Itineraria*, p.283: *Archaeologia* XVII, p.326. It is pointed out in *HKW* I, p.266, that the sheriffs of Middlesex were accounting as late as 1456 for the issues of 'a close in which a house of religious of the Celestine Order was intended by King Henry V'. So the Celestine site may not have been identical with the new site of Syon. Nevertheless, when John Ardene's lease of Shene, Petersham and Ham was renewed in 1438 it no longer included the Celestine site (*CCR 1437-45*, p.21). It seems possible that the empty site for which the Sheriff was accounting was in fact that abandoned by the Briggitines.
6 Rot Parl 10 Henry VI, pt 10, m 22 (which recites the terms of the petition).
7 BL Harl MS 231, p.71.
8 *CPR 1494-1509*, p.353-4.
9 *CLPFD Henry VIII 1519-21*, no.1151.
10 *CLPFD Henry VIII 1529-30*, no.6135 (13).
11 *CLPFD Henry VIII* 1546, no.1383 (87).
12 LR2/190 ff 100-102.
13 *Privy Council Acts*, vol 3, p.221. Compare p.52 above.
14 *CPR 1554-57*, p.229.
15 C 66/1113, Pat 16 Eliz part 6, 3 March.
16 The subsequent history of Twickenham Park is well described in Alan Urwin's *Twicknam Park* (1965), which is however confused as to the 15th and 16th centuries, ascribing to this park most of the references which in fact belong to Henry VI's new park in Shene, next to the Palace.

Chapter VIII: 'The King's Court should have the Excellence', pp.79-93

1 N.H. Nicolas, *Privy Purse Expenses of Elizabeth of York* (1830), pp.83-4.
2 Account by Somerset Herald in Leland's *Collectanea* IV, pp.258-64.
3 Garrett Mattingley, *Catherine of Aragon* (Cape, London, 1942), p.73.
4 Philip wrote from Richmond to King Ferdinand on 22 February, and a letter from him to James IV of Scotland, also from Richmond, was received on 9 March 1505/6.
5 Hall, *Chronicle*, p.501.
6 *Archaeologia* XVIII, pp.33-9.
7 G. Mattingley, *Catherine of Aragon*, p.87.
8 Hall, *Chronicle*, p.516.
9 *Ibid.* (the spelling and punctuation modernised by the present author).
10 *CLPFD* I i, p.370 no.670.
11 Hall, *Chronicle*, pp.516-7 (spelling modernised).
12 *CLPFD* I i, p.370 no.671.
13 *CLPFD* I ii, p.1016 no.2268.
14 *CSP Venetian* II, p.599.
15 *Ibid.*, p.606.
16 *Ibid.*, p.609.
17 *Ibid.*, p.624.
18 Hall, *Chronicle*, p.748.
19 *CSP Spanish* V i, p.332 no.112.
20 E101/517/23, no.11.
21 *CLPFD* III, p.1535.
22 *Ibid.*, p.49 no.152.
23 *Ibid.*, p.910.
24 *Ibid.*, p.1015.
25 *CSP Venetian* III, pp.123, 236; *CSP Spanish*, Second supp to Vols I and II, p.164.
26 *CLPFD* III i, p.314 no.873.
27 *Ibid.*, pp.332-3 no.896.
28 *CSP Spanish*, Second supp to Vols I and II, p.101.
29 *The Complete Poems of John Skelton*, ed. P. Henderson (Dent, 1931), p.350.
30 Stow, *Annales*, p.525.
31 *CSP Spanish* III i, p.209 no.119.
32 *SP Henry VIII*, I, p.150.
33 *Ibid.*, p.326.

NOTES: CHAPTERS VI – IX

34 *HKW* V, p.129.
35 Hall, *Chronicle*, p.703 (spelling modernised).
36 Cavendish, *Wolsey*, p.123.
37 *SP Henry VIII*, I, pp.325-6.
38 *CSP Venetian* IV, p.279, no.664. Hysteria is used here in its original sense of a disease of the womb.
39 *Ibid.*, p.287, no.682.
40 *CSP Spanish* V i, p.299, no.102.
41 *HKW* IV, p.228, quoting Bodleian MS Rawlinson D776, 777; and Nottingham University Library MSS Ne. 0. 1 and 2.
42 *CSP Spanish* V, ii, p.509, no.214.
43 *CSP Spanish* VI i, Intro p.xiii.
44 *SP Henry VIII*, I, p.637.
45 *CLPFD* XV, p.446, no.899.
46 *Ibid.* XVI, p.717.
47 *CSP Spanish* VI i, pp.305-6.
48 *Ibid.*, p.396.
49 Rymer, *Foedera* XIV, p.710.
50 *CFR* 1485-1509, p.250, no.581.
51 *CLPFD* III, p.1134, no.2694 (quoting 1518 grant).
52 *Ibid.*
53 *Ibid.*
54 This grant may have been made in the period 1521-7 for which the Richmond manor rolls are missing. Massie Villyard's previous occupation of the houses is stated in LR2/190, pp.100-2.
55 Quoted at E318/2026.
56 Quoted at *CPR* 1554-55, p.169.
57 LR2/190, pp.100-2.
58 *CPR* 1550-53, p.305; *Privy Council Acts* IV, p.37.
59 *CPR* 1555-57, p.186.
60 *Privy Council Acts* III, p.56.
61 *CPR* 1554-55, p.169.
62 Memo Roll, Mich 6 Elizabeth, rot 95.
63 E351/3326; see also *Privy Council Acts* II, pp.86, 149, 186, 207.
64 *Privy Council Acts* II, p.303.
65 *CSP Spanish* X, p.332.

Chapter IX: The Dissolutions and Refoundation of the Charterhouse, pp.95-115

1 The theory that Rich was not executed (followed e.g. in the *DNB* article on Elizabeth Barton) seems to derive from Bishop Gilbert Burnet's *History of the Reformation in England*. On p.252 of Vol.1 (1865 edition) he gave a list of those executed, omitting Rich, and commented, 'Rich is not named, being perhaps either dead or pardoned'. His source appears to be Stow's *Annales* (first published in 1580) which, although it had named Rich as an Observant Friar, condemned and pilloried with Elizabeth Barton, for some reason did not include him by name in a list of those executed on 20 April. However, Stow did name 'Richard Risby and another of his fellows of the same house', which appears to confirm that two Observants were executed, although suggesting that both were from Canterbury.
2 Edward Hall, *Chronicle* (1809 edition), p.807.
3 *The Lisle Letters* (Penguin edition, 1985), p.115.
4 *Chronicle of the Grey Friars of London*, ed. J.G. Nichols (Camden Society, 1852), p.37.
5 Dom David Knowles, *The Religious Orders in England* (Cambridge University Press, 1959), III, p.159.
6 Arundel MS 152, f 296.
7 *CLPFD* VI, p.369, no.835; p.479, no.1149 (2); p.589, no.1468 (8).
8 *CLPFD* VII, pp.242-3, no.622.
9 *Ibid.*, p.316, no.841.
10 *Ibid.*, p.320, no.856 (Letter of 19 June 1534 from Leonard Smith to Lord Lisle).
11 *Ibid.*, p.413, no.1057.
12 *Ibid.*, pp.423-5, no.1095.
13 The full story of the London Charterhouse is told in Dom Lawrence Hendricks's *The London Charterhouse* and in Margaret Thompson's *The Carthusian Order in England*.
14 Knowles, *op. cit.*, p.216, quoting Bodleian MS Don c42.
15 *CLPFD* VIII, p.441, no.1125.
16 *CLPFD* XIV, ii, nos.424, 425.
17 Statute 23 Henry VIII, c 27; E40/4758.
18 *CLPFD* XI, p.105, no.244.
19 *CLPFD* XX, i, p.263, no.557.
20 PCC 4 Wrastley (PROB 11/39).
21 *Privy Council Acts 1542-47*, p.161.
22 Augmentation Office Roll, 32 Henry VIII.
23 *CLPFD* XIV, ii, p.72, no.236 (6).
24 SC 6 Henry VIII, 3464, m 53.
25 *CLPFD* XVI, p.381, no.779 (7). (Particulars for the grant are at E318/572, f 15.)
26 *CLPFD* XVI, p.723, no.1500.
27 *CPR 1547-48*, p.172.
28 LR2/190, p.100.
29 *Literary Remains of King Edward VI*, ed. J.G. Nichols (Roxburgh Club, 1857), I, p.61.
30 *Privy Council Acts* II, p.384.
31 *Literary Remains of King Edward VI*, II, p.273.
32 *Privy Council Acts* III, p.452.
33 LR2/190, p.100. There are three quite different – and barely reconcilable – lists of the Shene lands, which are discussed in Appendix 4.
34 *CSP (Spanish)* XI, p.167.
35 *CSP Dom 1547-80*, p.54. This document is printed in *CSP (Spanish)* XI, p.159, as issued at Richmond on 8 August, but the date must be mistaken.
36 *CSP Spanish* XI, p.199.
37 *Ibid.*, p.242.
38 *Ibid.*, p.459.
39 *CSP Spanish* XIII, p.146.
40 *HKW* IV, p.229.
41 Thompson, *COE*, p.505, quoting Chauncey's *Passio*.
42 *CSP (Venetian)* VI, i, p.651, no.634.
43 *Ibid.* VI, ii, p.791, no.704.
44 *CPR 1555-57*, pp.354-5.
45 *Diary of Henry Machyn 1550-63*, ed. J.G. Nichols (Camden Society, 1848), p.160.
46 *CPR 1557-58*, p.438; Pat 5 and 6 P and M, pt 5, mm 7-8.
47 *CPR 1557-58*, p.439.
48 *CSP (Venetian)* VI, p.107, no.132.
49 Lucy Aikin, *Memoirs of the Court of Queen Elizabeth* (1818), I, p.217.
50 F. Madden, *Privy Purse Expenses of the Princess Mary* (1831), p.clxxxvii.
51 *Ibid.*, pp.cci-ccv.
52 Thompson, *COE*, p.501, quoting Chauncey's *Passio*.
53 *CSP (Spain)* I, p.77.
54 For the history of Sheen Anglorum, see Hendricks, *The London Charterhouse*, pp.284-348.
55 *Wills from Doctors' Commons*, Camden Society, vol.83 (1863), p.56.
56 The several references in Agnes Strickland's *Tudor and Stuart Princesses* to Adrian Stokes's occupancy of the Charterhouse in 1571-2 seem to be based on no.evidence, but simply on the assumption that this was part of the Duchess's property which he inherited. After his marriage to Anne Carew, the widow of Sir Nicholas Throgmorton (who died in February 1570/1) Stokes lived at Bradgate until his death in 1585.
57 *CSP For 1562*, p.83, no.170.
58 *CSP Dom 1547-80*, pp.200-18.
59 R.W. Sackville West, *Works of Thomas Sackville* (London, 1859), Appendix II, pp.xxxii-xxxiii.
60 *CSP Dom 1547-80*, p.318.
61 R.W. Sackville-West, *op. cit.*, Appendix II, pp.xxix-xxxiii.
62 *CSP Dom 1547-80*, p.320.
63 Hendricks, *The London Charterhouse*, pp.292-3, quoting a

manuscript 'Notitia Cartusianorum Anglorum' by Father James Long, which includes notes by Father John Suertis who joined the English Carthusians in 1571 and who related this story.
64 See the author's 'Charterhouse of Sheen' in *SAC* LXXI, 1977, pp.173-4.
65 *CSP Dom* 1547-80, p.610.
66 E310/25/142, p.49.
67 Pat 26 Elizabeth, pt 3.

Chapter X: The Palace under Queen Elizabeth, pp.117-149

1   *CPR 1558-60*, p.60. (See Chapter 11.)
2   S. Haynes, *Collection of State Papers ... left by William Cecil Lord Burghley* (1740) I, pp.364-5.
3   *CSP Dom* 1547-80, p.157.
4   Baron K. de Lettenhove, *Relations Politiques des Pays Bas et de l'Angleterre sous la Règne de Philippe II*, I, Brussels, 1882, p.505.
5   *CSP Spanish* 1558-69, p.175.
6   Haynes, *Burghley State Papers*, I, p.361.
7   The probable circumstances of Amy Dudley's death were convincingly explained in an article by Professor Ian Aird in the *English Historical Review*, vol.LXXI (1956), pp.69-79. He pointed out that some cases of breast cancer can cause a brittleness of the spine, which might result in a spontaneous fracture of the neck from no more of a jolt than that incurred by stumbling on the stairs.
8   *CSP Spanish* (*Simancas*) 1558-67, p.177.
9   *Ibid.*, p.178.
10 *Ibid.*, p.208.
11 *Ibid.*, pp.179-82.
12 M.S. Steele, *Plays and Masques at Court during the Reigns of Elizabeth, James and Charles* (Yale University Press, 1926), p.15, quoting A. Feuillerat, *Documents Relating to the Office of Revels in the Times of Queen Elizabeth* (Louvain, 1908), p.116.
13 *CSP Spanish* (*Simancas*) 1558-67, p.364.
14 *Ibid.*, p.367.
15 *Ibid.*, pp.460, 462, 465, 646.
16 E351/3203.
17 LR3/101/6, m 30.
18 *CPR* 1569-72, p.331, no.2440; C66/1082, m 14.
19 LR3/101/6, m 16.
20 LR3/101/6, m 1.
21 E310/25/140, p.17.
22 LR3/101/6, m 14. (Massie Stanton's house was probably the one which had been built by Nicholas Gray, on the south side of Water Lane.)
23 Confessions of the Duke of Norfolk (MSS Queen of Scots) quoted in J.A. Froude, *History of England IX*, pp.473-4.
24 SP12/4, no.57.
25 E351/3209.
26 E351/3219.
27 E351/3216.
28 Hatfield MSS, VIII, no.65.
29 E351/3218.
30 E351/3214.
31 E351/3225.
32 E351/3215.
33 E351/3210.
34 E351/3219.
35 E351/3223.
36 *CSP Dom* 1547-80, p.610.
37 E351/3225.
38 *Privy Council Acts*, XX, p.194.
39 E351/3223.
40 *The Office of Revels Documents* were published by A. Feuillerat (Louvain, 1908). The Chamber accounts were added by E.K. Chambers in *The Elizabethan Stage* (OUP, 1924), vol.IV, appx B. These and other sources were correlated and expanded in M.S. Steele, *Plays and Masques at Court during the Reigns of Elizabeth, James and Charles* (Yale University Press, 1926).
41 Feuillerat, *Documents*, pp.244 and 241.
42 *Ibid.*, p.350.
43 *Ibid.*, p.298.
44 *CSP Dom* 1547-80, p.682.
45 *Ibid.*, p.691.
46 E351/3216.
47 *Historical Manuscripts Commission*, 15th Report: gives the original French text; the translation is the author's.
48 Dr. John Dee, *The Compendious Rehearsal ... of His Life ...* (1592, printed 1851), p.516.
49 John Dee, *Private Diary*, Camden Society no.19 (1842), p.4.
50 *Ibid.*, 30 June 1578.
51 *Ibid.*, p.5.
52 *Ibid.*, pp.8-9
53 *Ibid.*, p.9.
54 *Ibid.*, p.19.
55 *Ibid.*, p.21.
56 *Ibid.*, p.32.
57 *Ibid.*, pp.36-37.
58 *CSP Spanish*, Elizabeth, III, p.198 (no.146).
59 A.J. Kempe, *The Loseley Manuscripts* (London, 1836), pp.300-2.
60 Letter from Lord Buckhurst to Sir William More, 2 August 1588, quoted in *Manning and Bray*, III, p.667.
61 I have not been able to trace an original use by Queen Elizabeth of this phrase, used in the above form in Agnes Strickland's *Lives of the Queens of England*, vol III (1844), p.286. Edmund Bohun in his *The Character of Queen Elizabeth*, 1693, says (p.373): 'She called this Royal Palace the Warm Box to which she could best trust her sickly Old Age'. Bohun's book is largely an anglicised version of Robert Johnstone's *Historia Rerum Britannicarum* (1655) in which the parallel passage reads (p.357): '*Senectutis suae Nidulum vocare consueverat*' (she was wont to call it a little nest for her old age). I am grateful to Dr. Stephen Pasmore for his help in tracing the phrase thus far.
62 Edmund Lodge, *Illustrations of British History* (1838), II, p.386, quoting Talbot Papers, vol.V, f 67.
63 Letter from Mrs. Wooley, dated Richmond, 5 September 1595. (*Loseley MSS* 316.)
64 Sir J. Harington, *Nugae Antiquae*, ed. T. Park (London, 1804), II, pp.215-18.
65 *Ibid.*
66 E351/3230.
67 E351/3231.
68 E351/3234 and 3237.
69 E351/3232.
70 E351/3236.
71 E351/3235.
72 Sir John Harington, *A new Discourse on a stale Subject, called the Metamorphosis of Ajax*, ed. E.S. Donno (London, 1962), p.61.
73 *Ibid.*, pp.177-8.
74 Sir John Harington, *Nugae Antiquae*, ed. T.Park (London, 1804), I, pp.239-40.
75 *Letters and Epigrams of Sir John Harington*, ed. N.E. McClure (Philadelphia, 1930).
76 *Letters written by John Chamberlain during the Reign of Queen Elizabeth*, ed. S. Williams (Camden Society, 1861), p.89.
77 *Ibid.*, pp.108-9.
78 Letter dated 7 April 1602 (NS) quoted by John Lingard, *History of England*, VI, p.633.
79 *CSP Dom* 1601-03, p.179.
80 Chamberlain, *Letters*, p.157.
81 *Ibid.*, p.170.
82 Sir J. Harington, *Nugae Antiquae*, ed. T. Park (London, 1804), I, p.320.
83 *Ibid.*, p.323.
84 Chamberlain, *Letters*, p.174.
85 M.S. Steele, *Plays and Masques at Court*, pp.126-7.

Chapter XI: Princesses and Potentates at Kew, pp.151-168

86 *CSP Venetian*, IX, 1592-1603, p.528.
87 *Ibid.*, pp.531-3.
88 *Ibid.*, p.554.
89 *Ibid.*, p.557.
90 Sir Robert Carey, *Memoirs*, written before 1627, but not published until 1759.
91 *CSP Venetian*, X, 1603-07, p.15.

Chapter XI: Princesses and Potentates at Kew, pp.151-168

1 This is based on an involved process of deduction from the early records which will be described in detail elsewhere.
2 *CLPFD* IX, p.157, no.479.
3 *Select Cases in the Court of Star Chamber*, Selden Society, No.16, 1903, p.237.
4 *State Papers* (*Spanish*), Supplement to Vols.1 and 2, p.26, no.4.
5 Richmond Manor Court Rolls: LR3/101/2, m 21.
6 *Ibid.*
7 Privy Council Signet Roll: C82/454, m 1.
8 PCC: 15 Porch.
9 John Leland, *Cygnea Cantio*, 1545, note on the lines: 'Chevam hospitio piae Mariae / Gallorum Dominae celebriorem'.
10 *CLPFD* XV, p.335, no.716.
11 CLPFD XIV, ii, p.336, no.782.
12 *Ibid.*, p.328, no.782; and BL Add Charter 49A46.
13 LR3/101/4, m 7 verso.
14 LR3/101/4, m 8 verso.
15 *Ibid.*
16 *Manning* I, p.448 (quoting Fox's Register V, f 4a).
17 PCC: 4 Porche (PROB 11/22).
18 E326/10605.
19 Feet of Fines, Surrey, 25 Henry VIII, no.983.
20 *Ibid.*, no.221.
21 *CLPFD* p.359 no.871 and p.459 no.1087(9); Statute 27 Henry VIII, c 26.
22 *DNB*, quoting *Spanish Chronicle of Henry VII*, ed Sharp Hume, p.72.
23 *CLPFD* XI, p.523, no.1291.
24 *CLPFD* XII, i, p.292, no.661, 16 March 1536/7.
25 *Ibid.*, p.357, no.806.
26 *Ibid.*, p.363, no.821.
27 Feet of Fines, Surrey, 30 Henry VIII, no.283.
28 *CLPFD* XIII, i, p.265, no.696.
29 *CLPFD* XIV, ii, p.323, no.782.
30 *CLPFD* XVII, p.103, no.220 (50); Feet of Fines, Surrey, 34 Henry VIII, no.366.
31 *CLPFD* XX, ii, p.232, no.496 (88); Feet of Fines, Surrey, 37 Henry VIII, no.464.
32 *CLPFD* XX, ii, p.188, no.427.
33 *CLPFD* XXI, i, p.152, no.302 (65).
34 Feet of Fines, Surrey, 40 Henry VIII, no.553.
35 *CPR* 1548-49, p.373.
36 *CPR* 1550-53, pp.323-4; Pat 6 Edward VI, pt 5, (roll 846), m 26.
37 *CPR* 1553-54, p.55.
38 *CPR* 1558-60, p.60; C66/941, m 18.
39 *CLPFD* XIII, ii, p.314, no.802.
40 *CPR* 1553-54, p.257.
41 *Privy Council Acts* V, p.29.
42 *CSP Dom* 1547-80, p.60.
43 *CPR* 1558-60, p.60; C66/941, m 18.
44 SC 6 Henry VIII, no.6164.
45 *Camden Society* vol 83 (1863), p.39.
46 *CSP Dom* 1547-80, p.109.
47 Folkestone Williams, *Domestic Memoirs of the Royal Family* (Hurst & Blackett, London, 1860), III, p.322.
48 LR3/101/6, m 7.
49 LR3/101/5, m 8.
50 LR3/101/6, mm 9, 11 and 12.
51 PCC: 6 More and 12 Chayre.
52 LR3/101/6, mm 3, 4, 12 verso and 14.
53 *CLPFD* XIV, i, p.594, no.1355.
54 *Ibid.* XIX, i, p.382, no.610.
55 *Ibid.* XXI, i, p.692, no.1383 (101).
56 PCC, 6 More (PROB11/37) and PCC 12 Chayre (PROB11/46).
57 Pat 36 Elizabeth pt 13, 2 September 1594.
58 *CPR* 1572-75, p.467, no.2877; Pat 17 Elizabeth, pt vi, no.31.
59 Ancient Deeds V, A13159.
60 Feet of Fines, Surrey, Mich 17/18 Elizabeth.
61 *CPR* 1572-75, p.467, no.2877; Pat 17 Elizabeth pt vi no.31.
62 See Chapter 9.
63 LR3/101/6, m 25 (attachment).
64 LR3/101/6, m 31 verso.
65 BL Add Charter 25512, 2 May 34 Elizabeth.
66 C2/ELIZ/P4/50.
67 BL Harleian MS, no.6850, f 90.
68 *Sydney State Papers* I, p.376.
69 LR3/71, p.1.
70 LR3/101/6, m 2.
71 *Ibid.*, m 11.
72 *Ibid.*, mm 5 and 6.
73 *Ibid.*, m 19 verso.
74 *DNB*, quoting *Letters from the Bodleian Library* (1813), II, pp.207-21.
75 LR3/101/6, m 38.
76 *Ibid.*, mm 25 verso, 29, 31, 32 and 38.
77 *Ibid.*, mm 25 verso, 38 and 39.
78 LR3/71, p.20.
79 Sir Roy Strong, *Henry Prince of Wales and England's Lost Renaissance* (Thames & Hudson, London, 1986), p.41.
80 *CSP Dom* 1547-80, p.18.
81 William Turner, *Herbal*, 1568 edition.
82 *CSP Dom* 1601-03, p.27.
83 *CSP* (*Venetian*), XI, p.278, no.513.
84 *Ibid.*, p.336, no.617.
85 *CSP Dom* 1603-10, p.552.
86 Agnes Strickland, *Lives of the Queens of Scotland and English Princesses* (1859), VIII, p.24.
87 LR3/71, p.6.

Chapter XII: James I's New Park, pp.169-178

1 Gunnar Sjögren, article 'Helena Marchioness of Northampton' in *History Today*, September 1978, vol 28, pp.597-604.
2 *CSP Dom 1595-97*, p.490.
3 Gorges appears to have obtained this lease by assignment from Lovell. He was already 'Lord of the Manors' on James I's accession (LR3/71, pp.1, 3 and 4).
4 *CSP Dom 1603-10*, p.13.
5 LR3/101/2, m 12.
6 The original grant to Hales has not been traced; it is referred to in the documents of 1547 and 1566.
7 *CPR 1547-48*, p.168 ff; E318/1816, m 13.
8 E326/B11224.
9 *CPR 1566-69*, p.25 no.114; particulars at E310/139/2, f 28.
10 *CPR 1578-80*, p.187, no.1511; Pat 22 Eliz pt 3.
11 LR3/101/4, m 6v.
12 E318/2026.
13 *Ibid.*
14 *CPR 1555-57*, p.186.
15 E310/25/140, p.5.
16 E310/25/141, p.8.
17 E310/25/140, p.24.
18 E310/25/140, p.10; CRES 38/1765.
19 *CSP Dom 1603-10*, p.199.
20 *Ibid.*, p.219.
21 *CSP Dom, Eliz and James I Addenda*, p.462.
22 Pat 5 James I, pt 26, m 20. (C66/1746.)
23 CRES 38/1765.

24 Devon, *Issues of the Exchequer*, James I, p.58.
25 LR3/71, pp.28, 40, 48.
26 LR3/71, pp.48, 223.
27 LR3/71, pp.27.
28 LR3/101/5, m 3v.
29 E351/3364.
30 E351/3366.
31 The Book of Architecture of John Thorpe is in the Soane Museum; see article by John Summerson in the *Walpole Society*, vol.XL (1966).
32 Colvin, *Dictionary of British Architects*; *HKW* III, pp.134-5.
33 HMC: *Calendar of Salisbury MSS*, XVII, p.202. (No year is given in the date of the letter. It could be 1606; but the King is known to have been in Richmond on 14-17 May 1605.)
34 E351/3373.
35 *CSP Dom 1611-18*, p.404.
36 Original receipt in Richmond Public Library.
37 E214/462.
38 E147/3/17.
39 E317/Surrey 46; see also E320/R28.
40 E315/173, P 49.
41 E317/Surrey 46.
42 Pamela Fletcher Jones in her *Richmond Park* (pp 15-18) mistakenly ascribes this survey to Charles I's park. She was in consequence puzzled about the lack of deer.
43 E315/173, p.24.
44 E320/R28.
45 *Mystery of the Good Old Cause* (1660), republished as *Sarcastic Notices of the Long Parliament* (London, 1863), pp.24 and 43.
46 SP29/5, no.58; *CSP Dom 1660-61*, p.71.

Chapter XIII: Richmond as the Seat of the Prince of Wales, pp.179-196

1 *CSP Venetian* X (1603-07), p.81, no.111.
2 E351/3239.
3 *CSP Venetian* X, p.300, no.453.
4 Thomas Birch, *Life of Henry Prince of Wales* (1760), p.74.
5 E351/3240.
6 E351/3242.
7 Birch, *Henry Prince of Wales*, pp.96-97.
8 E351/3243.
9 Birch, *Henry Prince of Wales*, p.330.
10 *Ibid.*, pp.75-6, quoting a letter of Ambassador La Broderie, dated 31 October 1606.
11 *CSP Venetian* XII (1610-13), p.142, no.217.
12 Roger Coke, *A Detection of the Court and State of England during the last four Reigns* (1694), I, p.70.
13 BL Harl MS 252.
14 Roy Strong, *Henry Prince of Wales and England's Lost Renaissance*, pp.153-60.
15 Pat 8 James I, pt 41, no.2.
16 For the information on Constantino de'Servi and on the palace project, the author is indebted to Sir Roy Strong's book, *Henry Prince of Wales and England's Lost Renaissance* (Thames and Hudson, 1986), pp.90-5. From this are taken the references to papers in the Archivio di Stato, Florence (ASF).
17 AO1/2021, no.3.
18 SP14/64, no.64.
19 Roy Strong, *op. cit.*, p.107; and *The Renaissance Garden in England*, p.98.
20 LR3/101/4, m 13.
21 LR3/101/6, m 17, m 25 (att).
22 LR3/71, p.12.
23 SP14/63 no.56.
24 SP14/64 no.63.
25 SP14/65 no.62.
26 SP14/65 no.55.
27 Philip Dixon, article 'Excavations at Richmond Palace, Surrey', in *Post Mediaeval Archaeology* IX (1975), pp.103-16.

28 E317/Surrey 48; published in *SAC* XXVII (1914), p.144 ff.
29 SP14/69, no.13.
30 ASF 4189.
31 *Ibid.*
32 ASF Mediceo 1348, f 194.
33 *Ibid.*, f 233.
34 BL Add MS 32464, ff 52-52*.
35 BL Harl MS 7009, ff 87-89.
36 ASF 4190, f 52.
37 ASF Miscell Mediceo 293, inserto 28, no.39.
38 ASF Mediceo 1229, f 286.
39 ASF Mediceo 1347, unnumbered folio.
40 Folkestone Williams, *Domestic Memoirs of the Royal Family*, III, p.18.
41 *HKW* IV, p.231.
42 *Archaeologia* XV (1806), p.17.
43 SP14/63 no.55.
44 E351/3244.
45 E351/3251.
46 E317/Surrey 53.
47 Landesbibliothek Kassel, MS Haas 18, f 79v.
48 Devon, *Issues of the Exchequer*, James I, p.179.
49 *Ibid.*, p.210.
50 *Hist MSS Comm 15th Report*, App2, pp.282-3. (*HKW* appears to include these works as carried out at the Palace, but 'Sheen' was no longer synonymous with 'Richmond'.)
51 E351/3245.
52 Pat 14 James I, pt 20, no.2.
53 Pat 14 James I, pt 10, no.3.
54 E351/3251 (pheasant house); E351/3254 and 3255 (repairs); E351/3256 (munition house and shuffleboard room).
55 *CSP Venetian* XV (1617-19), pp.271, 309.
56 *CSP Venetian* XIV 1625-26, p.130.
57 *CSP Dom* 1625-26, p.33.
58 *Privy Council Acts* 1625-26, p.126.
59 Recited at E214/462.
60 *CSP Dom* 1625-26, p.34.
61 Rymer, *Foedera* XVIII, p.685; Pat 2 Charles I, part 4, no.3.
62 *CSP Dom* 1628-29, p.329.
63 *Ibid.*, p.350.
64 LR3/71, p.156.
65 E351/3262.
66 E351/3265.
67 E351/3270.
68 AO1/2429/71.
69 Deputy Keeper of the Public Records, *Report* no.XIII.
70 *CSP Dom* 1637-38, pp.173, 376; 1638-39, p.460.
71 E351/3269; M S Steele, *Plays and Masques at Court*, p.263.
72 M.S. Steele, *op. cit.*, p.274.
73 AO1/2429/71.
74 M S Steele, *op. cit.*, p.275.
75 *CSP Dom* Apr-Nov 1637, p.129.
76 *CSP Dom* 1637-38, p.274.
77 Pat 14 Charles I, p.43; BL Add Ch 13590.
78 *CSP Dom* 1639, p.509

Chapter XIV: Charles I's New Park of Richmond, pp.197-206

1 Clarendon, *The History of the Rebellion*, I, p.77.
2 *CSP Dom*, Dec 1637 – Aug 1638, p.131.
3 The original is in the Museum of London. A much clearer 18th-century copy in the PRO is at MR 295, but contains a number of errors in copying. One of the landowners shown on the map had died by April 1632, so the survey must have been completed before then.
4 MPE 986.
5 Pat 10 Charles I, part 8, 5 May 1635.
6 Rymer, *Foedera* XIX, p.585; C66/2677 m 8.
7 *CSP Dom 1635*, p.25.

Notes: Chapter XIII – Appendix 1

8. E351/3407.
9. WORK 16/5/1 – a 19th-century 'abstract of contracts for the purchase of land in Richmond Park 1635 & 1636'.
10. C54/3430, m 26.
11. WORK 16/5/1.
12. *CSP Dom* 1635, p.479.
13. CRES28/1765.
14. E214/1398.
15. Surrey RO, 58/4/1/7.
16. E317/Surrey 31 and 45.
17. *CSP Dom* 1635, p.567.
18. *CSP Dom, Charles I Addenda*, p.511.
19. Raymond C. Gill, *Richmond Park in the Seventeenth Century* (Barnes and Mortlake History Society, 1990), pp.4-5; Mortlake Vestry Book I.
20. *Ibid.*
21. J.E. Anderson, *History of Mortlake* (1886, republished 1983), p.22.
22. *CSP Dom* 1635-36, p.331.
23. E351/3407.
24. E351/3409.
25. E351/3410.
26. E351/3414. (The undated payment warrant, attributed to 1630 in *CSP Dom* 1629-31, p.454, quite clearly refers to this work begun in August 1636. Its misplacing in the calendared papers has led some writers to believe that work on the park actually started in 1630.)
27. City of London Chamberlain's Vellum Book 1650, Vol.1/7, f 82.
28. The grant to Portland, quoted by P. Fletcher Jones, *Richmond Park* (1972), p.11, is recited at *CSP Dom* Jan-Sep 1644, p.234. For the deputies, see *CSP Dom* Apr-Nov 1637, p.555.
29. *CSP Dom* Apr-Nov 1637, pp.285, 555.
30. E351/3416.
31. WORK 5/176/4.
32. *CSP Dom* 1636-37, p.457.
33. J.P. Hore, *History of the Royal Buckhounds*, p.143.
34. Ham Manor Court 25 April 1637 (Sy RO 58/2/1/5).
35. *CSP Dom* 1636-37, p.388.
36. *CSP Dom* Sep 1638-Mar 1639, p.609.
37. *CSP Dom* 1641-43, p.50.
38. *Notes and Queries* (2) V, p.370, article on 'Richmond New Park', quoting a letter written by Colonel Edmund Whalley.
39. *Journal of the House of Commons* Vol.VI, p.246.
40. *Ibid.*, p.263.
41. *Ibid.*, p.365.
42. Chamberlain's Vellum Books: Vol 1/7, ff 82, 169b; Vol 1/8, ff 144, 193; Vol 1/9, ff 64, 144b; Repertory Vol 62, f 305b.
43. Chamberlain's Vellum Book 1651, Vol 1/7, f 167b, and similar entries in later years.
44. Common Council, Journal 41*, f 83b.
45. *Ibid.*, f 211b.
46. Repertory Vol 61, f 218, 13 September 1651.
47. Repertory Vol 63, f 204b, 7 November 1654.
48. Repertory Vol 62, ff 318b and 354, 21 June and 5 July 1653.
49. Common Council Journal 41*, f 232b, 7 May 1660.
50. *Ibid.*, f 234b, 2 June 1660. All the City of London documents noted above are transcribed in Sir Thomas J Nelson's *Richmond Park* (1883).

Chapter XV: Richmond in the Civil War, pp.207-211

1. *CSP Dom* 1640-41, p.333. The letter is undated, but the persons referred to were buried on 15 June (*Richmond Parish Registers*).
2. *Ibid.*, p.167.
3. *House of Commons Journal*, 18 September 1643.
4. *CSP Dom, Committee for Assessing Money* and *CSP Dom, Committee for Compounding*.
5. *Kingdom's Weekly Intelligencer*, 26 October 1647, quoted in *CSP Dom* 1645-47, pp.591-2.
6. *CSP Dom* 1648-49, p.156.
7. *Ibid.*, p.169.
8. *Ibid.*, p.171.
9. The Manor of Richmond, including Richmond Palace and Little Park: E317/Surrey 46; printed in *SAC* V, 1871, pp.76-85. (Substantial extracts, not wholly correct, in E.B. Chancellor, *The History and Antiquities of Richmond, Kew, Petersham and Ham* (1894), pp.xii-xix.) Sheen: E317/Surrey 53; printed in *SAC* LXXI, 1977, pp.187-92.
10. *CSP Dom, Committee for Compounding*, Pt 2, p.1526.
11. On the identification of these buildings, see Cloake, 'The Charterhouse of Sheen', *SAC* LXXI, 1977, pp.169-75, or *Richmond's Great Monastery*, Richmond Local History Society, 1990. The Sir John Dingley mentioned here is not the Parliamentarian appointed as one of the overseers of the Park in 1643 (see p.208). This Sir John had been Secretary to Queen Elizabeth of Bohemia. (See Margaret Toynbee's article in *Notes and Queries*, October 1953, pp.417-20.)
12. E320/R23.
13. E320/R28.
14. E315/173.
15. E320/R25.
16. Richmond Vestry Minutes, 5 January 1652/3.
17. LR3/71, p.335.
18. Register of St Paul's, Covent Garden.
19. LR3/71, p.343.
20. *Ibid.*, p.356.
21. SP29/5, no.58.
22. LR3/71, p.314.
23. *Ibid.*, pp.309-310, 312, 316, etc.
24. *Surrey Archaeological Collections*, XXVII, pp.144-6.

Appendix 1: The Belet Family in the 12th and Early 13th Centuries, pp.213-218

1. *Domesday Book: Dorset* (Phillimore, Chichester, 1983), 1 : 30; 57 : 1, 12, 13, 14, 19.
2. *Pipe Roll 31 Henry I*, pp.13, 15, 49, 51, 123.
3. *Ibid.*, pp.6, 86, 121.
4. *Pipe Roll 12 Henry II*, p.116.
5. *Pipe Roll 18 Henry II*, p.37.
6. *Pipe Roll 21 Henry II*, pp.15, 187, 203.
7. T.C. Banks, *Dormant and Extinct Baronage*, I, pp.31-2.
8. *Oblate and Fine Rolls*, pp.276, 287, 440. *Pipe Rolls 6 John*, p.139; *7 John*, p.211; *10 John*, p.14.
9. *Lincolnshire Feet of Fines 1199-1215* (Pipe Roll Soc NS29), pp.116-17.
10. *Oblate and Fine Rolls*, p.358.
11. *Pipe Roll 14 John*, p.20.
12. *Pipe Roll 13 John*, p.12.
13. *C Ch R* I, p.376.
14. *Red Book* II, p.758.
15. *C Ch R* I, p.376.
16. *C Ch R* II, p.302.
17. *Pipe Roll 31 Henry I*, pp.13, 15 (Dorset); 123 (Berkshire); 49, 51 (Surrey).
18. *Cartae Antiquae* II, p.197.
19. Manning (I, p.xxx) lists Robert Belet as Sheriff of Surrey in 1154 and John Belet in 1155. No evidence for this has been found, and they were not the Sheriffs mentioned in the Pipe Rolls.
20. *Pipe Roll 7 Henry II*, p.43.
21. *Pipe Roll 10 Henry II*, p.41.
22. *Pipe Roll 11 Henry II*, p.111.
23. *Pipe Roll 12 Henry II*, p.107.
24. *Pipe Roll 14 Henry II*, p.216.
25. *Pipe Rolls 11 Henry II*, p.111; *12 Henry II*, p.107, etc.
26. *Red Book* I, p.27; *Pipe Roll 14 Henry II*, p.144.
27. *Red Book* I, p.406.

28 A. Heales, *Records of Merton Priory*, p.25.
29 *Pipe Roll 22 Henry II*, p.134.
30 *Ibid.*, p.163.
31 *Ibid.*, p.217.
32 *Pipe Roll 23 Henry II*, p.195.
33 *Pipe Roll 26 Henry II*, p.39.
34 *Pipe Roll 29 Henry II*, p.101.
35 *Pipe Roll 1 Richard I*, p.180.
36 *Pipe Roll 2 Richard I*, p.31 etc.
37 *Pipe Roll 7 Richard I*, p.205.
38 *Pipe Roll 5 John*, p.139.
39 *Pipe Roll 6 John*, p.219.
40 *Book of Fees*, p.66 (see below p.217).
41 *Pipe Roll 32 Henry II*, p.197.
42 *Pipe Roll 6 Richard I*, pp.190, 193.
43 *Ibid.*, p.191.
44 *Pipe Roll 1 John*, p.231, to *9 John*, p.55.
45 *Records of Merton Priory*, p.29.
46 *Ibid.*, pp.28, 40.
47 *Pipe Roll 2 Richard I*, p.152.
48 *Ibid.*, p.155.
49 *Pipe Roll 10 Richard I*, p.149.
50 *Ibid.*, p.148; *Pipe Roll 1 John*, p.57.
51 *Pipe Roll 2 John*, p.217.
52 *Pipe Roll 6 John*, p.105.
53 *Pipe Roll 8 John*, p.116.
54 *Pipe Roll 9 John*, p.65.
55 *Book of Fees*, pp.343, 1153.
56 *Red Book* II, p.561.
57 *Book of Fees*, p.70.
58 *Ibid.*, p.66.
59 *C Ch R* I, p.43.
60 *CIPM* IV, p.11 (no.26).
61 *Manning & Bray* I, p.406.
62 *Pipe Roll 31 Henry I*, p.15.
63 *Red Book* I, p.311.
64 *Fine Rolls in Tower of London* I, p.71.
65 *Red Book* I, p.67.
66 *Ibid.*, p.93 and *Pipe Roll 6 Richard I*, p.257.
67 *Pipe Roll 5 John*, p.49, and *Red Book* I, p.143.
68 *Book of Fees*, p.254.
69 *Ibid.*, pp.846, 856.
70 *C Ch R* I, p.406.

Appendix 2: The Sites of the Old Manor House, etc., pp.219-222

1 SC6/1014/10-13.
2 Pipe Roll 36 Edward III, rot comp 6.
3 Foreign Account Roll 3 Henry IV, rot H.
4 E101/502/28.
5 E101/479/7.
6 Foreign Account Roll 45 Edward III, rot Dd, m ii; E101/494/17.
7 E101/494/28, mm 2-4.
8 *Post Med Arch* IX (1975), pp.103-116.
9 E101/517/23, no.11.
10 Bodleian, MS Rawlinson D776, f 119.
11 E101/479/7.
12 *Privy Council Proceedings* VI, p.32.
13 J.H. Harvey, *William Worcestre Itineraries*, pp.270-1.

Appendix 5: The Water Supply of the Palace and Charterhouse, pp.231-235

1 *SAC* V, p.80; E317/Surrey 46.
2 *SAC* LXXI, p.192; E317/Surrey 53.
3 *CPR 1461-67*, p.513.
4 Dr. A.A. Barkas, 'Our Ancient Springs', article in *Richmond and Twickenham Times*, 3 April 1920.
5 LR3/71, p.78.
6 LR3/71, p.343.
7 Surrey Record Office, 2353/51/16/62.
8 LR3/71, p.111 (April 1620).
9 *Privy Council Acts 1621-23*, p.29 (July 1621).
10 LR3/101, m 13.
11 E318/572, f 15.
12 Surrey Record Office, 5/16/15.
13 Surrey Record Office, 5/16/28; also E307/K13.
14 Surrey Record Office, 5/16/66 and 67.
15 LR3/202, p.138.
16 LR3/71, p.328.
17 LR3/71, p.343.
18 LR3/71, p.343.
19 'C G C', article 'Underground Richmond' in *Richmond and Twickenham Times*, 6 November 1909; and Barkas article *cit sup*.
20 Richmond Public Library L628 I, RA1, 026, p.63.
21 MPZ 2, plan B.
22 LR3/71, p.352.
23 LR3/71, pp.432, 514.
24 LR3/71, pp.44, 149, 158.
25 LR3/101/2, m 8 and LR3/101/4, m 3 verso.
26 LR3/85, p.74
27 LR3/86, p.159.
28 LR3/92, p.24.
29 Richmond Vestry Minute Book H, pp.395, 400, 493.
30 LR3/71, p.344.
31 Richmond Vestry Minute Book F, p.181.

Appendix 6: The Richmond Friary 1534-8, pp.236-237

1 John Stow, *Annales* (1631 edition), p.571. See also F.A. Gasquet, *Henry VIII and the English Monasteries* (1893 edition) 1, p.189.
2 *Privy Purse Expenses of Princess Mary*, ed. F. Madden (1831), p.70.
3 CLPFD VII, p.601, no.1607.
4 CLPFD V and VI – many references in 1532 and 1533.
5 Compotus Facultatum. Lambeth MS W19/1/1 (I am indebted to Noel Hughes for this reference). See also D.S. Chambers, *Faculty Office Registers 1534-1549* (Oxford, 1966), p.42.
6 Soc. Antiq. MS369, no.20. The drawing of the seal was engraved for Edward W. Brayley's *Topographical History of Surrey* (5 vols, 1841-8), III, p.78. Brayley gives the text of the inscription with 'Ord Minor' in place of 'Augustinor', but the engraving follows the text shown in the drawing.
7 Chambers, *Faculty Office Registers*, p.55.
8 *Franciscan History and Legend in English Mediaeval Art*, ed. A.G. Little (Manchester, 1937); chapter on 'The Seals of the Franciscans' by H.S. Kingford (p.97).
9 *Ibid.*
10 Chambers, *Faculty Office Registers*, pp.152 (Greenwich), 160 (Norwich), 164 (Chester) and 168 (Coventry).

Index

Black and white illustrations are listed by page number, in bold type. Colour illustrations are listed by plate number, in bold Roman numerals.

Aaron, son of Abraham, 10
Acton, Middlesex, 19
Acts of Parliament: Sequestration of alien priories (1414), 37; Separation of Isleworth from Duchy of Cornwall (1421), 75; Succession (1534), 97-8; Supremacy (1534), 98-9, 107; Treason (1534), 98-9; Suppression of lesser monasteries (1536), 99; Suppression of greater monasteries (1539), 100; Uniformity, etc. (1559), 111; Grant of Richmond Park to the City of London (1649), 205
Adder's Down Close, Mortlake, 249
Alexander VI, Pope, 73
alien priories, 37
Allen, Elias, mapmaker, 199, 242
Allen's Close, Kew, 158
Alnwick, William of, priest, 36
Amboise, Peace of, 121
Ancram, Earl of: *see* Carr, Sir Robert
Anglo-Saxon Chronicle, 3
Anjou, Dukes of: *see* Henry III, King of France; Francis, Duke of Anjou
Anne of Bohemia, Queen of Richard II, 24-6; statue of, 26, **26**, **II**
Anne Boleyn, Queen of Henry VIII, 87-90, 95-6, 97, 99, 146, 156
Anne of Cleves, Queen of Henry VIII, 90-2, 93, 171, 256
Anne of Denmark, Queen of James VI and I, 179, 183, **184**
Annesley, Ralph, 162
Anthony, monk of Shene, 44
Aquila, Bishop of: *see* Quadra, Alvaro de
Ardene, John, Clerk of King's Works, 32, 34, 75, 256, 276
Armada, Spanish, 134-6
Arniette's Lot, Shene, 37
Arthur, Prince of Wales, 52, 57, **57**, 79, 81
Arundel, Thomas, Archbishop of Canterbury, 27, 256
Asgill House, Richmond, 211, 219
Ashen (or Pond) Close, Mortlake, 250, 252, 253, 254
Athelstan, King of England, 1
At Were, Stephen, 152
At Were, family, 165; *see also* Ware
Aubrey, John, 165
Augustinian order, 36; Austin Friars, 98, 236-7
Aulus Plautius, Roman general, 2
Awberry, Morgan and wife Joan, 165
Awberry (or Aubrey), Richard, 165
Awberry, Dr. William and wife Winifred, 132, 164-5, **165**, 171, 172

Babbeworthpond, Manor of, 22
Babel, building the Tower of, **32**, **III**
Babington, Anthony, 133-4
Bacon, Edward, 77, 260
Bacon, Sir Francis, 77, 191

Bacon, Sir Nicholas, 77
Bagshot, Manor of, 4, 5, 7, 15, 214-5, 216-7
Bakare, John, friar, 236
Baker, ——, Steward of Wimbledon, 201
Balding Lane, Roehampton, 248
Baldry the Clerk, of Bagshot, 7
Baldwyn, Henry and wife Mary, 246
Ball, Henry, Vicar of Shene Charterhouse, 97
Bannockburn, Battle of (1314), 17
Banqueting house, Richmond, 80, 90
Banstead, Surrey, Manor of, 22
Barker, George, 258
Barn Elms, Barnes, 131
Barnes, Surrey, 2
Barnes, Thomas, 164
Barton, Elizabeth, the 'Nun of Kent', 96-7, 159
Barton, Thomas, 34, 256, 257, 259, 260
Basing, Robert de, 217
Battle Abbey roll, 4, 213
Baynes, Adam, 210
Beauchamp, Robert de: *see* Bello Campo
Beauchamp, Viscount: *see* Seymour, Edward
Beaufort, Henry, Duke of Somerset, 154
Beaumont, Oxford (royal house), 17
Beaumont, Comte de, French ambassador, 143
Beck, Edmund, 172
Becke, John, 155
Bedensford (?=Kew), 8
Bedford, John, Duke of, Regent, 31, 75
Bedyll, Archdeacon, 98
Belet family, 4-6, **212**, 213-8; lands: in Berkshire, 5, 7, 213-5; in Dorset, 4, 5, 7, 8, 10, 11, 213-4, 215, 217-8; in Lincolnshire, 213; in Norfolk, 213; in Northamptonshire, 213; in Oxfordshire, 6, 213-4, 215; in Surrey, 4, 5, 6, 7, 8, 10, 11, 213-5
Belet, Alfred of Hungerford, 218
Belet, Alice, dau. of Fulk d'Oyri, wife of John Belet (d.1204), 213
Belet, Alice, wife of Michael Belet of Shene, 6-9
Belet, Alice, dau of John of Shene, wife of John de Valletorte, 8-10
Belet, Amabil, wife of John Belet, then of Henry Fitznicholas, 8-9
Belet, Emma, dau. of John de Keynes, wife of Judge Michael Belet, 213
Belet, Emma, dau of John of Shene, wife of (1) Walter Oliver, (2) John Belet, (3) John Hake, (4) Robert de Meleburn, (5) William de Wilburham, 8-12, 14, 217-8, 255
Belet, Harvey (fl.1130), 213-4
Belet, Harvey (fl. early 13th cent.), 214
Belet, John I (fl.1130), 4-5, 6, 213, 214, 217, 255
Belet, John II (son of William II), 216-7
Belet, John (d.1204, son of Judge Michael), 213-4

Belet, John, of Shene (d.1230), 8, 9, 255
Belet, John, husband of Emma, 11, 217, 255
Belet, John, of Dorset (father and son), 218
Belet, John, of Hungerford, 11, 218
Belet, Matilda (wife of William II), 5-6, 215
Belet, Matilda (d.1229, dau. of Michael of Shene), 7-8, 255
Belet, Michael, Judge (d.c.1199), 6, 213
Belet, 'Master' Michael (d.c.1245), 6, 213-4, 217
Belet, Michael of Shene (d.1215), 4, 5-7, 217, 255
Belet, Ralph, 5, 215
Belet, Robert (fl. Dorset 1130), 218
Belet, Robert of Coombe (d.c.1199), 5, 10, 214-7
Belet, Robert of Shene (d.1197-8), 5, 216-7, 255
Belet, Robert of Dorset (son of William II), 5, 215-6
Belet, Robert (bastard of William II), 215-6
Belet, William I (fl.1085), 4, 213
Belet, William II (d.1174-5), 5, 6, 215-7, 255
Belet, William III (son of William II), 216-7
Belhaven, Viscount: *see* Douglas, Sir Robert
Bell Inn, Richmond, 130
Bello Campo (Beauchamp), Robert de, 6, 9-10
Bene, William, 164
Benedictine order, 36
Benet, John, 260
Bennett, Humphrey, 247, 249, 252, 254
Bennett, Richard, 208
Bennett, Thomas, 247, 254
Benson, Timothy and wife Katherine, 247, 248
Bentley, John, 178, 261
'Bentley Park', 178
Bergues, Sieur de, 81
Bernardin, Saint, 73
Berry Grove, Petersham, 243-5
Bertie, Peregrine, Lord Willoughby d'Eresby, 138
Bertie, Richard, 160
Beverley Bridge, 202, 249, 251
Beverley Brook, 202, 249
Beverley Closes, Putney, 249
Beverley Meads, Putney, 247
Bindon Abbey, Dorset, 12
Birch, Thomas, 180
Bird, Nicholas, 258
Black Death, 19
Black Ditch, Richmond, 235
Blacket, Richard, 151, 154, 164
Blackwell, Walter, 171
Blandford, Dorset, 10
Bletchingley, Surrey, 91
Blois, Treaty of, 126
Blount, Charles, Lord Mountjoy (later Earl of Devonshire), 142

Blount, Elizabeth, 87
Bocking, Father, 96-7
Body, Thomas, 50
Bokyngham, John, Prior of Shene, 223
Boleyn, Anne: *see* Anne Boleyn, Queen
Boleyn, Mary, 87, 146
Bolton, Thomas, 22
'Bond of Association' (1584), 133
Boseham, John de, 17, 255, 257
Bothwell, Earls of: *see* Hepburn, James; Hepburn, Patrick
Bourchier, Henry, Earl of Essex, 83
Bourchier, Robert, 76-7, 260
Bracebridge, Thomas, monk of Shene, 46
Bracebridge, William, 46
Bradshaw, Lawrence, 93
Brampton, Richard, 34, 92, 256, 257, 258, 260
Brampton, Thomas, 53, 92, 256, 258, 260
Brandon, Charles, Duke of Suffolk, 82, 83, 85, 103, 154-5, **155**, 160-1, 260
Brandon, Frances: *see* Grey
Brandon, Katherine (née Willoughby), Baroness Willoughby d'Eeresby, Duchess of Suffolk, 160, **161**
Bray, Sir Reginald, 72(n)
'Breikhouse of Shene' (brick kiln), 43
Brent, River, 2
Brent, Sir Matthew, 208
Brentford, Middlesex, 3, 8, 19, 171, 208; Battle of (1016), 3; docks, 2; ferry, 3, 15, 171; ford over Thames, 2-3, 151
brickmakers, **30**, 31, 73
bricks and brickwork, 31, 39, **64**, 72, 127, 175-6, 185, 202, 205
Bridget, Saint, 36
Briggitine order, 36-7, 75, 97
Brikeman, Hugh, brickmaker, 31
Briker, Henry, 39
Brimming, Henry, 172
Broke, Robert, 248
Brome, William, 178, 210, 261
Brompton, John, glazier, 22
Brooke, Henry, Lord Cobham, 167
Browne, Sir Anthony, 246, 257
Browne, Robert, 239
Bruce, Robert, King of Scotland, 17
Bryan, Sir Francis, 76, 260
Bryan, George, 239
Bryne, Roger, 258
Buckhurst, Lord: *see* Sackville, Thomas
Buckingham, Duke of: *see* Villiers, George
Budd, Richard and wife Patience, 252
Building materials, 22, 30-1, 39, 72; *see also* bricks; glass; half-timber; lead; plaster; stonework; tiles; timber
building techniques, **30**, **32**, **III**
Bull, Dr. John, musician, 181
Bun, Helen, 232

283

Burgh, Hubert de, Earl of Kent, 6, 9
Burghley, Baron: *see* Cecil, Sir William
Burghley House, Northants., 127
Burgundian influence at Henry VII's court, 70-2
Burnell, Edward, 14-15, 255
Burnell, Hugh (brother of Robert), 14
Burnell, Sir Hugh (fl.1415), 34
Burnell, Philip, 14
Burnell, Robert, Bishop of Bath and Wells, 12-14, 255
Burnt Close, Mortlake, 250
Burton Abbey, Staffordshire, 273
Burun, Roger de and wife Matilda (née Belet?), 6
Bury, John de (Senior), 257
Bury, John de (Junior), 34, 49-50, 51, 257, 260
Bushell, Edward, 187
Byfleet, Surrey, 17, 19, 29, 31
'Byfleet at Shene', 31-4, 49, 56, 219, 221-2; design and plan, 33-4; Chapel, 31-4, 73-4, 219, 222; cistern, 32; cloister, 32; King's and Queen's wards, 31; kitchen, 31; moat, 32, 219; stone towers, 31, 33; converted to friary, 73-4
Bynks, Thomas, carpenter, 72-3, 74
Byrche, William, 157
Byrkes, Anthony, 155-6, 157
Byrkes, Thomas and wife Ann, 151-2, 154, 155-6

Cadiz, Spain, raids on, 135, 138
Caen, Normandy, stone from, 30, 39
Calais, France, 31, 109, 120, 121, 136, 138
Campeggio, Cardinal, 95
Caneton, Walkelin de, 6
Carbery Hill, Battle of (1567), 124
Cardigan House, Richmond, 231
Carew, Sir George, 142
Carey, George, Lord Hunsdon, Lord Chamberlain, 146
Carey, Robert, 146-9, 191
Carisbrook, Isle of Wight: Castle, 209; Priory, 37
Carlile, Ludowick, 202, 203, 205, 261
Carlisle, Earl of: *see* Hay, James
Carmelite Friary at Shene (White Friars), 17, 184
Carpenter's Close, Roehampton, 247, 248
Carr (or Ker) of Ancrum, Sir Robert, Earl of Ancram, 177, 181, 191
Carrington Lodge, Richmond, 234
Carter, George, 211
Carter, Henry, 211
Carthusian order: origin and rule, 35-6, 97, 107; habit, **36**; lay brothers, 39, 40-1; monastery layout, 39; General Chapter (at La Grande Chartreuse), 35-6, 39, 43, 44, 72, 107, 108, 223, 224
Castle Inn, Richmond, 234-5
Castle Rising, Norfolk, 19
Cateau-Cambresis, Treaty of, 120, 121
Catherine of Aragon, Queen of Henry VIII, 52, 55, 57, **57**, 79, 80-2, **82**, 83, 84, 86, 87, 89, 90, **94**, 97, 152, 159; divorce of, 89-90, 95-6
Catherine Howard, Queen of Henry VIII, 91-2
Catherine Parr, Queen of Henry VIII, 92, **92**, 115, 171
Catherine de Medici, 120-1, 126
Catherine of York, Princess (dau. of Edward IV), 152
Caus, Solomon de, 183, 188-9, 191; designs for Richmond, **186**, **187**, 188
Cavard, Richard, 245
Cave, Mr., 86
Cavendish, George, 52, 89, 160
Cavendish, William, 160
Cavendish, William, Lord Mansfield, Earl of Newcastle, 196
Cecil, Edward, Viscount Wimbledon, 199, 200, 243, 247-52

Cecil, Sir Robert, Earl of Salisbury, 143, 167, 176, 183
Cecil, Thomas, Earl of Exeter, 242
Cecil, Sir William, Lord Burghley, 112-13, 117, 118, 119, 122, 126, 127, 130, 131, 137, 140, 166
Cecilia, Princess of Sweden, 169
'Cedar Grove', Richmond Green, 178
Celestine order, 37, 75, 276
Chabot, Philippe, Admiral of France, 86
Chalar's Grove, Ham Common, 244
Challoner, Sir Thomas, English Ambassador to Spain, 112
Chamber, Geoffrey, 257
Chamberlain, John, 143
Chambers, Dr., 207
Chapman, Edward, 246
Chappell Farm, Kingston, 247
Chappington, John, organ-builder, 127
Chapuys, Eustace, Spanish Ambassador, 91-2, 98
Charles I, King of Great Britain: as Duke of York, 167, **179**, 180, 191; as Prince of Wales, **190**, 191, 256; as King, 192, 194, 196, 204, 207-8; construction of Park, 197-203; execution, 205, 209; children of, 194, **195**, 207
Charles II, King of Great Britain: as prince, 194, 196, 207; restoration, 178, 205-6
Charles IV, Holy Roman Emperor, 24
Charles V of Castile, Holy Roman Emperor and King of Spain, 81, 84, 87, 95, 98, 105
Charles IX, King of France, 120, 126, 128
Charles, Archduke, 118, 122, 126
Charterhouse Grove, Coombe, Surrey, 108
Charterhouse of Jesus of Bethlehem of Shene, 29, 31; site, 37, 39; plan, 39-40, **40**; model of, **35**; building of, 37-9
Chapterhouse, 39, 108, 210; church, 39, 41, 108, 115, 210; Colet's house at, 46-8, 101, 108; endowment, 37; fisheries, 5, 37; Great cloister, 39, 41, 72, 108; James IV's body at, 45-6, 84; lands in Shene, **42**, 43, 100, 151, 172, 177, 225-9; lay brothers, 39, 210; library, 38-9, 275; murder at, 44; 'Pardon' at, 46; Priors of, 39, 223-4; privileges, 43, 46; reclusory, 38; refectory, 40, 210; seals, **44**; stones from, **38**; water supply, 40-1, 231, 232-4; Wolsey at, 52; **Dissolution**, 96-100; refoundation, 107-8, 111, 226; second dissolution, 111, 115, 169 (*see also* Sheen Place); Moses Glover's depiction, **210**; Parliamentary Survey, 209-10
Charterhouses in England: Axholme, Lincs., 36, 98; Beauvale, Notts., 36, 98, 100; Coventry, 36, 100; Hinton, Somerset, 36; Hull, 36; London, 36, 41, 97, 99, 100, 107, 223; Mount Grace, Yorks., 36, 37, 40, 41, 108; Shene (separate listing above); Witham, Somerset, 36, 108, 224; Dissolution of, 100
Charterhouses in Europe: Bruges (Val de Grace), 72, 100, 107, 111, 224; Grande Chartreuse *see* Carthusian order; Sheen Anglorum, 111, 115, 224
Chatillon, Cardinal: *see* Coligny, Odet de
Chatrousse, near Grenoble, France, 35-6
Chaucer, Geoffrey, Clerk of King's Works, 25
Chauncey, Maurice, Prior of Shene, 107-8, 111, 115, 224
Cheesman, John and wife Lydia, 245
Chertsey, Surrey, 50
Chertsey Abbey, 34, 37
Chertsey Bridge, 50
Chevreux, Duchess of, 192
Chichester, Bishop of, 156; *see also* Duppa, Brian
Childe, William, 250
Children of the Queen's Chapel, 127-8, 238
Children of St Paul's, 238
Chiswick, Middlesex, 27, 31, 39, 226
Christian IV, King of Denmark, 179, 191

Christina, Princess of France, 191
Church Hawe, Petersham, 226
Church Shott, Richmond, 226, 233
Cistercian order, 43
Clare, Gilbert de, Earl of Gloucester and Hertford, 11, 12, **12**, 255
Clare, Margaret, Countess of Cornwall, 17
Clarence House, Vineyard, Richmond, 232
Clarendon, Earl of: *see* Hyde, Edward
Clarke, Robert, 257
Claudius, Roman emperor, 2
Clement VII, Pope, 95
Clere, William, Clerk of the King's Works, 32
Clerk of Works' house, 50, 53
Clerk of Works' office and yard, 63
Clifford, Henry, Baron Westmoreland, Earl of Cumberland and wife Eleanor, 161
Clifton, William, 199, 245, 251
Cnut, King of England, 3
Cobham, Lord: *see* Brooke, Henry
Colchester, William, 246
Cole, George, 199, 244
Cole, Gregory and wife Jane, 198, 200, 201, 202, 242, 243, 244, 249
Cole, Thomas, 244
Coleman's Pit, Roehampton, 248
Colet, Dr. John, Dean of St Paul's, 46-7, 101
Colevill, William de and wife Matilda (née Belet?), 7, 8, 9
Coligny, Gaspard de, Admiral of France, 113, 120-1
Coligny, Odet de, Cardinal de Chatillon, 113-14
Commissioners for formation of Richmond Park, 200, 201, 244, 248, 249
Compton, Sir William, 82
Concordia, Lionel Bishop of, Papal Legate, 43
Condé, Louis Prince de, 120-1
Conduit Field, Richmond, 234
conduit heads, 226, 231-5
Conduit Shott: *see* Church Shott
Conduit Wood, Richmond Park, 231
Cook, Bernard, Clerk of Works, 20, 23
Coombe (Nevill), Manor of, 4, 5, 6, 7-8, 15, 199, 214-15, 216-17
Coose Eight, Ham, 245
Coote, Henry, goldsmith, 56
Cornwall, Earls of: *see* Edmund, Earl of Cornwall; Richard, Earl of Cornwall
Corporation Island, Richmond, 184(n)
Cottington, Francis, Lord Cottington, 197, 200, 203
Coupere, John, 22
Courtenay, Edward, Earl of Devonshire (d.1509), 152
Courtenay, Edward, Earl of Devonshire (d.1556), 159, 160, **160**
Courtenay, Gertrude (née Blount) Marchioness of Exeter, 159-60
Courtenay, Henry, Earl of Devonshire, Marquess of Exeter, 86, 156, 159, 160
Courtenay, Sir Hugh, 152
Courtenay, William, Earl of Devonshire, 152, 159
Covenanters in Scotland, 207
Coventry, Bishop of, 97-8
Coxford, Norfolk, 214
Crabbe, William and wife Margery, 252
Crane, Sir Francis, 200
Crane Piece, Richmond, 63, 65, 72, 172, 187-8, 211, 222
Crane Wharf, Richmond, 25, 50, 177, 183, 188, 221
Crane's Croft, Richmond, 93, 170-2, 174
Cranmer, Thomas, Archbishop of Canterbury, 96, 236
Creoun, Maurice de, Lord of Ham, 12
Crewe, Ralph, 248
Croft Mead, Kew, 226
Cromwell, Oliver, Lord Protector, 209
Cromwell, Thomas, Earl of Essex, 48, 52, 96, 97, 98, 99, 100, 155, 156, 157, 159, **159**, 236

Crossashe, Shene, 37
Crowet island, Ham, 34
Cumberland, Earl of: *see* Clifford, Henry
Cumnor House, Berkshire, 119
Cunningham, Sir James, 248
Cupbearer to the King: regular post, 213, 214, 217; serjeanty of, 5, 6, 9, 217
Cutler's Hill, Richmond, 73

Dacre, Baron: *see* Fiennes, Thomas
Dairy House, Kew, 158, 166
Dalle, William, 260
Danes, 3
Darnley, Earl of: *see* Stewart, Henry
Davy, Henry, 34, 256, 258, 260
Dee, Dr. John, 130-2, **131**, 148
deer, 50, 51, 52, 168, 178, 197, 203, 205
Delaber, Kenard, 162
Derby, Earls of: *see* Stanley, Henry; Stanley, William
De'Servi, Constantino, 183, 188-9
Despenser, Alice (m. Edward Burnell), 14
Despenser, Hugh, Earl of Winchester, 14-15, 255
Devereux, Robert, Earl of Essex (d.1601), 135, 137, **137**, 138, 142, 146; rebellion and death, 143, 145-6
Devereux, Robert, Earl of Essex (d.1646), 208
Devonshire, Earls of: *see* Courtenay, Edward; Courtenay, Henry; Courtenay, William
'Devonshire House', Kew, 152, 158-61, 166
Dieppe, France, 120-1, 138
Dingley, Sir John (Parliamentarian), 208
Dingley, Sir John (Secretary to Elizabeth, Queen of Bohemia), 210, 281
Dipere, Geoffrey, 6
Disdain, ship, 180
Ditton, Surrey, 6, 93
Diversbushe, Shene, 37
Doaker, Mr., 208
Domesday Book, 3, 4
Dormer, Jane, Countess of Feria, 109, 111
Dorset, Earl of: *see* Sackville, Thomas
Douglas, Sir Robert, Viscount Belhaven, 177, 191, 193, 195, 201, 242, 256, 257, 258, 261
Dover, Thomas and wife Alice, 124
Dowe, Anne, of Brentford, 118
Downton, Thomas, 239
Drake, Sir Francis, 128, 129, 134, 135, 136, 137
Drayton, Middlesex, 156
Dudley, Ambrose, Earl of Warwick, 121
Dudley, Amy (née Robsart), 102, 118-19, 278
Dudley, Guilford, 103, 105, 106, 118
Dudley, John, Viscount Lisle, Earl of Warwick, Duke of Northumberland, 101-3, **102**, 104-5, 118, 157, 158
Dudley, Robert, Earl of Leicester, 102, 113, 117-20, **118**, 121-2, 126, 129, 130, 133, 135-6, **136**, 137, **158**, **VII**
Duke's Yard, Richmond Green 93
Dundidge Grounds, Roehampton, 247, 248
Dune, Roger de la, 8
Duppa, Brian, Bishop of Chichester, Salisbury and Winchester, 194, **194**, 196
Duppa's Almshouses, Richmond, 235
Durham House, London, 79
Dutton, John, 238-9
Dutton, Lawrence, 239
Duwes, Giles, librarian, 259
Dyneleye, Robert de, 23, 255
Dysart, Earl of: *see* Murray, William

Earl of Derby's Company, 239
Earl of Leicester's Servants, 128, 238
Earl of Nottingham's Company, 239
Earl of Warwick's Servants, 238
East Molesey, Surrey, 6
East Shene (now East Sheen), 10, 197, 199, 203, 226
Easthampstead, Berkshire, 20
Eastwood, 7
Eaton, Alexander, 210

Index

Edge, William, 247
Edinburgh, Treaty of, 120
Edmund 'Ironside', King of England, 3
Edmund, Earl of Cornwall, 17
Edward I, King of England, 12, 13, 14
Edward II, King of England, 14, 15, 16, **16**, 17, 18-19, 184, 255
Edward III, King of England, **18**, 19, 20, **20**, **23**, 24, 29, 49, 72, 219, 255; death at Shene Palace, 24
Edward IV, King of England, 34, 41, 43, 46, 70, 73, 152, 256
Edward VI, King of England, 90, **91**, 92, 93, 101, 102, 104, 105, 157, 158, 159, 171, 174, 256
Edward, Prince of Wales (the 'Black Prince'), 24
Edwards, Humphrey, 211, 256
Eleanor of Provence, Queen of Henry III, 214
Elizabeth Woodville (or Widville), Queen of Edward IV, 34, 43, 46, 223, 256
Elizabeth of York, Queen of Henry VII, 55-6, 79, **80**, 152
Elizabeth I, Queen of England, **117, 119, 133, 135, 139, VI, VIII, IX**: birth, 90; as Princess, 104, 106, 109, **110**, 159; accession, 117; religious settlement, 111-17; marriage proposals, 117, 118-9, 122, 126, 130; relationship with Robert Dudley, 117-20, 121, 137; at Richmond, 118, 121-2, 126, 127-8, 130, 131, 132, 134, 135, 139, 143, 144-8; visits to Kew, 163-4; foreign policy, 120-1, 126, 128-30, 132-3, 137-8; and Mary Queen of Scots, 112, 124-6, 133-4, 146; small pox, 121; progresses, 138, **144**; death and funeral, 146-7, **148-9**, 149; other references, 46, 169, 256
Elizabeth (Stewart) Princess, Countess Palatine and Queen of Bohemia, 167-8, **168**, 180, 189, 191
Elizabeth (Stewart) Princess (dau. of Charles I), 194, 209
Eltham Palace, Kent, 20, 50, 70, 89
Englefield, Sir Francis, 115
Englefield, Sir Thomas, 109
Eric XIV, King of Sweden, 118, 169
Esher, Surrey, Wolsey's house at, 52
Essex, Earls of: *see* Bourchier, Henry; Cromwell, Thomas; Devereux, Robert
Evans, Agnes, Francis and William, 246
Evelyn, John, 244
Evesham, Battle of (1265), 11, 12
Exeter, Earl of: *see* Cecil, Thomas
Exeter, Marquess of: *see* Courtenay, Henry
Exeter, Marchioness of: *see* Courtenay, Gertrude

Fairfax, Thomas, Lord Fairfax, 208
Ferdinand I, King of Aragon, and V King of Castile, 57, 81, 84, 87, 152
Feria, Gomes Suarez de Figueroa, Count of, Spanish Ambassador, 111, 118
Feria, Countess of: *see* Dormer, Jane
Fernandez, Fray Diego, priest, 82, 152
Fernhills, Mortlake, 250
Ferrer, Thomas and wife Judith, 250
Ferry Hill (now Bridge Street), Richmond, 49, 232
Fetcham, Surrey, 215
Fiennes, Thomas, Lord Dacre, 113-14
fisheries, 3, 4, 5, 10, 37, 215-16
Fitzhugh, Sir Henry, Baron Ravensworth, Constable of England, 36-7
Fitznicholas, Henry, 8-9, 255
Fitzother, Walter, 4, 12
Fitzroy, Henry, Duke of Richmond, 87, 95
Fitzwilliam House, Richmond Green, 50, 70, 178
Fitzwilliam Museum, Cambridge, 70
Flanders, brickkiln in, **30**
Fletewood, Edward, monk of Shene, 100
Fletewood, William, 257
Flodden Field, Battle of (1514), 45, 84

Fossil, Dorset, 10, 12, 15
Fotheringay Castle, Northants., 134
Fox, Richard, Bishop of Winchester, 155
Foxe, John, Carthusian monk, 107
Framlingham, Suffolk, 104
France: relations with, 84-5, 86-7, 121, 126, 130, 134, 137-8, 191-2; situation in, 120-1, 126, 137-8; treaties with, 85, 89, 120, 121, 126; wars with, 31, 37, 75, 84, 89, 120-1
Francini brothers, 183
Francis I, King of France, 85-7, 154
Francis II, King of France, 120
Francis, Duke of Anjou (formerly Duke of Alençon), 126, 128-9, **129**, 130, 131; visit to Richmond, 128, 130
Franciscan order (Grey Friars), 73; Conventuals, 73, 236, 237; *see also* Observant Friars
Frascati, Italy, 183
Frauncys, William, Prior, 237
Frederick V, Count Palatine, King of Bohemia, 168, 189, 192
French, Jeffrey, 124
'Friars', The (house and land), 124, 183, 186, 210
Friars' Lane, Richmond, 123, 211
Friars' Stile, Richmond, 232
Friars' Stile Road, Richmond, 231, 235
Friars' Wharf, 86
Friary, Richmond (House of Observant Friars), 70, **71**, 73-4, 83-4, 92-3, 219; suppression (1534), 97-8; occupation in 1534-8, 98, 236-7; seal, 237, **237**, subsequent use of site, 107, 123-4
Frome Belet, Dorset, 4, 213
Fryer, Leonard, 140
Fulham, Manor of, 2, 3, 81
Fursey Close, Roehampton, 247, 248
Fysshe, Thomas, 34, 92, 256, 257, 258, 260

Gaddesby, John de, 15
Gallows Hill, Kingston, 200, 243
Gardiner, Stephen, Bishop of Winchester, 159
Gardiner, Thomas, goldsmith, 162
Gardyner, Robert, King's gardener, 27, 259
Garrett, Elizabeth, 245
Garrett, John and wife Lydia, 199, 242, 245
Garter, Order of the, 85
Gascoigne, William, 238
Gates, Sir Henry, 158
Gates, John, 158
Gedney, John, Clerk of the King's Works, 25
Gervoise, Sir Thomas: *see* Jervase
Gething, Maurice and wife Elizabeth, 250
Ghent, Abbey of St Peter, 37, 43
Gilbert the Norman, Sheriff of Surrey, 6
Gill, Raymond, 242
Gittin, Mr., 250
Glascock, Robert, 254
Glase, Edmund, 34, 256, 259, 260
Glasgow, Archbishop of, 79-80
glass, use in buildings, 22, 31, 32, 127, 175
Gloucester, Humphrey Duke of, Lord Protector, 31-2, 275
Gloucester and Hereford, Earl of: *see* Clare, Gilbert de
Godwin, monk of Shene, 45
Goion, John, 27, 256
Goion, Richard, 27, 256
Goldwyne, John, 251
Goodrick, William, 210
Gordon, Robert, Viscount Kenmure and wife Martha, 211, 256
Gorges, Sir Arthur and wife Elizabeth, 165, 166, **166**, 181, 191
Gorges, Sir Edward, 193, 256, 258
Gorges, Sir Thomas, 115, 165, 169-70, 172, 174, **174**, 175-7, 193, 201, 225-6, 256, 258, 260, 261
Grace, James and wife Elizabeth, 244
Grand Union Canal, Brentford, 2
Grandison Castle, Switzerland, 15
Grandison, Sir Otto de, 13-15, **13**, 255
Gravelines, France, 136

Graves, Richard, 257
Gravesend, Kent, 136
Great Chronicle of London, 56
Great Meadow, Shene, 177-8, 226
'Great Piece', Shene Warren, 170-1, 172
Greens: *see* Richmond; Kew
Greenwich: Manor of East Combe, 37; Manor of East Greenwich, 37, 99; Friary, 73, 97-8, 107; Palace, 74, 81, 86, 104, 129, 138, 183, 205, 207, 275; Priory, 37, 275
Greeves, Tom, 242
Gregory XIII, Pope, 35
Gregory, John, 232
Gresham, Sir Thomas, 113
Grey, Lady Catherine, 112, 121, 146
Grey, Frances (née Brandon) Duchess of Suffolk, 103, 112, **112**
Grey, Henry, Marquess of Dorset, Duke of Suffolk, 103-5, **105**, 106, 225
Grey, Lady Jane, 103-5, **103**, **104**, 106, 158
Grey, Lady Mary, 112, 121
Grey, Nicholas, Clerk of Works, 56, 72
Griffith, William, 258
Grobham, Sir Richard, 257
Guildford, Sir Henry, 83
Guise family, 120, 137
Guise, François, Duke of, 121
Guise, Henri, Duke of, 133, 137
Guldeford, John, 50
Gunpowder Plot, 179
Gunston, Percival, 124
Guzman de Silva, Don Diego, Spanish Ambassador, 121-2
Gyles, Thomas, 238-9

Hake, John and wife Emma (Belet), 11, 255
Hakelot, Shene, 37
Hales, John, 170-1
half-timber construction, 22, 29, 39, 72, 127
Halford House, Richmond, 234
Hall, John, 124
Ham, Manor of, 12, 13, 14, 34, 53, 91-3, 170, 172, 183, 191, 193, 198, 201, 203-4, 226, 242; Belet land in, 214; and formation of Richmond Park, 198-9, 200-1, 203, 242-4, 245-6
Ham Common, 198-9, 200, 203, 243, 244
Ham Cross, 199
Ham House, 191, 198, 201, 208
Hambleton, William, 246
Hammond, Robert, 156, 157
Hampton Court – Convent of St John of Jerusalem, 79, 86
Hampton Court Palace, 52, 86, 87-8, 88-9, 90, 121, 128, 138, 170, 172, 179, 197, 204, 205, 208-9; tennis court at, 70, 276
Handeforde, Thomas, 162
Harbord, Sir Charles, Surveyor-General, 200, 244, 245, 252
Harington, John, Lord Harington of Exton, 167-8, **168**, 180, 181
Harington, John, 2nd Lord Harington of Exton, 168, 181, **182**
Harington, Sir John, 140-2, **141**, 143
Harlington, Middlesex, 156
Harold, King of England, 3
Harris, Margaret, 248
Harrison, Robert, 246, 251
Hartington Combe, Manor, 162, 199, 244
Hartleton Farm (and Lodge), 199, 201, 202, 203, 244
Hartleton Hill, 199, 243, 251
Hartleton Lane, 251
Harvey, Henry, 53, 123, 124
Hastings, Henry, Earl of Huntingdon, 121
Hatfield House, Herts., 183
Hatton, Sir Christopher, 127, 129, 130, 137, 208
hawking, 51
Hayling Priory, Hants., 37
Hay, James, Lord Hay, Earl of Carlisle, 176
Hazel Pits Shott, Mortlake, 250
Heidelberg, Germany, 168, 191
Hele, Sir John, 167

Hemyng(e), John, 239
Heneage, Thomas, 89, 137
Henley-on-the-Heath, Surrey, 20
Henrietta Ann, Princess, 194
Henrietta Maria (Princess of France), Queen of Charles I, 192, 194, 198, 203-4, 207, 242, 256
Henrikson, Ulf, 169
Henry I, King of England, 4, 6, 17, 217, 273
Henry II, King of England, 9, 10, 36, 217
Henry III, King of England, 10, 12, 214
Henry IV, King of England, 27, 29, 35, 256
Henry V, King of England, **28**, 29, 31, 35-8, 43, 56, 256; foundation of monasteries, 29, 35-9, 75; 'King's great work', 29-30, 37
Henry VI, King of England, 31-2, 41-3, 75-6, 256
Henry VII, King of England, 34, 41, 43, 52, 55-7, **56**, 66, **67**, 72, 73, 76, 79, 80, **80**, 81, 82, **90**, 152, 154, 170, 219, 256; building Richmond Palace, 55-6; renaming Shene as Richmond, 56; death at Richmond, 82, 152
Henry VIII, King of England, 41, 45-8, 81, 82, 85, 86, 87, **87**, 89, 90, **90**, 93, **94**, 95-6, 101, 152, 154-6; foreign policy, 84-5, 86-7, 89; divorce from Catherine of Aragon, 89, 95-6
Henry III, King of France (formerly Duke of Anjou and King of Poland), 126, 128, 130, 132, 133, 134, 137
Henry IV, King of France (formerly King of Navarre), 120, 133, 137-8, 181, 192
Henry, Prince, son of Henry VIII, 83
Henry, Prince of Wales, son of James I and VI, 165, 167-8, 180, **180**, 181, **182**, **188**, 191, 256, **X**; grant of Richmond, 183; intended works at Richmond, 183-9; death, 189
Henry, Prince, Duke of Gloucester (son of Charles I), 194, 206, 209
Hepburn, James, Earl of Bothwell, 124, 125
Hepburn, Patrick, Earl of Bothwell, 79-80
Herbert, Baron: *see* Somerset, Sir Charles
Herbert, William, Earl of Pembroke, 130
Heriet, Richard de, 5, 216-17, 255
Herstmonceux Castle, Sussex, 33, **33**
Hertford Castle, Herts., 20
Hertford, Earl of: *see* Seymour, Edward
Hertford, Marquess of: *see* Seymour, William
Hertishorne, John, Comptroller of Works, 30
Hervey, William, 27, 260
Hewitt, heirs of, 248
Hill Close, Mortlake, 249
Hill Common, Richmond, 235
Hill Coppice, Mortlake, 249, 250
Hill Farm, Mortlake, 199, 249, 250, 251
Hill Field, Mortlake, 250
Hillesden Well, Shene, 41, 231
Hindley, Hugh, 178
Hinton, Cambs., 37
Holdenby (Holmby) House, Northants., 208
Holgill, Thomas, 256
Holland, Earl of: *see* Rich, Henry
Holland, Cornelius, 207
Holland, Miles, 254
Hollar, Wenceslaus, 186
Hollys, John, 246
Hook, Surrey, 7
Hopkins, John, 184
Hoppescourt, ——, of Bagshot, 217
Houghton, John, Prior of London Charterhouse, 98
Hounslow Heath, Middlesex, 208
Howard, Catherine (née Carey), Countess of Nottingham, 145, 146
Howard, Charles, Lord Howard of Effingham, Earl of Nottingham, Lord Admiral, 135-6, 143, 147, 149, 180
Howard, Sir Edward, 83
Howard, Thomas, Earl of Surrey, Duke of Norfolk (d.1524), 45, 84
Howard, Thomas, Duke of Norfolk (d.1554),

122, 125-6
Howe, Simon and wife Anne, 245
Howe, William, monk of Shene, 97
Howlett, Benjamin, 236
Huchynson, Richard, 101
Hudson, Goerge, 164
Hulyn, William, 34, 256
Humphrey the Chamberlain, 4
Hungerford, Berks., 218
Hungerford, Anthony, 172
Hunnis (Hunnys), William, 127-8, 238
Hunsdon, Baron: see Carey, George
Hunstanton, Norfolk, building of, **30**
hunting (of deer), 51-2, **51**, 76, 77, **119**, 172, 179-81, 197, 204, 209, **XI**
Huntingdon, Earl of: see Hastings, Henry
Hurst, Edward, 201, 246, 257
Hurst Castle, Hants., 209
Husdon, Thomas, heirs of, 254
Hussee, John, 96
Hussey, Patience (wife of Sir John Hussey), 249, 250, 252, 254
Hyde, Edward, Earl of Clarendon, 197, 201
Hyde Park, 205
Hynde, Augustine, 155, 161-2
Hynde, Hugh, 172
Hynde, John, 162, 165, 184
Hynde, Rowland, 162

Ikerne, Richard de, 18, 257
Ingleby, John, Prior of Shene, later Bishop of Llandaff, 43, 55-6, 72, 223
Innocent VIII, Pope, 43
Ireland: Tyrone's rebellion, 142, 146
Isabella of France, Queen of Edward II, 19-20, **19**, 23, 49, 219, 255, 257
Isabella, Queen of Spain, 57
Islands by Shene (Richmond) Palace, 17, 22, 24, 183-7
Isleworth, 10, 17-18, 19, 22, 29, 37, 52, 75-6, 101, 226; New Park of: see New Park of Richmond, Co. Middlesex
Isleworth ferry, 226
Ives, John, Prior of Shene, 223

Jackson, Timothy, 252, 254
Jacson, Robert, recluse of Shene, 38
James IV, King of Scotland, 45-6, 79, 84, 275
James V, King of Scotland, 45-6
James VI, King of Scotland and I of Great Britain, 46, 50, 53, 124, 134, 146-8, 149, 170, **173**, 178, 181, 191, 192, 208, 256; makes new park, 172-6, 197, 201
James II, King of Great Britain (formerly Duke of York), 194, 204, 206, 207, 209
Jane Seymour, Queen of Henry VIII, 90, 101, 156
Jeffreys, William, 254
Jennings, Mountain, 183-4
Jernegan, Sir Henry, 77, 260
Jervase (Jervoise, Gervoise), Sir Thomas, 178, 257, 261
Jewett, John, 232
Joanna, Queen of Castile, 81
John, King of England, 6, 7, 214
Jonbourne, John, Prior of Shene, 97, 224
Jones, Inigo, 183-7, 188-9
Josse, James and wife Elizabeth, 248
jousting, 61, 80, 81, 82, 83, **84-5**, 86, 102, 118
Joxeley, Mr., 247, 249
Joyce, Cornet, 208
Julius Caesar, 2
Jumièges, Abbey of St Peter, 37
Juxon family, 199, 201, 203, 250-1, 253, 254
Juxon, John (d.1626), and wife Judith, 248, 250
Juxon, John (son of above), 197, 250, 253
Juxon, Joseph, 250, 251, 253
Juxon, Thomas, 250, 253
Juxon, William, Bishop of London (and later Archbishop of Canterbury), 197

Keeper of Park's house, Richmond Green, 53

Keeper's Close, 177, 210
Kemp, Marjorie, 160
Kempe, Mr. of the Privy Council, 160
Kenmure, Viscount: see Gordon, Robert
Kenninghall, Norfolk, 104
Kent, Earl of: see Burgh, Hubert de
Kervour, Peter, carver, 31
Kew, Surrey: name of, xv, 8; battle at (1016), 3; plans of: (1500), **150**, (1600), **167**; 16th century at, 151-66; fishery at, 5, 215-16, 226; chapel at, 155, 158; Devon estates, 152, 155, 158-60, 161; Dudley estates, 118-19, 126, 158, 160-2
Kew Farm, 161-2, 163-4, 166, 167-8
Kew Ferry, 151, 171, 209; see also Brentford Ferry
Kew Field, 151, 154, 158, 166; Deane, 158; Foxholes, 151; Tinderland, 151, 154, 161; West Dene, 151
Kew Green, 151, 154, 162, 166
Kew Heath, 151, 162
Kew Meadows, 3, 151, 162
Kew Park, 154, 164-5, 166, 167, 171, 208
Kilkenny, William de, 11, 255
King Street, Richmond, 222, 232
'King's Great Work', 29-30, 37
King's Leas (or Lease), 170-1, 172, 177
King's Observatory, Old Deer Park, 39
King's Works organisation, 25; Clerks of, 25, 30, 32, 37, 72
Kingeslowe, John, recluse of Shene, 38
Kingsmill, Henry, 113, 114
Kingston Sheen (= Shene), 34
Kingston-on-Thames, 1, 3, 4, 14, 15, 50, 193, 199, 208, 209, 214-16; Manor of, 1, 3, 4, 19; and formation of Richmond Park, 198-200, 243, 246-7, 251
Kingston church, 6, 8
Kingston commons, 243
Knevet, Sir Thomas, 83
Knightley, William and wife Susan, 246
Knighton, Dorset, 5, 10, 12, 15, 216
Knollys, Lettice, wife of Earl of Leicester, 129
Kryer, John, 50
Kynwolmersh, William, 256

La Nayght (La Neyt), island by Shene Palace, 24-5
La Neyte, royal house near Westminster, 17-18
Lammas Mead, Shene, 226-9
Lancaster Herald, 52, 57
Lane, Nicholas, map by, 197, **198**, 242-53
Lanham (or Laneham), John, 238-9
Laski, Prince, 132
Latchmore Grounds, Kingston, 246, 251
Laud, William, Archbishop of Canterbury, 197
Lauderdale, Earl and Duke of: see Maitland, John
Lawrence, John, friar, 236, 237
Lawrence, Robert, Prior of Beauvale Charterhouse, 98
Le Havre ('Newhaven'), France, 120, 121
Lea, Robert, 245
Lead, use in buildings, 31, 37, 55, 101, 176
Leaver, William, 211
Leicester, Earl of: see Dudley, Robert
Lennox, Countess of: see Stewart, Margaret
Lennox, Duke of: see Stuart, James
Lennox, Earl of: see Stewart, Matthew
Leo X, Pope, 45
Lewes, Morgan, 171
Lewes, Battle of (1264), 11
Lewis, Edward, 257
Lewis, Robert, 257
Lewisham Manor, 37, 38, 99
Lewisham Priory, 37
Lezign, Guy de, 255
Lightfoot, Katherine, 24
Lire Abbey, Normandy, 37
Lisle, Viscount: see Plantagenet, Arthur; Dudley, John
Little Clay Shott, Roehampton, 248
Loanes (or Lones), Ham, 199, 203, 245, 251

Lodge, William, 247
London, Bishops of: Theodred, 1; Ridley, Nicholas, 104; Juxon, William, 197
London, City of, 10, 57, 181, 205-6
London, Tower of, 22, 27, 80, 129, 205
London, John (hedger), 50
London, John (landowner), 251
Lord Admiral's Company, 128, 144, 238-9
Lord Chamberlain's Company, 143, 238
Lord Hunsdon's Company, 239
Lord Strange's Company, 239
Lord's Cop (Grove?), Ham Common, 244
Lord's Pieces, Richmond, 53, 93, 170-2
Lote, Stephen, master mason, 30, 37, 275
Louis XII, King of France, 84-5, 154
Louis XIII, King of France, 192
Lovell, ———, gardener, 259
Lovell, Edward, gardener, 259
Lovell, George, 50, 123, 184
Lovell, Gregory, 93, 170, 256, 258, 260
Lovell, Joan, gardener, 259
Lovell, John (Senior), gardener, 50, 184, 259
Lovell, John (Junior), gardener, 259
Lovell, Katherine, 50
Loveney, William, 256
Ludlow, Shropshire, 79
Lydgold, Robert, 151, 154; heirs of, 162
Lyford, Henry, 252
Lyme, Dorset, 4, 213
Lynton, Anthony, 233, 234

Machell, John, 157
Machyn, Henry, 108
Maids of Honour Row, Richmond, 62, 222
Maitland, John, Earl (later Duke) of Lauderdale, 204
Maitland, William, Scottish Ambassador to England, 125
Maizières, Philippe de, **25**
Makyn, Robert, 151, 155
Malmesbury, William of, 1
Man, Henry, Prior of Shene (later Bishop of Sodor and Man), 97-100, 224
Man, ———, and wife Hannah, 246, 251
Manning, Edward, 200, 202, 203, 241
Manning, Rev. Owen, 5, 14, 213, 217
Mansfield, Robert, 257
Marbury, John, friar, 236
March, Earl of: see Mortimer, Roger
Margaret of Anjou, Queen of Henry VI, 32, 51
Margaret Tudor, Queen of James IV of Scotland, 45, **78**, 79-80, 112
Maria of Savoy, 189
Maria, Infanta of Spain, 191
Marlowe, Christopher, 128
Marshgate, Richmond, 235
Martin, James, 259
Mary I, Queen of England, **105**, **157**; as Princess, 46, 86-90, 104, 156, 236; accession, 104-5; marriage, 105-6, 159; religious settlement, 105-7, 108; at Richmond, 89-90, 105-6, 109, 111; death and will, 109-11, 117
Mary, Queen of Scots, **125**; marriage, 112, 121, 124; claim to English throne, 120, 121; abdication, 124; in England, 124-6, 128; plots to restore, 133-4; trial and execution, 134
Mary of Guise, Queen of James V of Scotland, 120
Mary Tudor, Queen of Louis XII of France, Duchess of Suffolk, 81, 82, 84-5, 103, 152, 154-5, **155**
Mary Stewart, Princess (dau. of Charles I), 194-5, 207
Mason (als. Wickes), Anthony, 162-3, 166
Mason, Sir John, 163
Maubane, Thomas and wife Amabil, 9
Maunsell (or Mansel), John, 11, 255
Maximilian I, Holy Roman Emperor, 83, 84, 87
Maybush Shott, Richmond, 231
Maydeston, Richard, 256

Meek, Walter, 259
Meleburn, Robert de and wife Emma (Belet), 11, 255
Meleburn, William de, 11
Mendoza, Bernardino de, Spanish Ambassador, 129, 130, 132, 133
Merchant Taylors' Schoolboys, 128, 238
Merston, Richard, 260
Merton Priory, 5, 6, 7, 9, 10, 108, 151, 162, 199, 215, 216, 244
Michell, John, Prior of Shene, 97-8, 100, 107, 224
Mochebrooke stream, Richmond, 234
Mollett, Elizabeth, 178, 211
Monasticism in England: state in 1413, 35; return in 1554-8, 107
Montfort, Simon de, 10, 11, 12
Moorbrook, Richmond: see South Park
Mordaunt, John, 1st Lord Mordaunt, 160
Mordaunt, John, 2nd Lord Mordaunt, 160-1
More, Sir Thomas, 96-7
Mortimer, Roger of Wigmore (d.1282), 10, 12
Mortimer, Roger, Earl of March (d.1330), 19
Mortlake, Surrey, 57, 130-2, 151, 226; Manor of, 2, 3; Commons, 199, 200, 243; fishery, 3; and formation of Richmond Park, 197-9, 200, 201, 203, 243, 249-51, 252-4; vestry, 199, 200, 252, 254
Mount Ararat Road, Richmond, 231, 232, 233, 234
Mountjoy, Lord: see Blount, Charles
Mulcaster, Richard, 238
Murray, Thomas, 191
Murray, William, Earl of Dysart, 191, 198, 200, 201, 203-4, 208, 242
Mylde Lands, Roehampton, 248

Nantes, Edict of, 138
Narbonne, John, 171
Nassau, Maurice of, Stadtholder of the Netherlands, 181
Netherlands: relations with, 132-3, **133**; situation in, 81, 120, 132-3, 134; treaty with (Nonsuch 1585), 133
Neufmarché Priory, Normandy, 37
Nevers, Duke of, 143
Nevill, Hugh de, 7
Nevill, Robert, brickmaker, 73-4, 276
Neville, Charles, Earl of Westmorland, 126
New Close, Mortlake, 250, 254
New Mead, Shene, 226
New Park of Richmond, Co. Middlesex (also known as Isleworth Park and Twickenham Park), 52, 76-7, **76**; referred to as 'Little Park', 52, 77
New Park of Richmond, Co. Surrey: see Richmond Park (Old or Little); Richmond Park (New or Great)
New Park of Shene (later Richmond), 49-53, 76-7, **76**, 170, 172, 174, 178; referred to as 'Great Park', 52
Newcastle, Earl of: see Cavendish, William
Newenden Bridge, Calais, 31
Ncwfield Close, Roehampton, 248-9
Newgate Cop, Meadow, Woods, Mortlake, 249, 250
Nicholas, Edward, 201
Noke's Hill, Kingston, 246, 251
Nonsuch (Nonesuch) Palace, 133, 138, 168, 209
Norborough, William, 257
Norfolk, Duke of: see Howard, Thomas
Norris, Sir Henry, 156
North Field, Kingston, 243, 246, 251
Northampton, Helena Snakenbourg, Marchioness of, 115, 149, 169, **169**, 172, **174**, 191, 193, 256, 258
Northampton, Marquess of: see Parr, William
Northorne, William, 22
Northumberland, Duke of: see Dudley, John
Northumberland, Earls of: see Percy, Algernon; Percy, Thomas
Norton, Sir Gregory and wife Martha, 211, 256

Index

Norton, Sir Henry, 211, 256
Nottingham, Earl of: *see* Howard, Charles
Noyon Priory, Normandy, 37
Nutsford, Dorset, 4, 213

Oatelands, Roehampton, 248
Oatlands Palace, Weybridge, 138, 179, 209
Observant Friars, order: 73, 97-8; suppression of, 98, 236; friaries: Canterbury, 96-7, 236, Greenwich, 73, 97-8, 107, 236, Newark, 98, 236, Newcastle, 236, Richmond *see* Friary, Southampton, 98, 236
Offley, William and wife Susan, 247, 248, 249
Old Deer Park, Richmond, 39, 235; *see also* Richmond Park (Old or Little)
'Old Friars' (house), Richmond, 124
Old Palace Lane, Richmond, 178, 187, 211, 222
'Old Palace Place' (house), Richmond, 124
Old Palace Terrace, Richmond Green, 41, 232
Oliver, Jordan, judge, 9
Oliver, Walter and wife Emma (Belet), 9, 255
Olney, Bucks., 76
O'Neill, Hugh, Earl of Tyrone, 142, 146
Onslow, Sir Richard, 208
Onslow Road, Richmond, 231-2
organs in Richmond Palace, 127
Osterley, Middlesex, 101, 113
Ottewell, George, 239
Oxenbrigge, John, 74
Oxey, Philip de, 5, 217
Oxford, 17, 208

Packe, Thomas, friar, 236
Paget, Sir William, 157
Palmer, Thomas, 93, 172
Pamber, Hants., 175
Paradise Road, Richmond, 233-4
Paris, University of, 47
Parke, Humphrey, 210
Parker, Sir Selwyn, 177
Parks (of Shene and Richmond): *see* Shene Manor House; Shene Palace (first); New Park of Shene; New Park of Richmond, Co. Middlesex; Richmond Park (Old or Little); Richmond Park (New or Great)
Parkyns, John, 162
Parliament, 205, 207, 208; sales of royal property, 177, 205, 209; surveys for sales, 177-8, 187, 209, 231
Parliamentary army, 208
Parma, Alexander Farnese, Duke of, 132, 134-5, 138
Parr, William, Marquess of Northampton, 169, 171
Partridge, Sir Miles, 157-8
Passelewe, Robert, 9
Paston, William, 46
Pate, John, 258
Paulet, Quentin, librarian, 259
Paved Court, Richmond, 232
Pearce (or Peirce), Stephen, 166, 258, 259
Peirce, Theobald, 259
Pembroke, Earl of: *see* Herbert, William
Pen Ponds, Richmond Park, 202
Penrith, William, friar, 236
Percy, Algernon, Earl of Northumberland, 209
Percy, Thomas, Earl of Northumberland, 126
Perkins, Henry and wife Thomazine, 201, 245
Perpoynt family, 254
Pesthouse Common, Richmond, 235
Petersham: brickkiln at, 31; chapelry of, 6; and formation of Richmond Park, 199, 200-1, 242-5; manor, 34, 37, 53, 91-3, 170, 172, 183, 191, 193, 198, 201, 203-4, 241, 242; weir and fishery, 37
Petersham Common, 200, 242-3
Petersham Lodge, Richmond Park (formerly Petersham Manor House), 199, 201, 202, 203, 244-5
Pett, Phineas, shipbuilder, 180
Peyton, Henry, 245, 251

Philip of Hapsburg, Duke of Burgundy and King of Castile, 81
Philip II, King of Spain, 105-6, **106**, 109, 111, 117, 118, 120, 128, 132, 138, 159
Philippa of Hainault, Queen of Edward III, 19
Philpot, Elizabeth, 93
Pickwell family, 232, 233(n)
Pickwell's Well (or Welway), Shene, 41, 231
Pinchon, John, 247
Pinkie, Battle of (1547), 158
Pius V, Pope, 126
plague, 19, 82, 86, 121, 138, 179, 192-3, 207
Plantagenet, Arthur, Viscount Lisle, 96
Plantagenet, Elizabeth, 157
plaster, use in buildings, 22, 29, 31, 39
plays, at Richmond Palace, 122, 127-8, 194-5, 238-9
Pleasington, Henry, 258
Pole, Reginald, Cardinal, Archbishop of Canterbury, 47, **47**, 97, 101, 106-7, **107**, 108, 109, 224
Pond (or Ashen) Close, Mortlake, 252
Pond Mead, Mortlake, 250
Ponde (als. Francis), William, friar, 237
Pont, John du, 259
Poole, John, 252
Pope, Hugh (father and son), 164
Pope, Thomas, 239
Porter, Arnald, mason, 39
Portland, Earls of: *see* Weston, Jerome; Weston, Richard
Portman, Sir Hugh, 162, 163, 166, 168, 184
Portman, Sir John, 168
Portsmouth Road, 199
Postell's Grove, Kingston, 247
Powerstoke, Honour of, Dorset, 216
Pratolino, Italy, 183
Price, John, 246, 251
Prustman, Roger, 11
Puckering, Sir John, 163-4, **164**
Putney, and formation of Richmond Park, 199, 200, 243, 247-9
Putney Common, 200, 243, 248
Putney Park, 199, 247
Putto, Richard, 162
Pye, Sir Robert, 195, 200, 244, 245
Pygeon, Edmond, 171
Pykwell, Nicholas, 233(n)

Quadra, Alvaro de la, Bishop of Aquila, Spanish Ambassador, 111, 118, 119, 120
Queen's Company (actors), 238-9
Queen's Stable, Richmond Green, 93, 172, 210
Queensberry, Duke of, 184(n)

Raimundis de Soncino, Raimundo de, Ambassador of Milan, 55
Ralegh, Wymund de, 7, 255
Raleigh (or Ralegh) Sir Walter, 137, 165, 167, 181
Randolph, Thomas, English Ambassador to Scotland, 121
Ravensworth, Baron: *see* Fitzhugh, Sir Henry
Raynford, Sir John, 171
Reading, Berks., 175, 208
Red Conduit, Richmond, 231-2, 234
Red Lion Inn, Richmond, 130
Red Lion Street, Richmond, 234
Redman (or Redmayne), Henry, mason, 73-4, 276
Redman, Lyonel, 258
Reigate, Surrey, 39, 209
religious changes in England: breach with Rome, 96, 98-9; return to Catholicism, 105-7; Elizabethan settlement, 111, 117, 126
Renard, Simon, Spanish Ambassador, 105, 107
Reynolds, Dr. Richard, 98-9
Rich, Henry, Earl of Holland, 209
Rich, Dr. Hugh, Warden of Observant Friars, Richmond, 96, 277

Richard II 'of Bordeaux', King of England, 24, **24**, **25**, **26**, 29, 49, 219, 255, **I**
Richard, Earl of Cornwall, 10, 11
Richbell, Ralph, 243
Richmond, Surrey: *see also* Shene; name adopted in 1501, 56; Manor of, 92-3, 170, 172, 183, 191, 193, 198, 210, 211; Court leet, 193; fields, 162, 170, 171, 172; and formation of Richmond Park, 198, 200, 242
Richmond Commons, 198, 199, 200, 231, 235, 242, 249
Richmond Ferry, 209. 210
Richmond Friary: *see* Friary
Richmond Green, 33, 41, 49, 50, 53, 61, 83, 92-3, 170, 171, 174, 178, 210, 211, 222, 234; conduit head on, 226, 231, 232
Richmond Hill, Richmond, 49, 231
Richmond Lodge, Old Deer Park, 175-6, **176**, 177, 195, 209-10
Richmond, Museum of, 35, 36, 39, 59
Richmond Palace:
 general and historic: building of, 56-73, 219; plan, 33, **60**, 219; model, **59**, **IV**; views of, **58**, 62-3, 65, 68, 69, 123, **186**, **V**; description by Lancaster Herald, 57-61; water supply, 58, 231-2; fire in 1505/6, 73; entertainments at, 52, 57, 61, 79-80, 81-2, 83, 109, 121, 122, 127-8, 143, 194-5; Wolsey, use by, 88-9; plays given at, 122, 127-8, 143-4, 194-5, 238-9; Queen Elizabeth's 'winter box', 138, 278; Prince Henry's plans for, 183-9; prepared for Charles I, 208-9; Parliamentary survey, 62, 69; sale and destruction, 205, 209, 211;
 features of: altarpiece, 66, **67**; bridges, 68, 69, 86, 90, 221; canted tower, 69-70; chapel, 61, 65-6, 72, 73, 180, 211; cistern house, 184-7; Fountain Court, 58, 65, 67, 72, 140, 180, 221, 222; galleries, 61, 70-2, 73, 90, 122, 127, 180; gardens, 61, 68, 70, 86, 127, 140, 180; gate and gatehouse, 62, 140; Great Court, 58, 62-3, 222; Great Orchard, 72, 221; Hall, 58, 63, 65-6, 72, 73, 122, 211; kitchens, etc., 61, 63, 65, 72, 127, 222; library, 189; Middle Gate, 63, 65, 72; moat, 67, 68, 69, 86, 187; organs, 127; pheasantry, 80, 191-2; Privy Lodgings (royal apartments), 61, 67-8, 72, 211, 219, 221; tennis courts, 62, 70, 72, 86, 90, 189, 191; towers and domes, 61, 67, 122; wardrobe, 62, 93; water-closet, 140-2, **141**
Richmond Parish Church, 11, 166, 178, 210, 234
Richmond Park (Old or Little), created by James I and known as 'New Park' until 1630s, 50, 53, 172-8, 179, 195, 205, 209
Richmond Park (New or Great), the present Richmond Park, created by Charles I, 194, 197-206, **198**, **204**, 208, 209, **XI**; expenditure on, 200-1, 202; acquisition of land, 241-254
Richmond, Treaties of: Anglo-Scottish (1501/2), 45, 79; marriage treaty with Spain (1508), 81; peace with France (1515), 85; peace with France (1525), 89; secret treaty with French Huguenots (1562), 120
Richmond Wells, 235
Richmond, Dukes of: *see* Fitzroy, Henry; Stuart, James
Richmond, Yorks., 236; earldom of, 56
Ridley, Nicholas, Bishop of London, 104
Ridolfi conspiracy, 126
Risbrooke, William, 258
Risby, Dr., Warden of Observant Friars, Canterbury, 96
Rithe, Christopher, 257
Roane, Robert, 258
Robin Hood Walk, Shene, 226
Robsart, Amy: *see* Dudley, Amy
Rochester, John, Carthusian monk, 107
Rochester, Sir Robert, 107, 108
Rockyngham, William, gardener, 27, 259

Roehampton, Surrey, and formation of Richmond Park, 198, 199, 200, 247-9
Rogers, Humphrey, 202, 203, 205, 245, 261
Rokeby, Thomas, 210
Roper, Sir William, 109
Rotherhithe, Surrey, 20
Roudham, Norfolk, 213, 214
Rough (or Row) Down, Kingston, 245, 251
Rudd, Dr. Anthony, Bishop of St David's, 139
Rupert, Prince, 208
Rutnells, Hartleton Farm, 244
Ryan, John, 259

Sackville, Anne, Lady Dacre, 113
Sackville, Sir Richard, 112-13
Sackville, Thomas, Lord Buckhurst, Earl of Dorset, 113-14, **115**, 140, 149, 162
Sagudino, Nicola, Venetian diplomat, 86
Saint Empire, Per, Marquis du, 234
St Evroult Abbey, Normandy, 37, 43
St James's Palace, 138, 181, 189, 209
St John, Oliver, Lord St John of Bletsho, 114, 210; 'Lady St John's Lodging', 210
St Michael, Wood Street, London, 45, 275
St Paul's Cathedral, London, 45, 57; land held by canons of, 2, 3
Salisbury, Earl of: *see* Cecil, Sir Robert
Sancto Romano, Dom Artaldus de, 11, 255
Sawyer, Sir Edmund, 244
Sayer, Thomas, 234
Scaramelli, Giovanni Carlo, Venetian diplomat, 144-5, 146
Scotland: relations with, 14, 79-80, 134; situation in, 14, 120, 124, 207, 209; treaties with, 45, 79, 209; wars with, 17. 45, 84
Scroope, Richard, Archbishop of York, 29
Scrope, Lady (née Carey), wife of Thomas Lord Scrope, 146-8
Sebastian, Master, 238
Selby, ——, former monk of Shene, 100
Selot, William, carpenter, 22
Serjeanty: of Bagshot, by veltrary, 5, 217; of Shene, by cupbearer, 5, 6, 9, 217
Seymour, Anne (née Stanhope), Duchess of Somerset, 101, 106, 107-8, 159
Seymour, Edward, Viscount Beauchamp, Earl of Hertford, Duke of Somerset, Lord Protector, **101**, **102**, **156**; at Shene, 101-3, 225-9, 233; at Kew, 156-7, 171; at Syon, 166; fall of, 158
Seymour, Thomas, Lord Seymour of Sudeley, Lord Admiral, 101
Seymour, William, Marquess of Hertford, 146, 207
Shakespeare, William, 128, 143, 239
Sharpe, Sir Montagu, 2
Shawe, Robert, 239
Sheen, Staffordshire, 273
Sheen (= Richmond), Surrey: *see* Shene
Sheen Grove, Richmond, 177
Sheen (or Shene) Place (or House), mansion formed from former Charterhouse, 105, 112-15, 162, 169, 178, 180, 193, 195-6, 208, 209, **210**, 227-9; royal stables at, 115, 127, 189, 194, 210
Sheep Hawe (or Sheepgape Close), Roehampton, 247, 248
Shene (later Richmond), Surrey: name, 2, 10, 273; early history, 1, 4-15; grants of manor, 19, 23, 27, 34; church, parish, of, 6, 8, 11; name changed to Richmond, 56
Shene Charterhouse: *see* Charterhouse of Jesus of Bethlehem of Shene
Shene fishery, 37
Shene (later Sheen) Lane, 49, 178
Shene Manor House, 1, 3, 4, 14, 17, 19, 20, 184, 219, **220**; the Douncourt, 19, 219; Park of, 14, 29, 49
Shene Palace, the first, built by Edward III: site and construction, 20-7, 219, **220**; destruction of, 25, 219;
 features of: chapel, 22, 26; clock, 21, 22; cloister, 21, 72; farm buildings, 23, 27; gardens, 21, 22, 27, 221; gate, 21, 22, 24;

Shene Palace, the first, *contd.*
  hall, 22; king's bath, 24; king's chambers, 21, 22, 24; kitchens, 22; moat, 21, 22, 219, 221; overcourt, 23, 27, 219, 222; park, 29; queen's chamber, 24; summer pavilion, 24; touncourt, 23, 27, 219; wardrobes, 22; wharf, 22, 25
Shene Palace, the second, built by Henry V and Henry VI:
  site and construction, 29-34, 219-21, **220**; plan, 33-4, 219, 222;
  damage by fire, **54**, 55;
  re-use of foundations, 31, 219;
  features of: chapel, 32, 55, 222; drawbridge, 34; garden, 32; great chamber, 32; hall, 32, 34, 222; moats, 32, 34, 221; outer court, 33-4, 222; parlour, 34; towers by chapel, 55
Shene Warren, 13, 14, 23, 27, 43, 49, 170
Shonk, Thomas, dauber, 22
Short Thorns, Mortlake, 251
Sibthorp, Robert de, Clerk of Works, 23
Sidmouth Plantation, Richmond Park, 202
Sidney, Sir Henry, 258, 260
Sidney, Sir Philip, 134, 138
Simier, Jean de, Baron de St Marc, 128-9
Siward, John, mason, 22
Sixteen Acre Close, Kingston, 246, 247
Skelton, John, 88
Skerne, Robert, 258, 260
Skipton, John, Clerk of Works, 30
Slades, Kingston, 243, 246, 251
Slaughterhouse Ground, Richmond, 170-1, 172, 177
Slawood, Mortlake, 251
Smith, Robert, 258
Smith, Thomas and wife Mary, 245
Smithy Croft, Richmond: *see* South Park
Smyth, Henry, Clerk of King's Works, 72, 74, 86
Snape, Nathaniel, 257
Snow, Lawrence, 50
Snow, Nicholas and wife Katherine, 50, 259
Somerset, Duchess of: *see* Seymour, Anne
Somerset, Dukes of: *see* Beaufort, Henry; Seymour, Edward
Somerset, Sir Charles, Lord Herbert, Earl of Worcester, 154-5
Somerset, Sir George and wife Thomasina, 154, 155, 164
Somerset, William, 164
Somerset House, London, 138, 183, 205
Somersett, John, 34, 256
Sonning, Berks., 175
South Park, Shene (otherwise Smithy Croft or Moorbrook), 49, 73
Southwark, Stephen, tiler, 22
Southwell, Sir Richard, 109
Spain: relations with, 81-2, 84, 87, 105-6, 128, 129-30, 132, 134, 191-2; treaties with, 81, 87; war with, 134-6, 137
Spencer, William, 238
'Spring Grove' (house), Richmond, 235
Spring Terrace, Richmond, 234
Squier, John, carpenter, 73
Staines, Surrey, 208
Stanhope, John, Lord Stanhope of Harrington, 138, 176
Stanley, Henry, Lord Strange, Earl of Derby and wife Margaret, 162
Stanley, William, Earl of Derby, 162, 166
Stanwell, Middlesex, 34
Staunton, John, 258
Staynford, Thomas, 154
Steete, Great and Little, Roehampton, 248
Stevenson, Hugh, 257
Stewart, Lady Arabella, 146
Stewart, Henry, Earl of Darnley, 112, 121, 122, 124-5

Stewart, Margaret (née Douglas), Countess of Lennox, 112
Stickles, Robert, Clerk of Works, 175-6
Stobart, William, 233
Stokes, Adrian, 112, 277
stonework, 22, 29, 30-1, **38**, 39, 72, 176, 185
Stony Close (also Croft Mead), Kew, 210, 226
Strand-on-the-Green, Middlesex, 3
Strange, John, Clerk of King's Works, 30, 37
Strange, Lord: *see* Stanley, Henry
Strong, Sir Roy, 165
Stroudes (Great Stroud Wood, Little Stroud Close, Great Stroud Meadow), Roehampton, 248
Stuart, James, Duke of Lennox, Duke of Richmond, 177, 196, 208, 209, 256, 257, 258, 261
Stubfield (or Stubble Fields), Roehampton, 247
Sudbrook, Petersham, 244, 245
Suffolk, Dukes of: *see* Brandon, Charles; Grey, Henry
Suffolk Place, Kew, 154-5, 160-1, 166
Surrey, Earl of: *see* Howard, Thomas
Sutton, Chiswick (royal house) 27, 31, 39
Swanton, John de, 20, 23, 27, 256, 257, 260, 274
Swanton, Thomas de, 27, 257, 260
Swanton, William de, 27, 256
Sweden, Eric XIV, King of, 118, 169
Swyft, Thomas, 259
Sydney, Sir Robert, 164
Symond, Adam, 256
Symonds, Lancelot and wife Jane, 249, 252
Symonds, William and wife Patience, 252, 254
Syon, Monastery of St Saviour and St Bridget of Syon, Isleworth: foundation, 37; change of site, 75-6, 276; dissolution, 95-6, 99; restoration, 108, 111; use as mansion, 101-2, 103, 104, 129, 132, 158, 159, 166, 204, 208, 209
Syston, Lincs., 214

Tare Snatch, Kingston, 246
Taverner, John, 175
Taverner, Richard, 162
Taylor, Hugh, lay brother, 107, 111
Templars, order of, 6
Thames, River: bridges, 2, 3; ferries, 3, 15, 171, 209, 210; festivities on, 57, 181; fisheries, 3, 4, 5, 10, 37, 215-16, 226; fords, 2, 2(n), 150; fortified palisade, **2**; reclamation of river bank, 183-7,**185**, 221; view from Richmond Palace window, **183**
Theobalds House, Herts., 127, 183, 192
Theodred, Bishop of London, 1-2
Thomas à Becket, St, Archbishop of Canterbury, 36
Thorpe, John, *Book of Architecture*, 175
Thorpe, John, 233
Thorpe Underwood, Northants., 214
Throckmorton conspiracy, 133
Throckmorton, Sir Nicholas, English Ambassador to France, 120
Thurbarne, Edward, 23, 255
Thurbarne, Ralph, 20, 23, 255
Thurley, Simon, 70, 70(n)
Tichburne, Richard, 247
Tilbury, Essex, 136
tilemakers, 39, 73
tiles, use in buildings, 22, 39, 175-6, 185
Tillières, Countess of, 192
timber, use in building, 22, 29, 31, 32, 39, 175, 185
Timber Hawe, Richmond, 72
Tower, Stephen atte, candlestick-maker, 22
Tracy, Ralph, Prior of Shene, 45, 224
Trafford, William, Prior of London Charterhouse, 100

Trained bands, 207, 208
Tremayne, Edward, 129
Treswell, Ralph, 242
Trevor, Sir John, 178, 261
Troyes, Treaty of, 121
Trumpeters' House, Richmond, 72, 219, 222
Trumpeters' Lodge, Richmond, 72, 219, 221
Turner, Dr. William, botanist, 166-7
Turner, Dr. William, lawyer, 232-3
Turnham Green, Middlesex, 19, 29, 37, 75-6
Turnor, Richard, 245
Twickenham, Middlesex, 19, 29, 37, 75-6
Twickenham Park, 77, 197, 276; *see also* New Park of Richmond, Co. Middlesex
Tyldesley, Will, librarian, 259
Tyler, Sir William, 56, 76, 170, 260
Tylt, Robert, 251
Tyrone, Earl of: *see* O'Neill, Hugh

Upper Neyland, Roehampton, 248

Vadstena, Sweden, 36
Valletorte (or Vautort), John de (d. 1301), 10-11, 13, 14-15
Valletorte (or Vautort), John de (son of above), 15
Valor Ecclesiasticus, 99
Valtort, John de (fl.1200), 6-10
Vanderdoort, Abraham, 189
Vane, Sir Henry, 207
Vautort, John de (fl.1350s), 15
Vautort, Richard de, 15
Venice, relations with, 85, 144-5
Vernon, Thomas, 257
Vesey, William, brickmaster, 31
Villa d'Este, Italy, 183
Villiers, Sir Edward, 259
Villiers, George, Duke of Buckingham, 192
Villyard (or Villiard), Massie, 92, 256, 258, 260
Vincent, David, 53, 77, 93, 171-2, 256, 258, 260
Vineyard, The, Richmond, 232

Wagstaff, William and wife Sarah (Juxon), 250, 252
Waleden, Humphrey de, 17-19, 257
Wales, castles in, 13
Walsingham, Sir Francis, 129, 131, 133-4
Walter, Sir William, 247, 248
Walton, Walter, mason, 37, 39, 275
Warbeck, Perkin, 45, 224
wardship, 5, 7, 8, 9
Ware Priory, Herts., 37, 43
Ware, James, 165
Ware Ground, Kew, 162
Warham, William, Archbishop of Canterbury, 96, 152
Warren, The, Petersham, 243
Warwick, Earls of: *see* Dudley, Ambrose; Dudley, John
water collecting chamber, Mount Ararat Road, Richmond, 233-4, **233**
Water Lane, Richmond, 49, 183, 232, 234, 276
water supply, **230**; Shene Palace (Byfleet), 32; Charterhouse, 40-1, 231, 232-4; Richmond Palace, 58, 231-2; proposed garden works, 184-7
Webber, Augustine, Prior of Axholme Charterhouse, 98
Weld (or Wilde), Thomas, 232
Welway: *see* Pickwell's Well
West, Henry, 203
Westerley, Robert, mason, 32
West Shene (= Shene), 10, 209
Westminster Abbey, 24, 25, 36, 66, 82, 108, 149, 164
Westminster Palace, 22, 37, 45, 57, 83, 209

Westmoreland, Baron: *see* Clifford, Henry
Westmorland, Earl of: *see* Neville, Charles
Weston, Frances, Countess of Portland, 247
Weston, Jerome, Earl of Portland, 199, 200, 202, 203, 247-8, 261
Weston, Robert, Earl of Portland, 199, 247
Weyman, Thomas, 257
Wheler, Richard, carpenter, 32
White, Henry, 199, 249, 251, 252, 254
White, Rowland, 164
White Ash Lodge, Richmond Park, 202
White Conduit, Richmond Park, 231, 232, 235
Whitehall Palace, Westminster, 138, 143, 181, 209
White Slade, Kingston, 246, 251
Whitfield, Thomas, 252, 254
Wilburham, William de and wife Emma (Belet), 12
Wilby, Mr., 211
Wildy, William, Prior of Shene, 223
Wilkes, Richard, 249, 252, 254
Wilkes, Simon, 254
William, lay brother of Mount Grace, 41
William of Orange, Stadtholder of the Netherlands, 132-3
Willoughby d'Eresby, Lord: *see* Bertie, Peregrine
Wimbledon, manor of, 2, 3, 22, 199; court rolls, 241; survey (1617), 242; and formation of Richmond Park, 199, 254
Wimbledon, Viscount: *see* Cecil, Edward
Winchester, Queen Mary married at, 106
Winchester, Bishop of, 37; *see also* Wykeham; Fox; Gardiner
Winchester, Earl of: *see* Despenser, Hugh
Windebank, Sir Francis, 195, 201
Windlesham, Surrey, 7
Windsor Castle, 4, 20, 27, 81, 205, 209; Horseshoe Cloister, 70, **71**; St George's Chapel, 66, 72(n)
Windsor Forest, 203, 214
Winfrith Newburgh, Dorset, 10, 12, 15
Winkfield, Sir Anthony, 124
Wolinne, widow, 6
Wolsey, Thomas, Cardinal, Archbishop of York: as Lord Chancellor, 84, 86, 87, **88**, 89, 95; and Hampton Court, 86, 88-9; and the divorce, 89, 95-6; at Richmond Palace, 88-9; at lodge in park, 47, 52-3; at Charterhouse of Shene, 47-8, 101
Wood, Sir Robert, 246, 251
Wood, William, 248
Woodsford, Dorset, 4, 213
Worcester, Earl of: *see* Somerset, Sir Charles
Worcester, William of, 34, 41, 52, 222, 274, 275
Wright, Sir Robert, 50
Wroxton Priory, Oxfordshire, 213-14
Wulfric, Thane, 273
Wyatt, Sir James, 159
Wydrington, John, Prior of Shene, 39, 44, 223, 275
Wykeham, William de, Bishop of Winchester, 20, **21**, 23
Wyndsor, Hugh de (father and son), 12, 13, 255
Wynferthing, Richard de, 18, 257
Wyngaerde, Antonis van, 61, 67, 69, 70, 122, 219, 221; drawings by, **58**, **62-3**, **65**, **66**, **68**, **71**, **113**

Yates, John, 244
Yevele, Henry, master mason, 22-3, 24, 37
Yorke, Bartholomew and wife Joan, 172
Yorke, William of, plasterer, 22
Young, Thomas, 200, 241

Zuche, William la, 12